From the Spitfire Cockpit to the Cabinet Office

for my late wife, Jane and for our children
Hilary, Marcus & Karen
of whom I am very proud.

From the Spitfire Cockpit to the Cabinet Office

The Memoirs of
Air Commodore J. F.
'Johnny' Langer CBE AFC DL

Pen & Sword
AVIATION

First published in Great Britain in 2016
and reprinted in this format in 2022 by
Pen & Sword Aviation
an imprint of
Pen & Sword Books Ltd
47 Church Street
Barnsley
South Yorkshire
S70 2AS

ISBN 9 781 39907 488 9

A CIP catalogue record for this book is available from the British Library

Typeset in Ehrhardt by
Mac Style Ltd, Bridlington, East Yorkshire
Printed and bound in the UK by CPI Group (UK) Ltd,
Croydon, CRO 4YY

Pen & Sword Books Ltd incorporates the imprints of Pen & Sword
Archaeology, Atlas, Aviation, Battleground, Discovery, Family History,
History, Maritime, Military, Naval, Politics, Railways, Select, Transport,
True Crime, and Fiction, Frontline Books, Leo Cooper, Praetorian
Press, Seaforth Publishing and Wharncliffe.

For a complete list of Pen & Sword titles please contact
PEN & SWORD BOOKS LIMITED
47 Church Street, Barnsley, South Yorkshire, S70 2AS, England
E-mail: enquiries@pen-and-sword.co.uk
Website: www.pen-and-sword.co.uk

Contents

Chapter 1	Schooldays	1
Chapter 2	Pilot Training	13
Chapter 3	'Wot! No Engines?'	30
Chapter 4	India	38
Chapter 5	Peace	53
Chapter 6	Fighters at Last	63
Chapter 7	The Far East	84
Chapter 8	Flying Instruction	98
Chapter 9	Singapore and Malaya	113
Chapter 10	Back On Fighters	129
Chapter 11	In the Doldrums	148
Chapter 12	Totally Becalmed	170
Chapter 13	How Green Was My Valley	184
Chapter 14	A Short Intermission at the Ministry	202
Chapter 15	The Far East Again	209
Chapter 16	The Last Post	231
Chapter 17	My Second Career	256
Chapter 18	Winding Down	271
Appendix A: Aircraft Flown		284
Appendix B: Naming the HS 1182 AJ		286
Epilogue		288

Chapter 1

Schooldays

I cannot remember much of my early childhood although a few incidents come readily to mind. For example, one day, when I was about three or four, my elder sister Jean and I were playing in the garden when we heard a screech of brakes and a yelp. Our nanny rushed out and took us into the house where our mother told us later that the family's much loved Scottish terrier had been run over and killed and was now buried in the back garden under an apple tree.

I also remember vividly that, when I was about six or seven, our mother would take Jean and me to the garden parties held in the grounds of the Putney Home for Incurables (a horrible name, still engraved on the building) which was on the opposite side of the road when we lived in West Hill. These were fundraising events and the ladies would dress up as if for Ascot with large hats, elegant dresses and pretty parasols. But what sticks in my mind was the horrific state of most of the inmates. Many of them were blind as a result of gas attacks, most of them had had limbs amputated and a few had neither arms nor legs. But the worst cases were those who had part of their faces blown away and were left with gaping holes. After these visits, and I can recall at least three or four, I had nightmares for several days.

The Langer family: Mother with Jean, baby Elizabeth and the author, John Francis.

* * *

My first school was of the nursery variety run by the Putney High School for Girls. I cannot recall any formal lessons: we spent most of the time doing clever things with plasticine or painting pictures of our houses, our mummies or our pets – to order. The school was very keen on eurythmics and free expression and whenever the weather allowed we were made to prance around the garden and to dance like trees or elephants or old men. I often wondered if I looked as foolish

The Langer family home, 12 St Simon's Avenue, Putney, London, SW15.

as I felt. It was all very Joyce Grenfell! My second school was the Convent of the Sacred Heart where Jean was already a pupil. The Convent took boys from five to seven years old but I stayed until I was nine. It was there that I was introduced to the three Rs. It was also at the Convent that I had my first fifteen minutes of fame.

One day the Reverend Mother Superior came to early morning prayers to address the school. After stressing the importance of religion in education she started asking questions about their faith to the assembled pupils. Hands shot up and satisfactory answers were given until she asked 'How much bread do we receive at Holy Communion?' Some of the girls hazarded answers in ounces and it was clear that the Reverend Mother was getting agitated. Thinking laterally I put up my hand and said 'We don't get any bread …'. Before I could go on she beckoned me towards her, and gave me a hug and enveloped me in her habit – which smelt strongly of mothballs and incense. Then addressing the audience she said 'Of course we do not receive any bread because during the Mass it was turned into the Body of Christ and I am surprised that it has taken someone as young as John to see that truth.' She then gave me a kiss on the forehead and swept out. If I blushed it was not because of the kiss in front of all those girls but because I was going on to say that the Communion wafer was not bread but biscuit.

From the Convent I went on to Donhead Lodge which was the preparatory school for Wimbledon College, the grounds of which were on the opposite side of Edge Hill. It had been a large private house so it had a homely feel about it which made it an excellent place in which to gently introduce us youngsters to the rigours of public school life. It was there that a few of us first met the dreaded *ferrula*, a thick piece of leather shaped something like the sole of a shoe. It was administered sharply to the palms of one's hands and hurt like hell. I remember clearly that I was awarded 'three of the best' for persistently confusing Britain with Briton and vice-versa. I never ever got that wrong again! Our form master was Father Millar, a grey-haired, tall, avuncular man who was much respected and well liked, except when he reluctantly decided that a little painful correction was necessary.

In 1936, when I was eleven, my class, all ten of us, moved across the road to Wimbledon College which had been founded in the mid-nineteenth century with the purpose of preparing Catholic boys for service as officers in the Armed Forces. Many served in the Crimea, the Boer War and the First World War, and the school's Roll of Honour was quite impressive. The College was run by the Society of Jesus, often referred to as the Catholic mafia. Founded in Rome in the sixteenth century but with houses and colleges around the world, the SJs were one of the strictest, most learned and influential of all the religious orders. Wimbledon College was a public day school, the associated boarding school being Beaumont College near Windsor.

The school was well endowed with sports facilities in that there were three tennis courts, a large gymnasium, a heated indoor swimming pool, two cricket pitches with practice nets, all in the grounds, as well as a separate sports field and pavilion at Raynes Park where there were three rugby pitches. The assembly hall, which was also the refectory, was quite grandiose, the chapel was beautiful, the science laboratories were well equipped but the classrooms were very spartan. The worst aspect of the school was the toilets, all with the original mid-Victorian plumbing which really deserved the schoolboy name of 'the bogs'.

Father Murray's class, Wimbledon College; the author is first left, back row.

Two years passed without significant incidence until, in second summer term, our form master became ill and was replaced by Father Rousel, who was on loan from Beaumont. He was a mild mannered, ineffectual man of whom we boys took full advantage: paper aeroplanes, chalk and rubber bands flew around his classes and the form became rather ill-disciplined. That all changed at the start of the following term when a new teacher took over.

When Father Murray arrived for the first class he entered the classroom amidst the usual babble of conversation with many of the boys lounging around. He walked up to the dais, turned and faced the class and waited until there was an awkward silence. He then said, 'I am going out of the room and when I re-enter you will all stand behind your desks in silence. I will go to the front and say "Good morning, boys" and you will say "Good morning, Father" and then sit down.' In that simple but firm manner Father Murray made it clear that he would stand no nonsense. Thereafter our class became the best behaved in the school. I was most impressed by the episode as it showed how easy it was for a group of boys to become an unruly mob when lacking firm direction and, more importantly, how all that was needed to knock them into shape was good leadership. It was a lesson I never forgot, especially when eventually I was in a position of authority.

By way of introductions Father Murray started by telling us a little of his own background. He then asked each of us to stand up, starting from the front row, to give our names, where we lived, our fathers' professions and what careers we intended to follow when we left school. And so it progressed towards the back row where I sat with my friends Mickey Hampshire and Robbie Burns. Most boys appeared to have little imagination and many simply opted to follow in father's footsteps: accountancy, banking, family firm, teaching and the Civil Service seemed to be the favourite occupations. Only Bernard O'Neil showed any originality by saying that he wanted to become a cricketer; which he did, playing for and eventually captaining Hertfordshire, one of the minor counties.

I was in a difficult position, firstly because my parents were divorced and secondly because, at the age of thirteen, I had given my future career absolutely no thought whatsoever. However I was an avid reader of Captain W. E. Johns' novels about that intrepid aviator, Biggles, and had recently seen an item on the Pathé News in the cinema about the Hendon Air Show and had been fascinated by the formation aerobatics. So when it was my turn I stood up and said 'John Langer, I live on Putney Hill, my father was a builder and I am going to be a fighter pilot in the Royal Air Force'. Whereas everyone else's statements had been well received, mine caused a bit of a titter and several boys actually laughed. My face went red and I hoped the ground would swallow me up.

At the end of the lesson Father Murray summoned me and asked why I thought the boys had laughed. I said that it was probably because I was not very bright and that they knew that entry standards for the RAF were very high. Father Murray then said, 'Pay no attention to them: it is now up to you to show that they were wrong. I am sure that you will prove to have what it takes.' When I left the classroom I felt ten feet tall.

The more I thought about it the more I became convinced that my choice of career was the right one. It was now 1938 and the threat of war was looming: so the chances were that, if it lasted long enough, many of us would be called up anyway. The possibility of a watery grave in mid-Atlantic did not appeal to me, nor did I wish to be blown to bits in the trenches, so the Royal Navy and the Army were out. I was determined to be a pilot but the transport, bomber and maritime roles had no attractions for me. I saw fighter pilots as being the last of the white knights engaging their opponents in an honourable and chivalrous manner – and usually getting back to base in time for tea.

Thus convinced I asked the Careers Master to find out what educational attainments were required before one could apply for entry to the RAF College at Cranwell. The answer was a good school certificate with a minimum of five subjects at credit level – and therein lay a problem. There was little doubt that I was not one of the brightest pupils in our class of twenty-one. In the end of term exams, Mickey and Robbie always vied for last place and I had never been far behind. Robbie was a bit dim, Mickey was rather lazy whilst, although not stupid, I was a day-dreamer with a short attention span. Clearly I would have to pull my socks up.

Fuelled by my newly-found ambition my class marks started climbing slowly but surely, especially in those subjects such as geography, Latin, science and geometry which I had always enjoyed: my least favourite subjects were French and algebra which I loathed. However, my attempts to forge ahead were becoming affected by problems at home. Although my parents had been divorced before I

The author with his elder sister Jean Rosemary in 1928.

went to prep school, my mother had been able to manage reasonably well on the income from taking paying guests. But our family fortunes started to plunge when she married Billy Doe and lost most of her capital by funding his unsuccessful building company which went bankrupt

By 1938 my mother had had to sell our lovely big house for a mere £2,850, most of which went to pay off debts. Our fairy godmother was Mrs Warren who lived opposite us in St Simon's Avenue and whose daughter, Doune, was a classmate and best friend of my sister Jean. Mrs Warren put up all five of us for several months until my mother found a suitable house to rent in Tideswell Avenue, a little farther down the hill, where she could resume taking paying guests. But worse was to come when the war started in September 1939 and her supply of foreign PGs completely dried up.

She now had no income whatsoever, could no longer pay the rent, had to vacate our rented house and we had become both penniless and homeless. By this time Mrs Warren had moved to Stoke Poges as her partner had moved his factory from Fulham to Slough Trading Estate where there were better facilities – so she could not help us. My mother was at her wits end and sought the advice of her old friend, the Mother Superior of the Convent at West Hill.

Strangely it was the advent of the war which most helped us to overcome our problems. Firstly, the pupils and teaching staff of the Convent had all been evacuated to a sister school in the country, taking Jean and my younger sister Elizabeth out of London. They could even stay there for the school holidays, so that was one less worry. Secondly, Linda Doe, Billy's step-sister, agreed to take my half-sister Edwina (Tweeny) into her home in Sussex as an evacuee: so that just left my mother and I with nowhere to go. Luckily the Reverend Mother and some of the other nuns had remained at West Hill: when she heard of my mother's plight she offered her the use of two offices in a building near the main gate which housed the gymnasium and domestic science classroom as well as a maisonette which housed Mr and Mrs Cheeseman, who both worked for the Convent, as gate-keeper/handyman and domestic servant respectively, along with their daughter Peggy who had been a pupil there and was now waiting to go to university.

The two offices now became our bedrooms, furnished by Reverend Mother with rather spartan iron-framed beds and, in my case, a desk so I could do my homework. These makeshift bedrooms were at the far end of the gymnasium on the first floor whilst downstairs the classroom was fitted with ovens, hobs and refrigerators and, thankfully, there was a toilet so we had all the necessary facilities to be able to live there. The only thing we did not have was any money. This was nothing new because we had been stoney-broke many times before. Indeed in the summer of 1938 Mater, Jean and myself, then aged thirteen, worked for two months in a seafront hotel in Shanklin on the Isle of Wight; Mater as the assistant housekeeper, Jean as a chambermaid and myself as the scullery boy. This was Mater's idea of a working holiday. I have no idea how much I was paid as Jean and I handed over our pay-packets to our mother. Jean sometimes worked as a waitress in the hotel's restaurant and was allowed to keep any tips but, as a backroom boy, I got nothing.

For the following Christmas holiday I managed to get a job as a porter at the Oatlands Park Hotel near Weybridge and I worked there every holiday until I left school. I was only paid £1 per week, with one shilling and four pence deducted for the 'stamp', but I was given accommodation and three meals a day. Oatlands Park was a very posh hotel with extensive landscaped grounds including a large lake. Many of the guests were wealthy permanent residents and most were quite famous. My favourite was a delightful old lady called Lady de Frece who, as Vesta Tilley, had been the leading male impersonator in the Victorian music-halls, most famous for her song 'Burlington Bertie from Bow'. Another was an even older gentleman, whose name I have forgotten, who was in his nineties and sadly going blind. Although very fragile and somewhat tottery, he was very mentally alert and asked me if I could read certain sections of *The Daily Telegraph* to him every afternoon, for which enjoyable chores he gave me a half-crown each time I did so – a small fortune!

Perhaps because I spoke 'posh', I soon became a favourite with the regulars who, when they knew my circumstances, were very generous whenever I did anything for them. But the best money earner was when I started looking after the cloakroom for the Saturday night dances in the hotel ballroom, which were open to the public and much frequented by officers from nearby units and their ladies. On special occasions, such as New Year's Eve, it was not unusual to collect up to £5 in tips. By now Mater was quite happy for me to keep most of the money I earned but on the understanding that it was to be spent on items of school uniform, my bus fares, such necessary books which were not provided by the school, etc. I even bought a second-hand bicycle for five shillings which saved on bus fares until I pranged it – but that is another story.

When we had settled in at the Convent, Mater tried to get a steady job but the only work readily available was as a temporary cleaning lady. It was very sad that in less than a decade she had gone from being a fashionable socialite with a big house and several servants to cleaning other peoples' homes but she coped remarkably well with no recriminations about her two husbands who had landed her in this financial mess.

It was remarkable how well Mater had coped from the time that the family's fortunes had started to wane. Her priority had always been to ensure that we children should have a good education. She had started to keep us at private schools by selling jewellery, pictures and silver to pay our fees and other expenses. When those resources began to run out she took in paying guests and now that our fortunes had plumbed the depths she was rolling up her sleeves and taking on even the most menial of tasks. I had, and still have, the utmost admiration and respect for her determination and courage.

One Saturday she told me that she was going for an interview and had high hopes of landing a job at a reasonable wage which would make life easier for us.

She told me she would be away for about two hours, leaving me to get on with my homework.

No sooner had she gone than I heard footsteps clattering on the wooden floor of the gym: at first I thought Mater had forgotten something but it turned out to be Peggy Cheeseman with whom we had become quite friendly. Looking over my shoulder she saw that I was struggling with algebraic equations and offered to show me where I was going wrong. Within a very short time she had completed all the equations on rough paper so I could copy them into my book. She then asked what else I had to do and promptly translated one of Ovid's poems from the Latin into English and a passage from English into French, leaving me to do the remaining geography homework which I said was no problem. I was most impressed but, of course, she was much older than me and about to go to university. Having helped me cover at least two hours work in about thirty minutes she invited me to sit beside her on the window seat where we talked about school in general and lessons in particular. I remember that we agreed that biology was one of the most interesting subjects and we had a giggle about the embarrassed way in which, during anatomy, our respective teachers had covered the reproductive process.

Peggy then asked whether I had ever done it. At first I was not sure what she was talking about and asked what she meant. Having explained, she then asked whether I would like to have a go. Hoping that my blushing was not too obvious, I replied 'Yes, rather', whereupon, continuing the academic theme, she gave me a practical demonstration, with audience participation, of how best to exploit the difference between boys and girls. After which I could but say 'Vive la difference'. At that time I was two weeks short of my fifteenth birthday.

* * *

When Mater returned she was very excited. She had been offered the job which was to prepare meals for the men of the Auxiliary Fire Service (AFS) Station in Wandsworth. There was however one snag: she was required to live at the station, where a small flat was provided, because meals might be required at any time of night or day. Unfortunately there was no way that I could live there also and neither Reverend Mother nor Mater would countenance my staying on alone at the Convent. However, Reverend Mother knew of a good Catholic family who took boarders in Cromford Road, only a short walk from the Convent, so off we went to see Mrs Cullinan who, having duly inspected me, said she would be happy to look after me on a half-board basis. When my mother and Mrs Cullinan had agreed terms we left with the promise that I would move in the following day.

Mrs Cullinan was a grey-haired, rather large woman of about sixty years of age with a crumpled face, a broad Irish accent and varicose veins. The only other member of the family living at home was daughter Eileen, a plump young lady in her early twenties who worked as a receptionist in an opticians in Putney High Street. The most important absent member was the husband who had been the

Regimental Sergeant Major of the Irish Guards for many years. He had retired after having had a very distinguished career, having been awarded the Distinguished Conduct Medal and Military Medal in the First World War. He had now been recalled to the Colours to help train new recruits at the Guards Depot. There were photographs of him in many rooms, displaying his magnificent waxed moustache and two rows of medals. He may have been away but his presence was still felt. There was also a son who was serving in the Army.

The only permanent border was a Miss Bullen, aged about seventy-five, who had worked as a nanny and governess for three generations of a wealthy, titled Italian family. She had reluctantly returned to England, where she had no family, when Mussolini made clear that Italy would join forces with Germany, and was now living on a meagre pension. Her room was fascinating, being packed with memorabilia of her fifty odd years in Italy where she had expected to end her days. Two other regular boarders stayed at No. 76 for short stays: one was a Mr Adlam, a solicitor's clerk, who was studying to become a Catholic priest and had to make regular visits to the seminary at Manresa House in Roehampton. The second was a Mrs Daphne Swinnerton, a widow of about thirty years whose soldier husband had been killed in France in the early days of the war. She was a nurse working as a sick-bay attendant for one of the shipping lines which still sailed between London and Cape Town. She would stay with the Cullinans for two days before going to visit her parents somewhere 'up North' and for two days before setting sail again. And now, of course, there was me.

When I moved in with the Cullinans, the Battle of Britain was just getting under way but, apart from the occasional condensation trails in the distant skies, there was little evidence of the battle from West London. My room was one of two in the attic and, fortunately, the window looked out to the East and, being on a steep slope of West Hill, I had a marvellous view over the adjoining roof-tops towards the East End and Docklands. Needless to say I wasted a lot of time that should have been spent doing homework, looking out in the hopes of seeing some of the action. However, all that was to change.

When I returned to the Cullinans after the summer holiday, spent mainly at Oatlands Park Hotel earning my bus fares, the Battle of Britain was virtually over as Hitler had ordered Hermann Göring to stop attacking the RAF airfields and to start bombing cities, mainly London. During my absence the Cullinans had cleared out the cellar and turned it into an air raid shelter which they had furnished with a settee, a few decrepit old armchairs and the odd bench. RSM Cullinan had decreed a golden rule that everyone in the house was to stay in the cellar from the warning siren until the all clear had been sounded. As the night-time raids became more frequent I obediently complied, much to the detriment of my homework.

I hated being cooped up in the cellar, not least because of the smell of coal dust mingling with the odours of sweaty bodies – and, as the ladies had all the most comfortable chairs, I usually had to make do with a bench. Eventually I managed to convince Mrs C. that I would be better employed in my attic room where, armed with a stirrup pump and two buckets each of sand and water and an old army blanket, I could watch out for and deal with any incendiary bomb that might come crashing through the roof. I told her stories about the many people who had emerged from their cellars at the all clear only to find the upper stories of their houses ablaze. Luckily where we lived had suffered few bombs of any description and I was able to spend most nights watching the searchlights trying to illuminate the bombers for the benefit of the ack-ack gunners whose shells exploding in the sky were just like fireworks. Occasionally I was able to see the odd bomb burst on targets along the course of the River Thames. It was all very exciting and, strangely, I felt no fear. Increasingly, however, the pyrotechnics palled, the weather got colder and I spent more time tucked up warmly in bed.

By the end of 1940 the London blitz was getting more personal as the Germans were not only targeting strategic targets, such as the docks, power stations, railway termini, etc., but were also regarding purely residential areas as fair game. East London still bore the brunt of the attacks but west London was where the bombers indiscriminately jettisoned any leftover bombs before heading southwards for their bases. There were raids over London virtually every night and this was beginning to seriously disrupt my ability to study. There were only about six months remaining before I would sit the School Certificate and I was way behind schedule. Thankfully, I discovered that I could do my homework in the reading room of Wandsworth's excellent public library which was a little farther down West Hill. I started going there straight from school and Mrs C. kept me something for tea when I arrived back usually about 6.30pm before the night's first air raid warning siren started wailing.

All was not gloom and doom during the blitz, which I have to admit I rather enjoyed. The spirit of the Londoners was magnificent and at school we vied with each other as to who could collect the most shrapnel from the ack-ack shells which rained down on the city every night. I particularly enjoyed the times when Daphne Swinnerton, whom I called the Merry Widow, was staying. She was a breath of fresh air in an otherwise rather dull household. She slept in the other smaller attic room and, when the all clear sounded she would come up from the cellar to my room to see if I was alright. She would sit on my bedside chair and tell me the latest risqué jokes that she had heard from her shipmates.

One night there was a raid during which only incendiary bombs had been dropped and, looking out of my window, I could see the glow of numerous fires way to the east. The raid seemed to be over when everything went quiet but the all clear was not sounded. After a while Daphne came upstairs, eventually coming into my room in her dressing gown. I teased her about being brave as the all-clear siren had not gone and she replied that the warden must have lost his whistle. Then almost immediately a second wave of bombers could be heard approaching and dropping their high explosive bombs into the fires to maximize destruction and casualties. Before long Daphne was cold and frightened so she got into bed with me – with the inevitable consequence. Just as things were getting interesting we heard the unmistakable whistle of a bomb coming down close to us, followed by a violent explosion which shook the house to its foundations. Luckily there was no serious damage although the bomb demolished two houses about one hundred yards away. There was no doubt that the earth moved for me that night.

I did not see Daphne again before the end of term and when I returned after the Christmas holidays I found that Mr Adlam, who was now studying full time at Roehampton, was installed in the room next to mine. When Daphne stayed she now had to double up with Eileen. I was disappointed, but my experience with Peggy and Daphne had convinced me that my next such adventure could be just around the corner. Little did I think that it would be over three years and many thousands of miles away.

The Easter term was given over to the preparations for our taking the School Certificate but, when I sat the mock exams, I did very badly, passing in only one subject. This prompted the Prefect of Studies, Father Sinnott, to write on my end of term report, 'For a boy with ambitions to become a pilot John's school work never got off the ground'. This stung and, with my mother in tears, I really got down to studying during the final term but, having sat the final exams, I could do no more than hope that, if I was lucky, I might just scrape through.

When eventually the results of those who had passed were posted on the school notice-board in descending order of achievement, I started at the bottom and worked upwards. Having got halfway I turned away believing that I must have failed until I was slapped on the back by one of my classmates who said 'Well done, Langer' in a rather incredulous voice. I turned back and found my name way up the list: one distinction (in history of all unlikely subjects), five credits and one pass (in French, of course). So I had exceeded the minimum academic requirements for Cranwell, which unfortunately had ceased its courses soon after the outbreak of war. But now there was nothing to stop me volunteering for pilot training as a war-time entrant.

By now I was still only sixteen years old and the minimum age for enlistment was eighteen and a quarter years. The careers master, Father Collinson, had suggested that I should take one of the Government-sponsored courses which would guarantee work until I could apply for pilot training. We decided on a radio technology course which might prove useful in my intended RAF career. In September 1941 I duly reported to the SW Essex Technical College in Walthamstow for the four-month course. I was billeted with another student, Harry Dyde, in very working-class digs. I got on very well with Harry, who was nearly a year older than me, not least because he was also bent on becoming a pilot. The course finished in January 1942 and Harry and I were posted to the HMV factory in Hayes, Middlesex, to work in a section devoted to diagnosing and repairing faults in aircraft radio sets which had been damaged in crashes.

The posting was very convenient as my mother had given up her AFS job in Wandsworth, after a dangerous and stressful eighteen months, and was now working as the housekeeper in a large country house in Farnham Royal, to which the Plant Protection Division of ICI had been evacuated after their premises in London had been bombed. She had a self-contained flat in which I was able to stay. Mater had been recommended for this job by her old friend, Mrs Warren, who lived with her family in nearby Stoke Poges.

After about a month the novelty of my job at HMV had worn very thin and I was hating every minute of it. The worst aspect was having to get up shortly after 6 o'clock in order to cycle to Slough Station to catch the 7.10am train which got to Hayes just in time to walk to the factory gates to clock on by 7.45am. Almost as bad was the utter tedium due to the repetitive nature of the task. I even joined the 17th Battalion of the Middlesex Regiment Home Guard because its volunteers were allowed time off for training. The only good thing about the job was the pay of £5 per week, even though most of it went to Mater for my keep and on train fares. However, the cost of living in those days was pretty low: for example I remember that lunch in the works canteen cost about one shilling – and that included the pudding.

The best thing about this period of my life was the weekends. Most days I managed to get together with Doune Warren and some of her classmates from St Bernard's Convent in Slough, where they were studying for the Higher School Certificate. We would go on long cycle rides, to the cinema, go swimming and play tennis. My tennis partner was usually Ruth Bowyer, grand-daughter of the founder of Bowyer's Meat Products, justly famous for their pork sausages and pies, who had a country house in Farnham Common. She was a delightful young lady, slightly older than me, with beautiful auburn hair and freckles. It was not long before she had become my first proper girlfriend in so much as we held hands in the cinema and kissed each other hello/goodbye, albeit strictly on the cheek. In those days my idea of heaven was our sitting in the shade of a tree with my arm around her and her head resting on my shoulder.

In May Harry became old enough to apply for pilot training and had arranged to go to Euston House in London for the usual interviews, aptitude tests, medicals, etc. I decided to go with him despite being a year too young. We were required to take our birth certificates, a copy of our scholastic results and, as we were minors, a letter giving permission from a parent or guardian. I got Harry to write my mother's letter which I signed 'Maud E. Doe', having practised her signature for weeks. The birth certificate posed a more difficult problem as there was no way I could change my date of birth from 1925 to 1924 without it being obvious. So I would have to go without it with a story about having mislaid it. To cut a long story short, we went up together, both passed all the necessary procedures and were accepted. We were then sworn in, or 'attested', and told to go home, join the Slough Air Training Corps Squadron and to await our call-up papers. Thankfully they had accepted that I had lost my birth certificate but told me to get another copy to present eventually at the Aircrew Reception Centre. I did not tell Mater that I had volunteered. It was just a matter of waiting – somewhat impatiently!

Chapter 2

Pilot Training

Having been warned of a possible year's wait for our call-up papers, I was delighted to receive mine after only three months. They instructed me to report to the Air Crew Receiving Centre (ACRC) in Regent's Park by noon on 28 September, only four days after the date on which the RAF thought I was eighteen and a quarter years old. This infuriated Harry Dyde who, in the event, had to wait the full year. My mother was very concerned about my going but I managed to convince her, as she had no idea that I had volunteered, that I was very lucky not to have been conscripted into the Army. Ruth knew that I had enlisted in May and, although unhappy about my leaving so soon, was mainly very proud. It was with great relief that I handed in my notice at HMV where my workmates held a whip-round and raised just over £20 to see me on my way. Despite having hated my time at Hayes, I nevertheless felt quite choked at their generosity and goodwill.

I duly reported to ACRC only to find that it was located in part of London Zoo, many of the animals having been redistributed to other, safer, zoos. We were a motley lot of young men mostly straight from university, public, grammar or state schools, as well as those who had worked in a variety of occupations since leaving school. There were also a few volunteers from the ranks of the RAF. We were given the rank of aircraftman second class, or AC2, but we were known as cadet pilots under training, or U/T pilots. Our pay was two shillings a day, of which I made a voluntary allotment of six pence a day to my mother.

Having booked in we were allocated into parties of about forty recruits and ours was marched to a large house in nearby Avenue Road where we were to be accommodated. There we were issued with three straw-filled 'biscuits' which served as the mattress on our iron beds. We were also given blankets, sheets, towels, pyjamas, mess tins, cutlery and a kitbag. We were then shown how to make up our beds and, more importantly, how to unmake them to prepare for the 'stand by your beds' kit inspections which were to be held every morning before breakfast. Woe betide anyone whose blankets and sheets were not aligned exactly as required. All our meals were taken in a dining hall in the Zoo. We had cups of tea with every meal which tasted decidedly funny. The rumour spread that we were being given bromide in the tea which was supposed to suppress our libidos and save us from the temptations of the wicked city.

The next three weeks were spent being issued with uniforms and everything else right down to vest, pants and socks. There were medical and dental examinations, not least the dreaded FFI (free from infection) examinations to check there were no sores on our private parts which required us all to drop our trousers whilst standing in a long line. There were various talks on a variety of subjects and most events were held in different places between which we had to march as a squad; so we also had to do a lot of drill training to ensure that everyone knew their left feet from their right. The communal aspects of this introduction to service life came as a nasty shock to many recruits; those who coped best were the ones who had been to boarding school and were used to sleeping in dormitories and to the mad rush to wash and shave in the totally inadequate ablutions, not to mention toilets.

Needless to say there was much queuing, particularly at meal times. In one such queue I talked to a young man who introduced himself as 'John Sharpe - with an E', who was eventually to become a firm friend and the best man at my wedding.

* * *

At the end of our three weeks at ACRC we were all posted to a number of Initial Training Wings (ITWs) all dotted around the country at holiday resorts where the Air Ministry had taken over many of the big hotels. I was amongst those going to No. 13 ITW at Torquay where they could not accommodate us for two weeks: so we were sent to Brighton and housed in the Grand Hotel where decades later the IRA attempted to wreck the Tory Party Conference, and hopefully kill the Prime Minister, Mrs Thatcher, by planting a bomb in one of the bathrooms. Whilst there we attended lectures mainly on the mathematics we would require to understand aerodynamics, meteorology and other aviation subjects. The top two floors of the Grand Hotel housed many Polish Air Force officers who had escaped before their country had been over-run by the Nazis. They were now studying English before being absorbed into the RAF.

In early November 1942 we eventually assembled for the ITW course at Torquay and were accommodated in another Grand Hotel. I was allocated to one of the penthouse suites which was rather spoiled by my having to share it with twenty other fellows. The six- month course was mainly academic with lectures on principles of flight, engines, meteorology, flight instruments, airmanship and air traffic control, all interspersed with physical training, drill, cross-country running, clay pigeon shooting and swimming. Everything we did seemed to be held at different locations and we were marched between them at 140 paces to the minute instead of the more sedate 120 paces which was usual elsewhere. The higher rate is acceptable on the parade ground but marching up and down Torquay's steep slopes played havoc with the shins and calf muscles.

I enjoyed my six months in Torquay despite the marching and our being whistled at by the girls. I had no problems with the academic aspects and even liked drill, which most people hated. Our drill instructor, Corporal Taffy Jones, a former Welsh miner, managed to combine absolute authority with a terrific sense of humour. Endless drill and interminable inspections were interspersed with fun such as the game 'Riley says' whereby we were marched around the parade ground with quick-fire commands to which we should only respond if prefixed with those two words. So if the instructor shouted 'Riley says right turn' we should turn right but if, for example, he shouted 'Halt' we should ignore the command. Anyone who got it wrong had to fall out until there was only one cadet left – the winner, who was suitably rewarded. I won the game on several occasions. It all sounds a little silly but it was, in fact, a serious test of our reactions. Much to my surprise, I also enjoyed clay pigeon shooting and found that, despite never having handled a shot-gun before, I was a natural shot. I often scooped the pool of the shillings put into the kitty by the twenty odd contestants, a windfall much prized considering our meagre pay. Clay pigeon shooting might seem an unnecessary part of our training but the pundits had long believed that the best fighter pilots were those who were good at shooting, squash and horse-riding: luckily I was not bad at all three.

Unless there was a church parade, Sunday was our only clear day off, Saturday afternoons being devoted to compulsory sport. Only those with private means could afford to 'hit the town' but even on my miserable two bob a day I could still afford to enjoy myself, not least because I neither smoked nor drank. A typical Sunday might begin with morning coffee in the solarium of the Imperial Hotel, one of the few still functioning normally. After lunch, I usually went to an afternoon concert in the Palace Theatre given by the Torquay Municipal Orchestra and perhaps the cinema in the evening. The local civilians were very hospitable and many of the cadets were invited into their homes for meals.

To my regret I did not go to any of the performances given by that great actor/manager, Donald Wolfit and his Troupe of Players when they were in town. I had been put off Shakespeare by having to study *Twelfth Night* as part of the English Literature exam for the School Certificate. Had I done so I might well have seen and fallen for one of the younger actresses, a Miss Doreen Newland Hodges, who also attended the Sunday concerts. When many years later I said to her 'If only we had met in Torquay in 1943' she replied in her usual forthright manner 'If we had met then I don't suppose I would have given you a second glance'. Oh, the woes of being a humble cadet!

* * *

The course finished towards the end of April and we cadets were dispersed to a number of Elementary Flying Training Schools around the country for twelve hours flying in the de Havilland Tiger Moth, a venerable aircraft first used in the RAF as a primary trainer in 1932. It was a biplane with two open cockpits and no radio, communication between instructor and student being by a hollow Gosport Tube and mouthpiece leading into the earphones in one's helmet. It had no brakes and no tail wheel, in place of which was a metal skid which slowed one down effectively when landing on grass. I was posted, with other cadets, to No. 16 EFTS in Burnaston near Derby. There we were told that, at the end of our twelve hours flying, we would be assessed as best suited for further training as pilots, navigators or bomb-aimers. This process was known as 'grading' and the news came as a nasty shock as we had all volunteered to be pilots.

The EFTSs were all grass airfields which in peacetime had housed civilian flying clubs. Our instructors came from a variety of backgrounds and were all very experienced pilots. My instructor was aged about forty and had had an RAF short service commission between the wars; his rather fancy name was Flying Officer de Vere Hunt. My first trip was an air experience flight intended to acclimatize us to the sensations of being airborne and seeing the ground from a bird's eye view. Towards the end of the flight I was asked whether I would like him to do a few aerobatics. Being mad keen I replied 'yes rather' whereupon he did a loop, a barrel roll and a stall turn before heading back to base. It was all very exciting but, unwisely, I had eaten a banana just prior to getting airborne and was now feeling rather queasy. I managed to hold on until landing but as soon as my feet were on terra firma I was sick on the grass: the first and last time that I was ever airsick.

Thereafter my training proceeded without incident until I had reached the take-off and landing stage. After about eight hours flying I was beginning to get the hang of things and hoped to be sent solo when disaster struck. The weather closed in, the Midlands was shrouded with thick mist and all solo flying was suspended. The remaining four hours, including my final handling test with the Chief Flying Instructor, were all dual and rather restricted by the weather. I wondered whether my not having gone solo would prejudice my being selected for pilot training. I asked Flying Officer Hunt how he thought I had done but he was rather non-committal.

On completion of grading we all assembled at the Air Crew Dispersal Centre at Heaton Park in Manchester where we would learn our fate. All the cadets were accommodated in the Nissen huts dotted around the park. About thirty were allocated to each hut with a single coke stove in the middle: thankfully we were there in June and July, so keeping warm was no problem. The worst aspect was that there was only one separate ablution block to every four huts, thus resulting in overcrowding and inconvenience, especially when it was raining. At Heaton Park I met up again with Johnnie Sharpe who had done his ITW course in Scarborough. After about a week we were all assembled in a local cinema to hear the results of our grading: luckily Johnnie and I were both selected for pilot training. We were then sent on embarkation leave to await notification to return to ACDC prior to travelling to Canada for the next phase of our flying training. Whilst on leave I stayed with my mother but, as she was working, I spent a lot of time with Doune Warren and Ruth Bowyer, of whom I was becoming very fond.

* * *

On return from leave Johnnie and I were delighted to learn that we were both in the batch of cadets being sent not to Canada but to America. Two weeks later we were driven to Liverpool where we embarked on the HMT *Louis Pasteur*, a former French cruise liner commandeered as a troopship. Hundreds of us boarded and were housed in various parts of the boat sleeping in either four- tiered bunk beds or in hammocks. I was lucky to be allocated into what had been the boat's library and I managed to get a bottom bunk. We sailed from Liverpool at night en route to St John's in Newfoundland and we expected to join up with a convoy but we learned from a seaman that former cruise liners made solo crossings as they were fast enough to outrun any submarine. Nevertheless, the boat was steered along an erratic zig-zag course to minimize the risk of interception. After about six very boring days we arrived in St John's in the usual thick fog, were disembarked and transported to Moncton in New Brunswick, where we stayed for a few days. Those of us who were going to training schools in Oklahoma, Arizona or Texas then boarded a train on which we stayed until we reached our various destinations. At Moncton, Johnnie and I found to our annoyance that, although we were both going to Oklahoma, we were allocated to different schools several hundred miles apart.

After three days and nights the train arrived at its first destination, Miami in the North East corner of Oklahoma, the home of the Spartan School of Aeronautics where No. 3 British Flying Training School was based. Eighty-seven of us were bussed from the railway station to the school: we wondered why eighty-seven but soon learned that we were to be joined by thirteen United States Army Air Corps cadets to make up our No. 17 course to a round hundred.

We were told that the course would consist of three phases each of two months: the primary phase consisted of seventy hours on the Fairchild PT19A, followed by the basic phase of sixty hours on the North American AT6C Harvard and finally the advanced phase of seventy hours, also on the Harvard. At the end of each phase the cadets would move up in the more senior barrack block and be given more privileges. The flying was to be interspersed with ground school and Link-trainer instruction. Most of the flying instructors were American civilians from a

The Cadet pilots of No. 3 British Flying Training School, Miami, Oklahoma, USA, in July 1943.

variety of backgrounds, such as flying the US Mail, barnstorming, crop-spraying and ferrying: many were quite old and all were very experienced. However the Commanding Officer was an RAF Wing Commander who had an administrative officer, an adjutant, three flying instructors and two ground instructors, all of whom were RAF officers. There were also four RAF SNCOs to look after armaments, drill and signals instruction.

The barrack block was T-shaped with the two junior phases in the cross-piece and the more spacious senior rooms at the foot. The overall facilities were pretty good, even the double-tiered bunk beds were very comfortable, but we got a nasty shock when we saw the ablutions where we found a long line of pedestal toilets without any partitioning between – a sure recipe for instant constipation. However, the food in the cafeteria was superb by UK wartime standards. Nothing was rationed in the USA and beef, chicken, ham, steak, eggs and salads appeared in unlimited quantities. At breakfast, in addition to the routine eggs, any style, and bacon, waffles and maple syrup etc., there was always a fruit bowl from which the cadets were meant to help themselves to apples, bananas, oranges and other exotic fruits, none of which were available in the UK – not even from Fortnum and Mason. What I remember most was the beautiful white bread, and unlimited butter, which was such a change from the tasteless grey loaves, with a scrape of butter or margarine, which was the norm in wartime Britain.

I had my first flight on 2 August with my instructor, Mr Bollar, a man in his fifties, who had flown planes delivering the US Mail for much of his life. He was like everybody's favourite uncle and he took a great interest in his pupils. On 9 August, more by good luck than good judgement, I was the first of my course to go solo. When I landed it was with tears in his eyes that he put his arm around my shoulders and told me how lucky I was to have a lifetime of flying ahead of me. He had four pupils, two of whom flew in the mornings, the others in the afternoons. I was paired with cadet J. R. 'Spud' Murphy, a typically chirpy Cockney from Eltham who had been a milkman for a couple of years before he joined the RAF. His proud boast was that his family lived a couple of houses down from that in which that great comedian Bob Hope had been born. Spud and I became good mates, not least because we were both Catholic and Londoners.

On the first Sunday after our arrival, Spud and I were the first cadets of the new course to leave camp as, being RC, we were excused Church Parade and were going to Mass in downtown Miami. As we went out of the main gate we saw a line of cars stretching almost as far as the eye could see: the first 'automobile' drove up and asked if 'we boys' would like to have lunch with him and his wife at their home. Spud replied that we would love to but we were on our way to Mass. No problem, said the driver who introduced himself as Pa Black, who took us to the Church in Miami, saying he would pick us up when the service was over. Having done so, we then drove quite a long way to Baxters Springs which was across the state border into Kansas. On arrival we were introduced to Ma Black and to their daughter Shirley, a rather plump sixteen-year old. Home was a rather rambling wooden shack set in several acres of wooded land that ran down to a rushing stream. After being shown around the property, we had a very good lunch of corned beef hash followed by apple pie and ice-cream. We then settled down to listen to the 'Charlie McCarthy Show' on the radio, a Sunday ritual in the Black household. After tea, Ma Black asked if we would like them to pick us up the following Sunday, to which we readily agreed.

Ma and Pa Black in Baxters Springs.

The Blacks not only picked up Spud and I that Sunday but also for every weekend until the end of the course. They really went out of their way to ensure that we enjoyed our time with them. We were driven all over the Middle West to view beauty spots, to visit Indian reservations and to other attractions. Pa Black gave us driving lessons as neither of us had driven before: he even let us drive his Ford on our own. He took us shooting in the woods for squirrels which Ma Black turned into delicious pies. The Blacks were not wealthy but whenever we ate out they would never let us pay. I will always remember their warmth, kindness and generosity. Spud and I were not their first RAF cadets; they had had five pairs before us. Needless to say, similar hospitality from other families was enjoyed by most of our cadets.

The primary phase of training was duly completed with only a few cadets failing to make the grade. We moved into the basic phase barrack rooms and were given the privilege of being allowed off-base after duty on Wednesdays instead of only on Sundays. Although the food in the cafeteria was good it was becoming a bit boring as the menu seldom changed and an institutional mess hall with 250 or so cadets queuing with trays and then sitting on benches at long refectory tables did not make for convivial meal-times.

On our first free Wednesday evening Spud and I went into Miami to eat at one of the town's 'diners'. We duly tucked into huge T-bone steaks with two eggs 'sunny side up' and mountains of 'french fries'. During dinner we noticed that two ladies at another table kept looking at us and laughing. Eventually they came over to our table and started chatting. They introduced themselves and Marjorie invited us to her house for coffee. Ellen did not seem so keen, nor in fact was I, but Spud, thinking we were on to a good thing, readily accepted. Then followed an embarrassing evening during which Spud and Marjorie larked about, played records, sort of danced and flirted outrageously whilst Ellen and I sat and nattered. Eventually Marjorie drove us back to base but not before giving Spud her phone number. I rather hoped that we would not be seeing those two not-so-young ladies again.

The author with Cadet
Percy-Smith in front
of the Fairchild Cornell
primary trainer.

By comparison with the Fairchild, which was rather too easy to fly, the Harvard, onto which we now converted, was a much more difficult proposition. It was bigger, heavier, more powerful, faster, more complex and had a number of vices which could only too readily catch out the unwary. However, it was remarkably robust and could withstand even the heaviest of landings but it did have a tendency to ground-loop when landing in a cross-wind and then often scrape a wing tip on the runway. My new instructor, Mr J. J. Hume was much younger than Mr Bollar and Mr Montague, my two primary instructors. Whereas they had been patient and good humoured, Hume was somewhat intolerant and irascible, quite rightly demanding the high standards necessary to master the Harvard. I was no longer paired with Spud Murphy but with a nice cadet called Charles Anthony Percy-Smith, known as Tony to his friends but as Percy to everybody else. It soon became clear that many of the cadets were having trouble coping with the Harvard and before long one or two cadets per week were being sent packing – back to Canada for retraining as navigators or bomb-aimers. Luckily I had no such problems and was thoroughly enjoying the flying, especially now that every other trip was solo.

One Wednesday in November Percy and I caught the bus to Miami to go to the cinema. I found the film, a typical Hollywood 'B' movie, very boring and the smoke-laden atmosphere quite oppressive, so I left, telling Percy that I would see him on the bus back to base. I walked around the town but there was little to interest me until I saw the United Services Organization (USO) reading room. I seemed to be the only person there so I settled down to read a *National Geographic* magazine. No sooner had I sat down than the lady 'minding the shop' came out from the office and to my surprise it was Ellen. She seemed pleased to see me and, having brought me a cup of coffee, she sat down and started to chat.

I had forgotten what a nice woman she was and before long we had laughed about our embarrassing first meeting and started talking about everything and nothing. I completely lost any sense of time but soon realized that I had missed the bus – and there was not another one for three hours. Ellen told me not to worry as she was being relieved soon and would drive me back to base. On the way I asked if we could meet again, perhaps to have dinner together. Ellen told me that it was a USO rule that their volunteers should not date servicemen and that we should not be seen out together – as much as she would like to do so. I then told her about the hole in the wall where, many courses previously cadets had created a breach in the fencing where they could get out of camp without being spotted. It opened onto a side road, not the famous Route 66 which ran in front of the main entrance and guardroom. Ellen said that she was free every Wednesday evening after her stint at the USO and that she could pick me up the following Wednesday at 8.00pm – and this she did every week until the end of the course.

Round about this time Flight Lieutenant Ayton Whitaker, the Navigation Officer, asked if I would be interested in reading for a part in the play he was planning to put on in mid-December. Apparently Whitaker had started to make a name for himself as an actor and director of stock and touring companies before the war. Since arriving at 3 BFTS he had formed a Dramatic Society and had already successfully staged *Rope* by Patrick Hamilton in the auditorium of the Miami High School. I told him that I had always steered clear of amateur dramatics at school because I was far too shy and that even now I would be a prime candidate for stage fright. He accepted my reservations but asked if I would be prepared to work behind the scenes as stage manager – to which I agreed.

The play was to be *Journey's End* by R. C. Sherriff, a good choice as all the action took place in a dug-out in the trenches during the First World War, so there were no scene shifts, and there were only eleven players. My job was to supervise the setting up of the scenery, to organize uniforms for the cast and to arrange the stage lighting with particular reference to the sound and light effects to denote bombardment. I was also to act as prompt for the rehearsals and performance and to prepare, and get printed, the advertising posters and the programmes. It soon became clear that I had too much on my plate, so, with Whitaker's agreement, I recruited two cadets, John Rayson as ASM to look after the prompting, and David Scatchard, an electrical whizz, to arrange all the lighting and sound effects. Through Ellen, I managed to get help from the USO who built the set, provided the uniforms and printed the posters and programmes – all for free.

The play opened, and closed, on Friday 17 December with every seat sold and was a resounding success. The star, as actor and director, was Ayton Whitaker but there was also an excellent performance by cadet Peter Shore. It was very brave of him to find time for the readings and rehearsals as he was struggling to make the grade and had already been put back a course, having a particular problem with instrument flying. Before the play I had spoken to the cast and the backroom boys prior to writing 'Who's Who in the Play' for the programme. I recall Shore telling me of his intent to become a Labour MP and that he had very strong political views. In his write up, amongst other things, I wrote 'He loathes the Conservative Party and has ambitions for a state of intellectual anarchism'. I do not know whether Peter ever got his pilot's wings, but he left the RAF as a Flying Officer in 1946. Having joined the Labour Party in 1945 he went on to have a brilliant political career, heading the Research Department for five years before becoming MP for Stepney in 1964. His appointments included being PPS to Prime Minister Harold Wilson, being Secretary of State for Economic Affairs, for Trade and for the Environment and also, when Labour was in opposition, Shadow Leader of the Commons. He was a persistent critic of the European Economic Union which may have been why he was an unsuccessful candidate for the leadership of the Labour Party. He was awarded a Life Peerage in1997 as Baron Shore of Stepney. I recall that, when I was in my tenth year as a Wing Commander and my once-promising career seemed to have gone pear shaped, I used to console myself that at least I had done better than Peter Shore who had only made the rank of Flying Officer.

When Ellen picked me up on Wednesday evenings our outings always followed the same pattern. Because Oklahoma and Kansas were 'dry' states she would drive hell for leather for the border with Missouri which was 'wet'. In dry states one could only buy alcohol from licensed liquor stores and then only drink it at home. You were allowed to transport unopened bottles in your car but if you were found with an opened bottle you would be fined heavily. Over the border, near the town of Joplin, Ellen knew a remote liquor store and bar and, having driven into the car park, one of us would collect the drinks. Our favourite was a 'Cuba Libre' served in a tall glass half filled with ice cubes over which a double tot of dark rum was poured, then the glass was filled with Coca Cola, topped with a thick slice of lemon. I was not fond of 'coke', but served like this it made a very refreshing drink.

We hardly ever said a word whilst driving as Ellen liked to keep her window wound down and to sing. She had a good voice and sang in her church choir and in the musicals put on by the local amateur dramatic society. Their next production was to be *Oklahoma* so she regaled me with songs from the show which was currently enjoying great success on Broadway. Her favourite was 'People will say we are in love', with which she used to tease me. At Joplin we always drank our drinks in the back of the car which was a Chevrolet two-door, four-seater coupé. The only side windows were those above the doors, so anyone in the back could only see forward but, more importantly, back-seat passengers could not be seen readily from outside unless someone actually peered in. Ellen was forever reminding me that we were not to be seen together or she might lose her job with the USO.

Once installed in the car with our drinks we talked incessantly. Ellen was very inquisitive and wanted to know all about me, including my parents, my siblings, whether I had any girlfriends, my school days, what sports I played, what my ambitions were, etc., etc. ad nauseam. In contrast she told me little about herself other than that she had graduated from Miami A & M College, had gone elsewhere to university and now worked in the local bank. It took me ages to find out that she was twenty-eight years old, almost ten years older than my real age. When I took her to task for always working our conversations around to me, she laughed and said that she loved to listen to my funny English accent. When we ran out of personal topics she showed great interest in the BFTS course and wanted to know, for example, what kept aircraft in the air. When I tried to gloss over her questions she said that she really wanted to know the detail so I had to explain the balance of the forces of thrust, lift, drag and weight coupled with Bernoulli's Theorem and the Laws of Isaac Newton. To my surprise she seemed to understand exactly what I was talking about and asked many perceptive questions. She was not only interested in the principles of flight but also in meteorology, navigation and engines. After a while I had a suspicion that she really knew rather more than she was letting on.

We had our last Wednesday outing the one before Christmas 1943 – which Spud and I were to spend with the Blacks. I had come to like Ellen a lot and I was grateful not only for her friendship and generosity but also for getting the USO to help with the staging of *Journey's End*, so, as she dropped me off at the hole in the wall, I gave her a Christmas present of a pair of Navajo silver-drop earrings encrusted with turquoise. She was both surprised and delighted and turned towards me to give me a kiss – which I rather botched by turning my head so she could kiss me on the cheek. She laughed and told me that I needed a few lessons in kissing – which she would put in hand after the Christmas break.

* * *

We had finished the basic phase of training in mid-December and had a few days break which Spud and I spent in Baxters Springs. Ground school was now finished and the advanced phase loomed. With no lectures to attend it was not unusual to have three or even four trips a day. We were no longer learning how to fly but how to apply our skills in such exercises as formation flying, combat manoeuvres, basic gunnery, night flying, low-level navigation and landing away on cross country flights. We wasted no time in ensuring that the course finished on time, even night flying on Christmas Eve – so Spud and I were unable to go to midnight Mass and the Blacks had to pick us up on Christmas morning for our three-day break.

Everything was now much more exhilarating than previously, not least because most of our flying was solo or with other cadets. Towards the end of January we had our final handling, navigation and instrument flying tests and sat the ground-school examinations. We lost several cadets during this phase until we were left with seventy-six out of the original one hundred. In the first few days of February we anxiously awaited the overall course results which were promulgated by the CO, Wing Commander Roxburgh, on the 5th. I tied with my friend Wally Murton for twenty-fourth place in the order of merit, which was disappointing as I had expected to do a bit better, but in the separate rating for officer qualities and

The author in the
cockpit of the North
American Harvard
advanced trainer.

leadership potential, which applied only to the RAF cadets, I came tenth, which was far better than I had hoped for, as a result of which I was commissioned as a pilot officer. I had given little attention to the possibility of becoming an officer as my immediate aim had been to qualify for my pilot's wings, so this came as a welcome surprise. I had not excelled in any particular aspect of the course, except perhaps on the athletics track and sports field, nor did I have a lot to say for myself as I was still pretty shy in public: maybe the staff mistook me for the strong silent type. The Blacks were just as delighted as I was the first of the many RAF cadets they had hosted to have been commissioned. Spud did well to come thirty-eighth, but Percy only just managed to scrape through and they were both promoted to sergeant.

The atmosphere was one of great excitement at the prospect of returning to the UK and going on to operational training. My joy was complete when, at my farewell interview with the Commanding Officer, he told me that I had been strongly recommended to go on to fighters. There was, however, one cloud on my horizon. Ruth had written to me every week since I had been away but her letters had tailed off in December and I had had only two since Christmas. Whereas previously her letters had been newsy, funny and bright, in these last two she seemed to be somewhat out of sorts. Her handwriting had changed into a barely legible scrawl and she seemed somewhat morose, writing that she desperately hoped that I would return soon – before it was too late. I realized that something was badly wrong – perhaps she was not well. I wrote telling her about my wings and commission and that I expected to be home on leave before the end of February.

We were awarded our wings by a Group Captain Bell, who had flown in from Washington, at a passing out parade which was followed by a Graduation Ball at which we had said goodbye to all our American friends. The following night we were getting ready for bed, somewhat earlier than usual as we were getting up at

5.00 the following morning to board the train back to Canada, when the phone in the barrack room rang. It was answered by one of the cadets who shouted out 'Langer, it's for you'. It was Ellen who asked if I could meet her in the hole in the wall in fifteen minutes time as she had something to give me. I said 'no problem' and quickly got dressed again. Mainly because of night-flying, we had had only three Wednesday outings since Christmas in which, true to her promise, Ellen taught me how to kiss, building up from the friendly to the positively seductive – all very tantalising! She also gave me a lot of advice on how best to court a young lady which could be summed up as behave impeccably, do not rush things, progress slowly but surely and, if things were to proceed to a natural conclusion, be gentle.

When Ellen drove up she asked me to get in the back seat as what she had for me was at her home. This surprised me as she had never invited me to her house and I did not even know her address – only her phone number. As we approached her road she asked me to crouch down so that, as she drove into the garage, no one could see that there was anyone in the back. Having closed the garage door, she took me into the kitchen, showed me where everything was and asked me to make two Cuba Libres whilst she changed into something more comfortable. When the drinks were ready she called for me to 'bring them in here'. 'Here' turned out to be the bedroom where, to my surprise, I found her wearing a dressing gown. We toasted each other. Putting down her drink, she kissed me and whispered in my ear 'I would like you to make love to me'. Being a boy brought up to be sensitive to the wishes of young ladies, I was only too happy to oblige.

When the deed was done and Ellen had got her breath back, I asked 'was that all-right?' 'All-right!' laughed Ellen. 'That was marvellous – the best ever.' Stupidly I said 'So you've done this lots of times before?' To which she replied 'Silly boy, of course I have – I've been married for seven years.' Oh my God, I thought to myself, she is a married woman: we have just committed adultery and that is a

The author is awarded his pilot's wings (and a commission) on 6 February 1944.

mortal sin! I asked why she had not told me she was married and did she not love her husband. She said 'Yes, I do love my husband and, believe it or not, what I have just done was for him.' I responded that it seemed a funny way to show one's love, to which she replied that she had never meant me to find out that she was married – it had just slipped out.

Seeing that I was distressed, Ellen went on to explain that they had been trying to start a family since they were married but to no avail. After about five years they had both been medically examined which showed that she was perfectly healthy and capable whereas he was found to have a very low sperm count. The doctors had said that it was not impossible that they might conceive but it was pretty unlikely. This inability was beginning to affect her husband, who blamed himself for their childlessness.

She then told me that when she and Marjorie first saw Spud and me in the diner they got quite a shock as I was the spitting image of her husband: same height, same complexion, same hair and almost identical facial features. She then went to a drawer and took out some framed photographs which she had hidden. It was uncanny: there was I in morning dress at the wedding, there was I in the cockpit of a Mustang fighter and in the uniform of a pilot in the Civil Air Guard and many others. Apparently her husband was an aeronautical engineer and test pilot working on aircraft production and only able to return home at weekends. Marjorie, who knew of Ellen's problem, had joked that, if she was to have an affair with me, any baby would be sure to look like her husband. She also told me how thrilled she had been when she saw on my 'dog tags' that my blood group was the same as her husband's. She said that, although originally it had all been a big joke, the more she got to know me the more she had been tempted – but she could not bring herself to be unfaithful as she had never slept with anyone other than her husband. She had only decided to go ahead at the eleventh hour when, by chance, my going coincided with her being at exactly the right time in her menstrual cycle.

Somewhat placated, I asked Ellen if she would let me know whether we had struck lucky. She said that it was best that I should never know and that, from her own point of view, irrespective of the outcome, she would have to do her best to forget me and what we had done. I tried to give her my mother's address but she refused to accept it saying that any future contact between us could be dangerous. The drive back to base was rather sombre but as Ellen dropped me off at the hole in the wall she kissed me and said 'Thank you for your friendship: I will miss you terribly but you must go back to your Ruth and forget all about me' and with that she drove off.

As I had not got into bed until the early hours, our 5.30am reveille came as a nasty shock. After a quick breakfast, we were all bussed to the railway station in Miami where, to our surprise, there were crowds of local people to see us off. The Blacks were there with young Shirley crying her eyes out. I looked around to see if Ellen was anywhere but wisely she had decided to stay away. Before long our train steamed in and we all piled on board for the three-day journey back to Moncton in New Brunswick. The contingent from No. 6 BFTS in Ponca City were already on board and to my delight I found that Johnny Sharpe had not only got his wings but also had been commissioned.

My emotions were very mixed as the train chugged its way towards Chicago and onwards into Canada. Initially my thoughts were with Ellen but I also remembered the Blacks and the way they had taken Spud and me into their hearts and their home, as indeed did many other American families who had showered the British cadets with such fantastic warmth and hospitality. But as the journey went on most of us became increasingly excited at the prospect of returning to the UK and our own families, not to mention girlfriends. I was also thrilled at the thought of becoming operational on Spitfires, Typhoons, Mosquitoes or whatever. Little did I realize what a shock I was in for.

* * *

It might be interesting to reflect that, in the early days of the war, pilot training in America was a very attractive idea much favoured by the RAF and top government officials. The advantages were many, including freedom from enemy action, unlimited supplies of cheap aviation fuel, better weather, and therefore shorter training courses, and the ability to utilize former UK training airfields for operational use. The initial problem was that the USA had not yet entered the war and was anxious to maintain at least the appearance of neutrality. Nevertheless, discussions took place at the highest level, eventually involving Prime Minister Churchill and President Roosevelt. Finally, the USA agreed to help and various schemes were discussed, of which that involving the setting up of six British Flying Training Schools was by far the most important.

The question of expense was paramount as the cost of the scheme was to be paid for in dollars, which were in short supply. However, the introduction of lend-lease provided a welcome method of financing these schools by deferring payment. The six schools were to be privately-owned establishments, run by civilians and the cost was to be an hourly rate of $25 for primary flying and $35 for basic and advanced flying – a bargain if ever there was one.

Paradoxically No. 3 BFTS was the first school to be set up, the first batch of cadets arriving on 10 June 1941 at the Spartan School of Aeronautics in Tulsa but moving to Miami on 13 July. According to the National Archives in Kew, a total of 2,124 RAF and 117 USAAF cadets started training and 1,493 graduated and were awarded their wings. That seems like a high wastage rate but it includes the unfortunate cadets on courses Nos. 26 and 27, whose training was never completed because of the end of the war. The real wastage rate was nearer to 25 per cent. The total output of trained pilots from the six BFTSs was about 9,000 – a great contribution to the war effort, at reasonable cost.

There were inevitably certain drawbacks. For example, in my six months of flying training, I never once flew in cloud: all my instrument flying was done under the hood or in the Link trainer. Map reading over the vast Mid-West, with its few roads and railway links, was completely different to that in the UK where roads and railways criss-cross the countryside with wild abandon. Navigation was also all too easy in the USA as all the major cities are linked by airways in which you can 'ride the beam'. All one had to do was to tune in to the relevant beam and maintain a continuous signal in one's headphones. If one's aircraft strayed off the beam to port the signal would become a morse A; if to starboard it became N; so slight adjustment to heading was all that was necessary to get back on track. Having said that, some of these disadvantages were prevalent in all those other countries, such as Canada, South Africa and Egypt, where aircrew training was carried out to take advantage of better weather which could halve the time taken to complete the various courses.

* * *

After three long days and nights we eventually arrived at the Personnel Depot in Moncton to await a troopship to take us back to 'Blighty'. My two priorities were, firstly, to go to confession and, secondly, to get kitted out in officer's uniform. Confession turned out to be a bit of an anti-climax. When I presented myself to the officiating RC Chaplain I went through the usual preamble until we got to the part where he said 'And what sins do you have to confess, son?' I replied somewhat hesitantly that I regretted that I had committed a mortal sin by sleeping with a married woman. Instead of being aghast, as I expected, he merely asked two simple questions 'How many times did you sleep with the lady?' to which I replied 'Just the once' and, secondly, 'Did you know that she was married?' to which my answer was 'No, I didn't'. To my surprise, instead of berating me, he simply said that there was no reason for me to be so worried but that in future I should try to be a little more careful. With that advice he spoke the words of absolution and gave me a penance of three Hail Marys.

Getting kitted out was equally painless as we brand new pilot officers were able to draw out a battledress top and trousers from the Equipment Section plus enough braid to sew onto the epaulettes. The No.1 uniform tunic and trousers and all the other items, such as the hat and leather gloves, had to be bought privately, so Johnnie Sharpe and I duly joined the queue to be served at the Moncton Family Outfitters which stocked a vast range of ready-made uniforms in just about every shape and size. In no time at all, for the incredibly low price of the Canadian dollar equivalent of £10, we were the proud possessors of a tunic and two pairs of trousers in good quality barathea. Despite many subsequent tailored uniforms from Messrs Gieves of Bond Street, I still maintain that that off-the-peg uniform was the best one I ever had.

Moncton in February 1944 was bitterly cold with temperatures well below freezing every day: it was so cold that it was decreed that it was a court-martial offence to go out not wearing ear-muffs because there had been so many cases of frost-bite. The countryside was covered with several feet of snow and we were restricted to remaining on camp or visits to Moncton which had almost nothing to offer by way of entertainment. Although we enjoyed the relative luxury of the Officers' Mess we soon got tired of playing cards, darts, snooker and any other indoor activity we could devise. The waiting for news of our troopship was very frustrating: we were not even allowed to write home unless our letters were intercepted which could give the U-boats an idea of when a troopship loaded with thousands of aircrew and Canadian troops could be sailing from St John's – when it would be at its most vulnerable. After more than a fortnight of champing at the bit we were finally embarked on the good ship HMT *Andes* which, being flat-bottomed and without stabilizers, rocked and rolled and pitched in the heavy North Atlantic seas – to the ruination of many a new proud uniform. After five days of high-speed zigzagging across the pond we arrived safely at the Port of Liverpool. Thus ended our North American adventure: it was now time for action!

Chapter 3

'Wot! No Engines?'

After landing from the *Andes* we were all sent off on disembarkation leave for fourteen days. Armed with first-class railway warrants, Johnnie Sharpe and I caught a night train to London from where we went our separate ways. I caught a train to Slough and then a bus to Farnham Royal where my mother was still working as housekeeper for the evacuated staff of ICI Plant Protection with a small flat in which I could stay. After a celebratory lunch I borrowed a bicycle from Miss Hannaford, the 'Head Girl' as I called her, and rode with some anxiety to Farnham Common to make a surprise visit to the Bowyers. When I arrived at their country house, the door was opened by Mrs Bowyer who seemed to have aged a lot in my nine months absence. She did not recognize me at first, being fooled by the uniform, but when she did her face lit up and she rushed forward to give me a hug. Then standing back she said 'You look so smart in your officer's uniform: Ruth would have been so proud of you.' I asked 'Where is Ruth?' Her face went as white as a sheet as she said 'Didn't you get my letter? Ruth died of pleurisy on the sixth of February.' When I asked her why they had not told me that she was ill she replied that Ruth had insisted that I was not to be worried at such a critical stage of my flying training, whereupon she burst into tears. I managed to hold back the flood whilst I comforted her over that great British cure-all – a nice cup of tea. But as I cycled home the tears cascaded down my cheeks: I hoped that nobody would see me or what would they have thought of an RAF pilot sobbing his heart out - and riding a lady's bicycle to boot!

The next few days passed in a bit of an aimless haze. I called on Mrs Warren at Stoke Poges and found that her son Derek had graduated from the Royal Military Academy at Woolwich and was now a lieutenant in the Royal Corps of Signals serving overseas. Also that her daughter Doune had joined the First Aid Nursing Yeomanry, inevitably known as FANYs, and was away on a driving course. So I was pleased when Mater asked if I would accompany her to London as she wanted to call on her old friend, the Mother Superior of the Convent of the Sacred Heart in West Hill. When we got to the Convent I left Mater and went off to call on my old landlady, Mrs Cullinan, in Cromford Road. On the way I popped in to see the Cheesemans at the gatehouse, not expecting to see Peggy as I knew that she was at university. When I asked how she was her parents told me that she had died of 'consumption' in January. Apparently, she had suffered from TB for many years: no wonder she had tried to live her short life to the full.

Mrs Cullinan was delighted to see me and, over a cup of tea, brought me up to date on her news. Her daughter Eileen was now married but still lived at home as her husband, Michael Smythe, was serving abroad and she was still working at the opticians in Putney High Street. Mrs Bullen had moved to the country to get away from the blitz and was now being looked after in a convent. Mr Adlam had recently been ordained and was now a parish priest 'up north'. I asked about Daphne, only to be told that her ship had been torpedoed en route to Cape Town and that there had been no survivors. I was badly shaken by this news: it was all too much of a coincidence – first Ruth, then Peggy and now Daphne. I began to wonder whether in some way I was to blame for their deaths: perhaps it was God's punishment for my having sinned. Obviously my Jesuit schooling was still influencing my thoughts. But as Mater and I stood on the platform at East Putney Station on our way home, I was brought down to earth by my first sight of a V1 flying bomb or 'Doodlebug'. Luckily for us it passed harmlessly overhead but we heard the explosion shortly afterwards. A timely reminder that my imagined problems were pretty small compared to what Londoners had had to put up with for the last few years.

* * *

I was glad when my disembarkation leave was over, not least because I was anxious to know to which operational training unit (OTU) I would be posted. I did not expect to be given any option but I had a 'wish list' of aircraft I would most like to fly, namely Spitfire, Tempest V, Mustang and Hurricane in that order. Such hopes were dashed when, along with hundreds of my contemporaries, including Johnnie Sharpe, I reported to No.1 Personnel Reception Centre (PRC) at Harrogate. We officers were housed in the Majestic Hotel, a dark, cold shadow of its former four-star self. Having booked in, we were instructed to report to one of the local cinemas the following day where we joined up with the sergeant pilots, who were billeted elsewhere in the town. Our spirits were high and there was a sense of camaraderie until the CO of the PRC, a wing commander, stepped onto the stage to address us.

The import of his talk was quite devastating! To summarize: he said that there was now a severe surplus of trained pilots and that there would be considerable delays in our being posted to the respective OTUs. The exception to this was that those destined to go as second pilots to Bomber, Coastal and Ferry Commands could expect to wait only weeks. Those destined for light bombers, reconnaissance and Army Co-operation would have to wait for months, whilst those going onto fighters could expect delays of at least a year. This was very frustrating, not least because the lucky ones were the cadets who had not done very well in their flying training, whereas those who had done best were having to wait the longest time to get operational.

The wing commander went on to say that those who had more than six months to wait could volunteer for various jobs which would make a vital contribution to the overall war effort. He then promised that those who volunteered would not lose their place in the queue for the OTUs. Then, to our astonishment, he explained that there were acute manpower shortages in the coal mines, on the railways and in farming. We could not believe our ears, especially when he gave us a pep talk on doing our bit for our country which did not go down at all well as we had all volunteered to do just that – as pilots. One of the sergeant pilots reflected our mood when he stood up and said 'I volunteered in the hopes of flying Spitfires, I'll be damned if I am going to volunteer to become a bloody miner, a train fireman or a flipping farmhand'. Someone else asked what would happen to those who did not volunteer, only to be told that the NCO pilots may not be given any option and officers would be dispersed around the country doing odd jobs on RAF stations. The wing commander then closed the meeting by saying that those who wished to volunteer should hand in their names and preferences to the PRC orderly room, whereupon he left the cinema hotly pursued by a babble of disgruntled voices.

Much to our surprise many of our peers did indeed volunteer but Johnnie and I agreed not to do so as it would be best to take a chance on being posted onto an operational station where we might be able to wangle the odd 'op' as supernumerary crew. After a week kicking our heels sampling the delights of Harrogate, about thirty of us were posted to RAF Credenhill, near Hereford, to attend the first course of the recently set up Aircrew Officers School. We did not know what to expect until we arrived in May when we discovered that we were to be instructed in air force law, administration and organization, RAF history, customs of the service and kindred subjects. The course was to last four weeks and there would be the inevitable exams at the end.

Most of our group were pretty cheesed off at the prospect of the course but I welcomed it as being a darned sight better than hanging around waiting for something to happen. I was probably the only one who intended to seek a permanent commission in the RAF after the war and I saw the course as a useful introduction to general administration. I took the four weeks seriously and, amazingly, I came top, with an average exam mark well in the 90s, and was awarded a distinguished pass which would have astonished but delighted Father Sinnott, the Prefect of Studies at my old school, Wimbledon College.

We had arrived at RAF Credenhill on a Saturday, so Johnnie Sharpe and I decided, after dinner in the Mess, to explore the delights of nearby Hereford, the idea being that we should sample the beer and the atmosphere of the local pubs. We tried out a couple before settling in the bar of the poshest hotel in town, close by the Cathedral, where we were joined by two other course members who suggested that we should go to the Corn Exchange where there was a dance. Johnnie was all for going but I was reluctant as I was still reeling from Ruth's death but, being outnumbered, I went along – and was very glad to have done so.

The dance was a pretty dreary affair with a four-piece band playing at one end of the hall, a trestle table with assorted drinks at the other and a motley collection of servicemen and local lads and lasses in the middle. Having paid one shilling each to get in and having quaffed our first drinks, we were about the depart when into the hall came a group of half-a-dozen Wrens. As always, Johnnie Sharpe was quick off the mark, having noticed a tall blonde, the best looker of the group, with whom he was soon dancing. The other girls were soon snapped up, but I noticed one who stood out from the others, not because of her size as she was all of five foot nothing but because of her bubbly personality. She was the sort of girl that you only had to look at to smile. When eventually we danced I found her every bit as delightful as she looked. We got on well and, having booked the last dance, I eventually escorted her back to the WRNS quarters, having made a date to take her to the pictures the following afternoon.

In those days Wrens were very much a cut above the other servicewomen as they had thousands of volunteers queuing up to enlist, perhaps because their uniform was so much more attractive than the other services', so the RN could afford to be selective and to set high standards. Patricia Wilkins was no exception; she was well spoken, well educated, well read, well everything and very pretty to boot. We met two or three times each week and by the end of the course we had become very close and Ruth's image was fading fast.

We were given a week's leave at the end of the course, which I spent in the Mess at Credenhill so I could spend time with Pat, and I then reported, not to Harrogate but to the PDC at Padgate near Warrington. It was a very frustrating time for all of us; D-Day had come and gone, the advance in France was well under way and there we were kicking our heels in that dreary place waiting for our postings hopefully to operational training.

In mid-July I was posted to RAF Church Lawford, near Derby, the home of No. 18 Advanced Flying School, where newly-graduated pilots were introduced to multi-engined flying on the twin-engined Airspeed Oxford. Having been recommended for fighters, I hoped that I was destined to fly Mosquitos or at least Beaufighters. But No! When I arrived at the RAF station I found that I was not on the course but was to report to the Chief Technical Officer who told me that I was to conduct a survey of the time that technical personnel spent away from their work-places on administrative matters, reporting sick, playing representative sport, having haircuts etc., etc. I had to record their every absence as part of a work study designed to review personnel establishments, manning levels and work practices so as to achieve greater efficiency. I found the work tedious in the extreme; it was a miserable time for me and after two months I was ready to volunteer for anything just to get away.

* * *

My misery was compounded when, at my request, the adjutant found out from the Air Ministry that I was unlikely to go onto operational training for fighters until well into 1945 – by which time the war in Europe could be over. Shortly after that news, a notice appeared in Station Routine orders stating that volunteers were urgently needed to augment the Glider Pilot Regiment for future airborne operations. What was not said was that there was a severe shortage of glider pilots because 229 had been killed and 469 had been wounded or taken prisoner at Arnhem. The only way this shortage could be made good quickly was by drawing on the RAF's surplus of trained pilots – such as myself. Apparently it had been agreed with the War Office that in future glider squadrons would be manned on a 50:50 basis of GPR and RAF pilots.

Without so much as a second thought I volunteered and within days things were moving. In mid-October I was posted to the RAF Regiment Depot at Bridgnorth in Shropshire for a two-week course of small arms, unarmed combat and fieldcraft training. There I met up with many of my flying training contemporaries, including my old mate Johnnie Sharpe. On arrival we were all issued with overalls for the training which was just as well as it rained virtually every day and the muddy assault course featured prominently in the syllabus.

From Bridgnorth we reported to No. 1 Glider Training School at RAF Croughton near Banbury where we were to fly ten hours on the Hotspur glider towed by the single-engined Miles Master. The Hotspur was a nice looking aircraft with a forty-five-feet wingspan, a two-pilot cockpit and seating for eight troops. It was made almost entirely of wood and one's confidence was somewhat undermined by the plaques on the cockpit doors which read 'Manufactured by Harry Lebus, furniture maker' or by 'Waring and Gillow'. I always felt a little happier if the Hotspur I was about to fly had been made by the latter company – at least they had a reputation for making first-class furniture.

I must admit that getting airborne, without an engine, on the end of a 300-foot rope took some getting used to. When the marshaller waved us clear to take off, the tug pilot would move slowly forward until the slack in the rope was taken up and he would then open the throttle fully and start trundling along the grass runway. Seconds later the glider started moving and within a very short distance

General Aircraft Hotspur gliders.

would get airborne, long before the tug had reached flying speed. The technique was to keep the glider just above the slipstream in what was known as the high-tow position. If the glider was too high the tug would not get airborne: if it was too low the turbulence of the slipstream would rock the glider with the danger of hitting a wing-tip on the ground or alternatively cause the tow rope to snap because of the increased drag. Once safely airborne, the glider would adopt the low-tow position just below the slipstream. Whilst on tow the glider flew rather sluggishly; when once the tow rope was released it handled beautifully. However, landing back at the airfield, in the right place, was quite difficult to judge as the Hotspur had neither flaps nor spoilers and tended to float. Nonetheless, everyone on the course made the grade without incident within the two weeks allocated.

In mid-November we all reported to No. 1 Heavy Glider Conversation Unit at RAF Peplow in Shropshire to convert onto the Horsa glider, designed and manufactured by Airspeed Ltd. By comparison with the Hotspur, the Horsa was a monster having a wing span of eighty-eight feet and seating for between twenty-five and thirty troops depending upon their equipment. It was also made mainly of wood but it weighed 15,250lbs whereas a fully-laden Hotspur only weighed less than 4,000lbs. It was built originally only at Airspeed's Portsmouth factory but after that was badly damaged in an air raid by a lone Junkers 88 bomber, work was sub-contracted to General Aircraft and the Birmingham Coach Works. The rope used to tow the Horsa was both longer and stronger than that used for the Hotspur being 350 feet long, 3.5-inches wide and waterproofed. At Peplow, the gliders were towed by a twin-engined bomber, the Albemarle, but at other schools and in other theatres Whitley, Halifax, Dakota and Stirling aircraft were used.

The kindest thing that can be said about the Horsa was that it flew like a brick-built outhouse. It was unbelievably heavy on the controls and very unresponsive. Two pilots were essential and it was usual for each to fly for no more than fifteen minutes before handing over to the other – in a state of exhaustion. For the course my second pilot was Sergeant 'Pete' Peterkin, a little fellow who could barely cope for ten minutes. However, the Horsa did have three very redeeming features; the first was that it had huge flaps, usually referred to as 'the barn doors'. They made the landing technique quite simple: the pilot would wait until the field had passed under the glider's nose when he would put down the flaps and push the control column fully forward until one appeared to be diving vertically. However steep the angle, the airspeed incredibly never exceeded 85 knots and, although it took both pilots to bring the nose up for landing, the speed decayed very rapidly and it was possible to land very accurately in the right place. The second blessing was that the Horsa was fitted with a cable-angle indicator, affectionately known as 'the angle of dangle', which showed the pilot the glider's position relative to the tow rope. This made it possible in cloud and at night to maintain the correct station vis-à-vis the tug aircraft. For night flying the tug aircraft was fitted with three little blue lights, one on top of either wing tip and one on top of the rudder. By maintaining the right triangle formed by the lights it was possible to maintain station but if one's attention was distracted it was easy to lose them amidst the stars.

Finally, if the Horsa came down in the sea, being made of wood, it was guaranteed to stay afloat for at least twenty-four hours. The ability to float would have been welcomed by the occupants of those off Sicily who were cast off by some of the USAAF tug pilots far from the designated landing zone (LZ). As a result sixty-nine of the gliders came down in the sea, thirty-four made it to the beaches but only twelve out of 115 reached the LZ. The glider captain has the sole responsibility to release the tow rope when he judges that he is in a position to make it to the LZ. Tug pilots were only supposed to jettison the tow rope in an emergency; that they did so because they came up against unexpectedly heavy ack-ack fire was an act of craven cowardice. The tug pilots who ditched their gliders should have been court-martialled for prejudicing the success of the operation. But knowing the Americans, it is more likely that they were awarded Purple Hearts for the hurt, hopefully, inflicted on their feelings by the contempt of those pilots who did not chicken out.

Whilst at Peplow we were given the opportunity to fly the American Waco glider, renamed Hadrian by the RAF. It had an all-up weight of 7,500lbs, about halfway between the Hotspur and the Horsa. It was made of tubular metal and fabric-covered wood and was usually towed by the ubiquitous Dakota. It could carry thirteen fully-armed troops or alternatively one Jeep or one 75mm howitzer and six men. Over a thousand were delivered to the RAF and were used mainly to

The cockpit of a Waco Hadrian glider.

replace the Horsas lost in early airborne operations; I flew three sorties in it and found it a delight to fly.

Our glider training was completed at the end of November and my log book shows that I flew fifty-six sorties in the four weeks allocated for a miserable total of less than twenty hours flying. Perhaps not too surprisingly as many of the sorties consisted of a take-off, a 180-degree turn onto the downwind and release of tow rope for the landing, the trip taking approximately ten minutes. I flew only about a half dozen sorties of more than thirty minutes, mostly on instrument and night flying. However, we were now considered to be 'proficient' and were despatched to No. 9 PDC at RAF Uxbridge to await our postings onto operational squadrons. About half of us, including Johnnie Sharpe and myself, were sent off on fourteen days' embarkation leave, which indicated that we were going overseas whilst the others would be posted to UK-based squadrons.

I spent that leave with my mother but managed to meet with Pat at Reading railway station to spend the day with her uncle and his wife who lived in nearby Caversham. After lunch they went off to play golf leaving us to do the washing up. Pat was quite upset to learn that I was going overseas and we discussed whether we should become officially engaged before I left. After much thought it was Pat who decided that we should not do so as the future was too uncertain for long-term commitment and who knows what might happen to either of us before the war ended. Amidst tears she asked if I would like to make love to her. This offer took me completely by surprise because, although she could be quite passionate, she had made it very clear that she would remain a virgin until marriage. Much to my astonishment I said that, whereas nothing would give me more pleasure, I would not do so as I knew that she would regret it.

Back at Uxbridge after our leave we were only required to report for a muster report at 10.00am to receive any news about future movements. The rest of the time was our own. Before long we were issued with tropical kit, including the 'Bombay Bowler' or pith helmet, which suggested that we were going to the Far East. I managed to meet Pat once more, again at Reading station. We could not go to Caversham as her uncle and his wife were away but, as we had four hours between her train arriving and her departure back to Hereford, we had time for a meal and to go to the pictures. Unfortunately, it was blowing a December gale, with the rain bucketing down, which prevented us from leaving the station: being in uniform, neither of us had an umbrella and we would have got soaking wet had we ventured forth. So we stayed in the refreshment room drinking countless cups of tea and eating sausage rolls and rock cakes. When our time was up and I kissed her goodbye, little did I think I would never see her again!

The following day about a dozen of us were told that we were leaving that night. Watch out, Hirohito, here we come.

Chapter 4

India

It was just getting dark as a dozen of us boarded the coach which was to take us on the first leg of our journey from Uxbridge to God knows where, although our having been issued with 'Bombay Bowlers' indicated that the Far East would be our final destination. We tried to find out where we were bound but nobody either knew or was prepared to tell us: instead we were regaled with the security slogans of the day so admirably cartooned by Fougasse, such as 'Walls have Ears' or 'Be like Dad, keep Mum'. As the coach trundled along Western Avenue towards London we tried to keep track of where we were going but all too soon we were enveloped in the stygian gloom that was the London black-out: we could not even read the street names.

Eventually we pulled into a railway siding close to a main-line station which I believe to have been Waterloo. There a train awaited us, consisting of only one passenger carriage, the rest being made up of freight cars. We were met by a sergeant from the Army Regional Transport Office who told us that the train was a 'special' bound non-stop for Bournemouth and that we were the only passengers. As soon as we had boarded, the train set off at a cracking pace and inside two hours we had arrived at our initial destination where we piled into the back of a 3-ton truck which drove to the airport at Hurn and deposited us alongside a waiting Dakota.

We were greeted by the aircraft captain, Flight Lieutenant Rose, who briefed us that we were bound for Gibraltar. He also told us that it would be a very long flight as he would be flying well out into the Atlantic to keep clear of the Bay of Biscay and to minimize the risk of interception by enemy fighters. We then clambered on board to find that the centre of the fuselage was piled high with battened-down freight and that the only seating was webbing seats which folded down from the side. Whilst the captain was starting up, the co-pilot issued us with 'Mae Wests', which were to be worn for the entire trip, and briefed us on emergency procedures should the aircraft have to ditch in the sea.

With that happy thought we settled in our seats for take-off and thus began a most excruciatingly uncomfortable eight-hour flight. The main problem was that the webbing seats had a tubular metal bar at the front which pressed into one's legs just behind the knee and resulted in 'pins and needles' after about thirty minutes. Most of us ended up sitting or lying on the floor when we were not walking around what little space was left in the fuselage trying to keep warm. The flight itself was quite eerie as the aircraft was flown without navigation lights and with no interior lighting outside of the cockpit. All we could see through the windows was the glow from the exhausts of the engines. It was with great relief that we approached Gibraltar just as dawn was breaking on the morning of 22 December 1944.

Having landed, we were taken to a transit mess for breakfast where we learned that we would be re-boarding the same aircraft when it had been re-fuelled for a flight to Cairo with stops at Oran in Morocco and Castel Benito in Tripolitania – albeit with a new crew under Flight Lieutenant Clay. So once again we had to endure the same discomfort, but at least it was now daylight and we were able to admire the grandeur of the Sahara Desert. We saw little of the Mediterranean after Oran as we were routed well inland to avoid the more sensitive coastal areas. Twelve hours later we touched down in Cairo, by which time we were well and truly knackered. We were accommodated in a pretty grotty commandeered hotel, right in the centre of the city, where, after a quick dinner, we all went to our rooms and flaked out.

Next morning we reported to the movements office in Hotel 'Grotty' and were told that we would not be continuing our journey until the morning of Christmas Eve, so we had all day to explore Cairo. Once again we were given no further information other than the fact that a coach would pick us up at the hotel at 8.30 the following morning. Armed with a street map, four of us made our way to Groppi's to sample their famous ice-creams. Sitting on the first floor verandah, we watched the incredible hustle and bustle of Cairo's streets, and our ears were assaulted by an unbelievable din: apparently Egyptians drive with one foot on the accelerator and one hand on the horn. We then made our way to Shepheard's Hotel for lunch. En route we were accosted by myriad small boys either demanding 'baksheesh' or offering the services of their sisters – or both. Shepheard's was absolutely heaving, mainly with Army officers from every imaginable regiment or corps, and it was virtually impossible to get to the bars. Luckily, we managed to book a table in the dining room where we were soon enjoying ice-cold beers.

There is an oft repeated story about an incident at Shepheard's when a group of RAF pilots were having a party and singing ribald songs around a piano. Needless to say, they were making a bit of a racket, much to the annoyance of several Army officers, one of whom got short shrift when he asked the airmen to stop. He then said, rather pompously in the manner of Colonel Blimp, 'Now look here; I am Lieutenant Colonel the Lord So and So and as senior officer here I order you to stop'. Whereupon a rather large moustachioed Irishman, complete with silk scarf around his neck, emerged from the crowd and said 'And I am Group Captain the Earl of Bandon and that's got you beaten on both counts, so we will continue'. Mind you he did not say 'beaten' he used a more descriptive word beginning with 'B' which gave the noble Lord apoplexy. Paddy Bandon, a wonderful character much loved by 'his boys' and everyone except the incredibly stuffy, went on to have an illustrious career ending up as a much decorated Air Marshal.

After lunch we wandered back to the hotel, taking in a few of the sights on the way, to indulge in a little horizontal PT under the fans in our bedrooms to conserve our strength for a planned tour of the cabarets about which we had heard so much. Although the beer was good and cold, the cabarets themselves were pretty mundane, all following a similar pattern of unfunny comedians, excellent acrobats, fumbling jugglers and very wobbly belly-dancers. We knew it was time to pack it in when we started to see the acts from previous cabarets for the second time.

Next morning we boarded the coach, each one of us nursing his kitbag, all the baggage allowed, and a well-deserved hangover. We were driven out of the city southwards along the west bank of the Suez Canal until we reached the widening waters of the gulf at the top end of the Red Sea where we stopped at a quay and noticed what we thought was an RAF Sunderland moored a couple of hundred yards off-shore. We expected to be met by service personnel but were approached by two men in the very smart white uniforms of Imperial Airways. They told us that the crew was already on board and that if we would be kind enough to board the waiting pinnace we would be ferried to 'our aircraft'.

We were greeted by the pilot, Captain Jones, in a be-medalled uniform looking for all the world like an admiral in tropical kit, an impression helped by his well-trimmed goatee beard. Two male civilians with their wives and children were already seated: we later learned that they were on their way to Basrah to work for the Anglo-Iranian Oil Company. They had bagged the seats at the front of the cabin but Johnnie and I spotted four seats with a table between right at the rear which would be ideal for playing poker or bridge with two of our card-playing mates, Derek Reeves and Ricky Richardson – so we made a bee-line for them. The cabin was pretty sumptuous, at least by Dakota standards, because the aircraft was a Short Bros C Class Empire flying boat, still in its Imperial Airways livery, from which the Sunderland was derived. Astonishingly Imperial Airways operated them between Egypt and India, a route along which there was no threat from enemy fighters. They carried a mixed bag of civilian and service personnel and we thanked our lucky stars to have been spared further air travel courtesy of the RAF – or worse still, by troopship.

No sooner had we taken our seats than the engines were started up and the aircraft taxied out for take-off, an exciting experience for those of us more accustomed to runways and wheels. Once the aircraft was at cruising height, Captain Jones came down from the cockpit and briefed us on the circuitous route which would result in our getting to our final destination, Karachi, in two days. He explained that the availability of landing, or should I write alighting, and refuelling facilities would dictate the lengths of the various legs which would average about three hours. We would be night-stopping in Basrah and meals would be served at the various stops and that only light refreshments would be available on board.

The first leg was fascinating as we flew north-eastwards from the Red Sea to Kallia on the Dead Sea to the west of Jerusalem. There was so much to see that we were rushing from the port to starboard port-holes so as not to miss anything – and our planned card playing was soon forgotten. The second leg to Lake Habbaniya, west of Baghdad was equally as interesting: as was the third leg to a one-night stop in Basrah. There we were accommodated in the luxurious Shatt-al-Arab hotel, albeit two to a room. That night, being Christmas Eve, there was a dinner dance to which we were invited with only our drinks paid for by ourselves: something we had great difficulty in doing as we were the only servicemen there and the locals, mostly expatriate civilians and their families, went out of their way to make us feel welcome. The highlight of a most enjoyable evening was a jitterbug competition which was won by Johnnie Sharpe who had the good sense to be partnered by the younger of our two air hostesses, albeit a lady in her mid-thirties. I think the judges were more influenced by their energy rather than by technique or style.

Next morning we set off for Bahrain but after about an hour's flying the wireless operator started receiving warnings of tropical storms ahead and a sea-state that was out of limits for landing – so Captain Jones had no option but to return. It was now Christmas Day, so we found the hotel very quiet, especially after the festivities of the night before, and we had the place virtually to ourselves. The weather en route had cleared up the following morning and, by way of Bahrain, Sharjah and Jiwani, we reached Karachi in the early evening where we bade a fond farewell to Captain Jones and his crew who had looked after us so well. In retrospect I have wondered whether our pilot was the famous Captain O. P. Jones who became the Commodore and Flight Director of BOAC.

At Karachi we were met by the RTO and the inevitable 3-ton lorry in which we were driven to the railway station where we boarded a first-class carriage in which six double-sleeper compartments had been reserved for us. The train was bound for Rawalpindi where it arrived in the afternoon of 27 December. Thus ended a journey of incredible up and downs but at all times exciting. But at least we were now firmly on our way to becoming operational in the airborne assault role.

* * *

When at last we arrived at our final destination, the airfield at Fathejang thirty miles south of Rawalpindi, we learned what the planners at HQ South East Asia Command (SEAC) had in store for us. They had formed two glider wings, each of three squadrons. No. 343 Wing, commanded by an RAF Wing Commander, was based at Fathejang with Nos. 669 and 670 Squadrons based there whilst No. 668 Squadron was located on the satellite airfield at Basal about fifteen miles away. No. 344 Wing, also commanded by an RAF officer, was based at the airfield of Dum Dum near Calcutta with its three squadrons alongside. All six squadrons were equipped with American Waco Hadrian gliders which had been shipped in crates from the USA and assembled in India at RAF Bhital before being towed to the various squadron locations. A number of RAF and USAAF Dakota squadrons, already based in India for supply dropping and other duties, had been modified for towing. Indeed a number of small glider-borne operations had already been mounted in Burma, albeit mainly by the USAAF.

To our great excitement we were also told that SEAC had already carried out forward planning for three possible airborne assaults; the first somewhere between Kohima and Imphal in north Burma, the second about halfway down the Arakan Mountain range and the third around Rangoon. Unfortunately, the first was likely to be cancelled as the Japanese had stretched their lines of communication too far in their quest to invade India and the Fourteenth Army, under General Sir William Slim, was at last beginning to push them southwards, aided by guerrilla successes in cutting their supply routes.

It was just as well that the first 'op' was cancelled as our Wing was far from ready for action. The airfield at Fathejang consisted of two runways and the usual hard standings but had no permanent buildings. In fact the only buildings were the three messes for the officers, the sergeants and the airmen which were being hastily constructed of wood. Everyone and everything was housed in tents or marquees. We twelve officers were the last to arrive (obviously they were keeping the best 'til last) and our tents had yet to be erected by squads of airmen who were unlikely to get around to ours before dusk. Four of us, Johnnie Sharpe, Derek Reeves, Geoff Drake and myself, decided to attempt to put up our own as Derek, a former scout, said he knew how. What he did not know was that our tent was an 'Egyptian Pattern Indian Produce', or EPIP, considerably larger than anything he had seen before. Our efforts were worthy of the 'Crazy Gang' at the London Palladium

The two 'Johnnies' enjoying the sunshine in India's North West Province at Fathejang.

but, with a little help from some earlier arrived friends, we finally made it. We were delighted at how spacious it was and, more important, how well it had been designed for use in the tropics. Tent erected, we were then issued with camp beds, sheets and blankets, mosquito nets, chairs, tables, locally made bamboo cupboards and Tilly lamps. When everything was in place it was really very comfortable.

From our operational point of view there were more serious problems. Firstly, the Wing had not yet got its full complement of gliders; secondly, none of the RAF pilots had converted onto the Waco Hadrian as we had all done the heavy-glider conversion course on the Horsa and thirdly, although sufficient Dakota squadrons had been modified for towing they were busy over Burma on supply dropping and other operational duties including flying over 'the hump' to supply the Chinese Army with weapons and ammunition for their fight against the Japanese.

When our Group HQ, No. 229 in Delhi, became aware of the problems they acted very quickly diverting our outstanding gliders to the airfield at Dhamial, east of Rawalpindi, to which Dakota crews were sent for rest and recreation from the Burmese front. They set up a crash conversion course which operated very efficiently: for example, in five days I flew no fewer than seventeen flights, albeit a total of only three hours and twenty minutes, and was duly graded as 'proficient' as eventually were all the other RAF pilots. Indeed on 1 February 1945 all three squadrons were declared fully operational with a full complement of gliders.

However, once the Wing was ready to go, so did the Dakotas which returned to their bases in Bengal and we were effectively grounded. Luckily, some bright staff officer must have recognized our frustration at not being able to fly and arranged for a number of de Havilland Tiger Moth aircraft to be made available so we could keep our hands in. These aircraft had been put into storage somewhere in India when the Elementary Flying School to which they belonged had been closed down. They were much in demand but I managed to wangle eight trips within the first month.

Flying a Tiger Moth in India was sheer bliss compared to in the UK where, because of the open cockpits and the temperate climate, we were required to wear clumsy great fur-lined boots, cumbersome sheepskin-lined jackets and trousers and two pairs of gloves – silk inners and leather gauntlets – and we still nearly froze to death. From Fathejang we flew in shirtsleeves with helmets and goggles – all very Biggles! However, because we were flying over tribal areas we had to be armed with our trustee Smith and Wesson .38 revolvers, a silk scarf with a map of the NW Frontier region printed on it and a 'goolie chit' which promised vast riches to any who returned a pilot who had had the misfortune to crash-land to the authorities in the 'entire' state. The tribesmen apparently had a nasty habit of neutering those infidels who fell into their hands. On one of my flights, by dint of refuelling at Peshawar, I flew through the famous Khyber Pass – a moment of history to relish.

* * *

On 23 February we were told that all 670 Squadron pilots were to attend a course at the School for Jungle Self-Preservation Training near Mahableshwar, a small town about sixty miles south of Poona (now Pune), the spiritual home of the Indian Army. The school had been set up by a Mrs Graham-Bower, an old Burma hand, who had smuggled out a number of families of the natives who lived in the Naga Hills, before the Japanese Army overran that region. She had then remained in the hills and had personally led many guerrilla raids against the Japanese. Her contribution to the war in the Far East has curiously been overlooked in the history books despite her being known as 'The Naga Queen'. The school was commanded by an RAF squadron leader and its purpose was to teach aircrew who might force land or parachute into the jungle how to survive, how to detect and evade Japanese patrols and how to navigate and, hopefully, make their way to Allied lines. The school had not been set up specifically for glider pilots but we were the ones most likely to need the skills they were to teach us. The school was the second one to be set up, the first having been in Manipur State in NE India. General Bill Slim, the commander of Fourteenth Army was so impressed by its training that he authorized and funded the second one, away from the war zone.

Two days later we boarded a train bound for Poona. An Indian long-distance train was a sight to behold, usually having two enormous great engines, one at the front, the other at the rear: a genuine case of push-pull which arrangement proved very necessary to cope with the steep gradients we were to encounter in the hill country. There were three classes of carriage: first-class where we officers had two-berth sleeper compartments well upholstered in leather with an en-suite rudimentary shower and a toilet; second-class where the SNCOs shared four-berth compartments with two toilets at either end of the carriage and third-class for the multitudes, which were little better than cattle trucks with wooden benches.

The most extraordinary thing about the railways was that the trains had no refreshment or restaurant cars so they stopped for about forty-five minutes at specified stations for breakfast, lunch and dinner. At these stations there were first- and second-class dining rooms but all other passengers had to make do with food stalls set up by peddlers on the platforms. It turned out to be a very efficient system as the conductor would wire ahead to the stations informing them of the time of arrival and how many people of which class required a meal – so everything was ready and waiting.

Although the train fairly rattled along across the plains of the North West Frontier Province and the deserts of the Sind, it could only chug slowly up the steep slopes when it reached the hills. The combination of stopping for meals and the fact that every state had its own railways, usually running on different track gauges which made it necessary in our case to change trains twice, made progress across country pretty slow. So our journey to Poona took three rather tedious days, during which Johnnie and I played a lot of cards; unfortunately we had no books as the RAF library services had yet to catch up with us.

The course, which lasted three weeks, was a delight. The school was located near Mahableshwar because that region of India was where the rain forests of the Western Ghats most resembled the Burmese jungle. The camp for the staff and the course members had been built in a clearing with wonderful views westward where the sunsets were really glorious almost every night. The Naga tribesmen had built their own kampong of houses on stilts using the materials readily available in the forest, mainly bamboo. In our first week there we were visited by an ensemble of Italian prisoner-of-war musicians who were touring British bases under the auspices of ENSA. I was no lover of chamber music but their choice of the most popular pieces was brilliant as was the setting. We all squatted on the ground in a natural amphitheatre listening to Mozart *et al* as the sun set slowly in the west amidst an incredible technicolour sky: it was magic! It was a night I will never forget.

The survival syllabus was virtually completely practical, our instructors being the tribesmen, a jolly bunch of little men whose average height was well short of five feet. They spoke no English, so they taught by showing us, for example, how to look for those plants in the forest, parts of which were edible. They demonstrated how to make snares for small animals and traps for larger ones. They showed us how to construct shelters out of bamboo and how to make them rainproof with fronds and leaves. In particular, they taught us where to find drinkable water. Everything they showed us we then had to do for ourselves and they would collapse with laughter at our early pathetic efforts.

We soon learned that survival in the jungle depended mainly on three things: firstly, a sharp machete with which we had all been issued; secondly, bamboo from which one could make snares, traps, shelters, crutches or stretchers if needed, cooking utensils, weapons and many other things; and, thirdly, the confidence that it was really quite simple to survive.

Finding water was absolutely fundamental to survival. It could be found in streams, it could be collected when it rained and it could be found in the centre of many plants. Food was essential but of less importance than water and, anyway, we soon learned that the forest abounded with edible berries, nuts and leaves. One tip was to watch what the monkeys ate because their food was likely to suit humans as well. Unfortunately, most food was way up in the tree canopy but luckily monkeys are messy eaters and a lot of their food would end up on the forest floor.

Having a machete, plenty of bamboo and confidence was not much use if one wandered around in circles. So we had to learn how to navigate towards our own lines. Our instructors in this were the RAF staff of the school, aided and abetted by troops who had served in Burma. Having even a rudimentary compass would be a great help but one might not always be available. Being able to see the sun would be useful but that would not always be possible because of the denseness of the forest canopy or in the monsoon season when it would be obscured by cloud – the same would apply to the sky at night. Even if one had a reasonable sense of orientation it was not always possible to travel in the desired direction because of the nature of the terrain. Having a map would be a help as it might indicate which mountain passes or river valleys to head for but that would depend on knowing more or less where one had crashed or baled out.

Having been warned of the problems we were then given advice on how to overcome them – and then it was time to put everything we had learned into practice. The course was split into teams of four: Johnnie and I were joined by Sergeants Jock Waterson and Dan Carver, our respective co-pilots. That phase started with each team being dropped off from the back of a 3-ton truck, shown exactly where they were on the map and told to make their way back to the base camp about three hours trekking away. This normally involved a few obstacles such as having to cross rushing streams, traversing tracks without being spotted and much trekking through dense undergrowth, taking turns to clear a path with our machetes.

The usual form was to proceed for about fifty minutes then take a ten-minute break to rest and, not least, to examine oneself for leeches which had a nasty habit of penetrating through the materials of one's trousers or through eyelets of one's boots. If allowed to get that far they would latch onto the soft, sweaty area of the crotch. If found they were easily removed by touching them with a cigarette end; pulling them off was inadvisable as the sucker might detach and could turn septic. In extremis there had been a few cases where a leech had penetrated the urethra and become bloated with blood thus making it impossible for the man to urinate. In those cases death would follow unless the poor fellow could be evacuated within three or four days.

The course ended with an exercise which, being spread over two days, required the teams to spend the night in the jungle. We not only had to make it to the base camp but also to evade patrols along the tracks and in the forest itself. If captured the team members would be treated as PoWs, subject to interrogation and rough handling until the exercise ended. Our team was lucky enough to be amongst the few to reach the base camp safely. One team got horribly lost until found by a rescue team the following day. We all agreed not only that we had all enjoyed the course but also that the lessons learned could be most useful when eventually we took part in airborne assaults in Burma.

My own excitement at getting ever closer to going into action was somewhat tempered by my concern that I had not had a letter from my girlfriend in UK, Wren Pat Wilkins, for six weeks. I was worried that something might have happened to her as she had written every week, and sometimes twice, since I had left in December. At long last a bumper crop of mail from Fathejang caught up with us, most chaps had four or five letters. I had only one but at least it was from Pat. My heart sank when I read that it was the most difficult letter she had ever written and that this was the umpteenth attempt to break the news to me kindly. She went on to write that her former childhood sweetheart, who was now a paratrooper, had lost a leg in an airborne assault in Europe and was being invalided out of the Army. He was taking it very badly, she had been comforting him, their former affection for each other had been rekindled, he had proposed and they were now engaged to be married. She admitted that her acceptance was prompted more by compassion than love and that she would never forget our love for each other. That night, at the farewell party in the mess, I got drunk for the first time in my life, finally collapsing fully dressed on my *charpoy*. Very early next morning good old Johnnie Sharpe, being unable to waken me, packed my kitbag and plonked it and me in the baggage truck of the convoy taking us to the railway station for our return journey. By the time we reached the train I had come to – but with the biggest hangover of my life.

* * *

When we got back to Fathejang we found that the adjutant had managed to book the squadron into the rest camp at Lower Topa, high in the Murree Hills. The camp served two main purposes: firstly to provide a place where RAF personnel could recover from injury or illness and, secondly, to provide respite for those serving on the scorching hot plains. The facilities for every sport imaginable were provided, with beautifully lush grass sports fields for football, rugby and hockey, whilst tennis and badminton courts were plentiful. What a delightful change from Fathejang where not a blade of grass was to be found and where such facilities as we had made for ourselves were of rolled latterite which was fine for hockey, reasonable for football and impossible for rugger. But the biggest difference was the climate: on the plains it was oppressively hot and not very conducive to exertion of any kind whereas at Topa it was warm by day and blissfully cool at night. But for some the biggest attraction was that, at nearby Upper Topa, there was a camp for WAAF personnel: never has any group of girls seemed so attractive as to we lusty males so long deprived of female company.

Within a couple of days we discovered that we could hire horses from a stable in the village for trekking in the hills. Several of us decided that we would try to ride every day which was a good move as a small group of WAAFs had the same idea – so we used to go out together. They were much the best of the bunch having pony club and gymkhana backgrounds and we had much in common with them. Indeed one of our number, good-looking, tall Geoff Webb, even got engaged to the best looking of the girls by the end of our stay. The horses were all ex-Indian Army polo ponies which had been retired and sold off to spend the rest of their lives on the pastures of the Topas. They were sturdy, sure-footed and loved to gallop across the pastures when not negotiating the twisting paths of the hills.

Our trekking was most enjoyable, not just because it gave us the opportunity to take in the magnificent scenery of the hills, lakes and pastures, resplendent with a background of the snow-capped foothills of the Himalayas, which was the most breathtakingly beautiful scenery I had ever seen – until I went to Kashmir, which was even more astounding.

Sport and pony trekking were not the only pleasures available from Lower Topa. For example, all of us officers were honorary members of the Murree branch of the Rawalpindi Club. There was a first-class bar with a huge verandah where we could sit admiring the superb view whilst sipping ice-cold glasses of Murree beer, which was really excellent. The Club also had a good restaurant with fierce-looking Indian waiters dressed in the club livery, including very imposing turbans. But our favourite eatery was Sam's, an Indian restaurant which also served very good English food. When our two-week stay was over, it was with a heavy heart but many happy memories of an idyllic time that we reluctantly wound our way back down to the sizzling plains.

* * *

When we arrived at Fathejang we were told that all the squadron's officers were to attend a course at the Indian Army's Officer Training School at Belgaum, about 120 miles south of Poona, but, unlike Mahableshwar on the eastern or plains side of the Western Ghats, not far from the Portuguese colony of Goa. Apparently there had been a change of policy regarding the role of RAF glider pilots. Originally we had been briefed that, once safely landed, our job was to make our way back to our own lines so that we would be available for any follow up airborne assault. Now we were to remain in the battle zone, having been trained to take over as platoon commanders should any of the Army lieutenants be killed or seriously injured. We thought that this change reflected the difference between operations in Europe and Burma. In fact it was more likely the result of the horrific casualties suffered at Arnhem, the 'bridge too far'.

So four days after getting back from the hills, during which time I managed to fly two trips in a Tiger Moth, we boarded the dreaded train for an even longer journey than before. However this time we were allowed to take our bearers with us, as Belgaum had servants' quarters. Johnnie Sharpe and I shared a bearer whom we called James as his Indian name was unpronounceable. He had worked for us since our first few days at Fathejang. A bearer's job was similar to that of a batman in the UK and was to look after our room in the mess, wake us up with early morning tea, make the beds, clean the shoes, wash and press our uniforms, carry water to our wash table and tin bath or anything else his 'sahibs' wished. James was first-class, not least because he spoke English, had a sense of humour and made excellent bacon and egg 'banjos' (sandwiches) when we did not feel like the long walk to the mess for breakfast.

The camp at Belgaum was an enormous place dominated by a huge parade ground surrounded by very unattractive barrack blocks. It was staffed by Indian Army Officers and SNCOs seemingly too old or decrepit for active service. Unfortunately, the training programme they had devised for us was equally archaic, more appropriate for operations in Afghanistan or the Khyber Pass, but totally useless for fighting in Burma. For example, we wasted a whole day being taught how to determine the direction and range from which enemy fire was coming by what they called the 'crack and thump' method. At the end, when questions were invited, one of us asked whether Robin Hood had used the 'twang and thud' method: the instructors were not amused!

We learned how to carry out flanking manoeuvres and how to storm buildings or pill-boxes. We were taught how to react when subject to enemy fire. Even now, sixty-odd years later, I can remember the mantra <u>DOWN</u> (i.e. lie prone) <u>CRAWL</u> (to a better protected position), <u>OBSERVE</u> (identify from where the fire came), <u>SIGHTS</u> (set the range on the rifles), <u>FIRE</u> (opportunist single shot or automatic fire). I can also recall the acronym for briefing one's platoon i.e. <u>GRIT</u> being Group (which section or sections), Range (for setting sights), Indications (nature and location of target), Type (of fire – single or automatic).

The best part of the syllabus was the weapons training in that we had the opportunity to fire most of the weapons issued to the Fourteenth Army. When we were tested at the end of that phase, I was graded as a 'marksman' on the .38 and .45 revolvers, the .303 rifle and the Bren gun and as a 'first-class shot' on the Sten gun and the Thompson sub-machine gun. We also fired the Vickers machine gun, rocket-propelled grenades and anti-tank weapons on which we were not graded.

The undoubted highlight of this training was a visit by an American team of 'cowboy sharp-shooters', which included a good-looking girl in the Annie Oakley mould, led by a white-haired old timer who claimed to have worked with Wild Bill Cody. They gave us an astonishing exhibition of sharpshooting and knife throwing: their accuracy was phenomenal but what impressed us most was their shooting from the hip without aiming. In fact, none of them fired from the hip, as in cowboy films, but held their guns in the centre of the body. When we tried this, which was quite contrary to anything we had been taught, we realized how easy it was to hit an assailant with sufficient accuracy to disable or kill him.

Shortly after the start of the course the news filtered through that Germany had surrendered unconditionally and that the war in Europe was over. This was great news and we were elated but we still had unfinished business in the Far East. Nevertheless, the Camp Commandant decided to hold a Gala Dance in the Officers' Mess to celebrate. Despite the elation, it was a pretty dreary affair but we, single, RAF officers did our duty and danced with the elderly and rather fusty wives of the senior staff as well as the few members of the Women's Army Corps (India), their ATS equivalent, who were based at the camp. There was one outstanding exception to this rather uninviting selection of ladies, a most attractive young girl of about eighteen years, small but beautifully proportioned, superbly dressed and made up – an excellent dancer to boot. Since my 'Dear John' letter from Pat Wilkins I had gone off girls so I paid little attention to her. Johnnie Sharpe, however, never one to miss an opportunity, tried to get a dance with her, only to be told that her dance card was already fully subscribed. Fully booked or not, the eyes of every red-blooded young pilot followed her every movement around the dance floor.

Towards the end of the evening I was inveigled onto the floor for a 'ladies excuse me' dance. Having changed partners several times I felt a tap on my shoulder and, when I turned around, it was her. I introduced myself and she told me that her name was Kaye Bailey, that she lived with her parents in Bombay and that she was staying with her uncle in Belgaum. When the band stopped playing I escorted her back to her table where I was introduced to her uncle, a much-bemedalled Indian Army major and his plump but extremely good looking Anglo-Indian wife, dressed in a magnificent sari absolutely dripping with jewellery. I learned that, when younger, she had been a star actress in the developing Bombay film studios but was now their leading make-up artist. I was invited to sit down and have a drink and before long I had been invited to tea at their bungalow the following day.

Next day, after tea, Aunty suggested that Kaye and I should go for a stroll through the woods at the back of their married quarters before it got dark. The woods were lovely, being mainly of pines with many large boulders scattered about. We stumbled across a grassy dell, sloping down to the west, so we sat down with our backs against a big rock to watch the sunset. Suddenly I sensed a movement at the edge of the wood nearby and three fox cubs came tumbling out into the open. They were playing at mock fighting and came to within a few feet of us quite oblivious of our presence. Soon afterwards a vixen appeared, saw us and barked sharply. The cubs stopped in their tracks and scampered towards their mother and cover. It was a magical happening.

Kaye was a delightful young lady. She was painfully shy in company and had very little to say for herself. But she was a good listener and wanted to know all about me and my family. We arranged to go to the camp cinema the following evening which was a bit of a disaster because, as we took our seats, she was

The author with his then girl-friend, Kaye Bailey, May 1946 at Juhu Beach.

bombarded with wolf whistles and catcalls by the Army squaddies in the audience. She was highly embarrassed and blushed bright pink. After the film the avuncular old SNCO who ran the cinema told me that, if we wanted to come again, he would let us sit in the balcony next to the projection room which was reached by back steps. We took advantage of his offer twice more before Kaye had to return home to Bombay – by which time we had become good friends, albeit no closer than holding hands and a good night kiss – on the cheek.

* * *

When we arrived back at Fathejang we found that the Wing had been put on stand-by for an airborne operation in July. This was exciting news but, although we felt better prepared after the course at Belgaum even if some of the syllabus was inappropriate, we still had some qualms about our ability to carry out a successful mass landing in Burma. The main reason was that we had flown so little in gliders since the conversion course onto the Waco Hadrian in January. For example, I had only flown two sorties in the last six months. Landing with accuracy in a confined space, such as a *padi* field in Burma, requires much practice of which we were woefully short. The Army glider pilots, who had more experience than ourselves, seemed to accept that any massed landing would be a series of controlled crashes with many casualties. We were more professional in our approach and were appalled at the current lack of briefing or discussion on landing procedures and tactics. We made our concerns known to Wing Commander Price, who managed to persuade the Army that the RAF pilots, at least, should practise a massed landing.

Eventually, on 20 June, sixteen Dakota tug aircraft were deployed and thirty-two RAF pilots from the three squadrons were selected to take part. The pre-flight briefing was very poor, concentrating as it did on the arrangements for the take-off and cross-country. Briefing for the landing was given by Flight Lieutenant Ben Kilvington, one of the flight commanders, who was to captain the leading glider. Virtually all he said was to watch for him casting off and then each following pilot was to do so himself ten seconds after the one in front and follow each other down.

I was flying in the thirteenth glider with Flying Officer Colin Brooke from 669 Squadron: we tossed up to decide who should do the landing and I won. Colin did the take-off and all went well, the tug/glider combinations forming up in loose line astern. We flew in formation for about fifty minutes to more or less replicate a real approach to a landing zone. Colin and I had taken it in turns to fly for ten minutes each, but I took over as we neared the LZ, which was an area marked out on the airfield by trucks parked at the four corners.

We saw the airfield on our port side and I watched to see the lead glider cast off: when it did, I could see that Ben had left it far too late and did not have a hope of reaching the LZ. The following pilots did as briefed and cast off at ten-second intervals. By now our own glider was in the ideal position so I ignored instructions and cast off. I turned towards the LZ, landed and came to a stop tidily in the far left corner, closely followed by the three following aircraft and one other who, having seen me cast off, followed and just made it. The remaining eleven gliders all landed well short but luckily the terrain was friendly and none were damaged.

Major Hafner, our squadron commander, drove up in his Jeep to congratulate us before driving off to berate Kilvington who had committed the cardinal sin of gliding by ignoring the adage that it is better to overshoot as you can always lose height (by side-slipping, fish-tailing or using the spoilers) but there is no way you can stretch a glide if you are undershooting. The shambles of that exercise did, at least, prove that our concerns were justified and led to discussions from which were evolved proper procedures to help solve the difficulties.

Preparations for the July operation were well under way. The mounting base for our assault was to be the airfield at Cox's Bazar near Chittagong to which an advance party had already been sent to organize accommodation and other facilities when disaster struck. Our two airfields were hit by a freak tornado which flattened tents and marquees and tore many of our gliders from their dispersals where they were picketed down, smashing some and badly damaging others. I was not at Fathejang at the time as I was recovering from a bout of dengue fever at Lower Topa but I was told what a frightening experience it had been. Luckily nobody was seriously hurt but nearly half our gliders were inoperable.

The planners acted quickly when they got the bad news. They cancelled the second planned operation and moved onto the third which was to be an airborne assault on Rangoon which was now scheduled for late August – if the Fourteenth Army kept up their present rate of advance towards the Burmese capital. The surviving Hadrians were to be shared by 668 and 669 Squadrons whilst our squadron, No. 670, was to relocate on detachment to the airfield at Raipur to which No. 298 Squadron of Halifax bombers had just flown in from the UK. Their aircraft had been modified for glider towing. Our squadron was to be re-equipped with Horsas which had recently been shipped to India.

It was with mounting excitement that we prepared to re-familiarize ourselves with the dear old Horsa when the Americans dropped the atom bombs on Hiroshima and Nagasaki and suddenly, and unexpectedly to us, the war with Japan was over. Whereas the news was greeted in general with much jubilation, many pilots including myself were somewhat frustrated that, after all that training and hard work, we had been cheated at the eleventh hour of the opportunity to go into battle for King and Country. We had volunteered to fly gliders as a shortcut to becoming operational to no avail.

Once again we boarded the dreaded train for yet another long, tedious journey, the fourth time in as many months. Back at Fathejang all the No. 343 Wing officers assembled at Sam's restaurant in Murree to celebrate with a Victory dinner. Wing Commander Price's speech was part triumphant and part commiseration for our failure to achieve operational service. Salt was rubbed into our wounded pride when we found that the pilots of the other Wing, No. 344, based in Bengal had qualified for the 1939-45 Star and the Burma Star medals as their Wing Commander, George Lillicrap, had arranged that they could fly, as supernumerary crew, with the local transport squadrons on supply-dropping and other operations. They only had to fly on one such 'op' to qualify – and good luck to them.

Chapter 5

Peace

The end of the Second World War did not mean that we could all pack up our kitbags and go home. Far from it, we had to join a long queue to be repatriated. Those servicemen who had served longest and had been in theatre for the longest time were given priority for such troopships as would be available. With only three years' service and less than a year in India, I was advised that I would have to wait for at least six months – not a prospect to look forward to! Some of us were lucky and were allocated to specific jobs: I was posted as adjutant to one of the recently-formed Air Booking Centres (ABC), that in Bangalore, whilst Johnnie Sharpe was posted to the one in Bombay. This was lucky because Johnnie had started an affair with the estranged wife of an Indian Army officer who happened to live in Bangalore whilst I was keen to get together again with Kaye in Bombay. We applied to swap jobs and this was agreed at the eleventh hour.

I managed to thumb a lift in an aircraft to Delhi where I spent three days marvelling at the architecture of Sir Edwin Lutyens and exploring the Red Fort. I then hitched another Dakota flight to Bombay where I arrived on 18 September. I was booked into a transit hotel and duly reported to the ABC the following day. I had no idea what to expect but was soon briefed by the CO, Flight Lieutenant Bill Warner. Apparently, the RAF transport force in India

The author, and two of the air Booking Centre's NCOs, putting out the fires after the 'Jai Hind' riots of 1945 in Bombay.

operated a network of scheduled Dakota flights between all the major cities, primarily for the carriage of service personnel and freight. It had been agreed that spare seats on these aircraft were to be offered to Indian businessmen to assist in the re-organization of industry, trade and commerce now that the war was over. The Air Booking Centres were responsible for the passenger manifests for all these aircraft and included an Air Priorities Board, consisting of RAF officers and Indian civil servants, who filtered and authorized the carriage of the businessmen who applied for tickets.

As adjutant I was to be responsible for the day-to-day administration of the centre, and, as imprest holder, for handling the money for the pay for the SNCOs and airmen and for that collected in fares from the civilians. This would require frequent trips to AHQ Bombay which was located about five miles away on Malabar Hill. The CO asked me if I had a civilian UK driving licence to which the answer was 'No'. He then asked if I could drive to which the answer was 'of course' – with my fingers crossed behind my back. He then suggested that a motorcycle might be the answer as I could be issued with a provisional licence. I agreed eagerly, despite the fact that I had never ridden a motorcycle in my life.

I duly reported to the MT section at AHQ and was allocated a Norton 500 – marvellous. I confided to the kindly sergeant in charge, that despite having driven staff cars and Jeeps, I had never even had a go on a motorcycle. He gave me a quick briefing on the machine and, taking his life in my hands, rode pillion whilst I weaved my way around the usual horrific Bombay traffic. Incredibly he was satisfied that I was not a danger to life or limb and issued me with a provisional licence. The motorbike was now mine for the rest of my tour, the only requirement being that I should only leave it, unattended, in the secure yard at the back of the ABC building or at night in the RAF MT compound, which was close to the officers' mess into which I was about to move.

Now that I was settled in at both the ABC and the downtown officers' mess, and had transport, it was the time to find out where the Baileys lived. I had their address but they did not have a telephone – so I could not let them know that I was now in Bombay. Armed with a street map I soon found Brady's Flats but there was no one at home so I waited, on the other side of the road, until someone turned up. After a while I saw a small group of schoolgirls, dressed in the uniform of the nearby convent. As they approached, I noticed one who looked like Kaye but was obviously much younger. I knew she had an elder sister and a younger brother but as they got close it became obvious that it was indeed Kaye. So I called out, whereupon she turned and saw me, burst into tears and rushed into the flat.

Her seeing me was obviously a bit of a shock so I waited a little while before knocking on the door. When it opened I saw that she had changed out of her school uniform, had combed her hair and put on some make-up. She was obviously much younger than I remembered, so I laughed and asked how old she really was to which she whispered 'I am nearly sixteen'. She told me that her Aunty in Belgaum had made her up to look much older for the dance and also before our every date.

To her relief, I was amused at having been fooled and before long we had caught up with each other's news.

Her mother, from whom Kaye had obviously inherited her good looks, arrived and made me feel at home by inviting me to stay for tea. I next met elder sister Renée who had just collected young Johnny from his school. I did not meet father, Jack Bailey, always called 'Bill', a lieutenant quartermaster in the Royal Indian Army Service Corps, as he was away on duty. Before I left I was invited to lunch the following Sunday. This set the pattern for the rest of the stay in Bombay: as Kaye's boyfriend I was treated as a member of the family.

One week I was invited to join the family for a picnic at Juhu Beach, a short train journey to the north of the city. There was a vast expanse of beautiful beach to which Kaye and I tried to go every Saturday thereafter. We found that if we took a short gharry ride to the northern end of the beach it became almost deserted where the sand gave way to dunes in which one could get lost. There was a rather rundown hotel where we could have lunch: it also had chalets scattered around its grounds which could be hired by the day as upmarket beach huts.

We would arrive as early as possible, rent a chalet, go for a swim, sunbathe in the dunes, before returning to the chalet for a shower and lunch. After lunch we would retreat to the chalet to escape the heat, Kaye usually lay on the bed under a fan whilst I sat in the shade on the verandah with a book. When it had cooled down we would have a final swim and another shower before returning to Bombay in time for Kaye to finish her homework.

As the weeks flew by Kaye and I became very close and sought every opportunity to be alone together. Then, just before Christmas at Juhu, we got too close for comfort – despite the heat. Thus I embarked on my one and only affair, as opposed to casual encounters, until about two years later when I met the lady whom I was to marry – eventually.

Despite the frustrations of my career to date I was determined to become a fighter pilot, so I applied for an extended service commission which would give me a further five years in which to achieve my ambition. In February 1946 I was promoted to the war substantive rank of Flight Lieutenant and given extra responsibilities as Security Officer for the ABC.

By that time the *Jai Hind* or 'Quit India' anti-colonial campaign was nearing boiling point and already there had been disturbances all over the sub-continent, mainly in the larger cities. Bombay was no exception, but the demonstrations had been largely peaceful, whereas in some cities there had been violent clashes with the police. AHQ Bombay decided that our offices in the prestigious Karimjee House building were vulnerable to attack as we were located in the heart of the banking and business centre of the city whereas all other RAF units were situated on the outskirts and within their own secure compounds. Moreover, we had a small complement of only fifteen personnel, being four RAF officers of whom one was a WAAF, one lady WAC(I) officer, one RAF SNCO and three airmen, with the remainder being Indian civil servants.

As security officer I was required to carry out a survey of the building, as a result of which bars were fitted to all the ground-floor windows, stronger locks and bolts were fitted to the double front doors and to the gates which led into the small yard at the back of the building. We were told not to fly the Union Jack from the flag-pole. It was also decided that the male officers should be issued with personal weapons, the trusty .38 Smith and Wesson revolver. I collected the guns and ammunition from the AHQ armoury and stored them in the safe in my office. I was also instructed that they were only to be used in dire emergency and only with the written permission of a magistrate – a ridiculous stipulation.

We did not have long to wait for trouble! About a week after our preparations were complete we heard the unmistakable noise of a riotous mob shouting and beating dustbin lids with sticks. I went onto the steps of the front door and saw a crowd of several hundred men, maybe even a thousand, approaching up Sir Pherozehah Mehta Road. I quickly withdrew, made sure that everybody was inside the building and closed the doors, gates and windows. I then phoned AHQ Bombay.

We hoped that the mob would pass us by but they stopped and gathered in front of our building where they were being harangued by their leaders who seemed to be inflaming the rioters who in turn started throwing stones, setting fire to a truck outside the side of our building and, to my horror, starting a bonfire up against our front door. I immediately opened the safe and handed out the guns and ammunition. I then phoned AHQ again to tell them that things were getting nasty and that if any one tried to break into the building I would have no hesitation in opening fire. The Provost Marshal to whom I was talking said 'You can't do that without the written authority of a magistrate' so I was rather scathing about our chances of getting such permission whilst surrounded by rioters. Somewhat taken aback by my reaction, he promised to request the Bombay Police to break up the disturbance as soon as possible.

A little later I went to the 'Gents' and heard a great commotion in the side street. Standing on one of the lavatory seats so I could look out of a high window, I saw one of the leaders of the mob, standing on an upturned galvanized dust-bin, inciting them to more violence and looting. He was a very tempting target, being only about twenty yards from the window. I thought better of shooting at him but I could not resist firing one bullet into the dustbin. The result was incredible: suddenly everything went eerily quiet and then, miraculously, the mob melted away.

Nobody in the ABC office heard my pistol shot, which was not too surprising considering the racket going on outside, so I told nobody what I had done. Nor did it come to light months later when I handed over the issued guns and ammunition to my successor as by then I had managed to replace the missing bullet.

When the police arrived ten minutes later they found me, and Corporal Sweet, putting out the fires. The press arrived shortly afterwards and the following day *The Times of India* featured front-page photographs of us with our buckets of water and sand. It was ironic that the only shot I fired in anger in three years of active service should have been in peacetime and in a civil disturbance.

After that incident nothing exciting happened until May when I was informed that my application to extend my service had been approved. Yippee! I was also told that I had been allocated a berth on a troopship home in June, news about which I had mixed feelings. I was delighted that I was about to start a new phase in my career but it was a wrench to leave Kaye behind. The Bailey family had no idea when they might be returning to the UK because it would depend on the future of those Britons serving in the Indian Army when, as seemed inevitable, the country would be granted independence.

* * *

In mid-June, after tearful farewells, I boarded the *Georgic*, a venerable troopship sailing from Bombay to Liverpool. To my delight I found that I had been allocated a very small cabin to myself and that it was on the starboard side as recommended in the old adage POSH (Port Out Starboard Home). As the good ship sailed out of the harbour I was very amused by the sight of a thousand Bombay Bowlers being thrown overboard to bob up and down in the wake. It was a long and boring voyage during which I reached my real twenty-first birthday as we approached the Suez Canal. Needless to say there was no celebration; I had no cards and no presents except for a box of Turkish Delights from a WAAF officer, the only person on board who knew about the milestone. She had bought the sweets from one of the 'bum boats' in Port Said. It was very sweet of her and I did not let on that I hated the stuff.

Towards the end of the voyage I found out that, if you spoke nicely, the purser would sell you a bottle of 'export only' Scotch at only a 'grey' market price. The only member of the family for whom I had not brought a present from India was Aunty Elsie, my mother's sister, who liked the odd nip – for medicinal purposes, of course. So I bought a bottle which I packed very carefully in the middle of my kitbag.

The next day we sailed into Liverpool and, complete with a first-class railway warrant to London, I disembarked en route to fourteen days' leave with my mother who now lived back in Putney in a house rented from Wandsworth Borough Council who had re-housed her under the mistaken impression that she had been bombed out. I was very happy to be back in England and astonished to be reminded just how green the countryside was as the train chugged southwards. When I arrived at East Putney station I decided to arrive home in style in a taxi. As the driver hoisted my kitbag into the baggage space he banged it against a lamp-post. When we arrived at my mother's house I paid the fare and he drove off. Only then did I become aware of the smell and realized that the whisky bottle had been broken.

I rang the door bell, my mother appeared and stepping forward to give me a hug she stopped, sniffed and said 'John, you have been drinking!' in a very disapproving voice: not exactly the reaction expected on the return of a prodigal son. Explanation over, I was given a tour of the house which was deceptively large, having four bedrooms, two of them doubles, which enabled my mother to take paying guests, now her only source of income. It was lovely to see much of the furniture, paintings, silver, ornaments, etc. which had been put into storage when we had become homeless in 1940. Although the semi-detached front of No. 15 Enmore Road looked very ordinary, the inside now looked rather grand, albeit a bit overstuffed in the Victorian style.

It did not take long for me to get fed up with being shown off to my mother's friends, usually at teatime with the inevitable cucumber sandwiches, so I was glad when I was able to keep a rendezvous with some old mates from 670 Squadron at the Captain's Cabin public house in the West End on the first Saturday of the month as arranged before we all dispersed from Fathejang. There were about a dozen of us all excitedly exchanging news. Some were still awaiting demob, others had gone back to the jobs they had been doing when they had joined up, which had been kept open for them – by law. A few had started new jobs and some were taking courses to gain qualifications. Johnnie Sharpe, for example, had gone back to working for an estate agent and hating every minute of it. Hearing their stories I was very glad that I was extending my service.

When the pub closed someone suggested that we might go on to a night club so four of us piled into a taxi, asked the driver's advice and landed up at The Windermere Club in Regent Street. As we paid the fare, the driver warned that we should not have anything to do with the hostesses as they not only charged for the pleasure of their company but were under orders to encourage the clients to spend money buying them drinks, corsages and cigarettes. Going down a rather dingy flight of steps we were told that the club was for members only and their guests. However, if one of us joined there and then we could all go in. So I stumped up five shillings, signed on the dotted line and duly became a member – a fact that was to have a very significant impact on my life – two years later.

In the subdued lighting the club seemed quite opulent, the band and vocalists were very good and the price of drinks not too exorbitant. But the best thing was that they served food as we were ravenous having eaten nothing but crisps and nuts since we had gathered in the pub. The hostesses looked very inviting but we took the taxi driver's advice and admired them from a distance. However, we did notice a very good looking young lady who was sitting with two Royal Navy officers on the other side of the dance floor. The naval men seemed to be ignoring her: indeed she was looking a bit glum to say the least. With his usual aplomb, Johnnie Sharpe asked if he could invite their lady friend to dance and they seemed only too happy.

After a couple of dances Johnnie brought her over to our table and introduced us. She told us that it was her twenty-fifth birthday and that she had been taken out to dinner by the two officers for whom she worked at the Admiralty, as their secretary. Dinner had been fine but since they had arrived at the club it had become clear that they were 'boy friends'; indeed we noticed later that they were holding hands surreptitiously under the table. We took turns to dance with Lady Windermere, as I named her because of where we were and her rather county voice. After a bit we felt somewhat guilty for monopolising her, so we invited the boys to join us and the evening developed into a right old party. Eventually we started to disperse as people rushed off to catch last trains, buses or Green Line coaches.

I was in no hurry as I had booked into the American Officers' Club in Holland Park where I could stay by virtue of having trained in the USA. When I found out that Lady W. lived in a flat in Notting Hill Gate, a stone's throw from the Club, I offered to take her home by taxi, to which her escorts readily agreed as they shared a flat in Victoria, in the opposite direction.

When we arrived at the flat, I paid off the taxi, as I felt I needed the walk to the Officers' Club. Elizabeth, Lady W's real name, asked if I would like to come in for a coffee which I politely refused but she seemed so genuinely disappointed that I relented. The flat was in the basement and rather dreary: in fact it was damp, dingy and depressing. When Elizabeth brought the coffee into the living room we sat on the sofa and she told me how much she had enjoyed the evening, thanks to the RAF. She went on to say that it had been one of the few times in the last year when she had not felt utterly miserable – and then burst into floods of tears.

Somewhat taken aback I asked what was wrong so she told me a sad story. She had joined the Wrens in 1940 and had eventually been posted to RNAS Yeovilton where she met and fell in love with a dashing young Fleet Air Arm pilot. They got married in 1944 and, because Naval officers were not allowed to marry non-commissioned Wrens, she was discharged but continued to work on the base. They had been blissfully happy until, in the last week of the war in Europe, he had been killed, not on operations but in a flying accident. She went into deep shock which developed into depression.

Elizabeth felt that she had to get away from Yeovilton, so she had transferred to the Admiralty and moved to London, where her family had lived before the war, and rented her present flat. I asked about her family and once again she started to cry. It turned out that her parents and younger brother had all been killed during the London blitz when their house in Kensington had received a direct hit. I did my best to console her and she ended up quietly sobbing with her head on my shoulder.

When she had recovered I told her that she needed to start a new life well away from her unhappy memories, preferably somewhere in the sun. I recommended that she might seek a transfer to one of the Royal Naval Dockyards overseas, such as those in Ceylon, the Caribbean, Hong Kong and Singapore. Although I did not say so I thought it vital that she should move out of that dismal basement flat and away from the loneliness of living on her own in a big city. Ideally she should marry again which she should have no difficulty in doing so as she was most attractive and would go down very well with the young bachelors in those remote parts where eligible young girls were at a premium. We talked for ages and she eventually fell asleep with my arm around her shoulders.

It was about 5.00am when, with much difficulty I managed to extricate myself without waking her. I got a blanket from the bedroom and covered her up. I then wrote a note saying that if she wanted to contact me she could write to my mother's address for forwarding and let myself out. I enjoyed the brisk walk to the Officers' Club and got the key to my bedroom from the night porter who did not seem at all surprised that I had arrived with the milkman. Tumbling into bed, I slept for a couple of hours but got up in time to have a hearty American breakfast of two eggs sunnyside up, bacon and waffle with maple syrup followed by toast and jello, washed down with cups of steaming coffee; just what I needed for the journey back to my mother's house where I was due to sort out her back garden.

* * *

Three or four days later I received a posting notice from the Air Ministry instructing me to report to reception at the de Havilland Aircraft Company at Hatfield to attend No. 2 Pilot Refresher Course at No. 1 EFTS which operated out of a grass airfield at nearby Panshanger. At last, I thought, this is a positive step towards flying fighters until I found out that the EFTS flew DH28 Tiger Moths. Refresher flying on powered aircraft was very necessary for those of us going onto operational aircraft after nearly two years of gliders – but on Tiger Moths? In fact the Air Ministry 'posters' were using the EFTSs as holding units for the likes of myself whilst the politicians and Air Force Board sorted out the post-war shape and size of the peacetime air force.

I was accommodated, with my fellow refreshers, in a beautiful Elizabethan manor house called Nast Hyde which had been de Havilland's 'gin palace' where they had put up and entertained foreign buyers pre-war. It had become an officers' mess in 1940 but was still owned and run by de Havilland. The other course members were a very mixed bag. Perhaps the most important were the dozen Fleet Air Arm observers who were re-mustering to pilot. They were to complete a seventy-five-hour course on the Tiger. The rest of us were a mixture of RAF personnel who had had their training interrupted by the outbreak of peace or, like myself, those who had flown gliders.

The EFTS was commanded by Squadron Leader 'Wispy' Turner and the flight commander was Flight Lieutenant Peter Lines, both of whom had been pre-war civilian pilots. After demob 'Wispy', so called because of the sparseness of his hair, became the manager of Exeter Airport whilst Peter became an instructor at a civilian flying club. Having looked at my log-book, Peter took me up for a flight check and assessed that I had little to learn other than instrument flying in the UK weather because my previous flying had been under the blue skies of America and India. He said that, apart from IF, I could do more or less what I wanted within the seventy-five-hour syllabus although, later on, he used me as safety pilot on IF and navigation sorties by the less experienced students.

Luckily Putney was readily accessible from Hatfield thanks to the superb Green Line coach service, so I was able to go home every weekend. Four weeks after starting the course I went home to find a letter from Elizabeth. In it she invited me to dinner at her flat the following Saturday. When I arrived she welcomed me with a kiss and a hug and was obviously very excited. It transpired that she had taken my advice, had applied for an overseas posting and was on her way to the RN base at Seletar in Singapore. Apparently there was a growing shortage of secretarial staff as more and more Wrens were demobbed, so her application had been very welcome. We had as delightful a meal as the continuing British rationing allowed and afterwards she showed her gratitude for my advice by giving me the gift that you don't tell your mother about. I never found out what the future held for Elizabeth but I hope she found happiness after the appalling bad luck which had befallen her.

It was a very frustrating time waiting for something to happen whilst I was merely keeping my hand in on the dear old Tiger Moth. I tried to get some worthwhile experience out of it, firstly by wangling myself onto an 'Introduction to Jet Engines' course run by de Havilland for RAF mechanics and secondly by attending a two-week Flying Training Command Ground Instructors' course, from which I emerged with an A2 category.

It was also frustrating, in more ways than one, not knowing when Kaye would be returning to UK. In the meantime, I had become friendly with one of the de Havilland employees at Panshanger, whom I will call Belinda. She was older than me, but we got along very well in a purely platonic way. She was a farmer's daughter and before I could take her to the cinema I had to ask her father's permission – in person, so I could be inspected and interrogated. He was a daunting mid-Victorian father figure who asked me what were my intentions towards his only child. Having replied that Belinda was merely a colleague and a friend and that I was already spoken for, he reluctantly agreed that we might go out together.

After our first night out together, he quizzed us about the film we had seen, about which bus we had caught and why it had taken eleven minutes to walk home from the bus stop. His suspicious attitude drove us to cheat by catching an earlier bus and spending the twenty minutes thus saved in one of his hay barns.

When Belinda learned that I went ice-skating at the rink in Richmond she was very keen to have a go herself – but it was too far to do so in one day. When I mentioned this to my mother, to my surprise she said 'why don't you invite her to stay the night here?' I explained about Belinda's tyrannical father and she said 'leave him to me'. When she 'phoned I was amazed how easily she was able to charm him into agreeing.

We duly went skating and Belinda was a big hit with my mother because she praised her cooking, admired the house and her belongings and generally buttered her up. At the end of that weekend my mother said she could come back any time she liked. My mother thought that she could do no wrong but what she did not know was that, when we had all long gone to bed, Belinda had crept into my room with naughty intent.

* * *

Life jogged along enjoyably until May 1947, by which time I had flown nearly eighty hours, when I was posted, not onto flying, but as assistant adjutant of No. 1 Polish Resettlement Unit at RAF Framlingham in Essex. The PRU housed those Polish Air Force officers who could not or would not return to their homes because they were in that part of Poland which was now under Russian occupation. Our job was to help resettle them by arranging emigration to other countries, mainly to Australia or South America, to find them jobs in the UK, to provide grants to enable them to gain professional qualifications and also, for relatively few, to absorb them into the RAF. Although very disappointed at not going straight onto operational flying training, I enjoyed working with the Poles whom I admired immensely – especially those who had the good sense to marry the daughters of well-heeled farmers and the like.

And then in August, at long last, I was posted to No. 2 Pilot Refresher Flying Unit at RAF Valley in Anglesey. Valley had been a wartime Coastal Command station, had recently re-opened after two years of care and maintenance status and ours was the first refresher flying course to operate from there. It was composed almost entirely of temporary buildings, mainly Nissen huts, and was a pretty bleak and forbidding place. Even in autumn it presented a dismal picture with such few trees as there were all leaning about 30 degrees away from the gale force westerly winds which seemed to blow most of the time. In those days Anglesey was a desolate place with no public houses, no cinemas other than a flea-pit in Holyhead and very little to do, on or off base. The nearest civilisation was the town of Bangor, a hired coach trip away across the Menai Straits. Little did I think that twenty or so years later I would return to Valley as the Station Commander.

It was, however, a joy to fly a proper aircraft again; none other than the ubiquitous Harvard which I had last flown two and a half years previously. I completed the course in four weeks and to my utter delight I was posted to No. 203 Advanced Flying School at RAF Keevil in Wiltshire – to convert onto the Spitfire. At last my dreams were about to become true.

Chapter 6

Fighters at Last

I arrived at Keevil in mid–September 1947 only to find that all flying operations had ceased and that No. 203 Advanced Flying School was in the process of moving to RAF Chivenor near Barnstaple in Devon. Even at the eleventh hour my finally getting to fly fighters was being bedevilled by delay. I was given a number of odd jobs, including acting as escort to the Squadron Leader, Administration, who was under close arrest whilst awaiting the possibility of a court martial for allegedly embezzling public funds. He was confined to camp but was allowed to go out for essential shopping accompanied by an escort. Luckily for me, he was an agreeable fellow whose one failing was his liking for the bottle. I went with him into Barnstaple three or four times where we spent ten minutes buying toothpaste and razor blades and two hours having a convivial lunch at one of the local hostelries. In fact, his case never came to court martial as an investigation found that no money had actually gone adrift but had been stuffed into drawers and filing cabinets – to be dealt with later. No wonder the books were in a shambles because, as a pilot, he had not got a clue about accountancy.

Amidst the chaos of the move the staff tried to run the ground-school programme for the course. My fellow students were all 'sprogs' straight from flying training at Cranwell and elsewhere and were either pilot officers or sergeants: as a flight lieutenant I was a bit of an oddity. The instructors concentrated on the various systems of the Spitfire such as the engine, the electrics, the hydraulics and the ancillary equipments such as the radio, the instruments, etc. We were each given a copy of the pilot's notes which we were expected to know almost by heart within a few weeks. By that time we had to know the cockpit inside out and were tested by being blindfolded and made to lay one's hands instantly on the throttle, the flap levers, the pitch control or any other switch, this ability to do so being vital, say, in the event of cockpit lighting failure when flying at night. Towards the end of October the move was complete and on the 27th the A Squadron Commander took me up for a flight in the back seat of a Harvard from where the forward view was not dissimilar to that from the cockpit of a Spitfire. He demonstrated the curved approach which enabled the pilot to see down the runway before levelling out to land. Having done a few circuits to his satisfaction, he then sent me off on my first solo.

Many pilots have written, more eloquently than I, about the joys of flying the Spitfire but even so I was not prepared for the reality. As I opened the throttle for take-off, I was pressed back into the seat by the power of the mighty Merlin engine. I had been briefed to expect a violent swing on take-off when the tail came up, because of the precessional force of the four-bladed propeller, but I found that it only needed a touch of rudder to correct and keep straight. Then when the aircraft reached the lift-off speed, I applied a little back pressure on the control column and it virtually leapt off the ground. I spent forty minutes at height putting the 'Spit' through its paces: operating the flaps and undercarriage at the recommended speeds, doing maximum-rate turns and carrying out all the manoeuvres which I had been briefed to complete before I returned to base to land. I knew that I would be watched from the control tower by the squadron commander so it had to be good: luckily I managed to 'grease it on'.

The aircraft was an absolute joy to fly, not least because the controls were so responsive to the touch and so well balanced. It did not seem to have any vices. Now I knew what was meant by the adage that one's first flight in a Spitfire was like losing one's virginity – life would never be quite the same again. There was no doubt about the Spitfire being a lady and a beautiful one at that.

The remaining ten weeks of the course just flew by – perhaps because I was enjoying myself so much. The syllabus was designed to prepare us for operational flying when we joined our squadrons. The exercises consisted mainly of close and battle formation, air to air with cine-camera against other aircraft or with .303 machine guns against a towed target flag, air to ground with cine and guns, dive-bombing with 25lb smoke bombs, low-level flying and tactical exercises. This was all new to me but I took to it like a duck to water.

Because I was a flight lieutenant with almost 400 hours in my log book I was regarded as being an experienced pilot but, if one disregarded my glider flying and the fact that about a quarter of my flying hours had been on Tiger Moths, I had no more experience than the sprogs. One day Chivenor was totally overcast with a cloud base of 300 feet above sea level. The Wing Commander Flying ordered dual flying only, from which restriction I was exempt, so the squadron commander briefed me to practise aerobatics prior to the start of the air-to-air phase.

When I took off the cloud base was down to 250 feet ASL and the cloud was about 1,500-feet thick. I was quite happy, little knowing that I was about to have the first of the relatively few 'dicey dos' of my career which could easily have ended in disaster. I had spent about twenty-five minutes putting together a low-level aerobatic sequence using the cloud tops as ground level when I was suddenly aware that there was no side-tone in my earphones and that I had not heard any R/T transmissions for several minutes. It was apparent that my radio had failed: I could neither transmit nor receive.

I had a rough idea where I was as I had kept a mental air-plot of my position but accuracy is somewhat dodgy during aerobatics. I knew that I only had to fly due eastwards for long enough to ensure crossing the Devon coast, beyond which I could descend and break cover over the sea. I lost height gradually until I was flying just above the clouds. When I calculated that I was well clear of the coast I let down gingerly, finally breaking cloud at 200 feet with, to my horror, ground beneath me and to my left and right I could see that the clouds were right down on the hills.

I recognized that I had come down just north of the Taw Estuary and had quite unknowingly flown right over the top of Chivenor whilst still in cloud. I flew a mile or so out to sea, did a quick turn around and flew down the dead side of the runway, rocking my wings to indicate radio failure. On receiving a green Very light I did a low-level circuit and landed. Once in dispersal, I found that all flying had been cancelled as the weather had deteriorated well below limits. About half an hour previously all airborne aircraft had been recalled but the control tower had been unable to contact me. The Wing Commander had been doing his nut and had begun to fear the worst when they heard the distinctive, unmistakeable sound of a Spitfire flying over the base. My safe return was a great relief and I became the flavour of the month.

One of the other delights of being at Chivenor was that I was able to resume playing rugger after a very long lay-off following my going to India in December 1944. After a couple of friendly games I was chosen to play for the Station XV as full back instead of my preferred position of wing three quarter. The team captain was Squadron Leader 'Black Mac' MacKenzie who commanded the other AFS squadron. Mac had been shot down over Germany in 1944 and had become a prisoner of war. In the prison camp he had feigned a nervous breakdown into a gibbering wreck. He put on such a convincing performance, including a chronic stammer, that he was repatriated to UK as part of the agreement whereby sick or badly wounded prisoners could be exchanged via a neutral country.

Once home Mac was medically examined and passed fit to resume full flying duties – but he found that he could not stop his stammer. Even at Chivenor he still stuttered quite badly but strangely he never did so when airborne. Under his captaincy the Station XV won the Fighter Command Rugby Cup but unfortunately we were knocked out of the RAF Cup in the second round.

All good things must come to an end and towards the end of January 1948 the course was complete, by which time I had flown fifty hours on the Spitfire – and loved every minute of it. We students were sent on a week's leave before reporting to our next postings, myself and a half-a-dozen sprogs to No. 226 Operational Conversion Unit at RAF Bentwaters near Ipswich in Essex to convert onto the Hawker Tempest II.

* * *

I was pleased with my posting because it meant adding another type of fighter to my credit and because all the Tempest II squadrons were in Germany, being units of the British Air Forces of Occupation (BAFO). But I began to have my doubts when I saw a Tempest II for the first time. By comparison with the beautiful, sleek Spitfire it was a bit of a brute. Its all-up-weight was nearly twice that of a 'Spit' and it was powered by a huge Centaurus 18-cylinder, double-banked radial engine with a massive five-bladed propeller. Getting into the cockpit was quite a struggle, involving pulling down a retractable step just to get onto the wing, then a clamber up to the cockpit, entering which required putting a foot into a recess and pulling oneself up using a handle in the cockpit. That manoeuvre wearing a parachute harness took quite a lot of effort but one soon got used to it.

The course at Bentwaters only lasted for five weeks, the first of which was spent in ground school learning all about the aircraft and its systems with the usual emphasis on getting to know the pilot's notes inside out. I was the first to go solo and found that the aircraft took a lot of flying as it was very heavy on the controls. Because of the power of the engine and the corkscrew slipstream from the propeller, every change of altitude, speed and power setting altered the balance of the controls and required adjustment of the aileron, elevator and rudder trimmers. However, one soon got used to the characteristics of the aircraft. I flew only eight sorties for a total of nine hours flying, was duly certified as proficient on type and was posted to join No. 33 Squadron based at RAF Gütersloh in Germany.

* * *

By this time I was well on my way to achieving my ambition of becoming a fully-fledged fighter pilot, but there was a black cloud on the horizon. Kaye and her family arrived back in July 1947, just over a year since I had sailed from India. I was able to take a few days leave and was on the quayside when their troopship docked at Liverpool. Despite it being early evening I spotted the family on the deck and soon we were waving frantically. Then it was their turn to disembark with Kaye leading the way, stepping gingerly down the gangplank before rushing to embrace me. She had not changed, still as lovely as ever, although it was strange to see her in heavy clothing after her flimsy *Vogue*-inspired creations in India.

I had booked into the Midland Hotel in the middle of the city and, as the Bailey family had been booked into a bed-and-breakfast establishment, I suggested that we should meet up later that night in the bar of the Midland. The Baileys duly arrived with a number of family and friends who had also come to welcome them home. They were a motley collection of Eastenders on Bill's side of the family and Irish on his wife's. The liquor flowed and before long the company got a bit boisterous. As pleased as I was to see the Baileys, who had been so kind to me in Bombay, I felt quite out of place, so Kaye and I sneaked off to the lounge to catch up on each other's news.

From that time onwards I began to realize that the Bailey family, in their privileged status in India, was rather different to the reality of life in the UK. For example Bill's brother had managed to find them rented accommodation in Westbourne Park. The flat was in one of the former elegant squares flanked by large Georgian town houses. Unfortunately, most of the houses had been turned into flats and now housed a majority of West Indian families who had little respect for the environment and had turned the square's central garden into a ramshackle children's adventure playground. The roads were littered with rusty old cars and loud reggae music filled the air. The council had tried to prevent this deterioration but had lost control and given up.

The family was now living on Bill's meagre Indian Army pension, so they had to find jobs. Bill got a job working in a betting shop; Mrs B., as I always called her, being a UK-qualified SRN went back to nursing; Renée became a shorthand typist whilst young Johnny attended a local school. Kaye was a problem as she had no idea what she wanted to do. Having been an air stewardess with Tata Airlines in India for nine months she would have had no difficulty in getting a job with one of the British airlines but she said that being a stewardess was too much like hard work – not a good sign!

Eventually one of her aunties talked her into training as a hairdresser, so poor old Bill had to stump up £300 to buy her a three-year apprenticeship with a hair salon with premises in Commercial Road. She would have to start at the bottom, sweeping the floor, making the tea and coffee, etc., before graduating to washing, perming, cutting and styling. She would be paid a weekly pittance which would slowly increase as she mastered the more advanced techniques. Once she had started mixing with the other apprentices, who were all from the East End, she began to become just like them. She never had had much to say for herself, but now all she could talk about was clothes, film stars, the latest dance craze, make-up and similar fripperies. Fairly early on, I took her to an Officers' Mess Ball at Framlingham and she was so tongue-tied and out of her element that it was embarrassing. I had hoped, that having left school and worked as a stewardess, she would have overcome her chronic shyness and grown up a bit.

To cut a long story short the main problem was that our aspirations were so very different. Despite a less than encouraging start I was still intent on a career in the RAF and would apply for a permanent commission in 1949 when eligible to do so. If granted I had hopes of promotion to wing commander or even group captain rank. On the other hand, Kaye's idea of heaven was that I would leave the RAF, get some deadly dull office job, marry her, live in a semi-detached bungalow in some ghastly suburb, have children and live happily ever after. This difference, coupled with Kaye's failure to mature in the way I had expected, was leading me to becoming increasingly exasperated.

Obviously this was beginning to show and one day, to my surprise, Mrs B. took me aside and told me that Kaye was not the right girl for me and that she thought I should break off our relationship, sooner rather than later. She said that Kaye would take it very badly at the time but she would soon get over it and look back on our affair with fond memories.

Despite that advice I was still reluctant to end the affair, not least because I felt very guilty. However Kaye's best friend, Joan, recently returned from Bombay, let slip that Kaye had had an affair with her Tata Airlines captain. That was the final straw, and two weeks before I was due to leave for Germany, I told Kaye that I no longer loved her and that it would be in both our best interests that we should end our relationship. As expected, Kay did take it very badly but within six months she had met and married an American and gone to live in California – I hope not solely on the rebound.

* * *

Towards the end of April, I reported to RAF Gütersloh to join No. 33 Squadron. It was a very busy station with four fighter squadrons: No. 2 which was equipped with Spitfires but was soon to convert to the jet-engined de Havilland Vampire, lucky blighters, and Nos. 16, 26 and 33, all equipped with the Tempest II. The Wing Commander was Frank Carey who had been awarded the DFC and Bar, a DFM and an AFC, not to mention two or three foreign gongs. Although a sergeant pilot at the time, Carey had been one of the highest-scoring aces in the Battle of Britain.

The No. 33 Squadron Commander was Bob Allen and the flight commanders were 'Bunny' Bunyan and Norman Gall, a New Zealander, and all three of them sported the DFC – which made me very jealous. The rest of the complement of eighteen pilots were either flying officers or NCO pilots with the exception of myself – a flight lieutenant. I was really the odd man out because, although senior, I had less powered flying time and far less weapon delivery experience than even the most junior of the pilots. I was determined to put this anomaly right, so I tried to fly as many sorties as possible, especially on the weapon ranges where, before long, I started to achieve above average results, particularly in rocket firing and

The author played rugby for RAF Chivenor and was in the team which won the Fighter Command Cup in 1947/48.

dive bombing. No. 33 was a day-fighter/ground-attack (DFGA) squadron but the emphasis in training was very much on the latter role.

Whereas I worked hard at flying I played sport even harder in an attempt to make a mark. Soon after arrival I played in an inter-squadron rugby match as a result of which I was picked to play for the Station XV in their last two matches of the season. I joined the bottom of the station squash ladder and within three months had climbed to third place and thereafter played regularly for the station team.

When the cricket season started I played for the Station XI as an all-rounder and managed in one such match to upset the Air Officer Commanding in Chief, Air Marshal Sir 'Tom' Prickett. He had been driven all the way to Gütersloh from HQ RAF Germany to watch their star batsman, Squadron Leader Roger Gebbels, play. Roger came in as their No. 3 and the first ball he received he hit for what should have been a certain boundary. I was fielding at cover point and, by throwing myself sideways, I just managed to catch it – and it jolly well stung like mad. So Roger was out for a duck and the AOC-in-C was not best pleased, but at least it got me noticed.

In August I was given the job of organizing the annual Station Sports' Day, probably because I had already run two such events in India when I was OIC Athletics at Fathejang. With a bit of luck I managed to win the hurdles, the long jump, to come second in the 100 yards and to anchor the squadron team when we won both sprint relays. As a result I was crowned *Victor Ludorum*.

In June 1948 RAF Gütersloh had a new Station Commander, Group Captain Laurence Sinclair, who had had a very distinguished wartime record during which he had collected a vast array of honours and awards including the GC, CB, CBE, DSO and Bar and several foreign decorations. At the same time, Bob Allen was succeeded as No. 33 Squadron Commander by Denis 'Splinters' Smallwood DSO DFC. Splinters had ended the war as an acting wing commander, temporary group captain but, like many other contemporaries, had to revert to his substantive rank of squadron leader.

I was lucky in that these two distinguished officers took an interest in me and my career. Both men, and their families, were madly equestrian. Splinters had become Chairman of the only RAF Riding Club in Germany, which was based at Gütersloh, of which Sinclair was already the President. The AOC-in-C's two daughters were also very horsey and often stayed with the Sinclairs and Smallwoods who, in turn, would invite me to join them at cocktail parties and dinners to help squire the girls. This was encouraging but nearly backfired badly when the AOC-in-C, perhaps prompted by his daughters, put in a bid for me to become his ADC. I told Splinters that I was horrified at the thought and he managed to convince Sir Tom that my career depended upon my completing a full two-year tour on the squadron because of my loss of powered flying experience resulting from my having flown gliders during the war.

* * *

In July the squadron was tasked to take part in a tri-service firepower demonstration on Salisbury Plain. Norman Gall was given the job of detachment commander and told to select the pilots. He chose Flying Officer Gerry Hill and Sergeant Charlie Randall for the rocket firing and himself and another experienced sergeant pilot for the dive bombing. Splinters intervened and told Norman that I should have been selected as, although inexperienced, I had had the best 'average error' results since joining the squadron.

We flew into RAF Thorney Island, from which we were to operate, in the late afternoon of Friday 9 July and, having hangared our aircraft, we caught a train to London to spend the weekend. By the time we arrived we just had time for dinner and a couple of drinks in the Captain's Cabin pub just off The Strand. When 'Time Gentlemen, please' was called Gerry suggested that we should go on to a night club. They had booked rooms in the RAF Club but, as I was going home to stay with my mother, I was not too keen. However, I was talked into it as I was the only one who was a member of a club, so we went to the Windermere in Regent Street. Had I not given in my subsequent life would have been very different.

The Windermere was much as I remembered it and, after I had booked in Norman and Gerry, I warned them not to have anything to do with the hostesses whose main job was to encourage them to spend as much money as possible and, what's more, charge for the pleasure of their company if they joined one's table. After a while Gerry became very taken with one of the hostesses but lacked the courage to ask her to dance, so he dared me to do so. When I approached her table another customer beat me to her so, not to be beaten, I asked the other hostess who had had her back to me. As she looked up and accepted, I felt a frisson of excitement for she was by far the most attractive girl in the club and I wondered why I had not noticed her before. She danced beautifully, was very well spoken and obviously quite unlike what I thought a hostess would be. So I disregarded my own advice and invited her to join our table. We had a jolly time, without any hassle to spend and she did not even ask for her fee. Eventually we all piled into a taxi to drop her off but, before we did so, I had kissed her and made a date for the coming Sunday.

We met in Leicester Square with a view to going to one of the cinemas for an afternoon matinee. She chose to see the Lawrence Olivier film of *Hamlet* which we both enjoyed. Afterwards we had an early dinner at the House of Hamburgers, an unlikely name for the best fish restaurant in the West End. I thought I was onto a good thing going out with a hostess but, away from the

The author meets Doreen 'Jane' Newland Hodges in the Windermere Night club in Regent Street.

environment of the club, this young lady seemed rather prim and proper – not quite what I had expected.

We talked over dinner and she told me that she was an actress who, having been 'resting' for some time, was hostessing in the evenings as a means of paying the rent of her flat whilst attending auditions during the day. It transpired that she had been a bit of a child prodigy, particularly as a singer and dancer, and had first been on stage in Shakespeare at Stratford-upon-Avon at the tender age of four. She had appeared in pantomime with Arthur Askey but most of her serious work had been as a member of Donald Wolfit's company. Wolfit was one of the last of the great actor-managers who specialized in taking Shakespeare's plays to the provinces. During the war, when she was with the company, he concentrated on playing to Service audiences in hangars and station cinemas around the country. She had accompanied him on two overseas tours, one to France and Belgium, the other to Egypt. Her last part after leaving Wolfit was as Violet Elizabeth Bott in *Just William* on tour and at the London Palladium. Incidentally, her name was Doreen Newland Hodges but she was now known to most as Jane – and she was twenty-one years old.

After dinner I escorted her to her flat in a handsome mansion block in Maida Vale where she invited me in for coffee. It was a sumptuous apartment in immaculate order for which she paid £36 per month which was almost as much as my monthly pay, after tax, as a flight lieutenant. We sat on cushions on the floor in front of the fireplace in the lounge where we talked, kissed and cuddled until I suddenly remembered that, being a Sunday, there were no late trains or buses and that I had no way of getting home. So I was invited to stay the night – for the prurient I would stress that the flat had three bedrooms. Next morning I was cooked an excellent breakfast and, when I left, I did not think that either of us expected to see the other again.

On Monday I met up with Norman and Gerry to travel back to Thorney Island. The next day we flew a recce of Westdown Ranges to identify our respective targets, the positioning of the spectator stands and the direction from which we should attack. We checked the air-to-ground communication, which was OK, so we were ready for tomorrow's demonstration.

A publicity photograph of Jane, who was a dancer, singer and actress. They were married on 25 October 1951.

Next morning, to our relief, there were clear blue skies so Gerry and Charlie, who were on first, had no weather problems and both scored direct hits on both of their rocket attacks. However, Norman and I were not scheduled until just before lunch by which time a cold front was rolling in bringing cumulus clouds with a cloud base of about 2,500 feet AGL. Ideally a Tempest should commence a dive-bombing attack from about 4,000 feet. Norman attempted to run in from below cloud, his dive angle was too shallow and his bomb impacted short of the 40-yard-square target area. I took a chance and climbed through the cloud to 3,500 feet where, very luckily, I found a break through which I could see the target, an old tank minus its gun turret, in the middle of the square.

I turned in with a dive angle of 60 degrees from the horizontal, lined up the gun-sight and made sure that the aircraft was perfectly balanced. By this time the speed was building up at an alarming rate and the altimeter was unwinding even faster so I pressed the bomb-release switch on the control column and then pulled back to recover. I was confident that I had done everything right so I was very surprised when the ground controller called to say that they had seen no impact and that perhaps I had a hang-up. I was about to call Norman to check my aircraft when the controller called excitedly 'Blue Two. Disregard my last message. You have scored a bullseye'. I turned to look at the target and could just see smoke coming up through the gaping hole left by the removal of the gun turret. To have scored a direct hit was just plain dead lucky as dive-bombing, from an aircraft like the Tempest, was a very inaccurate way to drop bombs – but it did my reputation no harm whatsoever.

* * *

At the end of the war in Europe, in accordance with the Yalta Agreement, Germany was divided into four zones of occupation, American, British, French and Russian. The capital Berlin, which was in the Russian zone, was also split into four zones for political and administrative reasons. This latter arrangement rankled with the Russians who decided to close the road and rail corridor checkpoints into Berlin, thus denying the Western Allies access to the city. The only access routes that they could not physically close were the air corridors. Thus began the Berlin Airlift.

By mid-1948 the Airlift was well underway and so successful in supplying essential commodities, mainly food, fuel and coal, that the Russians had begun to harass our transport aircraft. These aircraft, mainly Dakotas and Yorks, flew along the corridor into Gatow, the only airfield in the British zone. As a result the RAF fighter squadrons in Germany were tasked to patrol the British side of the border in the region of the corridor to make our presence felt and to deter further harassment.

At the beginning of August I had been flying one such patrol when my trusty Centaurus engine began to misbehave. It started with an occasional hiccup which gradually increased until the engine was seriously losing power. I turned towards RAF Wunsdorf, one of the airlift stations, and requested permission to make an

The author in the cockpit of a Hawker Tempest II of No. 33 Squadron at RAF Gütersloh in the British Air Forces of Occupation in Germany.

emergency landing – which was refused as the runway and taxiways were packed with transport aircraft lining up to take off every sixty seconds. This posed me with a problem because I doubted very much that I could stagger back to Gütersloh. If the engine failed completely I would have no option but to bale out.

As I flew over Wunsdorf at 4,000 feet I noticed that the parallel taxiway on the south side of the runway was clear so I made a 'May Day' call, saying that I had engine failure and requested permission to land on the taxiway. This placed Wunsdorf in a difficult position as a May Day message is a distress call to which recipients are bound by International Law to render such assistance as may be requested. Permission given, I closed the throttle and spiralled down to line up with the taxiway. I cut the engine when on the final approach, landed and came to a stop requesting that the aircraft be towed away.

By an incredible stroke of good luck the SNCO in charge was a flight sergeant engine fitter who was on temporary loan from No. 16 Squadron at Gütersloh to run Wunsdorf's station flight. He checked the engine and found, as I suspected, that one of the two magnetos had packed up. The second stroke of good fortune was that, because Wunsdorf had been a fighter station before being taken over for the airlift, there was a spare magneto in the equipment stores. He fitted it, checked the engine with a ground run, signed up the aircraft as being serviceable in the travelling form 700[*] and handed it over to me. Thus I was able to fly back to Gütersloh in time for tea.

---

* The Air Ministry form that was an aircraft's official record.

Shortly after that incident, Splinters Smallwood called me into his office and told me that the station had been asked to nominate someone to attend the Day Fighter Leader School course at the Central Fighter Establishment (CFE) at RAF West Raynham in Norfolk. Apparently a vacancy had arisen at short notice and the course was due to start in two weeks' time. He went on to say that he had recommended that I should go and the Station Commander had agreed.

Needless to say I was delighted to accept for several reasons. Firstly, because the course was designed for those pilots who had the potential to become fighter squadron commanders and most nominees had already been flight commanders – which I had not. Secondly, because the course was to be the first to fly the Gloster Meteor, as well as the Spitfire, and I had yet to fly a jet-engined aircraft. And, finally, because it meant returning to England for three months, enabling me to see Jane more often. I had already been home once since our first meeting and we had picked up where we had left off – at her flat.

CFE had many functions apart from being the home of the DFLS course and its night-fighter equivalent. It also administered the Air Fighting Development Squadron (AFDS) which had the job of keeping up with worldwide developments in aircraft design, aerodynamics, equipment, weapons and tactics. This entailed liaison with other countries' air forces and the aviation industry with a view to formulating operational requirements for future RAF fighter aircraft. CFE also held an annual convention which was attended by representatives of the air forces of Commonwealth countries as well as those of the USA and other major allies. Needless to say, the staff at CFE were all very experienced and most were highly decorated; in fact I had never seen so many 'gongs' in my life – outside of a Buddist temple. It was at West Raynham that I first met Wing Commander H. Bird Wilson DSO DFC AFC, always known as 'Birdy', who had been one of the Battle of Britain aces and who had already flown well over a hundred different aircraft types. Little did I think that he would one day become my commandant, my AOC and my good friend.

It was with some trepidation that I reported to CFE at the end of August, not least because I was very conscious of my lack of fighter experience and wondered whether I would be able to cope with the course. My fears were not abated when I met my fellow course members. There were twelve of us, consisting of three RAF squadron leaders who were to command squadrons after the course, one Belgian Air Force major, one RCAF squadron leader and one RN lieutenant commander, all of whom had had wartime fighter experience. The rest were all flight lieutenants, including one from Pakistan, who were already flight commanders and, finally, there was me with a mere six months' fighter experience behind me.

Thankfully my fears proved groundless as none of the course had flown jets before and because the Meteor proved incredibly easy to fly, the reason being that, having no propeller and therefore no corkscrew slipstream, there was almost no change of trim with variations in airspeed, altitude and power setting. The only slight problem was that the Meteor had two engines whereas most of us had only flown single-engined aircraft. As there were no dual Meteors at that time, we were each given two trips in an Airspeed Oxford to practise asymmetric flying on one engine and then sent solo on the Meteor 3, the successor to the Mark I which had seen squadron service during the war and had been most effective in bringing down the V1 'doodlebug' flying bombs. After eight trips in the Mark 3, to acclimatize us to the sensations and techniques of jet flying, we graduated to the Mark 4, with its uprated Derwent engines and a much superior all-round performance, for the rest of the course.

Approximately one third of the course was to be flown in the Spitfire Mark XIV, concentrating on the ground-attack role. The remaining two thirds was to be flown on the Meteor in the air defence role but with some ground attack thrown in. The course members were to be assessed on their weapon delivery and cine-film results and were to be marked on three end-of-course tactical exercises when leading a formation of four aircraft, two on the Meteor and one on the Spitfire. The marks were for preparation and planning, pre-flight briefing, conduct of the exercise itself and the debrief.

Flying the Spitfire again was an absolute joy and, until the very last sortie, I was more than holding my own. But for all of us it was the introduction to jet flying that represented the steepest learning curve because of the many changes to existing practices and tactics that ensued. We were introduced to open or battle formations, to cross-over turns and to, the most important innovation of all, the snake climb. This was the procedure whereby any number of aircraft could be controlled by radar to a position from which to attack enemy aircraft – despite the frequent need to fly through many thousands of feet of solid cloud.

For example, eight aircraft would line up on alternate sides of the runway. The leading pair (Blue Leader) would be scrambled and each following pair would take off at exactly ten-second intervals. Once airborne, Blue Leader would call when turning onto whatever heading had been passed to him in the scramble instructions ending his message with 'Turning Now'. The following pairs would follow at ten-second intervals all turning at 'rate one' (or 180 degrees per minute). The leader would respond to any other changes of heading and the rest would respond at the same intervals as before, until the last pair would call that they were clear of the cloud tops. The leader would then level out and throttle back to cruising revs and the following aircraft would close up into two battle formations of four aircraft, which would take about one minute.

During the course I flew in many snake climbs often through solid cloud from 1,000 feet to the tropopause at around 35,000 feet. Every single time the following pairs emerged from cloud in strict line astern at precise ten-second intervals. This was possible because, unlike piston-engined aircraft, all jet engines produce exactly the same power for a given rpm. So all the pair leaders had to do was to maintain climbing rpm, which tended to reduce with height, fly accurate headings and maintain exact timings which is not as difficult as it sounds.

Towards the end of the course we all had to lead a formation of four aircraft, one of which was always flown by a staff pilot, on tactical exercises on the execution of which we were assessed. Two were on the Meteor, the first being a low-level attack against an enemy target with attempted interception by an enemy fighter aircraft flown by one of the staff. The second was an air defence exercise involving a snake climb and being vectored on to an enemy bomber, usually an RAF Boeing B-29 Washington (Superfortress) with fighter escort. The Spitfire low-level tactical exercise was much the same as the Meteor one. The formation leader had to plan the operation including the navigation, give the pre-flight briefing, lead the formation on the exercise, recover to base without having lost an aircraft to interception and do the debriefing after landing.

When it was my turn I did reasonably well in both Meteor sorties, although I did lose my No. 4 to a fighter attack in the low-level exercise. I was the last course member to lead the Spitfire tactical exercise, which was an advantage as I had

The author in the centre of the front row of pilots returning from a sortie at the Day Fighter Leader School at RAF West Raynham.

already flown as No. 2 and 3 in the formations of other leaders, and everything went absolutely to plan. Despite flying at 250 feet above ground level at 420 knots I hit every turning point on the button. I also spotted two attempted enemy attacks in time to manoeuvre the formation to prevent the pilot bringing his gun-sight to bear, and identified the correct target on which all four of the formation were able to make successful attacks. As I recovered the formation back to base and called for permission to run in and break for landing, I must admit that I was feeling pretty pleased with myself.

Before I had called for permission to run in I had heard Air Traffic Control give landing clearance to another Spitfire which, from its call sign, I recognized as being from AFDS. When I was downwind I requested permission to land which was given but followed by ATC telling the lone Spitfire to clear the runway – but, hearing no response, I assumed that he was now clear. Landing was difficult as the duty runway was directly in line with the setting sun which was now bang on the horizon making forward visibility very hazy. I landed well up the runway and was slowing down nicely when there was a panic ATC call to me saying that there was still an aircraft on the runway. I immediately swung the Spit's nose to starboard so I could see ahead, only for my propeller to slice into the tailplane of that aircraft. Disaster had struck and I was brought down to earth with a bump.

I was feeling somewhat crestfallen when I got to the DFLS crewroom to do the de-brief. Luckily Squadron Leader Geoff Atherton DFC, an Australian serving in the RAF and second in command of DFLS, was flying as my No. 3 on the exercise, so he had heard and seen everything leading up to the prang. In front of the rest of the formation he told me not to worry as nobody in their right minds could blame me. In typical Oz fashion, expletives undeleted, he placed the blame squarely on the pilot of the AFDS aircraft, because no sooner had he landed than he had changed from the local control frequency so that he could speak to the AFDS 'ops' room and thus had not heard the ATC call to clear the runway. To his credit the pilot concerned, a squadron leader, sought me out the following day to apologize. He told me that he had been doing an air test and, because it was well after normal ATC closing time, he had assumed that he was the last aircraft to land, which was why he was doing a brake check on the runway.

Geoff was very complimentary after the de-briefing about the exercise and told me confidentially that, whereas DFLS did not usually tell course members their results, he wanted me to know that I had done pretty well and was in the top half of the order of merit despite my being the least experienced. So, with just two Meteor sorties and the farewell party left to the end of the course, my spirits were high again. In the twelve weeks of the course I had added sixteen hours on the Spitfire, thirty-seven hours on the Meteor and forty-five minutes on one trip in a Vampire to my log book, but I still had accumulated only a miserable 500 flying hours, including my glider time.

* * *

After a long weekend shared between my mother and Jane I managed to cadge a lift in a Dakota from Manston to Bückeburg and reported back to Gütersloh. In my absence there had been many personnel changes. Most importantly my champion and mentor, Splinters Smallwood, had been promoted and succeeded by Squadron Leader A. K. Furse, always known as Connie – for obvious reasons. Poor Connie had been a Blenheim pilot in Singapore and had become a prisoner of war when the Japanese had overrun the Malayan Peninsula in 1942. To his credit he had survived three years of ill treatment and malnutrition, but it showed! His fighter experience consisted only of conversion onto the Spitfire and Tempest, so he was ill prepared to command the squadron and had to rely heavily on his flight commanders.

At the beginning of December 'Bunny' Bunyan had to bale out of his Tempest and broke a leg on landing. As a result I was promoted to take over as acting A Flight commander, but Frank Carey, OC Flying, called me into his office and told me that, because Connie was struggling, it had been decided that a more experienced fighter pilot was needed to support him. So my hopes of being confirmed in post were dashed but he assured me that I would take over when Norman Gall vacated the B Flight commander post. Frank Carey also told me that he was on his way to a Group Captain appointment in a month's time. The next time we met I would be a Wing Commander myself and he the Rolls Royce representative in Sydney. In February I handed over to W. J. (Johnnie) Johnson, luckily an extremely likeable man who had played cricket for Northamptonshire.

The most important personnel change, however, was that of Lawrence Sinclair who had been promoted to Air Commodore and had become the Air Officer Commanding (AOC) of the newly reformed 2nd Allied Tactical Air Force (ATAF) with operational control of all RAF fighter, light-bomber and reconnaissance wings in Germany, including those of our allies, less the Americans. In mid-February the findings of the Unit Inquiry into the aircraft accident at West Raynham had landed on his desk and I was summoned to his office to hear the result.

He welcomed me warmly and then told me that the Inquiry had found that the blame lay principally with the AFDS pilot and with the ATC. However, they also found that I had been partially responsible for not having ensured that the runway was clear before landing the formation. In other words, the Inquiry had chosen to dismiss my statement, corroborated by Geoff Atherton's statement, that landing at dusk in hazy conditions directly into the setting sun had made visibility very poor. They also ignored the fact that the ATC had given me clearance to land, and had not warned me that the other Spitfire was still on the runway – until it was too late.

The AOC said that he shared my disappointment but the AOC-in-C of Fighter Command had agreed the findings and had instructed him to admonish me appropriately and to let him know how he had dealt with the matter. He went on to say that, coincidentally, he was looking for an officer to go to Sylt to initiate the arrangements to open up the old Luftwaffe airfield at Westerland as the 2 ATAF armament practice camp in place of Lübeck which was still being used for the

Berlin Airlift, which was in danger of becoming a permanent commitment. He expected me to be there for about a month and that my 'punishment' was to be taken off flying for that period. I was very annoyed at this turn of events, little realizing that, in what turned out to be an eight-week detachment, I would learn more about RAF organization and administration, and perhaps about myself, than I could possibly imagine.

Sylt is the largest of the islands of the North Friesian group off the western coast of Flensburg, very close to the border with Denmark. It is connected to the mainland by a long causeway along the top of which runs a railway line, the only access to the island other than by boat. It boasted only one town, Westerland, with two large villages, namely List on the north tip and Hörnum on the south of what is a narrow sand spit, with a bulge in the middle, which extends for about twelve miles. In peacetime, it had been a popular holiday resort because of its beautiful sandy beaches, one stretch of which was given over to naturism.

When I arrived at Westerland station in mid-February I was met by the Bürgermeister, who spoke no English whatsoever, and by an attractive young lady who introduced herself, in excellent English, as Rosel Hansen with the good news that she was to be my interpreter. We drove to the seafront hotel, which had been commandeered by HQ BAFO to be the temporary officers' mess, complete with an initial staff of one cook and one cleaner, as I was likely to be the only resident for at least two weeks. At the mess, the Bürgermeister handed over the keys of the Jeep which had been delivered two days previously for my use. The Bürgermeister bade me farewell and said, via Rosel, that he looked forward to our meeting in his office the following morning.

After tea, with Rosel as my guide, I drove around the disused airfield so that I could get my bearings. Disused it may have been but unused it certainly was not; every habitable building seemed to be crammed with people, mainly women and children and old men. Rosel told me that they were all displaced persons (DPs), mainly from that part of Germany that was now under Russian occupation. Some of them had been lucky enough to flee before the Soviet troops overran the region. Most of the other women, however, had been raped, many gang-raped, and their homes pillaged before they managed to get away. Many of the youngest children in the camp were the outcome of those atrocities before the Russian High Command put a stop to them.

We stopped so that I could take a look around and, before long, Rosel, who herself lived in half a hut on the camp, was talking to a crowd of women. I could see that the DPs had done wonders in making homes out of the ramshackle buildings and had created gardens and vegetable patches wherever the soil allowed. It seemed such a shame that they had to be uprooted yet again.

As I walked back to the Jeep I could see that Rosel was being given a hard time by the women who were shouting and gesticulating. They quietened down as I approached and Rosel told me that they were very upset at being moved and were demanding to know why. Asking her to translate for me, I addressed the crowd saying that the RAF was very concerned about the inconvenience and heartache that the move would bring about but that it was very necessary. I went on to explain that the Russians had closed all the road and rail corridors in Berlin and that the only way that the Allies could supply the German civilians in the city was by air transport. The winter had resulted in both food and fuel stocks becoming exhausted and we were having to increase the number of flights to prevent the civilians in the British zone from starving or freezing to death. This required that the RAF should open more airfields and Sylt was one that had been chosen. We were desperately sorry but there was no other way.

My words were well received and the crowd dispersed quietly. Rosel congratulated me on turning away their wrath as they now saw the Russians as being the 'bad guys' – not the Allies. However, what I did not tell them was that it was Lübeck which was vital to the continued success of the airlift and that Sylt was being opened as the Armament Practice Camp in its place because the fighter squadrons in Germany had been without that facility since the beginning of the airlift.

Thanks to the efficiency of the Bürgermeister, and the co-operation of the other DP camps in mainland Germany, the evacuation went smoothly. The buildings were cleared according to the priority which I had laid down and within a week about a quarter of all the DPs had been evacuated. Then I got a nasty shock when two 15-cwt trucks arrived on the airfield and out stepped four men in quasi-military uniforms. When questioned, they told me that they were from the Control Commission Germany (CCG) and that they had orders from their HQs to destroy the war potential of the airfield by demolishing such vital installations as the bulk fuel storage tanks. They were incredulous when I told them to go back from whence they had come as Sylt was in the process of being taken over by the RAF. They showed me their orders, which were dated only days previously and were reluctant to accept my word for it. It was eventually sorted out – but talk about the left hand not knowing what the right was doing.

By now I had been joined by two RAF officers of the Airfield Construction Branch (ACB) who were to oversee the refurbishment of the buildings and such repairs to the infrastructure as were necessary. With their arrival came the authority for me, as the imprest holder, to take on strength as many labourers as they needed. Information about the recruitment was circulated by the Bürgermeister's office and the senior ACB officer and myself, with Rosel in attendance, started to interview applicants in a room at the Officers' Mess. On the first morning a queue started forming at dawn and by 9.00 it stretched halfway round the block. We had put aside two hours, which we extended to three, but we only got through about a quarter of the applicants. I was concerned because, although we were only collecting personal information prior to selection, we had no way of checking their statements.

Rosel told me that there was a much respected ex-German naval officer living on the island who might be able to help. That afternoon we drove to the beach chalet where he lived. I was greeted in perfect English, which was not too surprising when he said that he had spent three very happy years at Oxford University in the mid-1930s. It turned out that he had joined the German navy on return from England and had specialized in submarine warfare. During hostilities he had been a very successful U-boat captain with Iron Crosses galore. He told me that he had become increasingly disillusioned during the war and had ended up an ardent anti-Nazi.

To my shame I cannot recall his name but I have an inkling that his Christian name began with a 'W' – so I will call him Wilhelm. I took an instant liking to Wilhelm and asked for his help which he was delighted to accept, despite the fact that I could only pay him as a labourer. I appointed him my PA and he became my right-hand man despite having been much my senior in rank and at least fifteen years older. It was a wise decision and he was absolutely invaluable, especially with the interviews.

By the end of the four weeks things were going so well that I was given authority to start interviewing women to select those most suitable to serve as waitresses and cleaners in the various messes. Rosel and I started to interview the first girl from the long queue outside the mess: she was a good-looking blonde who spoke no English. As we were coming to the end she whispered something to Rosel and left the room. When I asked what she had said, an embarrassed Rosel told me that she said that if she was selected she would let 'the officer' sleep with her. After this was repeated by several other girls, I instructed Rosel to open all further interviews by explaining what qualities we were looking for and that the offer of personal favours would disqualify applicants. Rosel explained that most of the girls were from the DP camp and that most of them had lost parents, husbands and boyfriends and many had been raped by the Russians. They were desperate to leave the camp but would only be allowed to do so if they had a job and could support themselves.

By now I had been joined by two more RAF flight lieutenants, one an 'equipper' and the other an accountant who thankfully took over the imprest which was becoming a bit of a chore as more and more people were being taken on strength. They were the first of the permanent staff of the APC to be posted in. The main runway had now been repaired and declared fit to use so the AOC flew in to check on progress. I took him on a tour of the airfield, the operational facilities and the domestic buildings and he was pleased with the progress. We then went to the Mess for lunch and to meet the other officers.

Two days previously, when I first heard that the AOC was coming, I had told the cook that we were expecting a VIP for lunch. He promised to produce as fine a meal as possible from the meagre resources available locally. However, I told him to serve a less than typical meal and we decided on brown Windsor soup, out of a packet, minced beef wrapped in cabbage leaves with mashed potato and carrots, followed by a sponge pudding, out of a tin, and custard. I knew that Air Commodore Sinclair was a bit of a gourmet and it was obvious that he was not impressed. I apologized for the frugality of the menu and told him of the limitations of having to buy local produce as we had no NAAFI or other nearby Service units who could help out. My cunning plan worked a treat and thereafter we had a weekly airborne delivery of 'goodies'.

As I walked with the AOC to his aircraft he congratulated me on a job well done, so I was emboldened to ask when I might return to Gütersloh as my month's penance was now up. He apologized for having forgotten to tell me that the Chief Gunnery Instructor of the APC, who was to take over from me, would not be available for a couple of weeks and would I mind staying on a bit longer – which I could hardly refuse. In the event the squadron leader concerned arrived three weeks later and, what with a week's handover, I had been away for two months.

Although I had missed out on a lot of flying I was, nevertheless, not sorry to have been diverted to a job which I had found fascinating and very rewarding – and one from which I had learned much about organization and personnel management. The last thing I did before I left Sylt was to write a loose minute, so it was on record, to the Station Commander-designate recommending that he should employ Rosel as his personal assistant and Wilhelm as the Mess Manager. I do not know whether my advice was taken as I was never to return to Sylt but I have heard from others that the Officers' Mess boasted the most glamorous waitresses in the RAF, many of whom got married to pilots on the APC course.

* * *

When I got back to Gütersloh I was determined to make up for lost flying time, only to find that the squadron, along with No. 80 (Spitfire) Squadron, had just been given early warning that they were to be deployed to the Far East. The move was because the Chinese Communists had finally overthrown the Nationalist regime of Chiang Kai-Shek and had proclaimed the Peoples Republic of China in Peking, with Mao Tse-Tung as Chairman. It was thought that Mao might want to flex his muscles by attempting to take over the Colony of Hong Kong. It was therefore considered necessary for the British to increase their forces in the Far East as a deterrent.

I received this news with mixed feelings. It was very exciting with the possibility of the squadron seeing some action but at the same time it meant being far away from UK for at least the rest of my tour – about eighteen months. Whilst on the DFLS course I had seen a lot of Jane and had, perhaps unwisely, allowed myself to fall in love with her – certainly against my better judgement for she was not exactly the convent-educated vestal virgin from a good, preferably wealthy, middle-class family that I had in mind for my wife-to-be. In fact, Jane's family can best be described as dysfunctional. Father, Wilfred, was a dour, not very successful farmer who was fifteen years older than her mother, Irene, who had been an exhibition ballroom dancer with many other artistic talents. Jane was the only child of that marriage but her mother went on to have more children with different partners. Luckily Jane inherited only her mother's talent for and love of dance. Moreover

I was not yet ready to consider marriage as my future in the RAF was uncertain, although I hoped to be granted a permanent commission.

There was no doubt that Jane and I had very little in common. Her main interests lay very much in the arts whereas mine were in sport and flying. But, as in magnetism, like poles repel whereas unlike poles attract – and attracted we certainly were! I had misgivings about whether she would be able to forsake the pleasures of her glamorous lifestyle with her many well-known thespian friends and accept the humdrum life of being a serviceman's wife. I began to realize that the impending separation now being forced on us might well be a blessing in disguise. If she could withstand that separation, and provided that we both felt the same about each other at the end of it, then there might be hope for us. But, quite honestly, I did not believe that she would stay the course.

No sooner had I arrived back at Gütersloh than I was sent off on leave as the squadron had been told to ensure that all personnel with leave outstanding were to take it before departing for Hong Kong; so much for my hopes of making up lost flying time because of my detachment at Sylt. But, at least it did give me the opportunity to break the news to Jane in person. She was not best pleased! However, I found that, after my return to Germany from the DFLS course, she had decided to give up hope of rekindling her theatrical ambitions and had left the flat in Maida Vale and returned home. Home was now a derelict mill in Shipston-upon-Stour which her mother had bought and was converting into a B and B establishment with licensed restaurant attached. She wanted Jane to become a partner in running the business – a prospect which she did not relish.

After my return to Germany the few remaining weeks flew by. Eventually all our aircraft were fitted with 100-gallon drop tanks under each wing and on 2 July 1949 we flew to the RNAS airfield at Abbotsinch, near Glasgow, to join the aircraft carrier which was to transport us to Hong Kong.

Chapter 7

The Far East

Having flown eighteen Tempest II aircraft into RNAS Abbotsinch (now Glasgow International Airport) the Squadron was told that the aircraft carrier HMS *Ocean*, which was to transport 80 Squadron and ourselves to Hong Kong, would not be sailing until 12 July so we pilots were sent off on an unexpected but very welcome seven days' embarkation leave. The 80 Squadron Spitfires, having arrived three days earlier, were already in the process of being winched on board and secured in the aircraft hangar but, because *Ocean* was also transporting numerous crates of diplomatic and service equipment and stores, including Army Air Corps Auster aircraft, there was no space left in the hangar for our aircraft. That meant that the engines had to be inhibited and the airframes cocooned to protect them against the corrosive effects of saltwater spray whilst they were tethered on the flight deck.

Having spent an enjoyable week with Jane and her family at The Old Mill at Shipston-upon-Stour, I reported back to Abbotsinch and going on board (not forgetting to salute the quarterdeck in memory of Lord Nelson – as tradition demands) I was pleased to find that the CO, Connie Furse, and we three flight lieutenants, Johnnie Johnson, Norman Gall and myself, had been allocated single cabins, whereas the junior officers had to double up. The NCO pilots were accommodated below decks and were to sleep in hammocks rather than the bunks we enjoyed.

The ship's company did their best to make us feel welcome and comfortable but the three-week voyage was a bit of a bore. It was enlivened only by our sailing through the Suez Canal and by the formal Saturday night dinners in the wardroom when, after the loyal toast, we raised our glasses to the Naval toast of 'to our wives and girlfriends', to which the response is 'and may they never meet'!

After about a week at sea, Connie was summoned by the Captain who informed him that a signal had been received from the Admiralty which notified him of a change of plan. It had been decided, at Air Force Board level, that whereas 80 Squadron was to continue to Hong Kong, our squadron was to be off-loaded at Singapore. Apparently there were two main reasons for this, namely shortage of accommodation at RAF Kai Tak and, more importantly, the outbreak of communist terrorism in the Federated Malay States which had started in 1948 but had now escalated. The Director of Operations had requested additional offensive air support, so it was appropriate that our squadron was being detailed because Tempests were more effective ground-attack aircraft than the Spitfires already in theatre. The decision may also have been influenced by the fact that our aircraft were on deck and that because our crates of spares had been the last to be loaded they would be the easiest to extricate.

The signal also stated that 33 Squadron was to be available to reinforce Hong Kong at short notice in the event that Chairman Mao should start rattling his sabre about the unification of the colony into mainland China. It would seem that we were to have the best of both worlds!

On arrival at Seletar Naval Base our aircraft were unloaded onto lighters and shipped to the nearby airfield where they were prepared for flight. The squadron remained at Seletar until all the aircraft were prepared and air-tested and our accommodation at RAF Changi was ready for us. At Changi we were to operate from a tented dispersal alongside the very short pierced-steel-planking (PSP) runway whilst the main long runway was being resurfaced and extended. RAF Changi was the home of Air Headquarters (AHQ) Malaya and of two Dakota transport squadrons which were temporarily based at RAF Tengah.

On 10 September the Squadron flew to RAF Butterworth on the Malayan mainland opposite to the Island of Penang. We took twelve aircraft and all our pilots to participate in the Armament Practice Camp where we carried out weapons training, principally rocket and cannon firing, on the ranges located on small uninhabited islands to the north of Penang to which the range controllers had to travel by high-speed launch. From the air the islands looked absolutely idyllic with beautiful sandy beaches, coral lagoons and incredibly blue and clear water. It was possible to see turtles swimming up to two fathoms deep. Our weapon skills having been honed, the Squadron returned to Changi on 6 October.

As the communist terrorist attacks seemed to be tailing off, AHQ Malaya decided that it might be a good time for the squadron to exercise its secondary role, i.e. the reinforcement of Hong Kong with a force of eight aircraft. Johnnie and Norman, the flight commanders, tossed a coin to decide whether A or B Flights should have the honour and Norman won: but much to my disgust I was detailed to be in charge of the advanced party of servicing personnel which was to be flown in a Dakota two days early to ensure that everything was ready for the arrival of the Tempests. That flight took nearly twelve flying hours with refuelling stops at Saigon and Tourane.

Kai Tak was a joint user airport as it operated both civilian and military aircraft and was located in the New Territories just north of Hong Kong Island. It had just one very long runway which jutted out into a bay for about half its length. It was in a valley and a common occurrence, when the wind was from the north, was for thick cloud to tumble down from the hills with little or no warning, making recovery of aircraft quite a problem. This was particularly serious for fighters flying in from Tourane in French Indo-China, because, having been given clearance to proceed when at the 'point of no return', the airfield weather could suddenly deteriorate and the fighters could not be diverted elsewhere in Communist China. The Air Traffic Controllers had worked out an emergency procedure with which all visiting pilots had to be familiar.

Shortly after our arrival I led a formation of four aircraft to test the procedure. This involved being vectored to the overhead position by radio direction finding (RDF) equipment and then out on a south-easterly heading which ensured that a descent at 500 feet per minute would miss all the myriad islands in the area. At around 1,000 feet above sea level RT contact with ATC would be lost. When clear of cloud, which could be as low as 150 to 200 feet ASL, the aircraft would turn onto a reciprocal heading and head back towards Kai Tak. As we approached land we were confronted by what appeared to be an impenetrable cliff face, the tops of which were up in the clouds.

We had been briefed to look out for that part of the cliff face which had been painted white. When I saw it looming up I flew towards the left-hand side. Only when getting perilously close was it possible to make out a narrow inlet between the cliffs through which it was possible to fly a formation in line astern. It required a lot of manoeuvring to follow the river but RT contact was eventually regained and miraculously the runway appeared straight ahead. Phew!

After just one week in Hong Kong the squadron set out to return to Changi and I persuaded Norman to let me lead the second formation of four aircraft on the return flight. The legs to Tourane and Saigon were uneventful. Having spent an enjoyable night in that lovely city, the rest of our return was a bit of a disaster. En route to Butterworth my No. 2 lost one of his 200-gallon drop tanks which made it necessary to return to Saigon as he would have had insufficient fuel to reach our destination. Luckily I was able to contact Norman, whose formation had taken off thirty minutes before mine, to let him know the score. More importantly I managed to contact the pilot of the rear-party Dakota just before he took off to tell him that we were returning and why. After a new overload tank was fitted, we set off again, reaching and refuelling at Butterworth without incident but on arrival at Changi my No. 4 suffered brake failure and ran off the end of the runway, luckily with little damage.

* * *

Two days later the squadron was tasked with its first operational strike against a CT (communist terrorist) target – a large clearing with several *bashas* (lean-to attap huts) under the trees. This was very exciting and Johnnie, Norman and I vied for the privilege of leading the formation. Connie decided that we should draw lots – and I won. This was somewhat appropriate as the target was in an area of rain forest with the Malay name of Ulu Langat. As the 't' is silent in Malay, phonetically the translation could be 'Langer's Jungle'. Norman insisted on flying as my No. 2 with Johnnie and his deputy flight commander flying as Nos. 3 and 4. Luckily for my reputation all went well: contact was made with Rover Charlie (the call sign of our ground controller), I identified the target on the first pass which we then attacked with rockets and cannon fire, setting alight the bashas and some of the secondary jungle. We saw no sign of activity but were informed later that, when the Army moved in, two terrorists surrendered and a number of locals, who had been forced to work the clearing for the CTs, were taken into protective custody. It was a good start for the squadron but, alas, relatively few subsequent operations had such a positive outcome.

* * *

It might be of interest if I briefly trace the origins of the Malayan emergency. The Malayan Communist Party (MCP) was set up in 1933 as part of a plan, sponsored by the Comintern, to spread communism throughout South-East Asia by infiltrating the labour force, fomenting industrial unrest and initiating strikes. This plan was put in abeyance when Russia joined the Western Allies in June 1941.

After the declaration of war with Japan, following the attack against Pearl Harbor, the MCP offered its services to the British authorities. This led to the formation of the Malayan Peoples Anti-Japanese Army (MPAJA) which co-operated with the British liaison officers who had already been placed behind the Japanese lines to co-ordinate the resistance movement. In December 1943 agreement was reached with the MPAJA that they would accept direction and orders from the Allied Forces: in return the British undertook to arm, train, equip and supply them. However, shortly after this agreement, contact between the Allied Forces in India and Ceylon was lost as a result of the speed with which the Japanese Army took control of the country.

Contact was regained in February 1945 when the tide of war had turned in our favour and no time was lost in arming and training the MPAJA. By the time the Japanese had surrendered it had become an effective, efficient and disciplined force now completely under the control of the British. Initially the MPAJA was kept mobilized and employed on 'watch and ward' duties, being fully rationed and paid by the British Army. However, in December 1945, they were disbanded with the understanding that all arms, explosives and equipment were to be handed in and its insignia of three red stars was never again to be used. In return each man was to be paid a substantial gratuity and given re-settlement aid. Some 6,000 men were disbanded and over 5,000 weapons were handed in.

What was not known was that the MCP, anticipating this outcome, had formed a secret arm of the MPAJA and that a large quantity of arms and ammunition, including Sten guns, carbines and pistols, along with many other weapons that had been supplied by air, had been picked up by the MPAJA unknown to the British Liaison Officers. All these weapons were now hidden in secret dumps throughout the country for possible future use by the MCP. This secret army numbered about 4,000 men.

After the war the MCP returned to its old policy of fomenting industrial unrest but, because of the remarkable political and economic recovery of Malaya, this policy resulted in communism becoming sidelined and the MCP failing miserably to attain political credibility. Accordingly, in March 1948, they decided to start an armed fight against the Government.

The ensuing campaign of violence included the ransacking and burning of the offices of rubber estates and mining companies along with the murder of British planters and mining engineers, as well as their Chinese, Indian and Malay workers. They also terrorized Malay *kampongs* (villages), stealing rubber, rice and other foodstuffs. In June 1948 the Federation proclaimed a 'State of Emergency' and passed special powers to deal with this outbreak of violence, the MCP being proscribed as an unlawful society and membership of it became a punishable offence.

* * *

From November 1949 onwards the tempo of operational strikes against the CTs hotted up and the squadron became somewhat itinerant. Although continuing to be based at Changi, we operated from other bases such as Kluang, Kuala Lumpur (KL), Tengah and Butterworth, dependent upon the location of the targets. Our main base remained Changi until the main runway resurfacing was nearing completion when we moved to Tengah before ending up at Butterworth.

Most of our targets were clearings located in the tropical rain forest (jungle) which covered more than three quarters of the country. The CTs were dependent upon these clearings for growing crops and vegetables which were usually worked by the natives under duress. Clearings were extremely difficult to locate, nestling as they did surrounded by trees of up to 200-feet high. It was very easy to pass one within 200 yards at an altitude of 500 feet above the treetops and still not see it. Our tactics were to fly in loose battle formation, so that four pairs of eyes could search, and as high as the inevitable cloud would permit. Success in locating clearings also depended upon the accuracy of the map references given by the Police or Army unit requesting the strike.

Occasionally we were tasked to attack caves in the many limestone outcrops in which the CTs were known or thought to be encamped. To be effective it was best to attack with rockets straight into the cave. This often involved flying directly towards the cliff face. It was up to the leader of a formation to decide exactly how a target should be attacked and to make the first run-in. On one such occasion I released, in pairs, all of my eight rockets, which disappeared satisfactorily into the depths of the cave, but it meant breaking away at the last moment. I pulled up hard, only to find that the cliff-face had a better rate of climb than my aircraft. I only just made it with my dear old Tempest brushing the tops of the trees. I then had to direct the other aircraft to attack at a 30-degree angle down the valley and only to release one pair of rockets at a time.

Very occasionally we were briefed to drop bombs and strafe with our cannon an area of jungle where there was no specific target. The purpose of these raids was to drive the CTs to evacuate their camps and, hopefully, walk into ambush traps set up at possible escape routes. It was extremely difficult to ensure that we were attacking the right area as one bit of jungle looks very much like every other bit. To help us get it right the Army unit concerned would float a brightly-coloured helium balloon up through the dense tree canopy and then pass us the target area in terms of bearing and distance from the balloon.

Eventually some bright spark at the Joint Operations Centre at Kuala Lumpur came up with the brilliant idea of dropping Chinese crackers, suitably modified to sound just like intermittent rifle fire. This proved very successful and put an end to the costly and far less effective use of bombs and cannon fire. Furthermore, these crackers could be dropped by the Army's own Auster aircraft.

By now the operational tempo was hotting up: for example, I flew three operational sorties in November, five in December and eleven in January 1950. This was all very exciting, but on 12 January the excitement got a bit out of hand. To mark the opening of a new airport at Labuan near Khota Kinabalu in Borneo, it was decided that FEAF should take part in a flag-waving fly past. Fifteen aircraft were to participate from No. 60 Squadron (Spitfires) No. 84 Squadron (Brigands) and ourselves – with Dakota aircraft in support carrying the ground crew.

Norman Gall was to be the Tempest detachment commander from Changi with myself as second-in-command. As we taxied out to the end of the runway, Norman called up to say that his aircraft had an unacceptable magneto drop and told me to lead the formation to Labuan and that he would follow later. As I took off I was aware that the runway appeared very bumpy just before lift-off. No sooner had I got airborne than the aircraft gave a sudden lurch and rolled rapidly to starboard until it was upside down. Instinctively I had pushed the control column fully forward to avoid the aircraft diving into Changi Creek and, having stabilized the roll, I managed to regain an even keel – but only with the stick right over to the side of the cockpit. ATC called to ask if I was in trouble as my starboard 200-gallon drop tank had fallen off just after take-off. I replied that I could maintain straight and level flight with difficulty but could only turn to the left. I had no option but to jettison the port drop tank which I did in shallow water off-shore, from where it was recovered. Having burnt off half my internal fuel I landed back safely. As I suspected the pierced steel plating (PSP) on a part of the runway was found to have become loose and, because the miscreant drop tank was never found, probably because it was buried deep in the mud of Changi Creek, it was assumed that the lug by which the tank was attached to the underside of the wing had snapped because of the vibration from the loose PSP.

I was then given an unexpected break. The RAF had recently introduced an instrument flying rating scheme and all pilots had initially to attend a course to have their instrument flying (I/F) standards checked and be awarded the appropriate rating. This was particularly important for fighter pilots as most fighters were single seaters and their I/F skills could not be checked. Connie decided that I should be the first from the squadron to attend, so I duly reported to the All Weather Squadron at Changi which had taken over our dispersal when we had moved to Tengah. The two-week course involved flying under a hood in the back seat of a Harvard and proving one's ability to carry out blind take-offs, flying two complex flight patterns, A and B, to within prescribed limits and be able to recover from unusual positions with the gyroscopic instruments 'toppled'. I was duly awarded a 'white' rating, despite having reached 'green' and 'master green' standards because, like most fighter pilots, I had insufficient experience of actual cloud flying. These ratings laid down the minimum weather conditions for take off and landing in terms of visibility and cloud base for each rating. From then on I logged every minute of cloud flying, which previously I had not done and eventually progressed to 'master green'.

From February the Squadron began to maintain a detachment at KL so that we could react more quickly to requests for strikes from the Joint Operations Centre (JOC). The station was dreadfully overcrowded and whereas, as detachment commander, I was given a room in the Officers' Mess, most of the others, pilots and ground-crew, were accommodated in marquees. The worst shortage was of ablutions and toilets, necessitating the construction, amongst other things, of outside earth closets. Despite these primitive conditions the Squadron's morale was sky high as we were closer to the action and playing an ever-increasing role in the offensive against the CTs.

At the end of May Norman Gall was posted back home and, at last, I officially became the B Flight commander, although I had virtually been running the flight since January. Norman was leaving the RAF at the end of his tour and returning to New Zealand, so he was quite content for me to do so.

* * *

Some time previously, AHQ Malaya had realized that the Malayan Police Forces had very little idea of exactly what the RAF could offer to assist their ground operations. They therefore decided that each of the Federated States should have an Air Liaison Officer and that the ALO should be a flight commander from one of the operational squadrons. For my sins I was appointed to the State of Kelantan in the far north-east corner of Malaya.

Accordingly on 14 June I was picked up at Butterworth by my old friend Flying Officer Johnny Dench, a Canadian in the RAF with whom I had scrounged flights in his Dakota whilst at Changi, for the flight to Khota Bahru, the capital of Kelantan. Johnny let me fly his beloved Dakota from take-off to landing – very trusting of him considering I had no twin-engine experience. I never saw Johnny again because several weeks later his aircraft went missing en route to Hong Kong in mysterious circumstances as there was no R/T or W/T message and no wreckage or bodies were ever found.

When we landed in the late afternoon I was met by a Malayan Police Inspector who drove me to the *Istana* (palace) of the Sultan who hearing of my arrival insisted that I should spend the first night at his home, which happened to coincide with one of his monthly parties for local big-wigs and expatriate foreigners who worked for the State. The inspector left, saying that he would pick me up at 8.00 the next morning. I was escorted to my room by a bearer, in Malay dress topped by a flamboyant turban in the State colours, who said he would collect me at 6.30pm and that the dress would be formal. Luckily I had packed my smart No. 6 tropical uniform, so I would not be out of place.

When I arrived at the party I was greeted by the Sultan himself who, speaking excellent English, introduced me to some of his ministers, most of whom had been educated in England. The party was fuelled by brightly-coloured drinks and a most sumptuous-looking buffet. Unfortunately, the drinks were all non-alcoholic and the food was mainly sickly sweetmeats into which the ladies were tucking with abandon. Luckily, the Chief of Police and many of his officers were there, and being expatriates and knowing the score, had, with the connivance of the Sultan, bought along a couple of bottles of gin which were added to the drinks on offer. The party broke up at about 8.00pm which suited me as I was pretty tired, so after a long walk around the lovely *Istana* gardens I returned to my room and slept like a log.

Next morning I was driven to the Police mess, where I was to stay for a couple of days, and then to their HQ where discussions lasted all day. Not least we decided on a programme for me which involved my being based at Gua Musang, a small town more or less in the centre of the State, from whence I would be able to visit many police outposts and encamped Army units. Gua Musang was famous, or perhaps notorious, for having been the only Malay town to have been taken over by the CTs until driven out in a major operation.

The journey to Gua Musang was a marvellous introduction to the difficulties of traversing the country. Our party consisted of an expatriate sergeant and six Malay constables as escorts. We left Khota Bahru in two Jeeps in the early morning and our first port of call was a rubber estate to meet the owner, an eccentric Englishman named Bill Bangs who had played a prominent part in the resistance movement during the Japanese occupation and was regarded as an expert on all matters Malay. He was a tall impressive man, dressed in a shirt and sarong, whose estate was the largest in Malaya. He made the sergeant and I very welcome but we turned down his offer of lunch. After leaving I asked why we had visited him and was told that he ran a network of his own workers and other Malays who provided the Police with invaluable information about CT movements particularly across the Thai/Malaya border.

We proceeded up the Nilgiri valley as far as our Jeeps could travel and then transferred to three long-boats with outboard motors. These boats were quite fast but our journey upstream was interrupted continually by white-water areas where the boats could not cross the rocks. The boats then had to be carried along jungle paths to the next navigable stretch of river. The journey took three days involving two night stops where we slept under attap shelters on beds of palm fronds – not the most comfortable way to spend the night.

Despite my having done the Jungle Survival Course in India, the reality of trekking for days through proper rain forest was a novel experience for me. Because of the great trees we were in permanent shade so it was not excessively hot but the atmosphere of 100 per cent humidity was such that even the slightest exertion produced copious sweat. We would walk for fifty minutes and then break for ten. The rest period was spent sipping water, smoking and checking ourselves for leeches. I was wearing jungle-green trousers, a long-sleeved shirt and jungle boots, but still the beastly things managed to get through onto the skin. They were ever-present but mostly in the area of small streams through which we had to wade. The leeches were particularly fond of the more sweaty parts of one's body, especially the groin. I found many, already bloated with my blood, on my legs. It was not advisable to pull them off as that left bits of them in the bite which could turn septic. The answer was to touch them with a lighted cigarette end which caused them to drop off intact.

The Malayan rain forest has abundant and varied wildlife which includes tigers, deer, elephants, buffalo, crocodiles and the ubiquitous monkeys. During my two weeks in Gua Musang, from which I trekked to visit numerous Police and Army units, I only encountered the monkeys and, on one occasion, a huge monitor lizard which must have measured at least seven feet from nose to tip of tail. We often heard many animals crashing through the undergrowth but the nearest I got to an elephant was when we stumbled upon a pile of steaming dung. The noises in the jungle were insistent, they never stopped even in the dead of night and the main culprits were the cicadas, the frogs and, of course, the chattering monkeys.

There were many snakes including huge pythons as much as twelve feet long but they seemed more afraid of us than vice-versa and slithered away when they sensed our approach. The jungle was eerie, but there were many compensations, particularly in the sight of beautiful butterflies and moths, incredible tree ferns and orchids. Many birds that one would normally only see in a zoo or aviary lived in their natural habitat: my favourite was the hornbill which lived in the treetops.

My visits to the outposts were always fun. I remember one to an encamped company of the Royal Hampshire Regiment where I stayed the night. In the marquee that was the Officers' Mess we dined on roast rack of lamb, which was carved by the company commander, accompanied by the odd bottle of a very acceptable Burgundy whilst the trestle dining table was adorned by two silver-branch candlesticks from the Regimental silver collection. In contrast, at a Police outpost I was more likely to be offered curried goat out of a billy-can whilst sitting on the floor. After my three weeks in the jungle I had nothing but admiration for the Police and Army personnel who were waging this most unconventional jungle warfare against the CTs. It was not only highly dangerous, but also carried out in the most uncomfortable and inhospitable environment imaginable.

My task at these units was not only to talk about offensive air support, how best to employ it and how to submit requests. I also explained what other services we could offer such as emergency casualty evacuation by Auster aircraft or the Dragonfly helicopter recently arrived in theatre on a trial basis. This involved an appreciation of the type and dimensions needed for airstrips and clearings. I told them of the psychological warfare capability such as the dropping of leaflets, usually offering amnesty terms to those CTs who surrendered with their weapons, and the use of taped broadcasts from aircraft. Finally, I told them of the very successful use of Chinese crackers dropped from aircraft in support of ground operations.

When I finally returned to Butterworth I had to spend three days writing a report for Group Captain 'Sam' Lucas, the AOC's representative at the Advanced HQ in KL. When next I saw him, he said that the report had proved useful and that my visits certainly seemed to have paid dividends as there had been many more bids for more types of air support for well thought out operations from Kelantan than ever before. Although I rather resented having lost four weeks flying, my visit was an experience I will never forget.

* * *

Shortly after my return the CO was informed that the Squadron was to be re-equipped with the de Havilland Hornet in the New Year. The Hornet was the fastest piston-engined fighter in the world and it was one that I had always wanted to fly – which now I would just miss as my two-and-a-half-year tour on 33 Squadron would be up in October. Hearing me bemoaning my fate, Connie said he would be very happy if my tour could be extended by six months. I was very tempted to apply but I turned down the opportunity as it would not have been fair on Jane who was having to endure too long a separation already – and it was always possible that I could be posted to a Hornet squadron on my return to UK. In the event I was glad that I did not extend as the re-equipment was delayed and I would still have missed out.

A little later that month the Squadron Commander called Johnnie Johnson and myself into his office to tell us, in the strictest confidence, that the squadron had been allocated a Distinguished Flying Cross (DFC) in recognition of its work during the emergency and that he was to nominate to whom it was to be awarded. He then asked for our views. Dear old Johnnie, bless him, suggested that it should be awarded to the pilot who had flown the greatest number of operational sorties – which he knew very well was me as we kept a tally in the squadron ops room. I took a rather different line querying whether the DFC was an appropriate award as, although some sorties had been quite hazardous, the danger was posed more by the weather and the terrain than by flying in the face of the enemy. I suggested that perhaps an Air Force Cross (AFC) would be more appropriate. I also suggested that, as the award was really for the squadron as a whole, irrespective of which award it was, it should be given to Pilot 1 Arthur Vine,* our senior NCO pilot who had flown the second most sorties, but it would have to be a DFM. This would

---

* The official designation for a flight sergeant pilot.

be seen as reflecting well on our dedicated, hardworking ground crew who had contributed greatly to the success of the squadron. Connie thanked us for our views and said he would speak with the AOC before making up his mind.

September was another busy month during which I flew eleven strikes. On the 13th, despite it not being a Friday, I had what turned out to be my 'diciest do' to date. I was leading a formation of four aircraft on a tactical Army Co-operation exercise when, having reached 15,000 feet there was a loud bang, the engine stopped and the cockpit filled with smoke. I immediately switched off the ignition, pulled hard to gain maximum height and turned back towards Butterworth. I then instructed my No. 3, Flight Lieutenant Dev Evans, my deputy flight commander, to continue with the exercise as I had a little problem and was returning to base.

I had no idea what the problem was but I was prepared for the outbreak of fire because of the smoke which was streaming back from the engine as well as filling the cockpit. I was having difficulty seeing out, so I opened the hood and almost immediately the smoke cleared. I then saw to my astonishment not only that the engine had stopped but also that the five-bladed propeller was in the fully-coarse position: in other words each blade was facing directly into the airflow.

By now I could see the west coast and Penang Island in the distance but too far away to attempt a dead-stick landing at Butterworth. So I called ATC, with a 'Mayday' prefix, told them of my predicament and that I intended to bale out when clear of the jungle. Having ensured that the aircraft was heading directly for the airfield and that it was perfectly trimmed to maintain 140 knots, the best gliding speed, I prepared for my first parachute descent.

The recommended way of leaving a fighter aircraft in a hurry is to slide back the canopy, undo one's harness, disconnect all other connections such as the R/T plug to the helmet, trim the aircraft fully nose-down, roll it over onto its back and drop out. However, as I had plenty of height, I decided to leave in a more sedate manner. As soon as I was clear of the densest part of the jungle and was over mainly *lalang*, or grass-covered areas, I called ATC to say that I was about to jump and gave them an estimate of my position. I then clambered over the side of the cockpit, lowered myself until I was standing on the wing but was blown by the airstream until my back was pressed against the fuselage. I then released my hold on the canopy rail and slid gracefully down – for about eighteen inches before I was jerked to a sudden halt.

To my horror I realized that my parachute harness had caught on the vertical hand-hold that helped pilots to climb into the cockpit. Thankfully, the aircraft continued gliding serenely towards Butterworth whilst I dangled feeling rather foolish. No doubt helped by a surge of adrenalin, I managed to get the heel of my right flying boot into the step recess on the side of the fuselage and, pushing up, was able to grab the canopy rail and pull myself up until I could disentangle my parachute harness. I then clambered back into the cockpit – for a rest.

Looking forward I could see Butterworth straight ahead and much closer than I could have hoped. Normally the Tempest II has the gliding characteristics of a brick-built outhouse but two things were working in my favour. Firstly, most drag comes from the wind-milling propellers and the resultant corkscrew slipstream. My engine was stopped and the propellers were in the fully-coarse position, so the airstream over the wings was at its most efficient and was creating maximum lift. Secondly the formation had taken off into an unusually strong easterly wind so I had a tail wind.

I called ATC to tell them that I was going to delay baling out as there was a possibility that I might just be able to land on the airfield. I would have to decide by 1,500 feet to ensure that I had sufficient height to bale out safely should my hopes prove forlorn. I therefore did not do up my straps. At that height I was confident that I could make it so I committed myself to landing. At 500 feet I selected 'undercarriage down': with no engine there were no hydraulics, so I activated the emergency air-pressure system. The port undercarriage locked down with a reassuring clunk, but the starboard one did not lock down and ATC told me it was stuck halfway. This was a recipe for disaster as, in that configuration, the Tempest had a tendency to turn over onto its back. So I selected 'undercarriage up', kicked the rudder violently to the right, lowering the aircraft onto the runway, hit the port wheel sideways forcing both wheels to retract and landed safely onto the grass beside the runway.

Before the aircraft slid bumpily to a halt, I had seen the station's fire engine, ambulance and lifting crane rushing down the taxi-track towards me but, as I climbed down from the cockpit, the first person to reach me – on a bicycle – was Aircraftman Dickens, the Squadron's odd-job man, who greeted me with the immortal words 'Will you be OK for soccer this evening, Sir?' I told him I would be – and we won!

The author's Tempest II which he just managed to scrape in onto the grass strip at RAF Butterworth after a disastrous engine failure. He was recommended for an AFC but was awarded only a 'green endorsement' in his flying log book in 1947.

Amazingly the aircraft looked relatively undamaged. The bottom two propeller blades had been bent backwards at right angles, the rocket rails and the tail wheel had taken the full weight of the aircraft and the bottom of the fuselage had not even been touched.

Having been lifted by crane back to the squadron dispersal, the aircraft was examined and it was found that the problem had been caused by a 'tuppenny ha'penny' locking washer which had disintegrated, allowing its nut to unscrew under engine vibration which in turn resulted in the loss of all the hydraulic fluid from one side of the constant speed unit (CSU).

As a result the propellers went into a fully-coarse position and the fluid splashing onto the air-cooled engine cylinders and exhausts had caused the smoke which had enveloped the aircraft inside and out. The propeller and CSU were changed, the engine was shock-tested and found serviceable, the undercarriage was checked, both with the hydraulics and a recharged compressed air bottle, and found to be fully operable, the rocket rails were changed and the aircraft was returned to service the following day. They don't make aircraft like that any more!

The rest of the month passed uneventfully, enlivened only by a party to celebrate the news that I had been granted a permanent commission in the RAF: thus was yet another of my ambitions realized. A few days later my successor as B Flight Commander, Flight Lieutenant Roy Austen Smith, an old rugby friend of mine, arrived. We completed the handover by the end of September but, as I was to remain at Butterworth until I was notified of my return flight to the UK sometime in mid-October, I did not want to get under Roy's feet. So, with Connie's blessing, I hitched a flight, as supernumary crew, in the scheduled Dakota flight to Hong Kong. It was a bit of a disaster in that we were delayed for two days in Saigon by unserviceability – but at least that gave me the opportunity to further explore that lovely city and to admire the grace and beauty of the young girls cycling around town in their long white gloves and chic flowing *ouzis* (trouser suits). On the flight to Hong Kong we were diverted to Tourane because of a typhoon. By the time we got to Hong Kong we were running three days late, so we had only one night there and I was unable to do my intended shopping. We returned to Changi in one very long day's flying.

Back at Butterworth I had two further Tempest flights, the last one being an operational sortie flying as No. 2 to Roy. Since our arrival in theatre the squadron had been tasked with just over 300 operational strikes and I had flown on sixty-two of them: no wonder I was considered a bit of an 'hour hog' – but then I had a lot of catching up to do. I had loved every minute of my time on No. 33 Squadron which had more than lived up to my expectations. I had enjoyed the excitement, the camaraderie, the adventure, the danger and, of course, the flying. I was sorry to leave but I was also looking forward to returning to the UK, not least to meet up again with Jane who had kept me sustained with a constant stream of long interesting letters.

I finally left FEAF on 26 October 1950, but the least said about that flight the better. The route sounded interesting taking in Negombo (Ceylon), Mauripur (Pakistan), Habbaniya (Iraq), Fayid (Egypt) and Malta. The problem was that the flight was in a Handley Page Hastings – referred to by cynics as the RAF's only three-engined transport aircraft because of the woeful reliability of its engines. So what should have taken four ended up taking seven long, dreary, boring days.

<u>Postscript</u>. In the 1951 New Year's Honours list I saw that my old friend, now Flight Lieutenant, Gerry Hill, had been awarded the DFC. I was very happy for Gerry who was a first-class chap and excellent pilot and who, at the time of my leaving the Squadron, had flown the third greatest number of 'ops' behind myself and Arthur Vine: but I must admit that I felt just a little bit miffed.

Many years later, when I was a Wing Commander at the Central Flying School (CFS), I met up again with the now Group Captain A. K. Furse, who was paying CFS a visit from MoD on some 'works and bricks' matter. Seeing the medal ribbon of the AFC I had been awarded whilst commanding No. 43 Squadron, he told me that following my forced landing at Butterworth he had strongly recommended that I be awarded an AFC for what he had cited as being 'an outstanding display of airmanship and skill in saving one of His Majesty's aircraft from certain destruction' (his words not mine). He was so confident that the AOC-in-C would agree that he decided to kill two birds with one stone and recommended Gerry for the DFC. The AOC-in-C disagreed, and all I got was a miserable 'green endorsement' in my log book. Unfortunately, Gerry did not live long to enjoy his honour as he was killed in an accident in a Meteor on his next flying tour.

Chapter 8

Flying Instruction

On arrival back home from the Far East I was given three weeks' disembarkation leave. I had to do a balancing act between staying with my mother in Putney and doing the-one-hundred-and-one odd jobs around the house and garden that she seemed to have saved for me, and getting together again with Jane. By this time she had moved down to her father's farm in Cornwall but was now working as the housekeeper of a small hotel in Looe. When, eventually, we were together we found nothing had changed between us despite our fifteen-month separation.

In the third week of my leave I reported to the Personnel Department of the Air Ministry to learn of my next posting. I was expecting to be posted as a flight commander on one of the Meteor or Vampire fighter squadrons in the UK, but I was in for a nasty shock! The Squadron Leader dealing with my case told me that I had been 'selected' to attend No. 123 Course at the Central Flying School (CFS) to train as a qualified flying instructor (QFI). CFS was, and still is, the longest-established military flying training establishment in the world, having been founded in 1912 and, quite rightly, enjoyed the reputation of being the centre of excellence in its field. To become a QFI could be a useful career qualification, but it was the last thing I wanted at that time.

I tried to convince my 'poster' that I needed to consolidate my miserable five months as a flight commander on a piston-engine fighter squadron with jet experience. I also reminded him that I had been assessed on the DFLS course as being a potential fighter squadron commander and therefore I needed more fighter experience before I could be considered for that role. My pleas fell on stony ground and I was told, in no uncertain terms, that if I was not prepared to go to CFS the only other posting on offer was as a ground instructor at the Apprentice School at RAF Halton, so somewhat reluctantly I accepted my lot.

I duly reported to CFS at RAF Little Rissington in December along with the other students on the course. We were a pretty motley crew, composed principally of RAF pilots from squadron leader down to six SNCO pilots. In addition there were three Royal Navy pilots and one Israeli captain. In all there were fifty of us.

I must admit that my first impressions were not very favourable, especially as the course started with a concentrated period of ground school. The syllabus covered all the usual subjects but in what I, and others, considered to be quite unnecessary detail. For example in 'Instruments' we were expected to learn the intricacies of the mechanisms of the altimeter, airspeed indicator, the gyroscopic artificial horizon, etc., etc. An appreciation of what could malfunction and possible remedial action was all that was really needed. Little did I think that many years later I would be in a position, as Chief Instructor of CFS, to completely rewrite, and rationalize, that same ground syllabus.

In 1950 the RAF was endeavouring to recover from wartime, during which the previous high peacetime standards of dress, discipline, drill and demeanour had understandably lapsed. The Air Board, in their wisdom, decided that the best way to influence the new generation of aircrew was via flying instructors who tended to become role models for their students. I was all in favour of the principle behind this thinking – the only trouble was that CFS was going about it the wrong way.

The principal butt of the students' antagonism was a certain Squadron Leader Dyer, the CFS officer responsible for implementing the Air Board directive. Unfortunately he was a bumptious, humourless, petty tyrant with the personnel management skills of a 3-ton truck. For example, he ordered all the officers on the course to parade in their overcoats and No. 1 uniform hats. He kept us standing to attention in a light drizzle whilst he walked up and down the ranks with a measuring stick checking that the hems of our coats were exactly fifteen inches above the ground. In Dyer's book any coat which was more than half an inch plus or minus the dress regulation height required replacing, at considerable expense, and then had to be produced for his approval. Needless to say a certain amount of coat swapping went on, not least because a new Crombie coat from Gieves, the military tailor in Bond Street, cost about the same as the monthly pay of a flight lieutenant.

Our hats in particular came in for similar scrutiny, perhaps with more justification, as many officers had removed the metal grommit, which prevented the sides from drooping, and had pummelled the hat into raffish shapes. Luckily, I had bought my hat from H. E. Bates of Jermyn Street who had produced hats without grommits which were approved by the Air Force Board.

Things cheered up when the ground school finished and flying commenced. My instructor was Flying Officer Joe Hulme, a QFI of much experience, albeit on twin-engined aircraft such as the Airspeed Oxford. He had just started at CFS and we were his first course. The students were paired off and I was lucky to have been paired with Flight Lieutenant Bill Scott who was as keen as I to do well on the course. To have the right 'mate' was very important because of the way CFS went about turning us into instructors, a pattern of training devised in 1912 by Captain Smith-Barry, the Chief Instructor, and little changed since.

Firstly, the instructor would give a model pre-flight briefing for the exercise about to be flown to both students; he would then demonstrate how the exercise should be put across in the air with each student in turn. They would then practise both the briefing and the flying exercise on each other, taking it in turns to play the instructor and 'Bloggs'. (For some reason it had become customary to refer to the supposed trainee as 'Bloggs'.) Finally the instructor would play 'Bloggs' and each student would reprise the briefing and flight and be assessed, criticized if necessary and given a mark. The series of exercises began with the *ab initio* basics such as 'Effects of Controls' and 'Descending' and so on to the advanced exercises such as 'Instrument Flying', 'Formation' and 'Aerobatics'.

Bill and I worked well together throughout the course. I was able to help him with aerobatics and formation, of which he had relatively little experience, and he helped me to smooth out my instrument flying – as I tended to fly 'by the seat of my pants!' The course lasted for four and a half months and involved about seventy-five hours flying. It was punctuated by periodic check flights with senior instructors, ground-school examinations, the final handling test and an instrument rating. The Course Dining out in the Messes coincided with the publication of the course results. Of the forty-seven of us who completed the course, Bill came second in the order of merit and I tied for fourth place: a very satisfactory result not just for us but also for Joe Hulme, our instructor, on his first CFS course.

Perhaps even more eagerly awaited than the results was news of our postings for various training units. I had hoped to be posted to the advanced phase of training for the flying although I appreciated that basic training would probably be a more rewarding experience. To my surprise I was the only student posted to a University Air Squadron (UAS) and Cambridge to boot! I knew very little about the UASs but having been congratulated by staff and students alike – maybe they thought it was a cushy number – I rather warmed to the idea. In particular I thought that it might be a nice relaxed atmosphere in which to introduce Jane to service life should we decide to get married. How wrong can one be!

* * *

Most of my fellow students on the CFS course had cars and were able to get away in the evenings and at weekends whereas I was dependent upon public transport or having lifts with others. So I started thinking seriously about buying a car before reporting to CUAS. Armed with £150 I started going around second-hand car dealers, but that sort of money would only run to rusty Ford Populars or similar clapped-out old bangers. I was about to give up when I found a two-seater 1932 Wolseley Hornet open coupé with an aerodynamic aluminium body. It had a six-cylinder inline overhead camshaft 1.5-litre engine with a very satisfactory throaty roar when running. At £135 I could just afford it so I road-tested it, put my money down and drove it from Islington to Putney two days before I was due to go to Cambridge.

There was a little problem in that I did not have a UK driving licence, although I had driven motorcycles, staff cars and 15-cwt trucks in the RAF. So I had no hesitation in setting off for Cambridge where I intended to take a driving test as soon as possible. The weather was sunny, the countryside was lovely and I was really enjoying the drive when the engine suddenly died for no apparent reason and my attempts to restart proved futile. So, having pushed the car off the road, I thumbed a lift to the Blue Boar Hotel in Cambridge where the adjutant had booked me in for three nights.

Having contacted a garage and arranged for them to recover the car, I was unpacking rather disconcertedly when I was called by the hall porter to say that two gentlemen were awaiting my presence in the bar. They were Flight Lieutenants Ken 'Dai' Rees and 'Taff' Bibby, two very Welsh CUAS instructors, who had kindly come to welcome me in the manner deemed appropriate – drinking rather too much beer! They finally left when it was too late for dinner in the hotel, so I walked around the Colleges and eventually found an Indian restaurant that was still serving.

Next day Dai drove me to the Squadron HQ to meet the CO, Wing Commander Philip Baldwin, who told me about the background to the formation of the UASs, of which there were now sixteen, four of which were Class 1 UASs (Oxford, Cambridge, London and Glasgow) commanded by wing commanders and the rest were Class 2, commanded by squadron leaders, and scattered about the country. The main difference was that the large UASs were authorized to recruit up to one hundred pilot cadets as well as up to twenty-five each of navigator and air traffic/fighter control cadets whereas the smaller ones were only allowed fifty pilot cadets.

The concept of University Air Squadrons was the brainchild of Lord Trenchard, the CAS of the RAF at the end of the First World War. His dream took years to come to fruition because of the opposition of the University Chancellors, despite there having been Army Officer Cadet Training Units for many years. However, when the first UAS, that of Cambridge, was launched in 1925, many other universities followed.

The thinking behind the concept, from the RAF point of view, was that in the 1920s military aviation was in its infancy and its potential capabilities were not appreciated by those in the corridors of power. It was also generally accepted at that time that many university graduates, especially those from Oxbridge, would go on to become Cabinet Ministers, MPs, Diplomats, Senior Foreign and Colonial Office officials, Captains of Industry, etc. Offering undergraduates the opportunity to learn to fly would result in their becoming air-minded and well disposed towards the RAF. This was particularly important in the 1920s when the Royal Navy and the Army were constantly lobbying for the disbandment of the RAF and the transfer of responsibility for fleet protection and ground support to themselves.

The CO went on to say that since the Second World War the RAF was no longer in danger of not surviving as an independent force and that the need to influence university graduates was much less important. The UASs remained a useful way of recruiting high calibre officers into all branches of the Service but were expensive to run and were no longer considered cost effective; so there was some doubt about their long-term future.

After my meeting the CO Dai drove me to Marshalls' Airfield, from which CUAS flew, to meet the Chief Flying Instructor, Squadron Leader Geoff Wright, and all the other instructors – and by golly were they pleased to see me! Not, I hasten to add, because it was me, but simply because they had been two QFIs short for some time. The QFI I was replacing, John Slessor, the son of MRAF Sir John, a former distinguished Chief of the Air Staff, had been posted away three weeks earlier and another QFI had broken an arm in a ski-ing accident. As a result, CUAS was way behind in its preparations for the summer camp six weeks hence.

I was, therefore, somewhat thrown in at the deep end. As I had not flown a Chipmunk before, my first flight was the statutory QFI check by Dai with my flying from the rear seat. I then flew a sector recce from the front seat to familiarize myself with the local flying area. I was most impressed with the Chipmunk and its de Havilland Gipsy Major engine: it was a delight to fly, not unlike the Cornell in America, but with a much better performance and a cockpit canopy – very necessary in the UK.

Having landed I found that I was scheduled for no fewer than six instructional flights on the trot. The way CUAS operated was as follows: the endurance of the Chipmunk was about two hours so two flights were flown with each refuelling with the students changing places with the engine still running. This maximized utilization but it only permitted pre-flight briefing with the first student. This made it difficult for any new QFI who would have to quiz the second student as to who he was and what exercises he had flown on his last dual sortie. As I had been allocated eighteen students, it took some time to get to know them all. However, I managed to cope reasonably well but, at the end of the day, by which time I had flown eight sorties, I was so whacked that, once back at the Blue Boar, I flaked out on the bed and missed dinner for the second night running. Thank Allah for that Indian restaurant.

It was clear that I could not afford to stay at the Blue Boar beyond the three days booked, so next day I managed to get the afternoon off to look for an affordable bed and breakfast establishment. Cambridge being a University town most landladies had no vacancies but I was lucky to find an acceptable room overlooking Parker's Piece, which was within walking distance of the Squadron HQ in Chaucer Road and on the bus route to Marshall's airfield. Unfortunately, it was a double room and the landlady reserved the right to let the second bed. She said it was unlikely that she would do so but one day I returned to find a US Air Force sergeant installed. That night was an absolute disaster: he was an insomniac who chain-smoked and wanted to talk all night! Luckily he was booked in for only one night – but I resolved that I would have to find somewhere else to live.

By now my dear old Wolseley Hornet had been fixed but I could not drive it legally until I had passed a UK driving test – so I arranged a test in two weeks' time. When I reported I went through all the necessary paperwork with a large, bluff, affable man who was to conduct the test. Everything went well until we walked out to the car and he noted that it had no doors and that one had to step over the side onto the seat and then slide down. His first reaction was 'I can't get into that bloody thing!' It took a lot of persuasion to get him to have a go, the operation being hampered somewhat by the fact that he had a wooden leg. By this time this affable fellow had become Mr Grumpy. He then proceeded to direct me to drive around town where the traffic was heavy and stopping was frequent. Oh, how my little car pined for the open road as the engine tended to oil up when idling and I had to keep revving up to prevent our being enveloped in white smoke.

When we had finished Mr Grumpy managed to clamber out with difficulty and much invective. He lost no time in telling me that I had failed, citing engine mishandling amongst other things. Luckily, I managed to book another test with a different examiner in a week's time. This time I borrowed Dai's battered old Ford Prefect and passed without adverse comment. I was now legal but there was no safe parking around Parker's Piece so I had to leave the car at Geoff Wright's house. As Geoff lived in a village several miles away, I could only use it on the CUAS day off – which was Monday.

Before long it was time for the six-week summer camp which was normally held on a RAF station in order to give our cadets a taste of service life: the base allocated in 1951 was RAF Hullavington in Wiltshire. The camp itself consisted of three periods of two weeks each and all of our undergraduates had to attend one of them. The idea was to take advantage of continuity of training and to pack in as many hours as possible. Needless to say, it was jolly hard work for the QFIs and, at the end of the camp, I was amazed to find that I had flown more than one hundred instructional hours, mostly in the Percival Prentice. HQ FTC had lent us about a dozen Prentices to help out at the camp. It was not a particularly nice aircraft to fly but at least it was one more aircraft type in one's log-book. However, it did have the advantage of three seats, useful for navigation exercises, and sufficient storage space for a large bag of golf clubs. One did me no favours towards the end of the camp when I had to make a precautionary landing at the disused airfield at South Marston (now the home of Honda UK) due to a magneto malfunction and a very rough running engine.

At the camp we QFIs worked hard but we also played hard, mainly at the Neild Arms in nearby Grittleton which had two distinct advantages. First, the landlords, Alan and Barbara Christian, a delightful couple who paid scant attention to the licensing laws, and the second being that we could drive there from the airfield by country lanes with little fear of bumping into a village Bobby. Needless to say it was the irrepressible, incorrigible rogue, Dai Rees, who led us astray. He had an endless fund of funny stories, many about his time as a prisoner of war in Germany, and a seemingly unquenchable thirst for best bitter. Yet for all the pints he sank I never knew him to be late for the early meteorological briefing or to show any signs of being the worse for wear – and at that time he was playing rugger for the RAF and for Wales.

Just before the end of the camp the CO, knowing of my accommodation problems, told me that he had arranged for me to stay in a room with en-suite facilities in St John's College, of which he was an 'old boy'. He apologized that it would only be available during the long vacation and that the refectory would be closed due to kitchen modernization. I was bowled over when I saw the rooms on the first floor of K staircase of New Court. It had wooden linen-fold panelling, antique furnishings and a superb view from the sitting-room window straight down the Backs – and it was all mine, albeit without breakfast, for less than half I had been paying at Parker's Piece.

* * *

One weekend when Jane and I were staying with her old actor friend, Howard Marion Crawford, I finally got around to proposing and was accepted. It must have had something to do with the Chianti Gran Reserva which 'Boney' plied us with at dinner! After much thought we decided to wed on 25 October 1951, two days after Jane's twenty-fifth birthday. Unfortunately, a couple of months later the then Labour Government chose that day for the General Election, thus giving rise to ribald comment that there would be no doubt who would get in that night!

As Cornwall was so remote, and most of our friends were in or around London, my mother offered to have the reception at her house in Putney so we made plans to be married at St Joseph's Church in Roehampton Village. Poor Jane, not being a Catholic, was required to have sessions of instruction before a 'mixed marriage' could be sanctioned. She started these in Cornwall with a delightful RC parish priest who spent most of the time talking about the theatre and Jane's career as an actress.

Unfortunately, the final session had to be with Father Turner, the parish priest at St Joseph's, at Manresa Seminary in Roehampton, to which she went with my mother. Father Turner was rather a dreary old stick who went through the duties of a non-catholic wife in an incredibly dull way, until, as an afterthought at the end of the session, added 'and don't forget that a good wife should never say "No" to her husband no matter how tired or how bad the headache'. It was all that my mother could do to keep a straight face until she and Jane were outside in the garden where they collapsed in a heap of helpless laughter. According to Azalea, my father's third and last wife, my mother was somewhat frugal with her favours, albeit she must have said yes often enough to have had six children.

The wedding went well and was blessed by reasonable weather.

The author in his morning suit with his Mother en route to the church.

Johnnie Sharpe was my best man and we wore morning dress. Jane had managed to get sufficient cream woollen material to have it made up into a simple but attractive dress with which she wore a Dutch cap – on her head! Her father was not able to leave the farm so Jane was given away by Leslie Heritage, an actor friend best known for having played Bob Dale in the radio soap *Mrs Dale's Diary*. Our mothers tried to outdo each other in sartorial elegance, a contest debatably won by Mrs Hodges thanks to her beautiful snow leopard fur coat.

The honeymoon did not go quite so well. We had been able to borrow Dai's battered old Ford as, fortuitously, he had been banned from driving for three months after being caught 'drunk in charge'. We planned to spend our first night at The Plough Hotel in Datchet

Signing the Register at St Joseph's Church, Roehampton Village.

but, as we neared the River Thames, we were enveloped in a thick fog and poor Jane had to walk in front of the car because I could not even see the kerb. We eventually arrived but worse was yet to come that night when Jane's elbow managed to collide with my right eye – and, no, we had not been studying the *Kama Sutra*. Fancy my becoming a battered husband on our first night of wedded bliss! Next day we met up with Jane's mother and her younger brother Keith at the Motor Show at Olympia by which time my eye was a delicate shade of black: not a very auspicious start!

The last day of our honeymoon was spent in Stratford-upon-Avon where we saw Richard Burton, then relatively unknown, in *Henry V*. It was an excellent production with Burton at his most impressive. After thus ending our honeymoon on a high, our arrival in Cambridge was back to reality. I had had great difficulty in finding somewhere suitable for us to live and it was literally at the eleventh hour that I had found accommodation that would do and which we could afford.

The 'Happy couple'.

It was the ground floor of a house with two front doors, one at each side: the owners occupied the first floor. It was a pretty miserable place which we shared with a mouse which lived in the gas cooker. Jane had to ask it to leave when she wanted to use the oven, which was not often.

It was incredible that more than six years after the war had ended many things were still rationed in England, notably meat, butter and other dairy products. Many other things, such as fruit, were not rationed but they might as well have been as they were seldom available in the shops. It was also incredible that, despite my being a flight lieutenant, and, being over twenty-five years old, entitled to a marriage allowance, just how poor we were. Our principal entertainment was the radio and we listened avidly to such programmes as *Saturday Night Theatre* and *A Book at Bedtime* which often

The Mothers: Mater in her Ascot 'Ladies' Day' finery and Jane in her Snow Leopard coat.

featured some of Jane's actor friends. We did try to go to the cinema once a week as our preferred seats in the circle cost only one shilling and ninepence. At the end of every month, if we had any money left, we would buy something for the house, such as a kettle or a coal scuttle.

This existence did not make for a good start to our marriage and was compounded by the way in which CUAS operated. To take advantage of our undergraduates' free time, we flew at weekends, having Mondays off. We also worked most Tuesday and Thursday evenings at the Squadron HQ giving lectures. I was responsible for airmanship and pilot navigation and had to attend most lecture nights. Jane did not take kindly to being left alone so often and was lonely and pretty miserable. Life in Cambridge was a far cry from her London days when she was wined and dined and danced the night away at The Windermere and The Coconut Grove. And matters were not helped when she became pregnant.

Meanwhile I was flying my socks off and loving every minute of it. I was rather surprised to find that I enjoyed instructing; there is a great sense of achievement in taking under one's wing a young man who has never flown before and guiding him into becoming a competent pilot. I felt rather guilty, knowing how lonely and unhappy Jane was – but there was little I could do about it. Jane always had many friends but she had little in common with the CUAS wives – who were a pretty dreary lot! I had hoped that she might offer her considerable stage experience to the Arts Theatre and maybe help them with their productions but she was reluctant to approach them. My hopes that UAS life would help to ease her into an RAF environment were proving quite wrong.

* * *

In early 1952 Wing Commander Baldwin called a meeting with all the instructors to tell us that he was about to attend a seminar at HQ Flying Training Command to discuss the future, if any, of the UASs. He was pretty pessimistic as the Treasury was looking for economies in the Defence budget and saw the UASs as an easy target. The CO asked if any of us could think of any way in which they could become more relevant and cost effective. Quite coincidentally, I had been talking recently to an old friend who had been the training officer of a Royal Auxiliary Air Force (RAuxAF) fighter squadron. He had told me that the RAuxAF was getting very short of pilots. Those former wartime pilots, who had become auxiliaries when demobbed so that they could continue to fly on a part-time basis, were now leaving in droves as they got married, started families and had to devote their time and energies to furthering their civilian careers.

I suggested that if we were allocated a few Harvards, still the RAF's advanced training aircraft, we could train our keenest third-year students to wings' standard and encourage them to join their local RAuxAF squadrons after graduation. Philip Baldwin latched onto this suggestion and presented it at the seminar where it was well received. To cut a long story short HQFTC authorized CUAS to conduct a trial by selecting three undergraduates to be trained but with the proviso that they should be assessed, alongside a normal graduating course at the FTS at RAF Feltwell, by sitting their ground-school exams and undertaking the final handling, navigation and instrument flying tests conducted by the FTS staff.

Our Harvards arrived in May and we chose Toby Robertson, Tony Back and Tony Lansdown as our guinea pigs. I was put in charge of liaising with Feltwell to ensure that we covered the same ground-school and flying syllabus and with monitoring progress and conducting independent checks. When our boys went to Feltwell we expected that they would do well but in the event they surpassed all our expectations. Toby came first in the order of merit of thirty-odd students. Tony B. came second and Tony L. fourth. Even more extraordinary was that, despite the end-of-term pressure in working towards these coveted wings, all three graduated from Cambridge with first-class honours. As a result, HQ FTC extended the scheme to all four Class 1 UASs (Oxford, London, Glasgow and ourselves) and the future of the UASs was assured for the immediate future.

The year 1952 saw many changes amongst the instructors. Geoff Wright had left before Christmas and Dai Rees acted as CFI until Squadron Leader John Leggett arrived in February. Unfortunately, he was a bit of a disaster, being humourless, ineffectual and a nit-picker of the first order. He seldom flew himself and cancelled flying for the rest of us whenever the wind blew or the clouds descended towards the limits: not too surprisingly he soon earned the nick-name of 'Granny'. When Dai was posted in March a lot of the fun went out of life. There were four new instructors, including Frank Forster, who had flown Hurricanes in India during the war. He was good news which was more than could be said about Stuart Winn. He was a tall, handsome, impressive-looking man who soon started to annoy as he had such an undeservedly high opinion of himself and his abilities, whereas he proved to be lazy and reluctant to pull his weight.

The 1952 summer camp was held at RAF Swanton Morley in Norfolk, a location negotiated by Leggett. It was not a good choice as it was a non-flying station which was hardly the environment to which we wanted to expose our budding pilots as an inducement to recruiting them into the RAF. The only advantage was that we had the grass airfield to ourselves which enabled me to clock up a record 132 flying hours despite Granny's attempt to limit the number of hours that instructors could fly every week – quoting health and safety regulations which only applied to airline pilots.

* * *

After the camp had been wrapped up I was able to take the four weeks' leave which I had saved up in order to ensure that I was around when Jane became due, probably in late August or early September. She had proved to be a model housewife who kept our half-a-house spick and span. She was also very good at making the most of our meagre ration of food; she even became a nominal vegetarian which meant that, whereas her ration book had no meat coupons, she got extra dairy products, principally butter and cheese. This worked very well as I usually bought our meat ration, always dressed in uniform, which often resulted in my being given more than my entitlement. I was also occasionally able to produce the odd rabbit or pheasant shot quite illegally on Marshall's airfield after night flying.

Jane had elected to put her confinement in the hands of Dr Eppel of Alford House, Park Lane, who had been her doctor when she lived in London. In the event this proved to have been a mistake. We were staying with my mother in Southfields when Jane's time came, so we reported to the Nursing Home in Avenue Road, St John's Wood, where it was found that Eppel had allowed the baby to get far too large for Jane's small frame: he should have induced the birth much earlier. He then defected and put the birth in the hands of an obstetrician. Eventually on 8 September Jane gave birth to a whopping great baby boy, weighing 9lbs 9oz, whom we named Hilary Jonathan.

When we returned to Cambridge to begin our 'ménage a trois' it became evident that Jane had little or no maternal instinct. She had already declined to breast feed, despite having the necessary wherewithal and having been advised of the health benefits to the baby. As she did the late evening feed, I volunteered to do the early morning one. I did not have the wherewithal but I soon became a dab hand with the bottle and Cow and Gate milk substitute. To her credit, Jane may not have had any maternal instinct but she did her motherly duty by the book. Luckily Hilary was a very well-behaved baby, never getting us up at night and seldom crying without good reason. I had hoped that Jane would welcome motherhood but having a baby, which further restricted her freedom, left her feeling disenchanted and even more lonely.

* * *

The year 1953 was a pretty good one for me from a professional point of view. It actually started in December when the CO told me that he had been asked by HQFTC to nominate someone to lead a formation of sixteen Chipmunks as part of a mass fly-past over Buckingham Palace to mark the Coronation of Queen Elizabeth II on 2 June. In view of my fighter experience and having flown in many thirty-six-aircraft formations whilst stationed at Gütersloh, Philip Baldwin said he would nominate me – if I agreed. I did not hesitate to do so for two reasons: firstly, being a bit of a Royalist, I considered it an honour to be involved, albeit remotely, in the pomp and panoply of the Coronation; secondly, I would not miss out on my third summer camp which was not due to begin until mid-June.

In January CUAS had a standardization visit from the Examining Wing of the Central Flying School, usually referred to as 'the Trappers'. Their job was to pay periodic visits to all training units and to fly with all the instructors and some students to ensure that standards were being maintained and that bad habits were not creeping in. Most units dreaded these visits as they could be disruptive, some instructors might be criticized and heads had been known to roll.

Before the Trappers arrived, the Chief Flying Instructor, John Leggett, told me that he had arranged for me to be tested as a potential Instrument Rating Examiner (IRE). Instrument ratings have to be renewed every year and when any CUAS rating was coming up for renewal the QFI had to fly one of the squadron's aircraft to CFS at RAF Little Rissington, take the test and return to base. This was inefficient as it meant the loss of one QFI and one aircraft for at least one day. However, if one of us was an accredited IRE the renewal tests could be done on the spot. I was not best pleased as it meant additional swotting for the CFS visit – but at least I was glad to have been chosen.

In the event the Trappers could not have been more helpful and all the QFIs, except one, were confirmed in their current categories. The exception was none other than the over-confident, self-opinionated Stuart Winn who was downgraded from his B1 category to B2 – defined as 'an inexperienced instructor of limited ability who requires supervision and may not authorize his own flights'. I am afraid to say that most of us were highly amused as Winn's constant bragging had become a bit of a bore.

I was one of the luckier ones, having passed the IRE test without difficulty. Moreover, when I was standardized, the report said that I was well up to A2 standards – by definition 'an experienced instructor of above average ability'. The only snag was that I was short by four months and about 100 flying hours of the minimum required to qualify as 'experienced'. The report recommended that I should take a re-categorization test as soon as I was qualified.

In March a combined Oxford and Cambridge University Air Squadron rugby team flew to BAFO to play a number of matches against teams from RAF stations in Germany. I regret to say that we lost all three, albeit narrowly, but we did enjoy ourselves and it was good for our undergraduates to experience life on overseas operational stations. Taffy Bibby managed the team and, as Dai Rees was long gone, I was the only officer in the team. I played in my favourite position of left wing three-quarter and managed to score a try and kick a couple of goals. Little was I to know that those matches would be the last I would ever play.

In April things started to go awry. Firstly, two of our stalwart instructors were posted and replaced by two newly-qualified QFIs straight out of CFS, one of whom had passed out as a B2 and was therefore on probation for six months. John Leggett did not like the idea of carrying two B2 QFIs during the very busy period leading up to the summer camp because of the limitations of what they could and could not do. The wretched man complained that he could not spare me for the briefings, rehearsals and the fly-past itself which were about to begin. He talked the CO into sending Stuart Winn, one of the B2 QFIs, in my place, although not as formation leader. I was rather cross as I had been looking forward to taking part in a little bit of Royal history and at having been replaced by the dreaded Stuart Winn. After the fly-past I was even more cross when he returned from the event sporting a Coronation Medal that should have been mine. Talk about a reward for ineptitude. Oh well! Winn some, lose some!

By May I had been a QFI for two years and had flown the requisite number of instructional hours so I flew to CFS for my A2 re-categorization test with Examining Wing. My instructor, Flight Lieutenant Green, was an Australian serving in the RAF and being an A1 category was obviously a first-class instructor with a lot of experience, but I regret that we just did not get on together. He seemed intent not on examining my knowledge and ability but on proving how clever he was. For example, part of the test was to examine how much one knew about the aircraft one was flying. The Chipmunk is a pretty simple aeroplane and I knew the answers to all Green's initial questions about the engine and airframe and such things as tyre pressures, 'g' limitations and the effect of icing on the flight instruments. For some reason, Green then started asking questions such as 'what is the longest piece of continuous metal in the aircraft?' I hazarded a guess that it was the main span of the wing but the answer was 'the copper wire of the primary winding of the generator'. After a few such silly trick questions I was moved to ask whether I was supposed to take them seriously.

The pre-flight briefings for the two airborne exercises went reasonably well. Once airborne, everything seemed to be going OK until I was asked to demonstrate a forced landing following total engine failure. When he cut the throttle, I did all the initial actions such as turning excess airspeed into height, turning into wind and selecting a suitable field in which to land. I did a tight circuit making a high approach and finally side-slipping to touch down in the right place. Green, however, chose to criticize my use of side-slipping, which is not suitable for all aircraft but perfectly suited to the Chipmunk, as a means of ensuring that one will not undershoot and end up in the hedge. When I told him that I had been a glider pilot for nearly two years, had made hundreds of landings, every one of which was a forced landing, and that I had successfully carried out three real forced landings in powered aircraft, always using side-slipping as a means of losing excess height, he was dumbfounded! But he insisted on showing me how it should be done. To my delight, he completely misjudged the wind-shear and had to abort the approach to avoid crashing through the hedge. Was Green's face red!

After landing and debriefing I was not at all surprised when he told me that I had not made the grade and that I should try again in six months' time. I was annoyed at this result as I am pretty competitive and dislike failure, but I was sure that it was due more to incompatibility than anything else. The Examining Wing of CFS had long had a reputation of being an elitist club in a 'holier than thou' sense and any dissent about their methods was badly received. When I returned to CFS as Chief Instructor a decade later this attitude was still prevalent. I had a difficult job convincing them that their future credibility would depend upon them being helpful and honest rather than having a reputation of being the inquisition.

The 1953 summer camp was held at RAF St Eval in Cornwall, one of the maritime bases which operated the Avro Shackleton. It was a good choice, largely because it was an operational station, unlike Hullavington and Swanton Morley, which was good for our cadets, many of whom were able to fly in the 'Shack' on some of their shorter sorties. Moreover, the nature of their operations seldom interfered with our flying. A bonus was that as Frank Forster was driving his car to St Eval he was able to take Jane and Hilary to her father's farm near Liskeard en route. It was a very welcome break for them and, and as the farm was in a low-flying area, I was able to amuse Hilary with a few aerobatics over the farm house.

The camp was unremarkable except that some of us were able to fly to St Mary's in the Isles of Scilly. That was a real experience because the airfield was not only very small but was also built on top of a steep hill. When landing it was advisable to approach the end of the grass runway at least 15 knots faster than normal and having landed it was then necessary to put on full throttle to prevent slipping back down the hill. Having rounded the top of the hill it was then necessary to put on hard brake to prevent careering down the hill and into the fence. I flew in and out four times and it never ceased to be a thrill.

From a personal point of view I shall remember the camp as where I clocked up 2,000 flying hours in my log book of which 1,000 had been spent instructing. In the six weeks I flew just over 120 hours and, because I was soon to be posted, that included seven IRTs and renewals. The boys must have thought I was a soft touch. A little earlier I had flown an IRT with John Leggett and, whereas I would have loved to have failed him fairly, his instrument flying was very good. Drat it!

* * *

Before going to camp, and knowing that I would be posted towards the end of the year, I had given a lot of thought to my next posting. I was worried about Jane, who had gradually become a shadow of her former self. Luckily she had been to see the CUAS honorary medical practitioner and told him of her various problems. He was a lovely man, a sort of Dutch Uncle, who reassured her that there was nothing seriously wrong, which cheered her up more than somewhat. However, he phoned me to say that she was probably suffering from mild depression and that the best thing for her would be an overseas tour in the sun.

Incredibly within a week there arrived a circular from the Personnel Department of the Air Military calling for volunteers to apply for appointment as training officer of the Singapore Squadron of the Malayan Auxiliary Air Force (MAAF). I had already found out that my next job was almost certain to be instructing so, although I would have preferred a posting back onto fighters, Singapore seemed the next best thing. The circular called for volunteers to have experience of both basic and advanced training, as well as a fighter background as the squadron had Spitfires and would eventually be re-equipped with Vampires. It seemed too good to be true but I applied for the job and got it. Alas it was too good to be true – but that is another story.

In many ways I was sorry to leave CUAS, not least because I had learned so much whilst there. I had joined as a sprog instructor and had progressed to being the senior QFI, the Instrument Rating Examiner and deputy Chief Flying Instructor. But more important I had found that I enjoyed instructing and seemed to have a talent for it. I had never had to fail any of my own students and had often been given other QFIs' problem boys to sort out, usually successfully. But it was now time to move on.

Chapter 9

Singapore and Malaya

Once my application to go to Singapore had been processed and accepted matters moved with indecent haste, which is more than I can say about my journey out there. I reported to RAF Lyneham on 1 September and clambered aboard a dear old Hastings. The first leg was to Idris (formerly Castel Benito) near Tripoli; on the second day we flew to Habbaniya in Iraq; on the third to Mauripur (Karachi); on the fourth to Negombo in Ceylon and finally to RAF Changi. So it took five days and thirty-seven flying hours whereas today, in the Jumbo Jet era, it can be done in one day and thirteen flying hours. But, at least, I was able to enjoy seeing something of the countries in which we night-stopped, including exploring a souk (Arab market) and swimming in the surf off Ceylon.

On arrival I was accommodated at RAF Tengah, where the Singapore Squadron was based, and was met by Flight Lieutenant 'Olly' Crookes, the training officer I was to relieve, and his No. 2, Flying Officer Holmes. Olly had originally been the No. 2 but, when the former training officer contracted a nasty tropical disease and was flown home, he was given acting promotion. I was not very impressed by either of them, a view reinforced when Olly took me to meet his wife and I found that they were living in near squalor in the servants' quarters of a big old colonial house. He even boasted that the rent was low enough to enable them to live on his local overseas allowance without touching his RAF pay – and it showed!

The next morning I went to AHQ Malaya at Changi to spend the day with my RAF boss, Wing Commander 'Bats' Barthold, the staff officer responsible for overseeing the four Malayan Auxiliary Air Force (MAAF) squadrons in Kuala Lumpur, Penang, Singapore and Hong Kong and to whom I was to report and who in turn would write the annual confidential report on me. I was a little surprised that Hong Kong had a MAAF Squadron: the first three made sense as it was assumed that, come independence, Singapore would join The Federated Malay States as one nation – but Hong Kong? The only thing it had in common was that it was a Crown Colony, as was Singapore, but Hong Kong could never become independent as the lease of the New Territories was due to expire in 1997 when they would be returned to China.

Barthold explained that the formation of the MAAF squadrons was a step in the direction of independence by fostering air-mindedness amongst the national youth and to create a pool of trained pilots should the new country consider the need for an air force. Singapore already had an airline, Singapore Airways, but it was manned entirely by expatriate foreigners – a very costly exercise. So the sooner it could be manned by nationals the better. Therefore the MAAF was serving both a military and civilian purpose.

After lunch the wing commander drove me into the city to meet an up and coming young politician named Lee Kwan Yew, the leader of the People's Action Party (PAP). Politically, Singapore was already well on the road to independence in that there was a Legislative Assembly headed by the Chief Minister, Mr David Marshall. The UK remained responsible for defence and foreign policy but Singapore was already looking after home affairs and the economy. He went on to say that Marshall's party was losing political ground and that the PAP would almost certainly take over before long so it was important to keep Lee informed about any proposed changes of policy which might affect the cost of running the Squadron. He explained that MAAF was a joint venture in that the Air Ministry did not charge for the RAF personnel involved or for the provision of the aircraft but Singapore paid for all running costs.

When we met I was very impressed by Lee Kwan Yew which was not too surprising as he had graduated from Cambridge University with double first-class honours. His clarity of mind, his ability to grasp quickly the nub of any problem and his concise expression were all extraordinary and I understood immediately the reasons for his rapid rise up the political ladder. We met several times before I left Singapore and I never ceased to be impressed.

During my takeover briefing with Crookes I was surprised, bearing in mind what Wing Commander Barthold had told me, to learn that we currently had twelve pilots under training, of whom only four were Singaporeans. The rest were all British expatriates working for British companies, often on five-year contracts. Of the Singaporeans, two were of Chinese origin and the other two were Indian. I was keen, therefore, to redress the balance by recruiting a couple of Malays. By chance, within days of my arriving I was told by an instructor from the Singapore Flying Club at Kallang Airport that a young Malay ATC cadet had just completed a flying scholarship of twelve hours on a Cessna aircraft and had shown great potential, having gone solo after eight hours.

I wasted no time in persuading Sulaiman bin Sujak who, on leaving school, had joined the Singapore Improvement Trust as an apprentice surveyor, to apply to join the squadron. MAAF HQ took ages to decide whether he was a suitable candidate because they considered that the Malay race as a whole were too laid back to make good pilots. Luckily I had already invited Sulaiman to Tengah where we had flown in a Tiger Moth and he had shown great aptitude, so I was able to persuade them to give him a chance. In the months to come, he far exceeded my expectations of him.

On my first training night at MAAF HQ in Beach Road in downtown Singapore I met most of the senior auxiliary officers – a motley crew! The CO was Wing Commander Bobby Drooglever, who had been an administrative officer in the RAF and was now chief accountant of an import/export trading company. His deputy was Squadron Leader Hugh Oates, who had been a fighter pilot in the

RAAF and was now the managing director of the Austin/Morris car main dealership. The flying squadron CO was Squadron Leader Ron Mumford, a former RAF pilot and now a commodities broker.

The Air Traffic/Fighter Control Squadron Commander was Squadron Leader Pelham-Groom, who had been a fighter controller during the Battle of Britain and had written a book called *Angels One Five* which had been made into a successful film. He was a bit past his 'sell-by' date and the power behind the cathode ray tubes was Flight Lieutenant Ken Meyer, now

The author briefing one of his Singaporean cadets before sending him off on his first solo flight.

an optician. I also met ex-Group Captain 'Dickie' Bain who looked after MAAF finances. He had commanded No. 43 Squadron, 'The Fighting Cocks', just prior to the Second World War, but was to become the bane of my life.

I sat in on two lectures that night; the first by Flying Officer Tommy Kingston on engines was excellent, the second by Flight Lieutenant 'Oz' Tomasetti on pilot navigation was pretty poor. Tommy had been a sergeant flight engineer in the RAF and was now the chief equipment officer of Singapore Airways. Oz had been a pilot in the RAAF and had been helping out at the squadron as a part-time flying instructor.

When the training night was over some of the officers took me to the food stalls in Beach Road to introduce me to the delights of satay, small pieces of chicken or beef on skewers which one dunked in bowls of hot satay sauce – absolutely delicious! Whilst there Hugh Oates asked if I wanted to buy a car as he had just got in a second-hand one which he could let me have with a substantial discount. Two days later I became the proud owner of a nearly-new Standard Vanguard for almost next to nothing.

Back at RAF Tengah the Squadron operated Tiger Moths as the basic trainer and Harvards as the advanced aircraft. When I asked about the Spitfires I was told that there had only been one which had been pranged by Tomasetti, as a result of which it was decided that MAAF was not yet ready for a front-line aircraft. I was also told that equipment with Vampires had been a long-term aim until the Legislative Assembly had been briefed, by Group Captain Bain, of the costs involved, whereupon the idea had been shelved. So the information I had been given about the squadron before I volunteered had long been overtaken by events. However, having seen the MAAF set-up, I could but agree that it was the right decision.

I was introduced to the RAF flight sergeant aircraft fitter who was in charge of the team of fifteen servicing personnel. They were a super group of chaps who worked strange hours willingly and never complained. I was their CO for disciplinary purposes but none appeared before me on a charge during my time on the squadron.

I flew just over fifty hours in my first two months, trying to fly with all our cadets and most of the officers; the only one who managed to escape my clutches was Tomasetti who seemed to have other things to do whenever I suggested a period of staff continuation training. I was beginning to settle in well when the Tengah OC Flying, Wing Commander Knight, told me that the CFS Examining Wing, the dreaded 'Trappers', were arriving for a standardization visit in a fortnight's time and wished to carry out tests on all QFIs on the station, including us. I was delighted for two reasons; firstly, my six months from my failure to re-categorize to A2 had now passed, so I was eligible to try again and, secondly, having flown with Holmes several times, I was beginning to suspect that he was not up to scratch.

When the Trappers arrived I flew with the team leader, Squadron Leader Ellis, who really put me through my paces but, thankfully, he said he was more than satisfied that I should be upgraded. When he asked who had taken me on my first attempt, he laughed when I told him, saying 'Poor old you! You might be interested to know that Flight Lieutenant Green had been posted from CFS after numerous complaints about his methods of testing'.

The CFS team flew with the three squadron instructors and five of our cadets and then summoned me to the final debriefing. Ellis started by saying that all five students had flown adequately considering the intermittent nature of their training, but they had developed certain bad habits which he outlined. He then dropped a bombshell: firstly Holmes had failed miserably and they had no option but to downgrade him to B2. Secondly, Tomasetti had fared even worse, so badly that Ellis had asked to see his RAAF log book. It revealed that Tomasetti had never been a QFI, but merely an instructor on an operational conversion unit. He went on to say that, between Holmes and Tomasetti, it was not too surprising that some students had developed bad habits.

Tomasetti took umbrage at the Examining Wing report and eventually resigned from MAAF. But I was left with the problem of Holmes. I was now responsible for supervising and authorizing all his flying and with carrying out regular staff continuation training sorties in the hope that, at the end of his probationary period of six months, I would be able to re-categorize him back up to B1. In the meantime, he could not authorize his own flights and I had to sit in on as many of his pre- and post-flight briefings as possible. To his credit, Holmes told me that he had finished near the bottom of his CFS course, had come straight to MAAF and had never done any staff continuation training with any other QFI, but he was prepared to buckle down to get up to speed and hoped he would not let me down.

So much for the bad news: the good news was that I had been informed that Jane and Hilary would be arriving in Singapore on board the troopship HMT *Empire Clyde* shortly before Christmas. So it became vital for me to find suitable accommodation to rent before their arrival. With the help of Tommy Kingston,

I looked at several possibilities and settled on The Waverley Guest House which was on the coast road near West Point Gardens with lovely sea views. It was also conveniently equidistant from Tengah and MAAF HQ. It was a bit out on a limb, but was only a temporary measure until we found somewhere more suitable. In the event, Tommy Kingston, having met Jane and Hilary, asked whether we would like to move in with him as he lived alone in a large two-bedroom flat with servants' quarters in Orange Grove Road near Tanglin Circus. He invited us to visit, we liked what we saw, discussed terms, accepted and moved in.

Jane with Hilary in West Point Gardens, Singapore.

It soon became clear that Singapore suited Jane. She made several friends and, thanks to a generous local allowance and a favourable pound/Singapore dollar exchange rate, we had enough money to live reasonably well. She did not like my absence on training nights, as at Cambridge, and was somewhat affronted when I told her that I would be serving lunch to the Squadron servicing personnel at Tengah on Christmas Day – but, of course, she was not familiar with this longstanding tradition as we had yet to serve on an RAF station. Taking Hilary for 'walkies' in his pram in Haw Par Villa Gardens with its myriad gruesome, gaudy concrete monsters was not exactly her idea of Christmas lunch – but then a temperature of 85°F and a humidity of 85 per cent does not exactly make 25 December feel much like Christmas anyway.

* * *

The year 1954 turned out to be a good one for just about everybody. Holmes worked really hard and, after three months of close supervision and advice, I was confident enough to let him off the leash. His tour was due to finish at the end of March, by which time he fully deserved to be upgraded – so I signed his log book to that effect. His successor was Flight Lieutenant Jack Challinor, who was not only an A2 QFI but had been awarded the DFM as an NCO pilot on bombers towards the end of the war. We immediately hit it off and his ability, experience, friendly character and quirky sense of humour made him the perfect No. 2.

There were several changes for the better at MAAF HQ. Both the Wing and Squadron Commanders resigned citing 'pressure of work' and were replaced by Hugh Oates and Mike Barlow respectively. Tommy Kingston, who had now qualified for his MAAF pilot's wings was deservedly promoted to Flight

Lieutenant and was made the squadron flight commander. At last we had a team with the necessary 'get up and go' to progress towards achieving the military and political aims.

Cadet Sulaiman bin Sujak was progressing so well and was so keen that I asked him if he would be interested in joining the RAF. He was surprised because he did not think it possible until I told him that he could apply for a Colonial Cadetship to the RAF College at Cranwell. He thought about it, discussed it with his parents and then told me that he was very keen to do so. It was a hard decision for him to make because, if he successfully completed the course, he would be awarded a permanent commission in the RAF and would only be able to return to Singapore on leave, although, later on, there was always the possibility that he might be posted to serve in the Far East.

Because applicants had to be sponsored by an organization rather than an individual, I set the wheels in motion by asking Group Captain Bain to request the necessary application forms from the Air Ministry. Dickie seemed to be reluctant to do so because, as he said, when he had been a Cranwell cadet in the 1930s the only colonials there were from Australia, Canada, New Zealand and South Africa. I argued that things had moved on since then and that, as Singapore was a Crown Colony, surely Sulaiman should at least be allowed to apply.

When the application forms arrived Bain rang me up to say, rather smugly, that Sulaiman did not qualify as he did not have the necessary educational qualifications. I immediately rushed around to MAAF HQ to read the papers for myself. I hit the roof when I read that the requirement was for the Oxford and Cambridge or London Boards' School Certificate with a minimum of passes in five subjects, of which English and Maths had to be of credit standard – or equivalent. I accused Bain of being utterly negative as I knew that Sulaiman, in his school-leaving exams, had passed seven subjects, all with grades equivalent to credits. Moreover, Sulaiman had already shown great pilot aptitude and had over fifty hours in his log book. When I told Hugh Oates about Bain's attitude he gave him an Australian style roasting whereupon the application forms were sent winging on their way.

Needless to say Sulaiman was accepted without demur for the three-year course starting in April 1955. Much to my satisfaction, and expectations, he did brilliantly, qualifying in the top ten of his course graduation order of merit, having been appointed as a junior under-officer and captain of badminton. Little did I know that Sulaiman would crop up many times in the course of my career.

Much to my surprise, CFS Examining Wing paid yet another visit to Tengah that October. I found out later that they always tried to visit Singapore towards the end of the year to do their Christmas shopping in town and at Changi Village because the cost of Japanese cameras, radios, watches and many other articles was less than half the UK price because of the strong pound and the favourable exchange rate. Normally, the Trappers only tested units every two years, but they asked to do the squadron again probably because of the fiasco of Holmes and Tomasetti last year.

Jack and I were confirmed as well up to A2 standard and, more satisfyingly, they wrote a glowing report about the six cadets with whom they had flown.

Around that time we were faced with two problems. Firstly, many of our cadets were about to be awarded their MAAF wings but, since the demise of the sole Spitfire, there were no operational aircraft for them to progress on to. I had suggested to MAAF HQ that they should consider purchasing a few Austers or Pioneers but, although Group Captain Bain had made enquiries about costs, nothing had yet materialized. Jack and I put our heads together and devised a cunning two-point plan. I would teach them fighter tactics, such as battle formation manoeuvring, cross-over turns, tail chases, quarter attacks on target aircraft and also close formation so that the MAAF pilots could take part in air shows and fly-pasts. Although we could only use the Harvard, the training would stand them in good stead should the squadron ever be equipped with fighter aircraft.

Jack would concentrate on pilot navigation with particular reference to reconnaissance tactics such as 'square searches' to locate jungle clearings used for growing crops and other possible signs of CT activity. To this end we flew many sorties to find and pinpoint the exact map co-ordinates of those clearings as already existed in the rain forests of South Jahore. We then compared notes to produce a master plan of the area to which we could send our pilots to locate and report them. With these two types of activity we managed to make them feel that they were progressing – which was vital to sustain keenness and esprit de corps.

The second problem was that we badly needed to recruit a new batch of cadet pilots. I knew that there were a few in the pipeline because I had insisted on sitting in on the selection boards. In the past MAAF HQ had made little effort to advertise, so I encouraged all our existing cadets to interest those of their friends whom they considered suitable. As a result we had a sudden rush of applicants.

Previously, MAAF HQ had inducted new recruits as and when they were selected. This was very inefficient as they were all at different stages of training. So I persuaded them to recruit intakes for a specific date so we could run a concentrated ground-school programme of four weeks before we started flying training and thereafter they would all progress more or less at the same rate.

I had told MAAF HQ that Jack and I could cope with a maximum of twelve new boys, given our aircraft resources, for a start date of 1 January 1955 and, assuming that each course would take two years to graduate, a further six

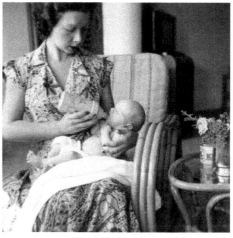

Jane giving Marcus his bottle in the flat we shared with Tommy Kingston.

cadets every year. With the approval of Wing Commander Barthold and Lee Kwan Yew, I had also stipulated that all recruits should be Singaporean nationals unless any expatriate applicants had a skill or experience that could help us with the training of the others. We did recruit a British Met Officer from Kallang Airport who became a godsend in the teaching of meteorology.

On the home front things were going well. Jane was pregnant again, a condition with which she coped with aplomb. What a difference having a nice home, friends, a good *amah* and plenty of sun made. The only snag was that neither she nor the doctors could work out exactly when the baby was due. The best guess was sometime in December! In the event Marcus was born in the RAF hospital at Changi on 20 December, weighing in at 8lbs and 9oz – and that meant our second Christmas in Singapore had gone a bit awry. However, the year ended on a high when the RAF promotion list was posted on New Year's Eve; much to my surprise, and I suspect that of others, I was promoted to Squadron Leader.

* * *

As welcome as it was my promotion did raise a few problems. We were due to start the new course in the first week of February and now there was a danger that I might be moved on. Indeed Wing Commander Barthold phoned to congratulate me and to ask whether I would be happy for him to request that I be allowed to complete my tour in post. I said I would be delighted to do so and he put the wheels in motion. However, the Personnel Department at the Air Ministry, whilst confirming that I was to complete the full two-and-a-half-year overseas tour, would only allow me to remain with MAAF for a minimum of three months or until a replacement could take over – whichever was the longer. In the meantime, AHQ Malaya was to find a suitable squadron leader posting for me in which to complete my tour.

In January Jack and I flew our socks off with the recently-qualified pilots before the new intake would take up most of our time. The fighter tactics element, despite being flown in the Harvard, was great fun and created lots of enthusiasm but it was the navigation and reconnaissance element that really paid dividends. Before long we had liaised with the Malayan Police Force HQ in Johore Bahru to offer our services which they gratefully accepted. We then started, for example, to fly to their airstrip to pick up one of their officers to carry out recce missions, to drop leaflets over those kampongs which were being threatened into supplying food for the CTs or to drop Chinese crackers in support of ground operations. These sorties gave the Squadron a real sense of purpose which was good for morale.

The new course duly assembled, albeit only nine of them due to last-minute withdrawals. They were all Singaporeans, five being of Chinese origin, two Indian, one Goan and one of white Russian/Malay parentage. Incredibly, the surnames of all the Chinese began with an L – no doubt an auspicious omen. They seemed pretty keen and we progressed rapidly.

Three months passed before I was officially informed that my successor would arrive on 10 May and that I was posted to the Advanced HQ in Kuala Lumpur with effect from 20 May. Jack and I hoped to have sent all the new boys off solo before I departed. I had four of them, of whom Leok was the most promising. He was the first to go solo on 7 May. As required I was in the tower to watch his first solo take-off, circuit and landing on the runway. Everything was going fine until, shortly after touch-down, there was a sudden gust of cross-wind which weather-vaned the aircraft to the left.

We had taught our students that once the Tiger Moth was well and truly on the ground the rudder became ineffective in steering the aircraft unless one opened the throttle slightly to increase the airflow over the tailplane. Unfortunately, Leok left it too late to correct the swing and to compensate opened the throttle far too much just as the aircraft veered off the runway onto the grass and then he froze. I was helpless to do anything, as the Tiger Moth had no radio, so I could but watch as the aircraft careered in a circle across the grass towards the control tower with its tail in the air. Luckily, it missed the tower and was hurtling towards the fuel tanks when his right wing hit an obstruction, causing the aircraft to tip forward onto its nose, eventually turning right over onto its back.

The wrong way to end up on one's first solo as demonstrated by Cadet Leok who went on to become the Chief Training Officer of Singapore Airlines.

I had neglected to say the instructor's prayer prior to sending a student off on his first solo which goes as follows 'Dear God, please don't let him prang but, if it is thy will, please let him do it where I can see it!' Nevertheless, Leok had given me a grandstand view.

I rushed to the aircraft and arrived just as the firemen started pouring foam over the engine to prevent fire. I did not think that Leok could be badly hurt as the aircraft had gone over fairly slowly but I was afraid that he might pull the harness release and drop down the several feet to the ground – onto his head. I dived under the aircraft, checked that he was OK and told him to release when I was in position to break his fall. Having lowered him safely onto the ground, we walked to the waiting ambulance where he was examined and pronounced completely unhurt – except, of course, for the inevitable Chinese loss of face.

The rest of that day was spent writing the accident report but, two days later, I took Leok up again and allowed him to fly an hour-long sortie without my once touching the controls. The final twenty minutes he spent doing circuits and landings including some where I initiated swing by kicking the rudder bar, with which he coped admirably. I then crossed my fingers and sent him off solo again and he never looked back. Indeed when I returned to Singapore some twenty years later I found that he was not only a senior pilot with Singapore Airways but also their Chief Training Officer.

My successor, Flight Lieutenant Van Cuylenburg, duly arrived and I spent two days to introduce him to everyone that mattered and flew the statutory instructor check with him before leaving him in the capable hands of Jack. I then flew five sorties with Leong who, having gone solo, was suddenly having difficulties as often happens. Having sorted him out, I attended my last training night at MAAF HQ where Hugh Oates, having said some kind words, presented me with a beautiful Javanese fruit dish. I managed to be suitably delighted and surprised because nobody else knew that Tommy Kingston and I had gone shopping to find something and I had chosen it.

I was extremely sorry to leave Singapore, not only because Jane and I had been very happy there but also because, with Jack's help, I had changed the Squadron from having been a rather disorganized outfit with a flying-club approach to an efficient unit with a sense of purpose. Indeed it had become a bit of an embarrassment as Bats Barthold had started quoting our achievements, in terms of flying hours, aircraft utilization, recruiting and training progress, as being those that the other MAAF Squadrons should try to emulate.

I drove up to Kuala Lumpur with a heavy heart and some apprehension, little dreaming that I would be back at Tengah before the week was out. After only three days away Jack got through to me at the JOC to say that Van Cuylenburg had gone down with 'flu and could I get back for the weekend to help out as all nine of our new boys would be at Tengah. Providentially the chap I was replacing was going to be there for another ten days so there would be plenty of time to complete the takeover. In the event I was able to fly down on Thursday in a Harvard that was due for second-line servicing and to fly back in a Percival Pembroke which would be ready to return to KL on Monday morning. So I managed twelve unexpected instructional sorties with my old students.

* * *

Back at KL I found that the air support the RAF could offer the ground forces was much greater than that available during my time with No. 33 Squadron in 1949-1950. It now consisted of offensive, transport and helicopter support, air observation liaison flights, photo reconnaissance (PR) and psychological warfare (PW) support. Command of the air forces allocated to the Emergency was exercised by the Air Officer Commanding (AOC) and his operational control was exercised through the Joint Operations Centre (JOC).

Requests for air support from the Malayan Police Force and by the Army units of HQ Malaya Command were submitted to the JOC where they were processed by a joint Army/RAF team consisting of a Major (GSO 2/Air) and a Squadron Leader (Sqn Ldr Ops and Int). The duty team was to decide on the suitability of the requests and to allocate priorities. The RAF member would then allocate aircraft and issue the operations orders to the appropriate units, which included an RAAF fighter squadron and an RNZAF transport squadron, both of which were under command of Air HQ Malaya. After the operations were completed the team were responsible for collecting, collating and disseminating the relevant intelligence.

I was to be the RAF member of one of the two teams and my Army colleague was Major Dickie Pote-Hunt RA, with whom luckily I was to get on very well. One team would be on duty or on call for one week and for the 'week off' I would be required to visit ground force units to advise on air matters, to assist in planning joint Army/Air operations and, most importantly, liaise with the RAF operational units.

The FEAF offensive support aircraft at that time included Lincolns, Hornets (No. 33, my old squadron), Vampires and Brigands; for transport support there were Vickers Varsities and Dakotas; for helicopter support there were Whirlwinds, Sycamores and the Sikorsky S-55; for AOP and light liaison there were Austers, Pioneers and Pembrokes; for PR there were Spitfires and Canberras on detachment from UK and for PW mainly Dakotas, modified for voice operations, assisted by Austers, Pembrokes and Pioneers for leaflet dropping. Additionally, parachute operations by 22nd Special Air Service (SAS) Regiment, which was pioneering the dropping of troops into the jungle canopy, were carried out from Varsities and Dakotas.

During my previous tour the CT threat was on the increase with many attacks, ambushes and assassinations. By 1955 the Security Forces had gained the upper hand thanks to the successful implementation of the Briggs' Plan initiated by the then Director of Operations, General Briggs, in June 1950 and to the current leadership and operational expertise of the GOC Malaya Command, General Sir Gerald Templer. The number of 'white areas', i.e. areas in which there was no longer any need to apply the Emergency Regulations, was steadily increasing.

The tactical flexibility and effectiveness of the Police and Army units had been much increased by the setting up of a number of jungle forts with adjacent airstrips in strategic areas and by the growing number of landing zones (LZs) and drop zones (DZs). These greatly facilitated rapid response, reinforcement, casualty evacuation and the removal of CT captives and cadavers for interrogation and/or identification for intelligence purposes.

With the help of my team-mate, Dickie Pote-Hunt, I soon settled in as an ops officer and had mastered the many procedures that dominated the day when we were the duty team. Although we were on call when off duty there were very few occasions when we had to report back to the JOC to initiate emergency operations such as urgent casualty evacuations. However, we often had to work pretty late in order to clear all the requests that had been received during the day. I found the work interesting and tiring – but not very exciting. I much preferred the 'week off' when I did my best to fly on every type of operation, usually as supernumerary aircrew. I particularly liked taking part in helicopter operations and before long I was being taught how to fly them – albeit very unofficially.

My immediate domestic concern was to find somewhere to live. RAF Kuala Lumpur had married quarters for which I could not be considered as I had less than a year before my tour was over. But eventually I was allocated a hiring, a bungalow at No. 24 Yap Quan Seng Road, which was adequate but rather remote from the city centre and shops.

At last I was able to take time off to drive down to Singapore to collect Jane and the boys. I elected not to travel by the coast road which was longer and, because of a ferry crossing, took much longer, in favour of the more direct inland route. Unfortunately my journey was dogged with problems: first I had a puncture in a remote location and had a wheel-nut which resisted my every attempt to budge it until I got some help from the first driver going in the opposite direction. That set me back about an hour and by then it was getting dark. Then, to my horror, I found that the Emergency Regulations had been re-imposed the previous day on a long stretch of the road because of reported CT infiltration into the area.

All the kampongs along the road were encircled by high-wire fencing and the gates across the road now had to shut and be locked from dusk to dawn. At the first set of closed gates I tried to convince the Malay policeman that I was on urgent military business. But, despite my being in uniform and armed, he was not inclined to let me through, perhaps because of the language problem, so I tried another tack by explaining, with appropriate gestures, that my wife was pregnant and expecting at any minute. That tipped the balance and I was let in and out, accompanied by the best wishes of the now assembled crowd. It was only a white lie in that Jane was indeed pregnant albeit not due for another seven months.

The scene was re-enacted at the next kampong but this time the policeman spoke good English and I not only persuaded him to let me through but also to phone ahead by land-line to the next police post and beyond. So I was virtually waved through the next three kampongs by which time I was back in a white area. I was exasperated and exhausted by the time I arrived home at 5.30am, having taken twice as long to complete the journey as the six-hour estimate. The return journey with the family was by the coast road and much more enjoyable with a night stop at one of the delightful Rest Houses along the route.

Life plodded on at the JOC for the next six months. I did not really enjoy the job but appreciated that it was valuable experience and would soon be over. I tried to fly as often as possible but what little I did only whetted my appetite for more. Then, out of the blue, came an expected opportunity. At a meeting to discuss a PR operation with the current Canberra detachment commander, I found that he was none other than Flight Lieutenant Olly Crookes whom I had relieved in Singapore. To cut a long story short he said that if I could get to Butterworth the following morning he would take me up on an air-test scheduled for around noon. Luckily Squadron Leader Jack Rumsey, one of the other JOC officers, wanted to go to Butterworth so I borrowed a Harvard from the KL Squadron of MAAF and flew him there.

The trip in Olly's Canberra was a real eye-opener. Once airborne, we swapped seats to let me fly it. I was astonished not only by the way it handled but also by its performance which, in all respects except manoeuvrability, was superior to both the Vampire and Meteor fighters I had flown. In particular, as part of the air-test, Olly took it up to 60,000 feet whereas the Meteor had to struggle to reach 45,000 feet. The view from nearly twelve miles up was truly sensational: luckily it was a beautifully clear day with only a few scattered fair weather cumulus clouds and I could see the whole of the Malay peninsula and most of Thailand. Once back on the ground, I just had time to visit 33 Squadron and to sit in the cockpit of one of their de Havilland Hornets, cursing my luck that the squadron's re-equipment with them had been delayed, and that I had missed, perhaps for ever, the opportunity to fly that most beautiful of piston-engined aircraft.

Christmas passed uneventfully and soon it was 1956, which was to be a bad year for the Langers. Our troubles started sometime in January when I started to feel a bit under the weather, mainly tiredness accompanied by a persistent cough and occasional bouts of dizziness. Eventually, at Jane's insistence, I reported to the MO who listened to my chest and immediately packed me off to the British Military Hospital (BMH) at Kinrara where I was diagnosed with pneumonia in both lungs and was admitted.

This could not have happened at a worse time as Jane was due in a couple of weeks and, moreover, my overseas tour would be up in March. At this awkward stage a guardian angel appeared in the form of the Station Commander of RAF Kuala Lumpur, Group Captain. K. R. C. Slater CBE AFC who, having been told of our plight, took steps to ensure that Jane was coping in my absence and even laid on a staff car to take her to a pre-natal appointment at BMH where she could visit me. Unfortunately, the rough road to Kinrara was so strewn with pot-holes and the ride so bumpy that it was decided that, in her condition, further visits were not advisable.

The Station Commander also suggested that I should apply for a six-month extension of my tour so that we would both have time to get fit for the journey home. A signal was duly sent to the Air Ministry, to which the reply was that an extension would not be granted as Squadron Leader Langer was to command a fighter squadron and that any delay could prejudice that appointment. That was marvellous news but it did not solve the problem that I was in hospital, Jane was about to give birth and there was no one to look after Hilary and Marcus. Once again Ken Slater came to the rescue by persuading one of the JOC officers, Squadron Leader Dave Frostick and his wife to 'volunteer' to take care of the boys in our absence.

Jane was brought into the BMH for an induction on 23 February whilst I was still there, on the mend but still undergoing treatment. That afternoon I was visiting Jane when the contractions started. I rushed to tell the Sister but she insisted that it would be hours before anything happened – but we knew better as Jane does not hang around when it comes to having babies! She never even got as far as the labour ward as Karen was born in the waiting room with me in attendance. When Jane was discharged we were driven back home with me on indefinite convalescent leave. Hilary and Marcus came home the following day.

I felt terrible, not least because, by my absence, I had let down the JOC who had to divert an officer to take over my duties at a very busy time. Jane was also feeling pretty ghastly, post-natal, and, although she did not realize it at the time, she had suffered a prolapse. To help us cope with the three children, we employed an Indian baby *ayah* who was pretty useless but, at least, was able to take the children off our hands whilst we prepared for the journey home. Our difficulties were compounded by our having to despatch the car for shipment to the UK. In the end we could not wait to be on our way; I do not think we would have been so keen had we known of the miseries yet to come.

Our journey began on 6 April when we flew from KL to Paya Leba (Singapore's civil airport) in a Dakota of Malair, the forerunner of Malaysian Airways. We were then driven to the RAF's transit camp at Changi Creek where we met up with Frank and Eileen Forster, our friends from Cambridge. Frank was on his way to take over as training officer of the Hong Kong Squadron of MAAF; what a small world! On 8 April we were called at the ungodly hour of 2.30am for our flight from Changi to Bangkok by an Eagle Airways Hermes IV aircraft, a civil variant of the RAF's Hastings. Having had a sort of breakfast at Changi we were offered another one, five hours later at Bangkok whilst the aircraft was refuelled, a process which seemed to take hours while we waited in a crummy apology for an airport lounge.

We then flew on to Calcutta where we had another long wait whilst technicians worked on the aircraft. Apparently the air conditioning was not working and could not be fixed. The new crew, or at least the captain, decided to press on to Karachi where there were better servicing facilities, a decision no doubt due to the fact that Air Ministry charter contracts always go to the lowest tender and therefore profit margins are very small. No air conditioning meant that we would have to fly below 10,000 feet across the Indo-Gangetic Plain in the heat of the early afternoon.

Needless to say, the turbulence for all of the six-and-a-half-hour flight was unbelievable. The aircraft was shaken almost to bits and, before long, very nearly every passenger was suffering from chronic air sickness. The cabin staff did their best to cope but they also succumbed eventually. After a couple of hours the floor of the cabin was awash with vomit and discarded sick bags. Being accustomed to the 'g' forces of aerobatics I was one of the few passengers to be unaffected, although the stench was absolutely revolting. Jane and I took it in turn to hold Karen upright but Hilary and Marcus had to look after themselves. They were marvellous despite being sick for the first time in their lives; they handled their sick bags very well, unlike most of the other children on board who were sick all over themselves or directly onto the floor. As we approached Karachi, and dusk, the turbulence abated considerably but the damage was already done. Having landed, all the passengers were driven in coaches to Mrs Minnewallah's Guest House where, thank the Lord, there was an overnight *dhobi*.

Next morning a fairly respectable looking and sweet-smelling crowd of passengers boarded the flight to Bahrain which was uneventful. The second leg to Beirut was also quite enjoyable by comparison, not least because of the fascinating landscape below being mountainous areas of desert with isolated villages where, unbelievably, beautiful Persian rugs and carpets are woven. The aircraft was supposed to be turned around quickly for the third leg of the day to Brindisi in southern Italy where we were to night stop. Having taxied out, the captain ran up the engines at the end of the runway – and promptly taxied back in again with an engine problem. We were kept on board whilst the problem was being fixed: it was suffocatingly hot and tempers were becoming somewhat frayed. At last we taxied out again, only to return to the terminal after another engine run. This time we were disembarked but, after the third futile attempt, we were eventually told that we would be spending the night in Beirut.

After what seemed to be hours of waiting around, the Eagle Airways agent told us that there was no hotel accommodation available in Beirut itself but he had arranged for a hotel in the mountains, which was normally closed until Easter, to be opened up but it would take time to get it ready for us. In the meantime, we were to be driven to another hotel on the outskirts of the city for an evening meal. When we got to the Eden Rock Hotel, a super-looking place, Jane was understandably fed up and in tears, the boys did not know whether they were coming or going and I was unable to find anybody in authority who could tell me what exactly was going on – the aircrew had just vanished.

We decided not to leave the coach in the hopes that the boys might be able to get some sleep when the hotel manager came to say that there was one family room available and would the Langers like to have it. We have no idea why we were singled out. It might have been due to the fact that an Army Medical Officer on board, who quite coincidentally had been the one who induced Jane, had put in a good word for us; it might have been because we were the only couple on board with three children and all under three-and-a-half-years-old, or simply that, by luck, I was the senior officer on board. Either way we were delighted, especially when we were led through the hotel onto a covered walkway along the adjoining cliff face to a cavernous suite carved out of the rock. It had two double beds, a lounge area and all the usual facilities, all to a sumptuous standard. Declining an evening meal, we gave Karen her bottle and put the boys to bed before collapsing ourselves. Unfortunately, it was a night to remember for all the wrong reasons. The poor boys, who were dead tired, confused and totally disorientated, both wet their beds, something neither of them had ever done before, so we took them into our bed – which again they wet. The only one to get a good night's sleep was Karen, now aged six weeks, in her carrycot.

The other fifty-odd passengers joined us for breakfast at 6.30am, having had a miserable night in an unheated and damp hotel in the hills. They had had only about five hours sleep when they were called for the coach journey to our hotel. Having been driven to the airport from where, with a new crew, we took off successfully for Brindisi where we had lunch; the final leg of our journey to Stansted took six and a half hours with a landing at 9.00pm local time. After the usual formalities, we were finally put on a coach for London and arrived at my mother's flat in Southfields at 2.30am.

The journey home was a total nightmare lasting from 2.30am on 8 April to 2.30am on the the 11th. It involved well over forty hours flying in the slow, uncomfortable old Hermes, with two night stops but precious little sleep, countless inappropriate meals, many of which we declined and hours and hours of waiting for something to happen. I found out later that it was Eagle Airways' very first return trip to Singapore under their newly-acquired contract and clearly they had yet to develop an efficient organization to cope with the inevitable contingencies.

Jane and I were neither really fit enough to travel under those conditions, especially with three young children, but despite the bed-wetting the boys were beautifully behaved, unlike many of the other, older children on board. However, there was light at the end of the tunnel in that I would soon be back on fighters – and as a Squadron Commander. Unfortunately things did not quite work out as planned.

Chapter 10

Back On Fighters

After two weeks of cramming our pint-sized family into Mater's half-pint flat, I reported to the Air Force Department of the newly formed Ministry of Defence (MoD) to talk to the 'posters' about my next posting. To my horror I was told that I was in a queue to become a squadron commander as the fighter squadrons of the Royal Auxiliary Air Force had been disbanded on 1 January 1956, and that the COs who had served less than a year in post were being given priority. I asked how long I might have to wait and was told that it could be as long as a year. I nearly hit the ceiling.

I berated the squadron leader dealing with my case by telling him that, in February, I had been refused an extension to my tour in the Far East on the grounds that any delay in my return would prejudice my getting a squadron. As a result, we had been required to fly home under atrocious conditions whilst I was convalescing from pneumonia and Jane was then only six weeks removed from childbirth – and with three children under three-and-a-half-years old.

I made such a fuss that I was passed on to the Wing Commander who told me that they were unaware of my reasons for requesting an extension and that, anyway, as I had been instructing on piston-engined aircraft for the last five years, I was required to attend two courses; firstly jet-refresher flying and, secondly, a Hunter conversion course, which together could take up to six months.

When I asked him what I was likely to do in the remaining six months if I had to wait a year, he replied that they had yet to address that problem but that, wherever I was held, it would be on a station where I could continue to fly. That was encouraging but I remained concerned about my future career in that I would be on courses or in supernumerary posts and would miss out on confidential reports upon which my career would depend. I left the 'posters' in no doubt about my opinion of their efficiency.

In the event I was posted onto No. 97 All Weather Jet Refresher Course at the RAF Flying College at Manby near Louth, Lincolnshire, where I flew Meteors Mks7 and 8 and renewed my Green instrument rating. Jane and the children joined me and we lived in part of The Rectory in the village of Withcall, several miles from Louth and even farther from Manby and Strubby airfields from which the course flew.

The Rectory had been redundant for many years and was now occupied by Lieutenant Colonel Field and his wife who ran it as a smallholding, breeding chickens and geese. By pure chance I had met Colonel Field in a pub in Louth and had asked him if he knew of any accommodation that might suit us. Our stay at Withcall was interesting to say the least, although Jane and the children were very isolated. Whilst there, in anticipation of our probable nomadic existence, I bought a farm trailer and had the car modified to tow it. It was to prove a godsend as we would be able to up sticks and move ourselves, and all our worldly goods, wherever fate and the RAF required us to go.

At the end of August I was posted to No. 23 Hunter Conversion Course at RAF Chivenor near Barnstaple where I found to my surprise that the first half of the course was to be flown on Vampires. This was an interim arrangement as the vast majority of students going through the course were newly-qualified pilots and the Vampire was a sensible way to

The author's Mother, who adored young children, was always pleased to babysit. Here she is with Marcus and Karen in 1957.

introduce them to jet flying and to teach them the basic skills of fighter operations before progressing onto the front-line Hunter F1.

The Hunter F1 was the original mark which had now been superseded in squadrons by the F4 with the Rolls Royce Avon 100 engine. It was somewhat underpowered but it had the same wonderful handling characteristics of the later models. It was a revelation to me, being the first aircraft with power-controlled ailerons and tail-plane that I had flown. It was as beautifully balanced as the Spitfire, with the added advantage that a jet engine does not produce a varying slipstream effect with different power settings, unlike a piston-engined aircraft and, therefore, there is no need for constant trim changes.

All the other students were required to attend regular physical training sessions from which I was excused. But, as I was not playing any sport and was now thirty-one-years old, I opted to take part in order to keep fit. I should have known better as, during one such session, the students ganged up on me with a cry of 'Let's get the Boss'. I ended up at the bottom of a heap of bodies and one of the lads got hold of my right leg and pulled. 'Crack' went my knee and the MO later confirmed that the cartilage had been torn and dislodged. On being told that an operation was advisable and that, as a result, I would be off flying for about six months, I asked him to keep quiet about it – and he agreed. Although it was painful, it began to ease with massage and exercises and I was able to continue to fly. The only real problem was that the joint could lock when my leg was in a kneeling position – but, as that posture was reserved for church and at bedtime, I was not too worried.

On completion of the course at the end of December I was posted, supernumerary, to No. 247 'China British' Squadron at RAF Odiham. This time the family did not come with me as Mater, appreciating our peripatetic existence, decided that she would go to the USA to visit my three sisters, thus leaving the flat vacant for us. This worked out very well as I could commute easily from Odiham at weekends. During her stay in Southfields, Jane started taking driving lessons which was a very good move as her having a licence soon became vital, especially after the children started school.

The CO of the Squadron was Squadron Leader R. A. 'Kit' Carson MC AFC who, having been shot down, had evaded capture and become a vital link in one of the escape routes by running a 'safe house', which in fact was a longboat moored in one of the canals in Holland. He was awarded the MC, a strange decoration for an RAF officer, for his work with the Dutch resistance. He was a very jovial fellow who was content to let his A Flight commander, Flight Lieutenant Chris Curtis, run the flying side of the Squadron's activities. Chris was a hunting, shooting and fishing sort of chap who was rather laid back – and it showed. The Squadron was a bit of a shambles and in my time with it I learned more about how not to run a squadron than anything else.

I was attached to B Flight which was commanded by Flight Lieutenant David Craig. David was four years younger than me but he had not joined the RAF until 1951 straight from Oxford University. Although he had been a member of the University Air Squadron he was pretty inexperienced. When I asked Kit why someone so lacking in front-line experience had been posted in as a flight commander he said that the station commander had told him that David had been singled out as someone who was going places in the RAF. Indeed David rocketed through the ranks and eventually ended up not only as Chief of Air Staff but also as the best Chief of the Defence Staff for many years. I met up with him many times during our careers and I always found him most friendly and a really nice man, completely lacking the traits of self-centred ruthlessness which often marks those who strive to reach the top. We still meet occasionally at the RAF Club, of which he is President. He is now Marshal of the RAF Lord Craig of Radley GCB OBE, Chairman of the House of Lords Select Committee for Science and Technology and all-round good egg.

In April I participated in Exercise FABULOUS, the then code name for Fighter Command's quick reaction alert (QRA) operation mounted at RAF Horsham St Faith. The day- and night-fighter squadrons took it in turns to provide twenty-four-hour cover of aircraft to intercept and report back to the Sector Operations Centres those unidentified 'blips' on the radar screens, usually at the extremities of the radar cover over international waters. As a day squadron No. 247 maintained a state of readiness from dawn to dusk – a very long day in the summer. Readiness involved a pair of aircraft parked on the end of the runway, plugged into ATC awaiting the instruction to 'scramble', the aim being to start up and get airborne within thirty seconds. Back-up was provided by two pilots in flying kit at the dispersal who would start up and taxi out to relieve the pair who had been scrambled. Their place at ten-minute readiness was then taken by a pair who had been at one-hour's readiness and the team was completed by a fourth pair who could be on stand-by in the Mess. In the event that the first pair was not scrambled they would be relieved after two hours and everyone would move up one state of readiness.

I was at Horsham for a week but was only scrambled once. The blip turned out to be a Canberra PR aircraft which had been routed to the edge of the radar cover to exercise the system. I had hoped it would turn out to be a Russian bomber, either a 'Badger' or a 'Beagle', the NATO codenames, which quite legitimately would fly into our radar cover to test our reaction. I hope they were impressed. Incidentally, FABULOUS aircraft were fully armed and, theoretically, could be ordered to shoot down a potentially hostile intruder into our airspace.

Halfway through the Hunter conversion course at Chivenor I had started ringing the 'posters' at MoD to find out whether there was any news of my posting. I continued to do so every two or three weeks with the deliberate intention of making a nuisance of myself. Perhaps because of this, in March, I was told that I had been selected to attend No. 38 Day Fighter Leader Course at RAF West Raynham. I kept quiet about the fact that I had already completed a DFLS course in 1949, albeit one flying Spitfires and Meteors. I believe that I am the only RAF pilot to have done the course twice.

I duly reported to the Central Fighter Establishment at the end of April. What a difference to the first course when I was the youngest and most inexperienced pilot who had to work jolly hard to keep up with the others. This time I was the senior RAF pilot with a wealth of experience and I found the course a bit of a doddle. We flew the Hunter F6 which was powered by the more powerful Rolls Royce Avon 200, which gave it much improved performance without prejudicing the beautiful handling qualities. And then, in May, my cup runneth over when I was told officially that I was to report to RAF Leuchars, near St Andrews in Scotland, after fourteen days' leave at the end of the DFLS course, to take command of No. 43 (F) Squadron, the 'Fighting Cocks'. I could not believe my luck; I may have been kept waiting for fourteen months since returning from the Far East but to end up with one of the most famous squadrons was certainly worth the wait.

* * *

When I arrived at Leuchars to take over the Squadron I was looked after by the incumbent CO, Major Ray O. Roberts USAF, who had been in command for the last two years on an exchange posting. He drove me around, introduced me to everyone and briefed me on how he had run the squadron and on the calibre of all the pilots. At the end of the week he handed me over to the tender mercies of the senior flight commander, Flight Lieutenant Peter Bairsto.

The author, now commanding No. 43 Squadron, the famous 'Fighting Cocks', briefing two of his pilots.

Peter was a little younger than I but had had a chequered flying career to date. He had joined the Royal Navy to train as a pilot in the Fleet Air Arm. He was within a few weeks of being awarded his 'wings' when peace broke out in 1945 whereupon the RN abruptly suspended all aircrew training. Peter, along with many of his contemporaries, immediately applied to join the RAF but was told that there were no vacancies. However, they were advised that if they enlisted in the RAF Regiment they would stand a good chance of re-mustering to pilot in about two years. Peter and a few others did so and were eventually commissioned. They must have been a very keen and talented lot as many of them, notably Air Chief Marshal Sir Peter Terry, achieved air rank.

Peter Bairsto was a very ambitious man, trying desperately to make up for lost time with which aim I was sympathetic. He was a very good pilot who led the squadron's aerobatic team, the 'Fighting Cocks', but he had a very different approach to mine on personnel management. He preferred to rule with a rod of iron, was a martinet on matters of performance and discipline and as a result was not the most popular of men. He also left me in no doubt that it was really he who had run the squadron for the last two years. He had even taken it upon himself to guide the 'officer qualities' of the squadron pilots, not only by strict observance of the customs of the service but also those of their wives by forming a Squadron

Wives' Club, run by his wife Kathie, which met twice a month so they could be taught bridge, flower arranging and the finer points of etiquette such as the leaving of cards, the wearing of hats and gloves, etc.

I am afraid it was very necessary for me to be very firm with Peter to show exactly who was 'Boss Cock'. He disapproved of my style of leadership and was appalled when Jane disbanded the wives' club, much to the relief of the young wives, many of whom had babies and toddlers and had great difficulty in finding and paying babysitters.

It should be the ambition of every red-blooded young pilot to command a fighter squadron, albeit it is a most demanding job and can be a make or break experience – as indeed I was to find out. I had been extraordinarily lucky to have been given No. 43 (F) Squadron, not least because of its glorious history in two world wars. In the First World War, equipped with Sopwith 1½ Strutters and later with Camels, it had the only two RFC pilots to have each shot down six German aircraft in one day. In the Second World War, equipped with Hawker Hurricanes, it had covered the Dunkirk evacuation by attacking the bases from which the Luftwaffe was operating. It then played a prominent role in the Battle of Britain and was credited, appropriately, with forty-three victories and many more 'possibles'. It went on to serve with distinction in the Desert Air Force, flying Spitfires, before covering the landings in Sicily, Anzio and Salerno. Thereafter, it concentrated on fighter-bomber operations in the Italian peninsula until the end of the war. It was briefly disbanded after the war but was re-formed at RAF Tangmere in 1949 with Gloster Meteors. In August 1954 No. 43 (F) was the first squadron to be equipped with the Hawker Hunter.

In the mid-1950s the Services were going through a bad patch in that the Treasury was pressing for cuts in the defence budget, despite the lessons of the Korean War, and the Defence Secretary was actively promoting the idea that it was only a matter of time before missiles would completely replace manned aircraft in both offence and defence. Needless to say, faced with the inevitability of severe cuts and reduction in career prospects, morale was pretty low.

When I took over the Squadron it had an establishment of twenty-two Hunters plus one Meteor 7 and one Vampire T11 and a complement of twenty-eight pilots. The other Hunter squadron at Leuchars, No. 222, commanded by Squadron Leader Jed Gray, had similar numbers. By the end of the year our worst fears had been realized in that No. 222 Squadron had been disbanded and we had been reduced to sixteen Hunters, one Meteor and twenty-one pilots. The two Leuchars-based Javelin squadrons, Nos. 29 and 151, the night-fighters, had also suffered similar cuts.

I had the onerous task of nominating those of my pilots 'with whom I would not want to go to war' in the words of the Fighter Command directive. Luckily at that time British airlines were expanding and were eager to recruit ex-RAF pilots. So, as an incentive to get pilots to leave, the RAF offered not only generous gratuities, but also financial assistance to help qualification for commercial and airline pilots' licences. As a result we lost more good pilots, who were rightly worried about their career prospects, than the less able ones. And, of course, those who went civilian were soon earning a darned sight more than me.

I must now digress slightly. Whilst I was on the DFLS course I was summoned to see the AOC of No. 13 Group, Air Vice Marshal A. Earle, under whose command RAF Leuchars came. He congratulated me on my forthcoming appointment and then told me that he was very disappointed with the performance of all the squadrons at Leuchars which were failing to meet Fighter Command's requirements, particularly in aircraft utilization but also in other areas. 'Tubby', as he was known affectionately throughout the RAF, told me that my principal task was to put things right with 43(F) Squadron and that I was to report my views to him on the reasons for past failures. I was rather worried about this latter task as it sounded a bit sneaky.

When I got to Leuchars I found out that the main runway had just been closed to permit resurfacing and that the Javelin squadrons had been detached to RAF Turnhouse (now Edinburgh Airport) as they could not operate off the shorter secondary runway, as could the Hunters. This work had been postponed until after Her Majesty The Queen had presented No. 43 (F) Squadron with a new standard. So once again I had missed out on another significant Royal occasion by a matter of a few weeks.

Thus I was able to report to the AOC that the performance of the squadrons in the immediate past had doubtless been caused by the preparations for the Royal visit and by the limitations on operations off the short runway because the ground controlled approach (GCA) radar was only lined up on the main runway and because crosswinds outside the Hunter limits were prevalent. But, of course, these reasons did not excuse earlier failures.

It soon became clear that the problems at Leuchars were largely due to the way the station was run. Group Captain D. F. Beardon, who was known as 'Cubey' because of his stocky build, had had no fighter experience and was more concerned with the smooth administration of the station than with its flying operations. He seemed to be stuck in the pre-war era. For example, he carried out a Station Commander's inspection every week, taking turns to inspect the Flying, Technical and Administrative Wings. When it was Flying Wing's turn, the squadrons had to stop flying by midday on Friday so that the aircraft could be washed and polished. He would be driven to the squadron in his staff car preceded by a bugler who would sound a fanfare to announce the imminent arrival of the great man. He would then inspect the line-up of aircraft, in front of which the pilots would be standing to attention in their 'best blues'. Then he would proceed to the crew rooms, the offices and the hangar, closely followed by the Adjutant with open note-book to record the Station Commander's dissatisfactions. Woe betide the squadron commander if any aircraft was dripping oil onto the tarmac, if the pilots' shoes did not shine brilliantly, if the floors were not washed and polished and if his white gloves detected any dust on a shelf or atop a door. Cubey was regarded as a bit of a joke; indeed it was quipped that if he was ever awarded an honour, which God forbid, it would have to be the QBE. However, the charade of these unnecessary and tedious inspections lost the squadrons at least one full day's flying every three weeks.

One day I was about to walk out to lead a formation of four aircraft on a high-level tactical exercise when the PA rang to say that the Station Commander wanted to see me. I asked the PA to say that I was about to go flying and could it wait until after I had landed? He rang back to say that I was to report at once. I then asked if I could go in flying kit as I hoped to get in the sortie before flying ceased and was told that I was to be properly dressed. I duly changed, which takes a long time, especially when wearing a survival wet-suit, and reported to the adjutant's office where I was kept waiting for twenty minutes.

When the Station Commander deigned to call me in it was to discuss a confidential report I had written on one of my technical SNCOs who was applying for a commission, an important matter which took all of ten minutes and was of no urgency whatsoever. I felt obliged to tell Cubey that I had to cancel a four-aircraft sortie, which had taken a long time to prepare and brief and, as a result, we had lost four hours' flying. He replied that I was in danger of being insubordinate.

About a month later the same thing happened again. This time I was due to fly No. 2 to one of our newer pilots in order to check his ability to lead a formation of four aircraft in the ground-attack role. He had completed his briefing and we were doing our pre-flight checks at the aircraft when my adjutant rushed out to tell me that the CO wanted to see me. I was darned if I was going to abandon this sortie as well, so I told the adjutant to say that I had already taken off. Having landed I was told I had to report immediately; when I did I found that Cubey had checked my time of take-off with ATC so he knew that I had disregarded his request – and was furious. He told me that I was under review and that if I stepped out of line again I would be posted.

Unfortunately, matters went from bad to worse at an Officers' Mess Meeting, which the Station Commander attended. I told the President of the Mess Committee that if we were to meet Fighter Command's targets it was necessary for the squadrons to fly over the lunch hour and asked if a room could be set aside in the Mess for aircrew to have lunch in their flying suits – as indeed was the practice at most fighter stations. The Station Commander intervened to say that under no conditions would he permit such a thing. So I then asked if the lunch hour could be extended from the present one hour to two in order to give us more flexibility. I explained that under present arrangements many pilots were unable to have a hot lunch and had to make do with packets of crisps and chocolate biscuits which we provided out of squadron funds. Once again I was refused and was told by the Station Commander that my proposals would lower standards unacceptably.

In early November the OC Flying, Wing Commander George Mason, told me that the Station Commander had been asking him about my abilities as a squadron commander and pilot and had seemed annoyed when he was told that I was doing a good job and was an above-average pilot in all respects. George said he believed that the CO was looking for reasons to have me removed from post as 'being unsuited to hold his present appointment' under the terms of the RAF Manual of Administration.

Towards the end of November the PA rang to say that the AOC wanted to see me at his HQ and that the Station Commander would fly me there in the Station's Anson: I was very apprehensive for both reasons. When we arrived the PSO showed Group Captain Beardon into the AOC's office. After about an hour Cubey stomped out, looking very unhappy and snarling that I was to go in. I swallowed hard and feared the worst.

However, as soon as I entered I knew that everything was alright. The AOC was beaming all over his rather chubby face, shook me warmly by the hand, told that he had been following my progress, that I was doing a first-class job and to keep it up. After a brief chat about this and that he sent me in his own staff car to catch up with the Station Commander who had gone ahead to book out with ATC and to do the pre-flight check. At the aircraft he was like a bear with a sore head and did not speak a word to me – merely grunting!

Two weeks later Cubey disappeared from Leuchars in a puff of smoke, unmourned and with no dining-out night or other occasion to mark his departure. Many years later the now Air Marshal Sir Alfred Earle told me that when Cubey was telling him of what he had objected to my doing it merely confirmed his suspicions that the problems at Leuchars lay at the door of the Station Commander. Also, that he realized that I had been trying my best to follow the instructions he had given me before I took command.

Beardon's successor was Group Captain Geoffrey Millington – and what a difference he made. Whereas Cubey had done nothing but obstruct, Millington's approach was simply 'Do you have any problems? What do you want and how can I help?' Morale on the station soared, a room for aircrew lunches was found in the Mess and a 'Greasy Spoon' café was opened in one of the hangars. The main runway was re-opened, the night-fighter squadrons returned from Turnhouse and aircraft utilization improved dramatically. Soon my squadron topped the Fighter Command achievement league table and stayed there for the next eighteen months.

* * *

The year 1958 was a good one for the squadron not least because, in February, we started to re-equip with the Hunter F6 with its uprated Avon 200 engine and changes to a number of the systems. As I had already flown the F6 at DFLS, I gave Peter Bairsto the job of running a short technical conversion course whilst I got on with the admin, which was piling up.

What a difference the F6 made; it significantly reduced the time to climb up to 40,000 feet and dramatically improved the aircraft's performance at altitude. For example, in the F4 it was almost impossible to intercept and take cine-film attacks on an Avro Vulcan bomber above 35,000 feet as it only had to open up its four engines to completely out-pace us. With the F6 successful attacks became a piece of cake.

In March the squadron was 'twinned' with a Royal Danish Air Force Hunter squadron based at Aalborg. The idea was to increase inter-operability and closer liaison with our NATO allied air forces. To get the ball rolling, Flight Lieutenant John Howe, the B Flight Commander whom I had poached from No. 222 Squadron when it was disbanded, and I flew to Aalborg for an overnight stay to discuss how best to implement the scheme. It was agreed that we should exchange a flight from each squadron for a week at a time to integrate and operate with each other. We flew back satisfied but rather worse for wear from our introduction to the dreaded Aquavit schnapps. We resolved to get our own back with single-malt whisky from our local distillery.

Also in March Peter Bairsto was given acting promotion to take command of No. 66 Squadron of Hunters at RAF Acklington. That squadron had languished for too long at the bottom of the Fighter Command achievement league table and the CO had been removed from post. As expected Peter went in like a bull in a china shop, sacking one flight commander and several other pilots. But to his credit he managed to drag the squadron up to the upper reaches of the league table – but it was not a happy squadron.

In May the 'Fighting Cocks' were put on stand-by to reinforce the RAF in Cyprus due to one of the periodic crises in the Near East resulting in the US invading the Lebanon and the UK pledging air support for Jordan should the situation get out of hand. This involved cancelling all leave for the stand-by period of three months and the preparation of an air-transportable pack of equipment and spares to enable the squadron to operate from Cyprus for up to three months. Cyprus had only one fighter squadron based there permanently, No. 208 Hunter Squadron, which Peter's 66 Squadron had already been sent out to augment. We would go only if a third squadron was deemed necessary.

Being on stand-by did not prevent us from normal training, and from taking part in Fighter Command exercises. I even managed to talk HQ 13 Group into letting us hold an armament practice camp at Leuchars in order that we would hone our air-firing skills and practise our armourers in case we became involved in dog-fighting should the situation in the Near East become nasty.

The camp was run by our newly-arrived qualified weapons instructor (QWI), Flight Lieutenant Bob Shields, a welcome addition to the squadron who did much to improve our scores. Another welcome addition in June was none other than Pilot Officer Sulaiman bin Sujak who, having graduated from the RAF College at Cranwell, had asked to be posted to the squadron knowing that I was the CO.

The squadron was due to stand down on 15 July when No. 74 (Tiger) Squadron was to take over the stand-by commitment. Two days earlier I was rung by an agitated staff officer from Fighter Command who asked if we could fly out to Cyprus on the 16th. Apparently the CO of No. 74 Squadron had made a horlicks

The painting of the author's personalized Hunter 'G', for George, flying over Leuchars; painted by Flt Lt Chris Golds, one of the Squadron's pilots.

of preparing to take over the stand-by. They only had six serviceable aircraft and had not prepared the equipment and spares and they could not be ready for at least a week. There was, it seemed, some urgency to send out a second UK-based squadron. Without a second thought I replied 'of course', despite realizing that by the time we got back nobody would have had any leave for about six months. I called everybody together and told them the news amidst loud cheering.

Much feverish activity followed, not least by Warrant Officer Simpson, the Squadron's engineer officer, and his merry men, who worked late into the night to prepare the ten aircraft for the flight to Cyprus but also to load the support Varsity with the necessary equipment and spares. We were really supposed to take twelve aircraft but the Air Board, in their wisdom, decided that we should leave two pilots with formation aerobatic experience and two Hunters behind so that Squadron Leader Roger Topp, the CO of No. 111 Squadron and leader of the Black Arrows, could train for and pull off the feat of looping twenty-two Hunter aircraft in order to beat the current record of sixteen aircraft by a team from the Pakistani Air Force. What some people will do to get into the Guinness Book of Records!

* * *

We were all ready to go in the early morning of 16 July but were informed by HQ Fighter Command that the *Mistral* was blowing up a gale in the Marseilles area and that the crosswind on the single runway at Orange Caritat, our second refuelling stop, was well outside Hunter limits. They stood us down until noon, which would still allow us to get to Malta, where we were due to night-stop, in daylight. At noon they told us that the winds had not abated but were expected to do so overnight.

As there appeared to be some urgency for our arrival in Cyprus I reviewed our flight plan and found that if we changed our 100-gallon drop tanks for 200s we could cut out the planned refuelling stops at Duxford and El Adem and get to Cyprus in one day. This would involve three legs of approximately two hours each: unfortunately six hours flying in one day was well above the limits laid down by HQFC. Jack Frost, who had recently taken over as OC Flying Wing, was reluctant to sanction my plan but the Station Commander, Geoffrey Millington, overruled him as his belief was that the limits did not apply to transit flights.

We took off next morning in three formations, John Howe and 'Bodger' Edwards, the A and B Flight commanders, each leading in a vic of three aircraft with me leading a box formation of four. We flew southwards in loose battle formation, reaching the English Channel after fifty minutes – and then the trouble started!

Unbeknown to us, French air traffic controllers had that morning gone on a 'go slow' strike which included refusing to speak English. When I called the Paris regional Air Traffic Control Centre they replied in a barrage of rapid French. I more or less got the gist of their message but I was damned if I was going to attempt to pass ATC messages in schoolboy French: it was much too dangerous. So I responded along the following lines 'This is the leader of a RAFAIR formation of ten fighter aircraft en route to Orange Caritat flying at angels 310 in accordance with our flight plan. We are about to cross the French coast over Cherbourg Peninsula. I shall continue to speak in the universally agreed ICAO ATC language which is English.' The response was 'D'accord: Bonjour Monsieur 'Rosbif; Bon Voyage.'

When I called ATC at Orange I was answered in English by an RAF sergeant air traffic assistant whom the Air Attaché in Paris had flown down in case we needed any help: very sensible. We landed as three separate formations. I was first to land and found that, whereas the French Air Force had swept the runway, the taxiways were still covered with sand, small stones and other debris blown across the airfield by the *Mistral*. I called the others to warn them and told them to maintain at least a fifty-yard separation between aircraft taxiing to dispersal in order to reduce the risk of 'foreign object digestion' (FOD) and damage to the engines from debris blown up by the exhausts.

The trip to Malta was uneventful and we refuelled and had lunch as planned. Before we left on our final leg I briefed the pilots on my intention to arrive in Cyprus in some style with a fly-past in close formation over the airfield of RAF Nicosia followed by an impeccable run in and break with two-second intervals between our ten aircraft. This was asking a bit much after six hours flying but the boys were all for it.

It was just beginning to get dark as we let down over the Mediterranean about ten miles west of Cyprus and headed towards Nicosia. I requested permission to do a fly-past, which was granted, so the pilots closed up into a tight formation and we then flew along the main runway at 500 feet before reforming into three sections in echelon starboard for the run-in and break. As I taxied into dispersal I was feeling very proud of my pilots – but they do say that pride goes before a fall!

As I clambered down to the ground I was expecting some sort of welcome and even congratulations on having flown to Cyprus in one day, the only fighter squadron ever to have done so, and from Scotland to boot. Instead I was confronted by a grumpy-looking Group Captain who said 'I am the Station Commander and I've had you fighter boys up to here (making the appropriate gesture) and, if I have any trouble from your lot, you'll be on the next aircraft back to England', with which encouraging welcome he turned on his heels and walked away.

He was Group Captain Bill Tacon, an Australian in the RAF, whose background was mainly in the transport role and who, as a wing commander, had been the senior pilot of The Queen's Flight. He stood about 5-feet 4-inches tall in his highly-polished shoes and had the aggressive approach not uncommon in Australians and small men. As I found out later he was not the most popular of COs and obviously resented the fact that his station had been invaded by the many RAF units that had been detached to the Near East at this time of political turmoil in the region.

I was, however, given a somewhat warmer welcome by my old friend, Peter Bairsto, who had arranged for a camp bed to be put into his room in the Officers' Mess. My pilots were not so lucky, as they all ended up sleeping on camp beds or mattresses on the floor of the squash court. Nothing had been done for their arrival as the Wing Commander Admin had assumed that we would not be there until the following day, despite HQFC having signalled to say that we were intending to fly out in one day. Luckily, there was sufficient accommodation available for my technical NCOs and airmen.

The following day, having settled the squadron into its dispersal accommodation, I reported to the station's operations centre where I met the Wing Commander Flying, 'Polly' Parrott, who had been CO of the squadron in Italy for five months before being shot down in March 1944. He was good news: at least he knew all about fighter operations. Polly explained that there were two unrelated reasons for the current political tensions in the Near East. The first was that the US marines had gone into Lebanon in an attempt to stop Palestinian terrorist groups from mounting attacks on Israel from their camps in the south of the country. This was of no direct concern to us, but it had contributed to the growing anti-western attitudes of the Arab peoples.

The second reason was that our staunchest political ally in the region, King Hussein of Jordan, was under severe threat, both internally and from the hostility of Iraq, Syria and Egypt. As a result the UK had a commitment to come to his aid, if required. Hussein (Harrow and Sandhurst and very pro-British) had narrowly escaped being killed when his grandfather, King Abdullah, had been assassinated in Jerusalem in July 1951. Since then there had been many conspiracies in Jordan culminating in the assassination of Hussein's cousin, King Faisal, in Baghdad in

July 1958. Following that event the British Prime Minister, Harold MacMillan, had reacted swiftly by sending 16 Parachute Brigade to Jordan to bolster Hussein against the possibility of a coup d'état. Coincidentally, I learned that the CO of the air element of that British contingent was a former colleague of mine, Squadron Leader Jock Dalgleish – of whom more later. It was the assassination of King Faisal which had also triggered the short-notice deployment of our squadron to Cyprus in case political matters further deteriorated.

Wing Commander Parrott went on to say that there was a third political problem which would be of no operational interest to us but would affect what we could and could not do whilst based at Nicosia. That problem was that the EOKA campaign for the independence of Cyprus from the British mandate to govern had turned to violence. It was being led by a Greek Cypriot renegade, Colonel Grivas, who was initiating increasingly frequent attacks against British interests, especially military bases and servicemen. These attacks were becoming more severe and, as a result, all servicemen were now confined to their bases and only essential road movements between units could be authorized – and then only when accompanied by an armed escort.

The three fighter squadrons based at Nicosia were required to maintain pilots and aircraft in a state of readiness to react swiftly should the need arise. They were also tasked to fly standing patrols in certain areas to detect hostile aircraft flying at low level below our rather limited radar cover. Any other serviceable aircraft could be used for routine squadron continuation training at the CO's discretion. When we had been joined by the two pilots and aircraft left in UK to take part in Roger Topp's twenty-two aircraft loop, I had my full quota of twenty-one pilots and twelve aircraft. The pilots now included an American officer on an exchange posting, namely Captain Al Wegman USAF, who was a qualified test pilot and a certified aircraft engineer: a very useful addition. The squadrons were required to maintain readiness from dawn to dusk; a fourteen-hour day so, unlike the other squadrons, I worked a two-shift system with A Flight doing the morning shift and B doing the afternoon one with an hour overlap: the next day this would be reversed whilst I floated between the two, usually from 8.00am to 6.00pm. This system gave the boys plenty of time to play sport, mainly squash and tennis, and to swim in the station pool. Unfortunately, the curfew meant that we had no opportunity to explore the beautiful beaches, the Troodos mountains or the many historic sites.

I cannot speak too highly of the sterling efforts of my technicians and groundcrew, who also worked a two-shift system supervised by Al Wegman and Warrant Officer Simpson. It was quite usual for them to have nine out of twelve aircraft on the line every day; very often we had more serviceable aircraft than the two other squadrons put together. In fact, because of the extended flying day and the glorious late summer weather, we were flying more hours than we would have done at Leuchars.

By mid-August the political situation seemed to have quietened down so we were taken off permanent readiness, fewer standing patrols were considered necessary and the squadrons took it in turn to have the odd day off. I persuaded Polly Parrott to authorize the occasional visit to Kyrenia on the north coast of Cyprus so that we could carry out dinghy drill in the sea. This still required an armed escort but that was no problem as the RAF Regiment, who would provide the escort, were as keen as ourselves to visit what is, debatably, one of Cyprus' best beauty spots and a welcome change from dusty old Nicosia in the summer.

Although we took a couple of dinghies and several 'Mae Wests' with us, we did little survival training. A typical day there would be for us to swim from 'The Slab', the sea wall at the base of Kyrenia Castle, then to retire for lunch at the Harbour Club which was run by a former Shakespearean actor and his wife. The walls of the club were hung with photographs of thespians, including many of Judy Campbell most famous for her singing of 'A Nightingale Sang in Berkeley Square' in a West End theatre revue in the 1940s. Because of her likeness to the photos, I assumed that our hostess was Judy Campbell but about fifty years later when I met the real Judy Campbell, in a revue at the Jermyn Street Theatre, she told me that it was her sister.

After lunch, usually of steak tartare and many cold beers, we would descend into Clito's Wine Cellars where we would taste all of his local wines before deciding of which two we should buy casks, one for us pilots and one for the ground crew. We also took the opportunity to visit St Hilarion, a ruined castle dating from Crusader days which was being beautifully and sympathetically partially restored. We also went to Belapais Abbey, where I found a tree grafted to produce oranges, lemons and limes. Our journeys back to Nicosia, in the back of an open 3-ton truck, were usually hilarious events accompanied by much singing of ribald ditties.

Towards the end of August it was decided that it was no longer necessary to maintain three fighter squadrons in Cyprus and we were told that we would be returning to the UK at the end of September. Moreover, the police and security forces seemed to have the EOKA terrorist threat under control and many restrictions were lifted. To celebrate the lifting of the curfew, I arranged a lunch for the squadron pilots at the Hotel Berengaria near the summit of Mount Troodos. At 6,000 feet ASL, the views in all directions were absolutely stunning but what I remember most was my first taste of that famous Greek delicacy, moussaka.

Finally, on 27 September I planned a twelve-aircraft formation flypast over RAF Akrotiri and Nicosia and one over Kyrenia to say goodbye to the Harbour Club. At the last moment one of our Hunters went unserviceable so I had to make do with eleven. On the 30th we began our flight home along the route we should have come out, which included the night stop in Malta.

We found out later that our return may have been somewhat premature as there was another assassination attempt on King Hussein in November. Perhaps lulled into a sense of false security at home and abroad, Hussein decided to visit his mother whom he had not seen for many months as she lived in Switzerland. On 11 November he took off for Geneva, flying a Royal Jordanian Air Force (RJAF) de Havilland Dove, with Jock Dalgleish as his co-pilot. The most direct flight plan involved flying through Syrian airspace which was closed to RJAF aircraft. However, clearance for this special flight had been obtained by the UN Representative in the Middle East. As he approached Syrian airspace, Hussein contacted the Damascus air traffic control centre and was given permission to proceed. When the Dove was well inside their airspace Damascus ATCC ordered the aircraft to land immediately at the capital's airport.

Jock Dalgleish, an experienced fighter pilot, took over control and headed back to Amman at 200mph, flying at tree-top height to evade Syrian radar. Then two MiG-17 fighters appeared and started to swoop on the Dove. Although their speed was more than double that of the Dove, it could out-manoeuvre the MiGs and Jock managed to evade every potential attack by turning inside them before they could align their gun-sights. This harassment continued for about twenty minutes, by which time they were well inside the Jordanian airspace. Hussein, who was only twenty-two-years old at that time and had already survived several assassination attempts, called this incident 'the narrowest escape from death I had ever had'. He learned later that a party of about 200 Jordanian rebels had been gathered together at Damascus airport with the intention of lynching him. Jock, who was by then seconded to the RJAF as a wing commander, was made a Knight of the Holy Sepulchre by the Greek Orthodox Church for protecting 'the Keeper of the Holy Places', one of Hussein's traditional titles.

* * *

The next day we arrived back at Leuchars where it seemed that our landing was being watched by the whole station. As I taxied into dispersal I caught a glimpse of our three children being looked after by Sulaiman, who had come back in a Varsity with the advance party. I could not see Jane because she had been taken up into the control tower to get a better view of the landings. When eventually we got together I was shocked by her appearance; she had lost weight which she could ill afford, her eyes had dark shadows and her face was drawn. It turned out that whilst we were in Cyprus she had been suffering from a badly prolapsed womb, which was going to require major surgery in the near future. Obviously she had had too many children too close together and far too big for her slender frame. I felt rather guilty not only at having been away for so long but also for having enjoyed myself. I knew that she was having gynae problems but I had no idea that they were so serious.

After two further consultations with Professor Walker at Dundee Royal Infirmary, which I attended, it was decided that she should have the 'op' in the new year, so I took some long outstanding leave and we all went to Torquay where Jane's mother owned a hotel. The plan was to leave Marcus and Karen there until Jane was well enough to look after them again. Hilary was to return with us to Leuchars where he was to be looked after by Maggie Morgan, wife of the Senior Medical Officer. Whilst in Torquay, I received a 'phone call from John Howe congratulating me on having been awarded the Air Force Cross in the New Year's Honours list.

I felt a little bit guilty about that too as the award was really for the achievements of the squadron as a whole. I had been lucky to have been blessed with a team of excellent, eager pilots, and, even more so, with a ground crew team of dedicated, hardworking and extremely competent technicians. Perhaps my major contribution was to have imbued them with enthusiasm to attain high standards whilst 'running a happy ship' – as my Naval friends would say.

In February Jane had extensive surgery and was recovering well when, to our horror, she became pregnant again. Unfortunately, she had had problems with contraceptive devices, so had been recommended to use the 'safe period' method. As we had often joked, after having three children in three and a half years, we had only to share the same bathwater for her to become pregnant. Professor Walker was also most concerned as childbirth so soon would not only wreck his surgery but be dangerous. So he strongly recommended a termination and hysterectomy, which solved all our problems.

My term as squadron commander was due to end in July, so I was determined to make the most of what little time I had left. We managed to cram in two armament practice camps, in March and April. In the first I achieved a 36 per cent hit rate on the target flag, thus putting my young 'hot shots' in their place. In the second I actually managed to shoot down the flag, the first time anyone could remember that happening.

In March our AOC, AVM 'Tubby' Earle was promoted and before he left he asked me to call on him at 13 Group HQ, which I did on 1 April. He told me that he had been watching my career very carefully and had been impressed. He went

The author, in the middle of the front row, handing over to Squadron Leader Scrymgeour, in July 1959.

on to say that he had strongly recommended to the Air Member for Personnel that I should be put on the 'accelerated promotion' list, the so-called 'fast stream'. Needless to say, I felt highly elated but secretly hoped that I was not being made an April Fool. Tubby went on to great things, ending his career as Deputy Chief of the Defence Staff in the rank of Air Chief Marshal.

In May I was given a very unusual task. The Shah of Persia/Iran was about to pay an official visit to Great Britain. Iran was the most pro-western of all the Middle Eastern countries and was, of course, vital to us because of our reliance on the Anglo-Iranian Oil Company for the bulk of our supplies. As a reigning monarch, the Shah was to be accorded an eight-aircraft escort and my squadron was given the job of providing it. I was briefed to take station on the royal aircraft as it climbed after take-off from Orly (Paris) Airport and to escort it until it began its descent into Heathrow (London). With a little help from Paris radar, I spotted the aircraft in just the right position for us to swoop on it and take station with military precision, thanks to the Hunter's marvellous airbrakes. We formed a Vic on the aircraft with my four aircraft in echelon starboard and John Howe's to port. And there we stayed for about twenty minutes before the aircraft started its descent when we signed off with a pre-planned aerobatic flourish.

Several weeks later I received a small packet in which was a letter from Sir Martin Charteris of our Royal Household saying that His Imperial Majesty the Shah of Iran was graciously pleased to appoint me to the Order of Hamayoun (4th Class). And there, in the satin-lined presentation box, was a magnificent solid-silver medal in the shape of a star with the central figure in enamel of a lion waving a sword above its head. It was accompanied by a length of the medal ribbon which was a rather garish green and orange. I later discovered that the fourth class was, more or less, equivalent to the British OBE.

My last adventure of note was a detachment to Denmark to visit our twinned RDAF Hunter squadron for NATO interoperability training. I took eight aircraft to their new base at Skrydstrup and my Danish opposite number took the same number to Leuchars. We each took part in exercises run by the other's control centres and it all worked out very well.

It had been arranged that we would spend the weekend in Copenhagen and the RDAF had booked us accommodation in the university campus. We spent most of the time sightseeing, not least at the Little Mermaid, but on Saturday evening we met up with some of our opposite numbers in the Tivoli Gardens – and drink was taken. On our way back to our rooms John Howe and I came upon a huge statue of a bull on top of an enormous plinth and we decided that we should climb onto its back – because it was there! A few Danes gathered and cheered us on: luckily no policemen appeared. I wonder how a couple of Danish air force officers would have fared if they had tried to surmount one of the lions in Trafalgar Square as Big Ben chimed the midnight hour.

My two years as 'Boss Cock' of No. 43 (F) Squadron was about to come to an end in July: my very last flight was to take part in a Fighter Command exercise with Sulaiman as my No. 2. Those two years had been the most enjoyable and rewarding of my career to date and I doubted whether I would ever again find such satisfaction in any appointment: luckily I was to be proved wrong.

The year 1959 had been very kind to me and was crowned by my promotion to Wing Commander after only four and a half years as a Squadron Leader. Thank you, Tubby!

The author, with Jane and eldest son Hilary, who was just old enough to be allowed to attend the Investiture at Buckingham Palace when Her Majesty the Queen presented his father with the Air Force Cross (AFC).

Chapter 11

In the Doldrums

As pleased as I was to have been promoted I was not too keen on my new appointment as the first Wing Commander, OC Cadet Wing of the RAF Technical College at Henlow in Bedfordshire. Henlow was an old 1920s station with a small grass airfield. Since the end of the Second World War it had become the centre of excellence for most of the RAF's engineering training.

Before the war the RAF was run almost entirely by General Duties Pilots. All those with permanent commissions were required to specialize after several years of squadron flying, in one of the four disciplines of engineering, signals, navigation and armaments. However, the Second World War had resulted in tremendous advances in the complexities of aircraft, airframes, engines, signals, including radar, and weapons systems. It therefore became necessary to form an Engineering Branch of dedicated technical officers. Initially the new branch was composed of mechanical engineers, known as 'plumbers' and electrical engineers known as 'fairies' (derived from fairy lights – I hasten to add).

During the war engineers were recruited mostly from industry, universities and technical colleges and from the ranks of former RAF aircraft apprentices. After the war it was decided that there should be an engineering equivalent of the college at RAF Cranwell which ran three-year courses to produce young pilots with permanent commissions. That equivalent was the Cadet Wing of the RAF Technical College, now in its fifth year of running three-year courses for direct entrants and one-year courses for university graduates with engineering degrees.

When I arrived at Henlow I was briefed by Group Captain Richard Brousson, the deputy commandant, who told me about Cadet Wing and explained that when he first arrived he realized that there was a very important element of cadet training missing, that of officer and leadership training. He went on to explain that the Education Branch officers of the instructional staff tended to treat the cadets like sixth-form schoolboys, whilst those of the Engineering Branch treated them like apprentices. He had therefore campaigned for an aircrew Wing Commander, with operational experience and the necessary qualities, to take on the job of officer training.

I next met the Commandant, Air Commodore Norman Rutter, a small and rather pompous person with almost no sense of humour – as I was to find out! Amongst other things, he told me that the long-term aim was for the Cadet Wing to merge with Cranwell. When I asked why, if that was so, was a new Cadet Mess about to be built at Henlow? He replied 'because it may never happen.' Funny!

My own staff consisted of two squadron leader pilots, one flight lieutenant navigator and another flight lieutenant who was the adjutant. The first three were the 'housemasters' who looked after the one hundred or so cadets on a day-to-day basis on matters of discipline, drill and initiative training by running escape and evasion exercises while camped under canvas in the Welsh Mountains. They also supervised cadet sport. This was a good start but a far cry from the sort of training I had in mind, such as personnel management, Air Force Law and Administration, leadership, command and control, etc.

I firmly believe in leadership training by example. Most of the cadets were aged around seventeen or eighteen years, a very impressionable time of their lives when they are susceptible to seeing their instructors as role models, so I was determined that my own staff should set high standards. I also believed in leading from the front, a trait potentially fraught with disaster. For example, shortly after my arrival the senior course was scheduled for a five-mile cross-country race. I had run many such races when under training myself, without any previous long-distance training, so I decided to take part. I managed to keep up with the leaders for the first couple of miles before the agony started biting.

I developed cramp and a chronic stitch and slowly but surely I was overtaken by the rest of the cadets. However, I was determined to finish so I stumbled on, hoping that not everybody had left the finishing post. To my astonishment everyone was still there to cheer me on and, what's more, I was not last: Cadet Coggins, a rather large and plump young man to whom I was most grateful, finally crossed the line well behind me.

However, I got my own back on the squash court where I was only ever beaten by two cadets, one of whom, Peter Stokes, went on to become the RAF Champion – a title he held for about a decade. But I think I first earned the cadets' real seal of approval when, at my first 'dining-in' night in the Cadets' Mess, I managed to drink a yard of ale successfully without spilling it all over my mess kit or being sick afterwards. A yard of ale is made of glass in the shape of a post-horn with a large bulb on the end. It is three-feet long, hence the name, and holds just over a pint of beer. The secret of success is to tip the yard very slowly, taking care not to break the stream.

The cadets themselves were a mixed bunch from mainly public and grammar schools, plus several who had already completed the three-year apprentice school at RAF Halton and had done so well that they were selected to become technical cadets and, if successful, engineer officers. As a general rule the school boys were academically more gifted; however, the ex-apprentices may not have been quite so bright but they had the advantage of their previous training and were more accustomed to discipline and service life in general.

The one thing they all had in common was prodigious appetites. Jane and I tried to have all the cadets to dinner, at least once, six at a time in our married quarter. We started by serving a meal of, say, prawn cocktail or jellied consommé followed by blanquette de veau and a lemon soufflé or fruit salad, all of which flew off their plates in a thrice. On one occasion I was carving a joint and the vegetables were being passed around: when I had served all six Jane said 'please start before it gets cold' whereupon they all finished before we had even sat down. After that we concentrated on quantity rather than fine dining with such things as minestrone soup, spaghetti Bolognaise and steamed puddings. Sometime later we found out that some cadets had even had high tea before coming for dinner.

One of the events to mark the graduation of our senior course was a dance (I hesitate to call it an end-of-term ball) in the apology for the cadets' mess which was in fact a converted airmen's barrack block. The dance floor was in the dining room and the bar and buffet were in the ante-room. Jane and I were amongst the guests of honour and were seated with the other VIPs.

It soon became clear that the cadets had no idea how to organize and run such an event and, in particular, were hopeless on the dance floor: they merely smooched about with their girlfriends. Jane did her best to entice a few onto the floor, much to the detriment of her feet. I realized that it was necessary to make them aware of their duties as hosts, of the need for escorts to look after the guests and of other aspects of social etiquette. But, most importantly, I arranged for them to have ballroom dancing lessons. This did not go down too well until they found out that I had also arranged that they were to be partnered by sixth-form girls from a nearby convent.

There was one other member of the Cadet Wing Staff whom I have yet to mention, namely the Flight Lieutenant Chief Flying Instructor – an imposing title for our one QFI and his four Chipmunk aircraft. The senior technical cadets, who were

MRAF Sir Thomas Pike, then Chief of the Air Staff, was the Reviewing Officer at the graduation of No. 5 (University) course at RAF Technical College, Henlow, where the author (third from right in front row) was Officer Commanding Cadet Wing as a Wing Commander in July 1960.

medically fit, could volunteer for flying training to private pilot's licence standards, mainly in their free time in the evenings and at weekends. The best of the bunch could compete for the de Havilland Trophy and could also volunteer for flying training to the award of RAF pilot's 'wings' followed by a year on an operational squadron. This meant that those chosen would only get around to practising their engineering and man management skills after five to six years under training of one sort or another. In the case of ex-apprentices this could be as long as eight years.

I was not very impressed by the QFI or by the way in which the flight was being run and I was appalled by the length of time some cadets would take to begin working as engineers. I made several changes within my purview and managed to persuade the Commandant that all cadets should go, immediately on graduation, to engineering appointments and that those really wanting to go onto pilot training should only be able to apply after a minimum of one year in post. This ensured that only the keenest would apply and, as a result, the number applying dropped by more than half.

Luckily my QFI qualification on the Chipmunk was still valid so I could still instruct. I flew with many of the cadets, flew several staff continuation sorties with the QFI, who needed them badly, and carried out all the final handling tests for the de Havilland Trophy. We also had a commitment to give air experience flights to CCF and ATC cadets, in which task I was only too pleased to help out. A further bonus was that there was a RAFVR ATC Gliding School based at Henlow, flying Sedbergh and Cadet III gliders. Needless to say, I managed to wangle a few trips, going solo on the Cadet and managing to stay airborne for eighteen minutes by finding a convenient hot air thermal above the Officers' Mess – well it was lunchtime!

The graduation of Nos. 6 (Henlow) and 8 (University) Courses passed without a hitch, which was just as well as the reviewing officer was MRAF Sir Thomas Pike, the Chief of the Air Staff. We had many high-ranking officers visit Cadet Wing in my time there, not least the one-armed Air Vice Marshal 'Gus' Walker, who refereed our two home games of rugby with the RAF College, Cranwell. The most notable exception was Air Chief Marshal Sir Wallace 'Digger' Kyle who, as AOC-in-C of Technical Training Command, was our ultimate boss. He was invited several times but declined to visit for as long as his son, Richard, was a technical cadet. The AOC-in-C was an Australian who had won a Colonial Cadetship to Cranwell in the 1930s. His grandfather had been a gold digger in Western Australia but, not finding any, he had eked out a living as a grave-digger – so how could Sir Wallace be called anything but 'Digger'. When he retired from the RAF he was appointed Governor General of Western Australia – how appropriate!

After a very enjoyable year or so at Henlow I got a nasty shock. A wing commander from the Air Secretary's Department rang to tell me that I was to attend No. 51 course at the RAF Staff College at Bracknell in January 1961. Apparently the careers of those officers in the 'fast stream' were reviewed from time to time and they had just realized that, despite having passed the qualifying exams several years previously, I had yet to attend the course. The year 1961 was my last chance to do so as I would be older than the upper age limit by the following year. So my time at Henlow was to be a bare eighteen months; a pity as I believed that I was beginning to achieve a few worthwhile results. However, I suppose that, in the interests of my own career, it was time to move on.

The building of the new Cadets' Mess was progressing well and was in the decorating and furnishing stage by December 1960. It was quite exciting for not only was it architecturally pleasing but also it was to be furnished with a brand new range of furniture which, if it found general approval, would be used in all RAF messes. The Commandant, his deputy, Group Captain Kelly, who had taken over from Dick Brousson, and I formed the committee that had the final say on the selection of furniture and all other aspects of the decoration.

One day Air Commodore Rutter and I were in the dining room, which had a very high ceiling, tall narrow windows and a minstrels' gallery, to select the curtain materials and decide where to hang the pictures. We had the usual ones of the Queen and Prince Philip in RAF uniform and several aviation oil paintings which we had scrounged from various sources. The Commandant told me that he was very concerned about the blank spaces which would remain on the upper walls, even after the pictures had been hung. We dismissed the idea of papering over the light-cream emulsion which was in the process of being applied by the painters using mobile scaffolding.

Recently I had admired some reproductions of Leonardo da Vinci's aeronautical drawings which hung in the Commandant's residence. I suggested that a chosen few could be projected onto the walls using an epidiascope mounted on the scaffolding and then, using the projected images as a template, much enlarged reproductions could be painted onto the walls. The Commandant was very taken with this idea, so the job was done and looked not only unique but also very effective and appropriate.

As the date of my leaving approached I was pondering what I could present to the Cadets' Mess to mark my departure. The problem was solved when I was watching the demolition of an old building to make space to build the new Cadets' Mess squash court when I saw a very decrepit long piece of wood which was being placed in a skip. On examination it proved to be a twin-bladed propeller, possibly from a First World War fighter aircraft. Having been stored in the rafters of the building it was covered in decades of dust and cobwebs but seemed to be in good condition So I paid to have it stripped, sanded, stained and French-polished in the workshops. When finished, it looked superb in its laminated glory so I had a battery-operated clock inserted into its central hub aperture and fixed a shiny brass plate detailing by whom presented and the date. The Cadets moved into their new mess about six months after my departure whereupon it was announced that the Cadet Wing was to move to the RAF College at Cranwell in around two years' time. I have often wondered where my lovely propeller clock ended up

I left Henlow with mixed feelings. Jane and I were not sorry to leave the area which we rudely referred to as 'cabbage country' because of the perpetual smell of rotting vegetables. But I had enjoyed working with the cadets who were a lively bunch of boys with great promise: indeed many went on to achieve air rank which is pretty good in the Engineering Branch. The only thing I held against the cadets was that they made me feel old, especially when I found that everyone on No. 7 course had been born after I had joined the RAF.

* * *

I will gloss over the eleven months at the Staff College because it was probably the least enjoyable period of my career. It certainly started badly when, on arrival, I found that we had been allocated a miserable semi-detached type V married quarter. I assumed that all we students had been given similar accommodation but I soon found out that nearly everyone else had been housed in larger detached type III and IV quarters. Squadron Leader Peter Latham had even been allocated two – but then he and Barbara did have eight children!

Something had gone very wrong so I went to see the administrative staff to ask why I had been allocated such an inappropriate quarter despite being the second most senior officer on the course. The Squadron Leader (Admin) tried to flannel by saying that it was all due to the luck of the draw. So I asked to see their nominal roll of the students and found that, due to a typing error, I was down as being a squadron leader but with my seniority as a wing commander, which made it appear that I was one of the most junior officers on the course.

I hit the roof and said that if I was not moved to a type III quarter within the month I would take my complaint to the Commandant. Within a week I was notified that one of the Directing Staff (DS) was vacating his quarter and that, as his successor was going to live in the mess, I could have that house. Thus we ended up next door to our old friends from RAF Leuchars, Jack and Shelagh Frost.

The course itself was a mixture of lectures, exercises, the writing of theses on politico/service subjects, the giving of 'small talks' (twenty minutes on a subject of one's choice), putting on a forty-minute presentation with three other students on a service subject and, of course, masses of syndicate work. I must admit that I found it all rather tedious, perhaps because I am a 'doer' rather than a plodding thinker. And having had my fair share of command I was anxious for more because it was becoming clear that leadership was my forte.

I am not suggesting that I had nothing to learn; I learnt a lot, particularly in the art and craft of service writing which was to stand me in good stead for the rest of my career and beyond. Nor am I saying that there was nothing to enjoy; there was, especially the visits to service units. Perhaps what I most resented was that Staff College was yet another period of marking time in furthering my career – but it was, of course, a necessary evil.

The course ended in December 1961 and in my final interview with the Commandant, Air Vice Marshal Maurice Heath, he congratulated me on having done well and said that he had annotated my course report as my being eminently suited to return as a member of the DS. I thanked him, with my fingers crossed behind my back, and thought to myself 'over my dead body'!

* * *

I was one of the lucky ones in that the vast majority of the course members were posted into staff jobs at various HQs. Not only was I posted to a flying job but it was as the Chief Instructor at the Central Flying School at RAF Little Rissington – a prestigious appointment. Although I was delighted to be going back to flying I was disappointed that it was not onto fighters or at least to an operational rather than a training role. In peacetime, the vast majority of wing commanders have only one flying appointment and very often it is that job which dictates one's subsequent career path. So it was now most likely that postings relating to flying training would be my fate. As it turned out that was probably a blessing in disguise.

As I had been off jet flying for two and a half years I had to attend a jet-refresher flying course at the RAF Flying College at Manby. There I flew Meteors to requalify as a jet QFI and renew my master-green instrument rating. My so-called 'instructor' was Flight Lieutenant Douglas 'Puddy' Catt, reputedly an excellent former fighter pilot who was clearly very bored with Meteors after two tours on Lightnings. His main job was to act as safety pilot for 'refreshers' like myself whilst we practised our instrument flying skills under the dreaded hood in the rear cockpit of the dual Meteor 7. He was also overweight, over-confident and ill-disciplined.

On a number of occasions he took control, ostensibly for safety reasons but really to buzz other aircraft – strictly against the rules. This was very annoying as he would do so, for example, whilst I was attempting to fly the complicated pattern 'B' within the limits necessary to renew my master-green rating. Eventually I read him the riot act and said that I would report him to the OC Flying if he messed me about again. He behaved himself for the next few sorties but on 29 January he could not resist making a quarter attack against another Meteor. As he swooped on the other aircraft he manoeuvred violently, toppling all the gyroscopic instruments and leaving me totally disorientated for the first time in my life. As a result I was unprepared to brace myself as he pulled about six 'g' in the final stages of the attack. Suddenly, I felt a sharp pain in my lower back as if I had been stabbed. I let out a yell, told Catt he was a stupid oaf and ordered him to return to base immediately.

Back in dispersal I suffered the indignity of having to be helped out of the cockpit as the pain was excruciating. When I was examined by the Senior Medical Officer he said that I had, most probably, pulled a muscle which had gone into spasm. He gave me painkillers and muscle-relaxant tablets which improved matters and I was able to complete the course, albeit with much discomfort.

As I was not due to report to CFS until April, I was attached firstly to No. 5 FTS at RAF Oakington to familiarize myself on the Vampire and secondly to No. 3 FTS at RAF Leeming to fly both the piston and Jet Provosts. I managed to cope fairly well but whenever I tried to stop or reduce the number of tablets I was taking the pain became pretty intolerable; so I realized that something was badly wrong.

When I reported to CFS and saw their SMO he arranged an appointment for me with the consultant orthopaedic surgeon at the RAF Hospital at Wroughton who, after examination and x-rays, told me that I had slipped a disc. To cut a long story short, after manipulation, the fitting of an orthopaedic corset and exercises to strengthen my back muscles, I more or less regained reasonable fitness but the damage done was to plague me for the rest of my life. In particular it took all the fun out of flying as I was warned that high levels of 'g', as in aerobatics, should be avoided to prevent recurrence.

When the dust had settled on this most annoying episode, I rang my old friend, Wing Commander 'Knobby' Clark, the OC Flying at Manby, and asked him to let Catt know just what a problem his ill-discipline had caused and requested that he should give him a right rollicking from me. Knobby said that nothing would have given him more pleasure but Catt had recently left the RAF and was now flying Lightnings for the Saudi Air Force at a salary greater than both of ours put together. There ain't no justice!

* * *

When I arrived at CFS in April 1962 the Commandant was Air Commodore 'Pat' Connelly, a delightful Irishman with a very laidback approach to life. His equanimity was put to the test in July when CFS celebrated its fiftieth anniversary as 'the oldest flying training establishment in the world'. Her Majesty Queen Elizabeth The Queen Mother, the Commandant-in-Chief, was the guest of honour at the celebrations. As a result, RAF Little Rissington was to be invaded by a long list of VIPs, including the Lord Lieutenant of Gloucestershire, the AOC-in-C of Flying Training Command and the Minister of State for Air.

The Commandant took the preparations for this grand event in his usual relaxed stride. He calmly delegated all responsibility to others; for example, the Station Commander was responsible for the appearance of the station, his PSO was responsible for all the protocol such as the seating plan for the lunch and the provision of escorts for the VIPs; the PMC and the Mess Manager for the lunch menu and the reception etc., etc. My job as Chief Instructor was to organize a static display, on the sports field in front of the Mess, of as many as possible of the aircraft operated by CFS since its formation in 1912 and to arrange a flypast of a mixed formation of all our seven current aircraft types and displays by our two formation aerobatic teams, the Jet Provost 'Red Pelicans' and the Chipmunk 'Windrushers'.

On the day we were all very relieved that everything had gone extremely well from Her Majesty's arrival up until lunch time. The 'Queen Mum' had clearly enjoyed her day and was in good form as she was introduced to those of us lucky enough to be invited to lunch. The Mess Manager, the excellent Mr Gray, had done a wonderful job and the tables looked magnificent, resplendent with the highly polished CFS silver. The starter and fish courses were delicious but when the main course, chicken cordon bleu, was served disaster struck.

The 'Queen Mum' helped herself to the pepper pot from the condiment 'bandstand' but, alas, the silver top fell off covering her plate with its contents. Without any to do, the Commandant took her plate and replaced it with his own, which was in turn replaced by a passing steward so quickly that very few people noticed but wondered why the Queen Mum suddenly got a fit of the giggles. I met Her Majesty many times in my subsequent career and she always recalled that incident with much mirth.

The 'Windrushers', the formation aerobatic team of the Central Flying School (CFS).

In November 1962 the then station commander, Group Captain Richard de Burgh, with whom I had never got on, was replaced by the newly-promoted Henry Chinnery who was even more laid back than 'Uncle Pat, which made for a very happy station as we wing commanders were allowed to run our own squadrons without any undue interference. Henry Chinnery was an old Etonian, where he had been captain of cricket and squash, and had been Equerry to Prince Philip for two years. He was a bit of a charmer and we got on very well.

This was all to change when Pat Connelly's tour came to an end and Air Commodore H. Bird Wilson CBE DSO DFC and Bar AFC and many foreign decorations took over. 'Birdy' had been a Battle of Britain ace and had had a distinguished career in other theatres of operation and in peacetime appointments – all in the fighter world. He had had no flying training experience whatsoever and his selection to be Commandant of CFS was somewhat unusual.

Although I admired and liked Birdy, I regret that, at first, we did not see eye to eye. This was his first posting as an Air Commodore and he had difficulty in appreciating the role of a commandant and tended to meddle in matters which were, strictly speaking, in the purview of the station commander, on whose station HQ CFS was a lodger unit. This often sent Henry Chinnery up the wall. Nor was I spared his pernickety attentions.

For example, when I had first arrived at CFS I was not best pleased with the condition and appearance of the various pilots' crew-rooms. They were dingy and dirty and festooned with pin ups of well-endowed near-naked ladies. I managed to wangle enough money to buy tins of light pastel emulsion to paint the walls which were of the worst shade of dark brown and green. The squadron commanders were given the job of supervising the work which had to be done by staff and student pilots – out of working hours. At first I was not very popular but eventually, when the work was completed and the naked ladies replaced by aviation pictures, everyone agreed that the job had needed doing.

Her Majesty the Queen Mother, Honorary Commandant in Chief of CFS, arrives at RAF Little Rissington to celebrate the 50th Anniversary festivities, escorted by Air Cdre 'Pat' Connolly.

The work took a couple of months to complete and the pilots had done a pretty good job but, within weeks of Birdy's arrival, he told me that he was dissatisfied with the appearance of the crew-rooms and wanted them all redecorated. Luckily Henry Chinnery knew just how much effort had already been put in and managed to persuade the Commandant that all the crew-rooms really needed was updated 'coffee bars' which he would provide out of station public funds.

On another occasion, during the Friday 'happy hour' in the Officers' Mess, Birdy announced that in future the first aircraft airborne every morning could beat up the airfield. Apparently he had been reading about the history of CFS and noted that, in the 1920s, that had been the practice. The following Monday morning I was surprised to see the instructors and students literally rush to their squadrons when Met Briefing was over. Monday mornings were not normally marked by keenness to get airborne! Ten minutes later I was astonished to see a Chipmunk flying upside down at 200 feet along the main runway. I rang the primary squadron commander and told him to send the miscreant pilot to my office immediately after landing.

An hour later the young Flight Lieutenant Derek St John Homer was standing to attention in front of my desk whilst I gave him a right rollicking about his irresponsible action. I gave him no opportunity to follow up his 'but Sirs' before I dismissed him. The following morning a Jet Provost did the beat up so I rang Peter

Hicks, the squadron commander, to ask when on earth was going on, only to be told that the Commandant had authorized the early morning beat ups.

I was furious that Birdy had done so without consulting me first. Had he done so, I could have told him why it was a bad, yet alone dangerous, idea. The principal reason was that the early-morning sorties were being wasted as the pilots were rushing to their aircraft without doing the pre-flight briefings which were an intrinsic part of every training sortie. Moreover, it encouraged them to skimp the requisite pre-flight aircraft inspections and to taxi across the grass to take off from halfway up the runway – with flight safety implications. When I explained all this to the Commandant, he apologized for not having spoken to me because if he had done so he would not have acted so rashly. At the next Met Briefing I informed everyone that the Commandant had changed his mind about the wisdom of reviving that ancient tradition. From that time onwards Birdy and I got on much better and, whereas he continued to take an interest, he ceased to interfere and left me to run Flying Wing my way.

I must admit that, although I enjoyed the prestige of being the Chief Instructor at CFS, the job itself was not exactly my cup of tea – for several reasons. I had enjoyed all my previous instructing, which I found very rewarding, but teaching already qualified pilots how best to instruct was a different matter. Moreover, I found CFS rather hidebound by tradition and that little had changed for many decades. And although I flew quite often, usually on intermediate and final-handling tests with students and staff continuation training flights with instructors, I never really enjoyed the flying mainly because of the pain in my lower back during high 'g' manoeuvres.

* * *

There were, however, many compensations, not least being the visits to other air forces. In 1963 there were three, the first of which was to the Royal Norwegian Air Force at their basic flying training school at Vaernes near Trondheim to discuss aircrew selection, training syllabi and methods. The RNAF were extremely hospitable and I flew two sorties in their Saab Safir trainer which was a delight, being similar but far superior to our piston Provost which, thankfully, we were about to phase out in favour of all-through jet training.

The second was at the invitation of the German Air Force which was becoming very concerned about the very high accident rate they were suffering in operating the Lockheed F-104 Starfighter aircraft, so high that the aircraft was being referred to as 'the widow-maker'. The GAF wanted an independent survey of their training methods and engineering practices. As Chief Instructor and a former fighter squadron commander, I was to be team leader with Flight Lieutenant Derek Bryant, my Gnat project officer, and an engineering officer from HQ FTC as members.

Before we left for Germany, I contacted the Canadian and Belgian Air Forces who also few the F-104 in the ground-attack role and found that their accident rates were surprisingly low. I also managed to scrounge a flight in an English Electric Lightning aircraft as I had never flown an aircraft capable of going supersonic in straight and level flight: the dear old Hunter could only reach Mach One in a dive. We were made very welcome at the GAF base at Nörvenich, the operational training unit (OTU) for the F-104. They also gave us unrestricted access to the material we requested, such as servicing records and accident reports. Derek and I also flew two sorties each in the Starfighter during which we joined the 'Mach 2 Club', albeit in a steep dive. We both found the aircraft surprisingly easy to fly in the fighter-bomber, low-level penetration role, considering that it was originally designed as a high-level interceptor. Nor did we find any apparent difficulties or potential vices in its operation.

Analyzing the accident reports, we found that the majority had been classified as being due to 'pilot error'. However, we soon discovered that many of them arose from system malfunctions due to servicing inadequacies with which the pilots had been unable to cope. It did not take long for us to establish that the root cause of the problem lay in the recent history of the GAF. After VE Day in May 1945 the Luftwaffe was disbanded and all its air and ground crews were dispersed to civilian life, except those unlucky enough to fall into Russian hands, many of whom were kept in prison camps for several years.

In the 1950s it became clear that the main threat to the Western Alliance was Russian communism and that West Germany, having been absolved of its Nazi past, should be invited to join NATO and be permitted to re-constitute its armed forces. The High Command of the new German Air Force jumped at the chance to prove their worth and started recruiting old Luftwaffe personnel and young volunteers. Pilot training was carried out in America and Canada whilst engineers and technicians were sent on crash courses at various manufacturers.

The High Command then made an understandable but unwise decision to equip its front-line squadrons with the Lockheed F-104, which the Belgian and Canadian air forces were already operating in Europe as fighter-bombers capable of delivering tactical conventional and nuclear weapons. In this they were encouraged by the Americans – always keen to secure substantial aircraft contracts. The GAF would have been better advised to cut its jet teeth on relatively simple but still very effective aircraft like the Hunter or the F-86 Sabre. The F-104 was a step too far for an air force whose only previous jet experience had been for a small cadre of pilots and technicians who had operated the Me262 towards the end of the war. Moreover, the on-board electronics were all 'state of the art' equipment of which the GAF had no knowledge, having lost a decade of experience. To sum up: the GAF senior officers were old and out of date whilst its young men were just too inexperienced. They had no middle ground; no wonder they found it difficult to cope.

Returning from that visit I put together a diplomatic report for HQ FTC to forward to the GAF. I had few recommendations to make about the flying and training aspects; indeed Derek and I were impressed by the organization of flying wing and, in particular, by the calibre and keenness of the pilots. However, our engineer officer did have a number of worthwhile comments and recommendations which I incorporated in the report. In my conclusions I wrote that the only element missing in the operation of the F-104 was experience and that it would only be a matter of time before the accident rate descended to acceptable levels. And so it proved: within two years of the CFS visit the GAF F-104 accident rate was even lower than those of the BAF and the RCAF.

The third visit of 1963 was a major one. The RAF had a longstanding arrangement with the RAAF and RZNAF that their respective CFSs should exchange visits every two years; so this was a once-in-four-years opportunity which I was determined not to miss. The CFS team was to be led by the Commandant with myself and Squadron Leader Stan Pomfret, one of the 'trappers', in support along with Wing Commander Jim Corbishley, my opposite number as CI of the helicopter element of CFS at RAF Ternhill.

On 6 November we flew out from Lyneham to Paya Lebar (Singapore) in an RAF Comet C4 with a night stop at Khormaksar (Aden). The RAF had taken over BOAC's Comets after the disastrous crashes which effectively ended civilian use of the world's first jet airliner. After the Royal Aeronautical Establishment at Farnborough had established that metal fatigue had been the problem and a few essential but fairly minor modifications, the RAF operated the Comet as a transport aircraft for many years without a single accident. Moreover, the basic design was still flying four decades later, in the form of the Nimrod maritime aircraft, an updated version of which was scrapped by the UK government in a cost-cutting exercise that left the UK without an effective airborne maritime reconnaissance and anti-submarine capability. What a wasted commercial opportunity which allowed American civil aircraft to dominate the jet market.

After a day spent in Singapore we continued our journey to Sydney via Darwin in a BOAC Boeing 707, where we spent the night before proceeding to Canberra in an ANA Fokker Friendship. In Canberra we were looked after by the British High Commission, which gave us a guided tour of that, then, rather soulless capital city. The ring of lakes around the centre of the city were being excavated, but we could appreciate the difference they would make when flooded.

On the morning of 12 November we flew to Melbourne where we were met by staff officers from the HQ of the RAAF Flying Training Department, who gave us the itinerary which they had planned for the main party and for Jim who would be independent from us. They stressed that, in our presentations at the various bases, we should concentrate on why we had decided to adopt all-through jet training and our experience to date of so doing. Later that afternoon we boarded a TAA Lockheed Electra for the flight to Perth – a distance equivalent of London to Istanbul.

We arrived in Perth in the early evening of a Friday where we were met by a RAAF corporal driver who to our surprise drove us to a hotel in the city rather than to Pearce Air Force Base, the home of the Advanced Flying Training School. His parting words were 'I will be picking you up at 9.00am on Monday morning and don't be late as the Base Commander is a stickler for punctuality'.

There were no messages waiting for us at the hotel so clearly we were being left to our own devices. Luckily Birdy had an old Australian friend who, after a distinguished career in the RAF ending as an Air Marshal, had retired to the family home in Western Australia. Once contacted, he drove about a hundred miles to pick us up on Saturday morning. He and his wife looked after us marvellously, having arranged a family picnic at a beautiful sandy cove on the west coast before driving us inland to give us a glimpse of the aboriginal desert, taking in a vineyard, where we tasted some remarkably good wines, and many of the local beauty spots and deserted old mining villages.

On Monday morning we were picked up and driven to Pearce where we were greeted by the Adjutant who told us that the 'Boss' was not available but would be back shortly. We were kept waiting for well over an hour. Birdy, being a stickler for protocol, was becoming increasingly agitated, when eventually Group Captain Podger finally turned up in flying kit with the words 'Sorry to have kept you guys waiting but I had the opportunity to fly this morning; a chance I never turn down'. And then, to our astonishment, said 'Now what is it you chaps want?'

Somehow Birdy managed to keep his cool and said that we wanted to follow the programme which he knew had already been sent to Pearce by their HQ. Podger then buzzed for the Adjutant and asked if he had seen anything on the subject, whereupon he was reminded that he had been given the letter the previous week. He then called in the OC Admin Wing and told him to make the necessary arrangements. We were then given a guided tour of the base – by the Adjutant.

Worse was still to come! Eventually we were taken to a conference room in Station HQ where an audience of about twenty awaited our arrival. I soon realized that they were odd personnel who had been press-ganged to attend and that there was not one pilot amongst them. I took OC Admin Wing aside and reminded him that we had been asked to talk to Flying Wing and that unless every pilot who was not flying was rounded up we would have no option but to report the matter to their HQ.

After a further embarrassing wait, a respectable number of instructors and students, mostly in flying kit, were assembled and our presentations went ahead. Birdy did the introductory talk, I spoke on most of the subjects which we had been asked to cover and Stan Pomfret did a short burst on how the RAF went about ensuring that flying standards were maintained, not just at flying training schools but also on operational squadrons. The presentation was reasonably well received, albeit questions were few because we were in danger of missing lunch. We were then escorted to the officers' mess where there was no 'top table' with the station commander – indeed we never saw him again before we left. Instead, we queued with our trays for a rather dreadful cafeteria lunch.

After lunch Birdy, Stan and I split up and went to visit the three squadron crew-rooms. I asked the CO if there was any chance of a sector recce so that I could have a look at the local area from the air. He said 'no problem' and called over one of his flying instructors who was to take me up. Whilst I was putting on flying kit, I saw them talking furtively and laughing and I was just able to hear the CO say 'sort out the Pom good and proper'.

Flight Lieutenant Dunn and I clambered into a de Havilland Vampire T35 and he gave me an excellent recce, showing me Freemantle, the major port of Western Australia, and then flew up the west coast where I was able to show him where we had picnicked on Saturday. He even flew well into the outback where we searched for wild camels but, unfortunately, we did not find any.

Turning back towards Pearce, Dunn told me that he was the aerobatic display pilot for the base and that he would like to show me his sequence. The penny dropped – I was about to be sorted! In the event he put on a pretty good show, even if he kept looking to see how I was taking it. Luckily, I had put on my orthopaedic corset so my back was OK and I am not prone to airsickness.

When he had finished he asked for my opinion. With my tongue in my cheek, I said that the display was quite good and that it was similar to the sort of sequences that I used to do in Spitfires but that it did not take account of the two advantages of the Vampire: firstly that a jet engine does not flame out under negative 'g' as do piston engines and secondly that, because of its compact design, the Vampire had higher 'g' limits. Saying 'let me show you' I went into a short sequence which careered from plus 6- to minus 3-g and included a roll off an outside loop and three turns of an inverted spin, neither of which manoeuvres Dunn had ever attempted before and which left him feeling somewhat the worse for wear. Indeed, after landing he rushed off to the ablutions, his face a delicate shade of yellow. I think Dunn had been well and truly done but when he returned it was with a new air of respect.

Later that afternoon, when we had returned to the Officers' Mess, Birdy came into my room and said that he could hear sounds of some sort of a party getting underway. So, thinking that it might be drinks in our honour, we quickly changed into our smart No. 6 tropical uniforms and went downstairs. We located the noise as coming from the bar where we saw an unbelievable mêlée of RAAF officers, six deep, crammed around the bar waving empty pint mugs whilst three bartenders were stretching out trying to fill them from hose-pipes. The scene was more like a petrol station than an officers' mess. It was, in fact, the 'Five O'Clock Swill', resulting from the Australian government ruling that all bars had to be closed at 6.00pm, with the result that people normally knocking off work at 5.00pm would endeavour to drink as much as they could in the hour remaining. It could hardly be called a 'Happy Hour' because of the resultant high incidence of road traffic accidents on the way home.

At 6.00pm, without as much as a 'Time, Gentlemen, please', the shutters came down on the bar and all the Aussies drank up and disappeared into the night. We were left alone in the Mess, our only company being the station duty officer and the mess cat. After a dreadful supper, we played a few games of table tennis and retired uncharacteristically early as the staff car taking us to the airport was coming at 6.00am. Needless to say no one saw us off – except the cat!

The final insult was yet to come. Our travel arrangements within Australia were the responsibility of the British High Commission in Canberra which was guided by UK Treasury rules. So some petty deputy assistant clerical officer had issued us all with economy-class tickets because the rules stipulated that only air vice marshals and above could travel first-class on domestic flights, notwithstanding the fact that our trips to Perth from Sydney via Adelaide and return were the equivalent of flying from London to Istanbul via Malta. At the airport we met up with two RAAF flight lieutenants who were travelling first-class which indeed all their officers did when on duty and flying by Australian airlines. They were amazed that we were flying 'steerage' and took pity on us by bringing their free drinks for us. Luckily, we were sitting in the front row of economy class so there was no bother. Australian sparkling wine never tasted so good!

Our antipodean tour continued with a visit to RAAF Laverton, a fighter base flying the French Mirage aircraft. It followed the same disorganized and disinterested pattern as we had encountered at Pearce. But things improved greatly when we arrived at RAAF East Sale, the home of their CFS, where we were well received and looked after. Our presentations went down well and useful discussions followed. I had the dubious pleasure of flying the RAAF basic trainer, the Winjeel, which was undoubtedly the worse aircraft ever built. We were told that the Australian Government had a policy of restricting imports, be they cars or aircraft, unless those items were assembled under licence in the country so whenever an Australian manufactured product became available it was snapped up. That was why the Winjeel was forced upon the RAAF, despite the fact that the engineering company concerned had never previously manufactured anything bigger than a lawn mower.

The Australian part of our tour ended on 23 November when we flew from Sydney to Wellington in New Zealand. As a result of our 'down-under' experience so far we were a little apprehensive as we deplaned but we need not have worried because we received the warmest of welcomes, generous hospitality and, more importantly, the keenest of interest in everything we had to say. The whole visit was extremely well organized wherever we went.

We spent the first two days in Wellington being looked after by HQ RNZAF before beginning the tour proper in North Island with visits to the stations at Wigram and Ohakea. Our presentation to personnel from both bases was scheduled to be given in a cinema and when we arrived we found that we had a full house. We discovered that all aircrew, except those on duty, were obliged to attend and any available ground crew were invited to do so. Our presentation was similar to that given in Oz with a few extras specifically requested by HQ RNZAF. The cinema was booked for an hour and a half but, such was the enthusiasm and interest of the audience, we were kept on stage for nearly three hours.

Most questions dealt with flying training in general but we were surprised at how many were directed to us as individuals. For example, Birdy was asked about his experiences in the Battle of Britain and in his subsequent career. Even

I was quizzed about my two tours in Malaya during the emergency to which the RNZAF had recently contributed a fighter/ground-attack squadron of Vampires and a transport squadron of Bristol Freighters. It was relevant as many in the audience were due to start tours on those squadrons shortly. We subsequently found that our CVs, which had been sent out prior to the tour, had been circulated within the RNZAF. We were delighted at everyone's keenness and interest; such a relief after the 'don't want to know' attitude of the Australians.

Even more astonishing was their hospitality and keenness to show us their beautiful country, of which they were understandably very proud. I flew on two trips from Wigham and once from Ohakea, all in the dear old Harvard, on sector recces to be shown the mountains, the hot springs, the geysers and the coastline with its wonderful coves and beaches, such as Hawke's Bay.

On 29 November we flew to Whenupai on South Island where everybody seemed intent upon going one better than the 'Northerners'. For example, for our first lunch we were flown by Sunderland flying boat to the middle of Lake Taupo where we picnicked on board on smoked salmon and champagne and fished the waters until we had each caught a trout, which teemed in the lake.

The following day we gave our second presentation, again in a cinema, and again we were kept for nearly three hours, so keen was the audience. On our last day, we were asked what we would like to do and Birdy opted to go water-skiing, with dire consequences as he hit rocks in shallow water and sustained some nasty cuts and bruises. I was luckier as, during our picnic on Lake Taupo, I told the aircraft captain that I had never flown a flying boat and would love to do so one day. So I was taken to the base at Hobsonville where there was a Sunderland awaiting my pleasure. The captain demonstrated the taxiing, take-off, circuit and landing procedures just once before we changed seats and I flew two circuits to his satisfaction. For the rest of the hour I flew circuits and splashes to my heart's content whilst the crew played cards in the back.

The South Island was even more wondrous than the North, not least because their mountains were higher and, despite it being the antipodean summer, there was still snow on the peaks – but then the southern tip is not that far from the Antarctic Circle. The New Zealanders and their country restored our belief in the value of these liaison visits and this second part of our tour is something I will never forget.

On 4 December the team flew back from New Zealand to Singapore, via Darwin and Djakarta, courtesy of Qantas, where we had a day to wait, before flying to Lyneham, via Gan and Khormaksar, courtesy of the RAF Comet C4 fleet. We had been away for thirty-one days.

* * *

My first job back at Rissy was to draft the visit report for Birdy to approve and forward to HQFTC. After the obligatory staff continuation training flight, I then started to carry out a number of final-handling and progress checks on course students. However, most of my time began to be taken up with the Air Force Board decision to form a new RAF formation aerobatic team using the recently introduced Folland Gnat advanced trainer to replace the existing CFS Red Pelicans team who flew Jet Provosts.

The background to this decision was as follows. The deservedly famous Black Arrows of No.111 Squadron, flying Hawker Hunters, had been the RAF representative team for many years until the Hunter squadrons were re-equipped with English Electric Lightning fighters. In due course, the Black Arrows were replaced by the Flying Tigers of No. 74 Squadron and they, in turn, by the Blue Diamonds of No. 92.

Unfortunately the Lightning, despite its terrific performance, was not a good display aircraft and, more importantly, it was found that display flying was using up its fatigue life at an alarming rate. So the responsibility for providing the RAF's representative team was passed from Fighter Command to HQFTC – with the subsequent formation of the Red Pelicans from CFS flying Jet Provosts. They did the best they could with their limited power and straight-wing configuration, but were far from impressive. The introduction into service of the high-performance, swept-wing Folland Gnat, which had originally been designed as a single-seat light-weight fighter, was a golden opportunity to recapture the glory days of formation aerobatics so badly missing since the demise of the Black Arrows.

HQFTC duly tasked CFS with the job of forming the new team. The then AOC in C, Air Marshal Sir 'Batchy' Atchelor, laid down only one stipulation: that Flight Lieutenant Lee Jones, the leader of RAF Valley's unofficial team, the Yellow Jacks, already flying the Gnat, was to be the leader. This made sense as Lee was a very experienced formation aerobatic pilot, having flown with the Black Arrows for three seasons.

My first task was to muster the volunteers from whom we would select the team of seven pilots plus one reserve for what was to be a seven-aircraft team. I contacted the Chief Instructors of all the flying training schools that had aerobatic teams and laid down a few candidate guidelines which included formation aerobatic experience, qualification and suitability to become CFS instructors and their Station Commanders' recommendation. Needless to say, we had an abundance of applications whose possible selection had to be cleared with the Air Secretary's Department lest the individual was due for promotion or a posting which would take precedence.

Eventually Birdy and I whittled down the applications to a short list of about a dozen pilots whom we called in to attend a selection board at which we were joined by Lee Jones. We duly selected the team but there was a small problem in that neither Birdy nor I thought highly of Lee Jones as a team leader. There was no doubting his flying ability but we did not like his anti-authority attitude, his over-confidence and rather slap-dash approach. Quite independently, we both considered Flight Lieutenant Ray Hanna, the current leader of RAF Manby's Macaws team, a much better bet. Birdy expressed our concerns to the AOC-in-C but he was over-ruled and told to get on with it.

Jones wanted the new team to be called the Yellow Jacks, but we did not agree for several reasons. Firstly, yellow jack is the name given to the flag flown by ships when under quarantine; secondly we had found that yellow aircraft did not show up well in murky conditions and, finally, we did not like the connection between yellow and cowardice. We wanted the team to be worthy successors to the Black Arrows so we proposed the name Red Arrows, which suited the arrow shape of the swept-wing Gnat – and this proposal was agreed by the Air Force Board.

The rest is history. Selection over, the chosen applicants, except Bill Loverseed who was already in post as the CFS Meteor QFI, continued in their current positions until the late autumn when they too would be posted to Little Rissington. The Yellow Jacks, of which four pilots including Lee Jones had been selected, completed a full display season at the end of which their yellow Gnat aircraft and three more from the reserve pool were transferred to No. 5 MU at Kemble to be painted in the new colour scheme of the Red Arrows. The team, with its own technical and administrative support, including a non-formation flying-team manager, Squadron Leader Dick Storer, took up residence at Kemble. The work-up for the 1965 display season went very well and their displays were enthusiastically received with the result that they were authorized to add two further aircraft, as nine gives more scope for complex formations and enables the team to split for synchronized displays. The only blight on the season was that Lee Jones' leadership came under scrutiny for frequent violations of the international rules that laid down minimum height and other safety procedures. As a result, Birdy sacked him at the end of the season with the agreement of the new AOC-in-C, Air Marshal Sir 'Gus' Walker. He was succeeded by Ray Hanna who led the team for the next three seasons and proved to have been one of the best ever leaders of the Red Arrows.

* * *

No sooner had I returned from 'down under' than I started to feel decidedly ropey: even the least demanding sortie left me feeling completely drained. I tried to carry on normally but, when I was beaten at squash by the Commandant, I realized that something was very wrong. The Senior Medical Officer could find nothing amiss, so he sent me to the RAF Hospital at Wroughton to see the consultant gastro-enteric surgeon, Wing Commander Jimmy Harris, who, having subjected to me a series of indignities, found a lump.

On 17 January 1964 I was admitted for exploratory surgery the following day. The good news was that it was not a tumour as Jimmy had expected. The bad news was that it was an abscess on the base of the colon which had obviously been there for some time as it had done a fair amount of damage. Jimmy had to excavate diseased flesh and, in removing an anal fistula, had to cut the two lower rings of muscle of the sphincter. Even worse news was that a second operation would be necessary and, in the meantime, I was to stay flat on my back in bed for ten days to allow the excavations to granulate and the muscles, which had been sewn together with Chinese silk, to join up again (which regrettably they failed to do). To make matters worse I was put on a very low residue diet for obvious reasons. (Yuk).

Three or four days later I began to see flashes of light in my left eye. When I told Jimmy he said that this was probably a not uncommon reaction to anaesthesia and that it should soon disappear. Unfortunately, it got steadily worse until the sight of that eye started to distort and its colour perception changed until everything appeared a muddy brown. Luckily, the ophthalmic surgeon from the RAF Hospital at Halton was holding a clinic at Wroughton two days before my second operation. When looking into my eye he muttered a very disheartening and unprofessional 'Jeez'. He told me that I had the largest swelling on my retina that he had ever seen which was preventing the blood vessels from doing their job. He explained that, under normal circumstances, I should have a massive dose of steroids to reduce the swelling as soon as possible but I could only be given a small dose to prevent the swelling getting worse as a high dose would inhibit healing after surgery and could have serious side effects. So I would have to be admitted to Halton as soon as possible after discharge from Wroughton.

When I was allowed to sit up I was determined to do something useful, so I got my adjutant, Flight Lieutenant Dick Griffin, to bring writing materials and certain documents for me to work on. I started by reviewing and revising the ground-school syllabus to cut out those aspects of it which were historical but now somewhat outdated. I then wrote a staff paper with the exciting title of 'Planned Flying/Planned Servicing at CFS' in which I outlined a system whereby aircraft take-off and landing times were synchronized with the availability of 'turn-round' teams. I worked out that by staggering take-offs, particularly in the morning where currently there was a mad rush to get airborne, it would be possible to achieve up to 25 per cent more sorties without any increase in the number of servicing personnel or aircraft. The drafts of these two proposals were typed by my PA and submitted to the squadron commanders for comment. Eventually, the finalized papers were submitted to the Commandant for his approval ten days before I was due to leave hospital. Birdy wasted no time in approving them and told me that he had fended off an MoD attempt to replace me as he wanted the proposals to be implemented as soon as I was available to supervise them.

I was discharged from Wroughton on 31 March after nearly three months of incarceration. The surgery was very much on the mend but my medical category had been downgraded from A1G1Z1 to A5G3Z5, the lowest possible without being dead, which meant no flying except as a passenger, no stressful ground appointments and service restricted to UK only. A total career-ending disaster, unless the ophthalmic people at the RAF Hospital at Halton could sort out my eye problem.

After ten days back in the office I reported to Halton for a four-day stay. On arrival I was given a thorough examination and, being found to be free from any condition which could be aggravated, I was put on a three-day course of steroids, which meant taking tablets at four-hour intervals, day and night. I was carefully monitored for any side effects but the only one was total inability to sleep – so I spent the nights sitting with the duty sister enjoying countless cups of tea.

At the end of the course the consultant subjected my left eye to a rigorous examination. He told me that the swelling had completely subsided but, unfortunately, it had left an area of the retina where the photoreceptors were impaired due to damage of the nerve cells – a condition called serous retinopathy which left me with a black hole, luckily just off-centre near the macula and some distortion. He said that the condition could not be cured but he expected some improvement with time. When I asked about my medical category he replied that it would remain A5G3Z5 subject to six-monthly reviews at the RAF Central Medical Establishment in London.

Shortly after my return from Halton I was sitting in my office morosely pondering my future career prospects and wondering whether I had any when I received a 'phone call from Group Captain Danny Clare, an old rugby acquaintance, who now worked in the Air Secretary's Branch. He started by commiserating about my loss of a flying category and went on to say that I had been 'pencilled in' to be the next Station Commander of RAF Linton on Ouse, the home of No. 1 FTS, with the acting rank of Group Captain. However, as that was a flying appointment, I had been ruled out because the ophthalmic consultant had told him that I was very unlikely to regain a flying category in the near future. My heart sank but he cheered me up by saying that, as I had been cleared for promotion, the Air Secretary had told him to see whether there were any suitable non-flying group captain posts coming up within the next few months. This was very encouraging but he advised me not to let my hopes get too high.

Ten days later he rang to say that the post of Deputy Captain of The Queen's Flight was becoming vacant and my name would be put forward if I agreed. Agree! Under the circumstances it seemed a perfect solution – especially for a fervent Royalist like myself, but there were two hurdles to be crossed: first, I had to be acceptable to the Captain, Air Commodore John Boulting, and, secondly, I had to be approved by the Palace who would have the last say. Danny advised me not to tell anyone about this possibility, even Jane, as the Palace had a very nasty habit of rejecting applicants who publicized their appointment before having been given their blessing.

A meeting with the Captain was arranged at RAF Benson; he told me that the Deputy was responsible for organizing the travel arrangements and looking after the protocol aspects for the minor Royals and for accompanying them on visits to service units in the UK and on official visits overseas. I was invited to stay for lunch in the Officers' Mess; no doubt he wanted to check my table manners. Once back in the Captain's office I must have passed muster as John Boulting told me that he would be pleased to have me as his deputy and then passed me over to his PA who gave me a couple of lengthy forms to fill in with the information required for the personal vetting of myself and, unusually, for Jane as well.

On return to Little Rissington I found it very difficult to hide my elation and not to tell Jane of our next posting. Luckily, I resisted the temptation because I was rung a few weeks later to say that, despite my twenty-two years' service, it had just dawned on the posters at MoD that I had never done a staff job. They therefore considered that it was in my best career interests to be posted to a staff appointment at HQ FTC, followed by attendance at the Joint Services Staff College at Latimer. There was nothing I could do about that decision, so I just had to like it or lump it. As it happened, my old friend Dickie Peirse got the Deputy Captain job and ended his career as the Defence Services Secretary and as Air Vice Marshal Sir Richard Peirse KCVO. There but for the grace of MoD might have gone I!

I saw out my time at CFS feeling somewhat like a lame duck, for what good is a non-flying chief instructor. However, I did, at least, have the satisfaction of supervising the introduction of the PFPS system and finding that it lived up to my expectations of it. It had the wholehearted support of the technical staff which was not too surprising as I had discussed my ideas with Wing Commander Denny Dent, the OC Engineering Wing, some months previously and had incorporated many of his suggestions. It took longer to convince the pilots but they came around when the benefits of higher aircraft utilization and the achievement of more sorties in the average day became obvious.

I duly handed over to my successor, Wing Commander Eddie Edmunds, in June 1964 and moved out of No. 6 Smith Barry Crescent, the married quarter which went with the job, into No. 1, which luckily was vacant at that time, until we could move into a MQ at HQFTC. This was at the suggestion of the Station Commander, Henry Chinnery, who had been very supportive during what had been a very difficult time for me.

Although my CFS story did not have a happy ending, our time at Little Rissington was not without benefit. Perhaps most importantly Jane was able, for the first time in our life together, to become more involved in station affairs. This was due largely to the fact that Hilary and Marcus were settled at boarding schools, Ratcliffe College and Grace Dieu Preparatory School respectively. Although reluctant to do so, she became a very effective Chairwoman of the Wives' Club. Because of our proximity to Stratford-upon-Avon she was also able to go back to her theatrical roots and to get together with her old friend, Donald Sinden, whom she persuaded to give a talk to the Wives' Club. Not too surprisingly, he wowed them. Karen, who was now nearly nine-years old, was being taught ballet by Lizzie Hill and was showing promise. I wondered whether she might follow in her mother's, and grandmother's, footsteps as a dancer?

The Commandant of CFS, Air Cdre Patrick Connolley, thanking the Managing Director of Folland, Mr Digby Brade, who had just presented CFS with a silver model of a Gnat.

Chapter 12

Totally Becalmed

In July 1964 I arrived at HQ Flying Training Command, based at Shinfield Park, now a campus of Reading University, leaving Jane and the family at Little Rissington until I was allocated a married quarter. No sooner had I settled into the Officers' Mess, the PMC of which was my step-cousin, Wing Commander Bob Doe DSO DFC of Battle of Britain fame, than I was given an appointment to attend the Central Medical Establishment in London for my first six-monthly review. My left eye's sight was still distorted, slightly blurred with a blank hole luckily off-centre. However, there had been some improvement and I had no difficulty in driving but I was pretty sure that I would not gain my flying category this time; and so it proved. I pinned my hopes on better luck next time, not least because if I did not regain my full category then I would forfeit flying pay – and that would be serious.

It did not take me long to get to grips with my first-ever staff job as Wing Commander (Flying Training). I had a rag-bag of responsibilities which included giving the air staff presentations to visitors to the HQ, carrying out pre-AOC inspections, looking after the staff aspects of the management of the Red Arrows, liaising with all FTC flying units, etc. All pretty mundane and rather tedious, but there was one job that I really enjoyed and that was preparing the briefs and accompanying the Air Officer Commanding in Chief on his visits to flying units. The AOC-in-C was none other than Air Marshal Sir Augustus Walker KCB CBE DSO AFC MA, whom I had first met at Henlow when, as AVM 'Gus' Walker, he had refereed a couple of my cadets' rugby matches.

'Gus' was all of five feet nothing, of very slight build and had lost his right arm during the war. He made up for his lack of stature by boundless energy and a marvellous approach to leadership. For example, when I was preparing his briefs for visits, I had to find out just about everything about the Station, Wing and Squadron Commanders and of their wives and children as well. Thus armed he might say to an officer 'I understand that your son has just won a Duke of Edinburgh gold award. Please give him my congratulations'. He had a fantastic memory for putting names to faces but, of course, he could not remember everyone, so one of his tricks would be to say 'I am afraid that I can't remember your name,' whereupon the chap would say 'Smith, Sir', or whatever. Then Gus would say 'Oh I know that: I mean your Christian name'. Thus he had the ability to make his subordinates feel ten-feet tall by showing such an interest in them.

My second and most critical eye examination was carried out at CME in January 1965. The consultant examined both my eyes and then asked me to read the test card with my good right eye which I did without faltering. He then told me to cover up my right eye whilst he changed the test card. I changed my hands but not my eye more for a laugh than anything, expecting him to say 'naughty, naughty' but, incredibly, he failed to notice so I thought 'what the hell'. When asked to read the first three lines, I did so rapidly then hesitantly read the fourth, but getting it all right, before stumbling a bit over the fifth, making two deliberate mistakes, before giving up on the sixth. The consultant was surprised that I had done so well, considering the state of my retina, but confirmed that he was content that my full flying category should be restored and that he would inform MoD and HQFTC.

I was delighted and very relieved but did not feel at all guilty for having cheated because I knew from driving that with both eyes I could see perfectly well and that my depth perception was as good as ever. It was only when my good eye was covered that my sight was blurred and distorted, but both those defects were steadily improving. To celebrate I wangled myself onto a Staff Officer Helicopter Familiarization course at Odiham where I flew fifteen hours, including going solo on the Westland Whirlwind Mark 4, the much loved 'Willy Four', and also flew the Bristol Sycamore and the Bell Sioux.

By now Air Marshal Sir 'Paddy' Dunn KCB had taken over from 'Gus' Walker who had been promoted to Air Chief Marshal and had become the Inspector General of the RAF, an inspired appointment. I was sorry to see Gus go, even if he was a hard taskmaster and was very intolerant of those staff officers who did not measure up. Luckily we had got along well and even more luckily I got on just as well with Paddy Dunn, who was a much more relaxed character. As a result, when he was invited to visit USAF flying training establishments in America he took me along, much to the annoyance of my immediate boss, Group Captain George Petty, who was expecting to accompany him.

We flew into New York on 21 September courtesy of BOAC. Thereafter our visit was organized most efficiently by the USAF. Our programme included visits to a basic and an advanced flying training school and to the US Navy's Flight School at Pensacola in Florida. However, the highlight of the tour was the visit to the USAF Academy in Colorado Springs. Everywhere we went we were looked after extremely well and every visit was meticulously planned, most interesting and enlightening. We attended many formal lunches and dinners where we found that, wherever it was held, the menu was almost always the same. The starter was prawn cocktail, followed by chicken of some sort, and finished off with apple-pie and ice cream. It was always delicious, but we did get rather tired of the same old thing, so whenever we had the chance to eat in restaurants we would chose something completely different which usually disappointed. The only exceptions were their steaks, but being mostly of the porterhouse or T-bone variety they were too enormous for words.

Throughout the trip we were impressed by the resources available to the USAF; it was obvious that no expense had been spared. As one might expect, the most opulent unit was the Academy which was the equivalent of the RAF College at Cranwell in so far as the aim was to turn out an elite cadre of permanent commissioned officers, albeit their course lasted four years against Cranwell's three. But I was shocked by the USAF approach to officer training whereby, for their first year, the cadets who came from a wide range of ethnic and social backgrounds were knocked into shape by a regime of bullying and abuse not just by staff but also by cadets senior to them. On arrival they had their heads shaved, were dressed in fatigues rather than uniforms and had to run everywhere except when marching as a squad. In addition they were subject to what was called 'hazing', a system which allowed senior cadets to punish minor demeanours, real or imagined, by giving them arduous or degrading tasks. Those cadets who survived the rigours and indignities of the first year, and there were many dropouts, were then built up by the gradual award of privileges and responsibility and were accorded improved conditions and accommodation each year.

We talked to many cadets from each year who, when spoken to by officers, had to stand rigidly to attention, stare straight ahead and answer every question in a specific, clipped manner. For example, when asked from which state they came the answer would be 'Sir. Alabama. Sir' or whatever. We came to the conclusion that the aim of the USAF was to turn out officers cast in exactly the same mould. Indeed, it was uncanny but the fourth-year cadets all looked the same, spoke in the same perceived military manner, wrote with identical handwriting and were indoctrinated to do everything 'by the book'. In other words they had lost all individuality and personality and, I suspect, all initiative when faced by the unexpected.

A bonus for me was that, when I told Sir Paddy that I had a younger sister living and working in New York, he arranged for me to be flown to and from New York by the USAF so that I could spend our one free weekend with her. On our first evening, Liz took me to the Rainbow Room at the top of the Empire State Building where we wined and dined looking down on the cloud tops and up at the stars. The next day she gave me a tour of the city in a chauffeur-driven limousine, which included lunch at Murphy's bar and restaurant, a favourite haunt of actors and journalists. I was amazed that everywhere we went Liz was greeted by so many people. Perhaps I should not have been surprised as she was, at that time, the personal secretary of Mark Goodson, one of the founding partners of Goodson-Todman, who created the TV game show concept and held the national monopoly of game show productions. When the company moved to Los Angeles, Liz became Vice-President of the company.

When we returned to HQFTC I learned that I was to attend the six-month course at the Joint Services Staff College (JSSC) starting in January 1966. The Air Secretary's Branch was certainly honouring their promise to me made when I was denied acting promotion to Group Captain on the grounds that I lacked staff experience. So, after a mercifully short stint at Shinfield Park, I hoped that I was about to tread on the final stepping stone to that promotion.

* * *

In due course I reported to Latimer House, the Officers' Mess and HQ of JSSC. As we were able to retain our married quarter at Caversham, I was to become a weekly boarder, returning at weekends. This was convenient as Karen was a pupil at the excellent St Anne's School. Hilary and Marcus were boarding at Ratcliffe College and at their preparatory school, Grace Dieu, respectively.

I was to find that I enjoyed the JSSC course as much as I hated that at the Staff College. There were several reasons for this, the first of which was the location at Latimer which had a fascinating history both ancient and modern.

The front of Latimer House where the author was a student when attending the Joint Services Staff College.

The village of Latimer is situated in the beautiful Chess Valley, a fertile area which had been farmed for centuries by ancient Britons and by the Romans during their occupation: indeed there are still traces of a Roman villa nearby. The Saxons succeeded the Romans and discovered deposits of iron ore which they exploited.

The first mention of a manor at Latimer was recorded in 1194, then lived in by the Chenduit family until the estate was transferred to Queen Eleanor in 1284, becoming the home of the two daughters of Edward I in 1290. In the turbulent times which followed, ownership changed frequently, for example, in the fifteenth and sixteenth centuries the tenure of the manor was held by many well-known families including the Nevills, the Willoughby de Brokes, the Grevilles and the Sandys.

In 1615 the Sandys sold the manor to Lord William Cavendish, who became the first Earl of Devonshire. Various members of the Cavendish family lived there for the next 300 years but in 1834, during the tenure of John Compton Cavendish, the fourth Lord Caversham, the manor was badly damaged by fire. The architect Edward Blore was given the task of rebuilding it which he did in the style known, unkindly, as Victorian Gothic: however he did retain the sixteenth-century chimney stacks which survived and replaced those that did not with replicas. By now the manor was known as Latimer House.

At the beginning of the Second World War the then Lord Chesham lived in one wing of the house to allow the rest to be used, first, as a hospital for the treatment of Metropolitan Police air-raid casualties and then for military occupation by the Northamptonshire Yeomanry and later by the HQ of the IVth Army Corps as offices and as the officers' mess. For security reasons Lord Chesham moved out, having first bought the Old Rectory in Latimer Village – which eventually was to become the residence of the Commandant of JSSC.

In 1942 a military unit known as No. 1 Combined Services Distribution Centre took over. This was in reality a very important organization where high-ranking German and Italian prisoners of war were interrogated for intelligence purposes before being held elsewhere. Its real title was the Combined Services Detailed Interrogation Centre (CSDIC). The unit required many purpose-built facilities, such as blocks of cells, which were spread around the grounds. These were ideal for use by JSSC as syndicate rooms, the lecture hall and model room.

After the war Lord Chesham emigrated to East Africa in 1946 leaving Latimer House and grounds to his son who in turn sold it to the Government in 1951 thus ending 336 years of ownership by the Cavendish family.

The second reason why I enjoyed the course was that my fellow students were a very congenial crowd. Altogether there were ninety-six of us, the majority from the UK's three services with a few from the Civil Service and the police. There were also the overseas students from the USA and the older Commonwealth countries, plus one or two from Africa. We were split into three groups, each under one of the Senior Directing Staff (SDS) and each group was further split into syndicates of around eight students. The composition of the syndicates was changed every two months.

The majority of the students were of lieutenant colonel or equivalent rank and we were supposedly all 'high fliers'. Indeed the Chiefs of Staff directive to the Commandant of the first JSSC course in 1946 began:

> The object of the course is to train officers, who are already qualified in the staff work of their own services, for staff appointments on Joint Staffs and for higher appointments in their own services … .

Sometime later the directive was amended to state that the course was to be a prerequisite for attendance at the Royal College of Defence Studies. One of the best things about the course was that, unlike at Staff College, the DS treated us very much as equals.

The third, and perhaps the most important, reason for my appreciating the course was the level and calibre of the high-ranking politicians and service officers who came to talk to us. In my opinion the two star performers were Admiral Sir Michael le Fanu, then CNS (designate) and Air Chief Marshal Sir 'Sam' Elworthy, then CAS who went on to become CDS. But perhaps the most likeable and interesting was Lord Alexander Douglas Home, the Foreign Secretary, who joined us for dinner one night and then held court in the lounge where he talked and answered questions for about two hours.

There were only two exceptions, the first being Mr Enoch Powell, then out of government, who gave us his own views on the United Kingdom's place in world politics. His theme was that the UK, having lost an Empire, had yet to find its place which he reckoned should be akin to playing football in the third division. Needless to say, his pessimistic view was not well received and he was peppered with questions to which he replied by demolishing the speaker along the lines of 'the fact that you should have asked that question reveals your total lack of appreciation of the problem'. A typical politician's gambit, which went down like a lead balloon.

The second flop, I am sorry to say, was by an RAF officer who was Director of Air Plans at MoD. He clearly had done no homework whatsoever and only spoke for about ten minutes before inviting questions which he failed to answer with any conviction.

As a weekly boarder I lived in an accommodation block, one of the temporary wartime buildings, known as the 'Cardboard Castle'. There were about two dozen of us and we got to know each other very well. I was able to play lots of squash and managed to stay in the top ten of the squash ladder. However, there was one player whom I should have been able to beat but never succeeded in doing so. He was Group Captain Tommy Burne, the SDS (RAF), who had lost a leg during the war. Tommy played on his disability with great skill and monopolized the centre knowing that nobody would have the nerve to barge him out of the way.

Another advantage of being a boarder was that I had plenty of time to make full use of the comprehensive JSSC library. This was a great help as we students had a lot of written work to complete in our own time. The major task was to write a paper of between three to four thousand words on a political subject of one's own choice. I chose to write on 'The Implications of the Sino-Soviet Dispute' in the form of an appreciation for presentation to the Joint Chiefs of Staff Committee. As

the source of all information had to be referenced, this required a lot of research and without constant access to the library would have been impossible. Most students chose less complicated subjects but I had done a lot of study of Chinese communism at Staff College, not least because of interest resulting from my having been engaged in the Malayan Emergency. My paper was one of the five shortlisted for the course 'Essay Prize' but, alas, I was pipped at the post by an Army officer – fancy being beaten by a 'pongo'!

I also wrote a paper on the required service subject of between fifteen hundred to two thousand

The author standing by a large statue of a Russian soldier in East Berlin when he was a student at the Joint Services Staff College in June 1966. Even the squirrels were red ones – how appropriate.

words on 'The Problem of Wastage in Flying Training' which, thankfully, I could do without any need to refer because I had already dealt with that problem exhaustively at CFS and HQFTC.

Towards the end of the course I had the usual final interview with the Commandant, Air Vice Marshal Stewart Menaul, who told me that I had done well and that he would recommend that I should return, eventually, to Latimer as a member of the Directing Staff. His recommendation did not fill me with foreboding, especially as I thought it might be as SDS (RAF).

We UK students awaited the news of our next postings with bated breath. When the list was promulgated, I was delighted that I was going to a NATO appointment, on the staff of HQ AIRCENT, then based at Fontainebleau, forty miles south of Paris, but disappointed that I was not to be promoted. The only RAF student going to a group captain post was my old friend Geoff Cairns who was six months junior to me. Nevertheless it sounded like an interesting job in a very agreeable place – and, as a family, we were ready for another overseas posting after ten years in the UK.

* * *

On 23 August 1966 I travelled by train and ferry to Fontainebleau to take over my new job, leaving behind Jane and the car in which she would join me later. My first priority was to find somewhere for us to live and, as no married quarters were provided, officers had to make their own arrangements. Luckily Wing Commander Peter Thompson, from whom I was taking over, was moving out of his house in two weeks' time and nobody had put in a bid for it. Peter took me to meet his wife and to look over the house, which was a quaint three-storey building situated by the main gate in the grounds of a 'grand mansion' in the village of Avon, a suburb of Fontainebleau. Peter took me to see the owner, Madame Versaire, a stout retired Parisienne milliner of indeterminate age camouflaged by illiberal applications of rouge and lipstick. She lived in the big house and had a British Army colonel and his German wife in an apartment within the house and an RAF group captain living in the stable block at the other end of the grounds. Peter warned me that she had been known to reject potential tenants if she did not like the looks of them, so I was on my best behaviour and, before long, we had agreed the rent.

My job, which was officially 'Air Operations Plans', promised to be very interesting. For example, I was to take over the chairmanship of a working party of the NATO Allied Group on Aviation Research and Development (AGARD) tackling the problem of pilots suffering 'flash blindness' as a result of the use of tactical nuclear weapons. I was also a member of another AGARD working party which was developing the use of the forward-looking radar in the nose of the F-104 as an aid to low-level penetration at night using a 'hands off' terrain-following system. I would also be involved in tactical route-planning and many other kindred subjects.

The main offices at HQ AIRCENT were at Camp Guynemer in an enclosed site on the edge of the forest. The staff consisted of officers from no fewer than seven nations, being the USA, Canada, the UK, Germany, Belgium, the Netherlands and France. The numbers from each country were more or less proportionate to the size and importance of the operational units contributed.

After what seemed like ages, at last everything was ready for Jane to come out with Karen. She had done a marvellous job in handing over our married quarter at Caversham, of packing up and doing the hundred-and-one things necessary when moving overseas. I travelled to Calais by train and was on the quayside when the ferry docked. After an agonizing wait I saw our Morris 1800 being driven gingerly down the ramp. My having to leave Jane behind was asking a lot but she had coped extremely well with a little help from a few friends and the RAF movements staff.

I took the wheel for our drive to Fontainebleau where the girls were fascinated by our mid-nineteenth-century French house which was charming, albeit with very quirky and unreliable plumbing and electrics. It was full of typically French 'meubles' (furniture) which had seen a great many better days, for example, the chairs in the dining room were held together with piano wire. The house had no corridors, so going anti-clockwise from the hall you went through the dining room into the lounge, through the kitchen and back into the hall. Upstairs it was the same, through a small bedroom into the master bedroom, through a third bedroom via the bathroom and loo and back onto the landing – a perfect setting for a French farce. We did not have access to the third storey, which was used by Madame Versaire's younger sister for storage.

Having got used to the peculiarities of the house we became very fond of it and we loved the overall location. Perhaps the greatest attraction was the Fôret de Fontainebleau which was literally on our doorstep. It was a magical place to explore at any time but particularly in the autumn when the leaf colours of red, gold, yellow and brown rivalled those of New England. Dotted throughout the

The author's daughter, Karen, seeing off her two brothers on their return to school in England after the summer holiday in Fontainebleau.

forest were outcrops of rocks, glades and streams, all of which added to its beauty. Hidden in its midst was the village of Barbizon, a very attractive place with an artists' quarter and many excellent restaurants. Another advantage of our location was that it was only an easy forty-minute drive from Orly Airport to which Hilary and Marcus would fly when they came out for the Easter and summer holidays.

Our stay in Fontainebleau nearly came to a sticky end when Jane and I were invited to dinner with the Deputy C-in-C, Air Chief Marshal Sir Edmund Huddlestone. The other guests were his PSO, Wing Commander Freddie Yetman and his wife, his PA, Flight Lieutenant Jim Baldwin, and his wife, with whom we had become friendly. It was Jim's farewell party and he had been invited by Lady Huddlestone to bring a couple of friends. At dinner I sat next to Sir Edmund, who clearly had had a lot to drink. After the ladies had withdrawn he started ranting and raving about those 'bloody fools' who got themselves into trouble attempting to cross the Atlantic in small boats, climbing on Snowdonia with inadequate preparation or taking part in similar 'stupid' activities. He could not see why the RAF should waste time and money sending out air-sea rescue launches, helicopters or mountain rescue teams to go to their assistance.

I should have known better, but I suggested that the RAF should be grateful for the opportunity to practise their skills for real and would thus be better prepared should an aircraft ditch in the Irish Sea or crash on Snowdonia. He seemed taken aback that anyone should disagree with him. When we joined the ladies he sat on the arm of the chair in which Jane was sitting and began holding forth in such an 'effing and blinding' manner that Jane got up and moved away. As soon as possible, we thanked Lady Huddlestone, who was charming, for an excellent dinner and bade our farewells.

The next day Air Commodore Denis Rixon, the Senior RAF Staff Officer and my boss for administrative matters, called me to say that ACM Huddlestone had told him that he did not want me on his staff and that I was to be sent packing. I explained the circumstances of the previous evening and Rixon told me that he was well aware of Huddlestone's drink problem and consequent tirades. He advised me not to worry, but to keep my head below the parapet until the Deputy C-in-C, who was due to be relieved in about three weeks, had departed. Imagine my relief and pleasure when the new man turned out to be none other than ACM Sir Augustus Walker.

Unfortunately, our stay in Fontainebleau was cut short anyway when President de Gaulle withdrew from NATO and demanded that all its units should leave France as soon as possible. This came as a nasty shock and initiated a mad scramble to find alternative locations elsewhere. To facilitate this, the HQs of NAVCENT, LANDCENT and AIRCENT were disbanded and reformed as the slimmed-down, tri-service HQ AFCENT. Various locations were investigated but, eventually, the site of an abandoned coalmine was chosen. This was at Brunssum in Suid Limburg, the southernmost province of the Netherlands. This sounded pretty grim after the splendours of Fontainebleau.

Once this decision had been taken the married officers of the other nationalities were given time off to go and find accommodation for their families. However, the RAF personnel were told that HQ RAF Germany would undertake to find suitable hirings for us within the constraints of the local overseas allowance (LOA). This sounded helpful but not too encouraging as our LOA was the lowest of all the other nations. I later found out that my LOA as a wing commander was less than that of a corporal in the RCAF.

To cut a long story short, after a couple of months HQ RAF(G) gave up and we were left to make our own arrangements. I hurried to Brunssum and found that the only accommodation still available was either totally unacceptable or way above my allowance. I returned to Fontainebleau rather cross, worried and disheartened.

Amidst the turmoil of the merger of the three HQs and the imminent relocation a team from the Air Secretary's Branch arrived in Fontainebleau to give a presentation on new procedural arrangements for postings and promotions. All RAF officers had been forewarned and invited to let the team know in advance of any career concern which they would like to discuss. I had applied on the grounds that I had been in line for two group captain appointments in 1964 yet, nearly three years later, I was still a wing commander. My concern was not helped by the fact that the team leader, Air Commodore Roy Austen-Smith, had been two years junior to me when he had taken over from me as flight commander on No. 33 Squadron.

After the presentation I was interviewed by my case officer, a Wing Commander Navigator, who gave me a load of old codswallop about promotion being the luck of the draw and being in the right place at the right time. I got a little cross and asked him to stop flannelling and to tell me what was holding me back. Were my annual assessments below par? Was there something I had done – or not done? I had now been a wing commander for seven years, whereas the norm for those in the fast stream was between five to six years. I told him I realized that I could not have the Station Commander job as I had temporarily lost my medical flying category but I could not understand why I had been refused the post of Deputy Captain of The Queen's Flight as the lack of staff experience quoted at the time seemed rather spurious.

My interviewer, who was getting a bit hot under the collar, asked whether I really wanted to know the reason to which I replied 'of course'. He continued, 'the truth is that, whereas you were considered eminently suitable for the job, your wife was not acceptable to the Palace.' I asked why on earth was that, and he replied because of two aspects of her past, not least the fact that she had been a night-club hostess. I then remembered that she had been subject to personal vetting after my interview with the Captain of TQF, when he had said that he would be pleased to have me. I was totally dumbstruck by this news and by his final word that I was no longer on the accelerated promotion list.

I was shaken by this news; it was so unfair, not just for me but particularly for Jane. I was furious that some starchy old courtiers, who had probably never been to a night-club in their lives, should have ruled her out. Admittedly there were good and bad clubs and perhaps the hostesses of the latter did have a certain reputation but the Windermere and The Coconut Grove were both very respectable. Jane had gone through a very difficult time after leaving Donald Wolfit's 'troupe of players' and deciding to go it alone. That coincided with her mother and father breaking up and getting into financial difficulties. Her going home to help out resulted in a unfortunate, long break in her career at a critical time.

When she returned to London she had initial success playing Violet Elizabeth Bott in *Just William* during which time she rented a flat in Maida Vale. When *Just William* closed she ran out of luck, largely because she refused to travel the 'casting couch' route to securing parts. On occasion she was the director's choice for the part but lost out to the producer's girlfriend. In desperation, she turned to hostessing to earn enough to pay the rent whilst leaving the days free to attend auditions, as had been done by many actresses before her. Had she been interviewed, as I had been, she would have passed with flying colours. Jane may not have been a typical senior RAF officer's wife but she was a darn sight better than most – as indeed she was to prove later on.

I had been very disheartened by that interview as my career seemed to be in tatters. My mood was one of utter despondency, not helped by the turmoil of the move to Holland and the mess that HQ RAF(G) had made by failing to find suitable housing before it had all been snapped up by the other nations. I think I must have been going through a sort of mid-life crisis – and it showed. Jane was very concerned, but I decided not to tell her the real reason as I did not want her to feel in any way responsible.

HQ AFCENT came into being at Brunssum on 1 November 1966. I drove up in the Fiat 500 which I had bought for £50 and took the first available opportunity to go to the accommodation office where the sergeant in charge shrugged his shoulders and said there was nothing new. However, the corporal on the next desk piped up and said that the offer of a brand-new furnished bungalow had just come in. I took one look at the photograph, read the prospectus and knew that it would be perfect for us – at a rent only just above the LOA. I drove immediately to the village of Kunrade, met the owner, viewed the house and shook hands on the deal. One of the clouds on my horizon had suddenly lifted.

It was with great regret that we left Fontainebleau with its many attractions, such as the Sunday market and the wonderful *charcuteries*, *fromageries* and *patisseries*. It was with some foreboding that we approached the former coalmining area of Brunssum. However, it did not take us long to realize that there were many compensations. First, the area was not as bleak as we had expected. Several years previously the Dutch government had taken the brave decision to close down all their coalmines in favour of relying solely on the vast reserves of natural gas in the North Sea. They had then carried out a radical programme of environmental improvement, which included the grading and planting of all the slag heaps. As a result the area was now surprisingly attractive.

The second advantage was the location at the conjunction of many countries. For example, we were able to take visitors on a drive which encompassed Holland, Belgium, France, Luxembourg and Germany and still get back in time for tea. In addition, cities such as Aachen and Maastricht were only a short drive away and the boys would be flown by charter aircraft into RAF Wildenrath, which was just over the border into Germany.

The third and, from my work point of view, the most important was that the HQ was now within only a relatively short distance of all the operational units under command. For example, we could now hold meetings, conferences, seminars, etc. and most delegates would be able to get to and from Brunssum in one day whereas Fontainebleau was so remote that many delegates would be away from their units for three days.

On the domestic side, our bungalow was a delight and our landlord was most helpful. There was an excellent Officers' Club and Karen was able to transfer from the Fontainebleau école to the International School at Brunssum without difficulty. I thoroughly enjoyed my job which gave me greater responsibility and freedom of action than anything comparable in the RAF. Moreover, for the first time in my career, I was able to take my full leave allowance and we went on some wonderful holidays, usually when the boys were with us. The living was easy and time passed quickly but my lack of promotion still rankled. After that fateful career interview I was not surprised that I did not feature in the 1967 January and July promotion lists. In the end I decided that I should do something about it, so I sought the advice of the Deputy C-in-C.

We had become quite friendly with ACM Sir Gus Walker and his wife, Brenda. We had been the first to invite him to dinner – within days of his arrival in Fontainebleau and since the move I had done a number of jobs for him with which he had been pleased. For example, I had made all the arrangements for the visit of Bill Bedford, the Chief Test Pilot of Hawker Siddeley, and for the presentation he gave on the Harrier 'Jump Jet' aircraft. I had also become the Secretary of the Netherlands Branch of the Cormorant Club (ex-students of JSSC), of which Sir Gus was the senior member, and had arranged an inaugural dinner in the Officers' Club which he had enjoyed. I also knew that he had a soft spot for Jane – in the nicest possible way.

When I had plucked up courage to seek an interview, Sir Gus listened intently to my tale of woe. He said he remembered why I had lost the job of Station Commander in 1964 as he had been my C-in-C at that time. However, he had not known about my being in line to become Deputy Captain of TQF and was very surprised and highly indignant that I should have lost that job because Jane had not found favour with the Palace. He told me that when he next visited the MoD in London he would speak to the Air Secretary on my behalf. When he returned from that visit he told me that the Air Secretary had been sympathetic and had promised that my career pattern would be subject to review and the findings relayed to HQ AFCENT. Another cloud had lifted, even if I did not have high hopes.

After what seemed like an eternity Sir Gus summoned me and said that he had had a letter from the Air Secretary who asked him to apologize to me for a serious error by his staff. As indeed I knew, I had been quite rightly taken out of the fast stream when I lost my flying category but had not been reinstated when I regained it. The letter went on to say that my subsequent annual confidential reports were being re-assessed and that he thought it most likely that I would be promoted at the end of my present overseas tour which would be in February 1969 – provided I kept up the good work. I thanked Sir Gus profusely and floated out of his office with my head in the clouds.

I realized that everything was now up to me, so for the rest of my tour I set out to make the best possible impression by getting things done quickly and efficiently – never an easy task in any multi-national HQ. I began to be co-opted onto a number of working parties and committees and to be given tasks that no one else wanted. Working in a multi-national tri-service HQ had been a bit of a culture shock, but I had soon learnt that, whereas the German and US officers outnumbered everyone else, if you wanted something done well you gave it to the British or Canadians. The Germans tried hard but as they were all Second World War veterans who had been demobilized for more than a decade they were not only old but also out of date. I had expected that the Americans would be prominent but they seemed to be interested only in filling the senior posts and there were relatively few at the 'coal-face' where the work was done. There were too few Belgian or Dutch officers to make any impact.

Most of our friends were German, Lieutenant Colonels Kaufman, Kretschmer and Lindner to name but three – perhaps because of my name and Prussian ancestry. We got to know few Americans as they had their own clubs and seldom mixed outside of work. In fact, many people considered that General de Gaulle kicked NATO forces out of France because he was affronted by the way the Americans did little to help the French economy. It sounds unbelievable but they flew in all their own supplies for their clubs, messes and stores, even lettuces, bread, cheese and meat. Their wives shopped almost exclusively at the BX and PX shops where everything American for the families was available. Every officer was entitled to have a new car flown in and then back home again at the end of his tour. The one exception to this was our friend Lieutenant Colonel Dan D'Andrea, who thought his compatriots were crazy. He and his wife, Betty, loved France and everything about it, but then he was really an Italian in disguise. It was he who introduced us to the AFCENT Touring Club which visited vineyards, châteaux and historic towns and indulged in gourmet dining.

Towards the end of my tour I was beginning to think that I might have done well enough to have reasonable hopes of promotion in the January 1969 list but my hopes were dashed when the posting notice arrived: I was to join the Directing Staff of the JSSC not as SDS (RAF) but as a Wing Commander syndicate leader.

Jane and I made the most of our remaining few months by revisiting some of our favourite places, such as Baden-Baden and the Black Forest, Oberammergau and Bavaria with its wonderful castles and baroque churches and Amsterdam with its canals – our favourite weekend haunt with the children. But all good things must come to an end: I was dined-out at the Club and Sir Gus said some nice things, then, at the beginning of March 1969, I reported to Latimer House to take over my new job, to collect my 'homework' before the next course started and to arrange accommodation. Unfortunately, there were no available married quarters, so I was allocated a hiring, a newish small house in Little Chalfont, as a temporary measure. I then returned to collect Jane and Karen and such little baggage as we had accumulated, all of which fitted easily into our capacious Morris 1800.

The Commandant of JSSC was now Vice-Admiral Denis Mason CB CVO, a very likeable and relaxed man with a charming wife. The SDS (RAF) was now Group Captain R. P. Harding and all other members of the DS had also changed since I had been on the course three years earlier. Unfortunately, most of the exercises had been rewritten so I could not rely on having wrestled with them before. I therefore had to do the new exercises myself to find out the pitfalls before I could pontificate on my syndicate's efforts. There was no such thing as the DS ideal solution for as the saying goes 'there are more ways than one of skinning a cat', none of them exclusively perfect.

So I was a very busy boy for the first three months of No. 37 course and was caught by surprise when I was promoted in the July list. The Commandant broke the news to me, and to Dusty Miller who had also been promoted, and told us that we would not be posted until the end of the course.

It soon became clear that I was being treated with kid gloves; perhaps the Air Secretary was trying to make amends for his Branch mishandling my career over the last five years. One of his air commodores rang to say that the post of Deputy Captain was coming up later that year and to ask whether I would like the job. I replied that, whereas I would have welcomed it in 1964 because of my loss of flying category, I now wanted to get back into the mainstream, preferably as a Station Commander.

There was no guarantee that I would get a station; poor old 'Dusty' was posted to HQ No. 1 Group as a staff officer. It was also taking a bit of a risk because being a station commander can be a 'make or break' posting. Do well and a bright future beckons, whereas to make a hash of it could be the end of the line. So I waited with bated breath to see whether my gamble paid off, which it did – with bells on! I was to become Station Commander of RAF Valley in Anglesey in January 1970: I could not have wished for a more appropriate or demanding appointment. I would soon be in a position to make up for five years in the wilderness and to attempt to recover from having fallen so far behind my expectations.

Chapter 13

How Green Was My Valley

Needless to say, before I could take over at Valley I had to undertake the usual refresher flying as I had been in ground appointments for five long years. However, during that time I had done my best to keep my hand in: in fact in the four years since I had regained my flying category I had managed to wangle over thirty hours on a variety of aircraft. The most enjoyable were two trips in a Hunter F7 when I was chief umpire at the NATO weapons meet at the RCAF base at Laarbruch. But by far the most rewarding were two trips in a Lockheed F-104, the first in an RCAF aircraft when I was able to try out the low-level cross-country route my committee had planned to train pilots in the use of radar prediction for night sorties with terrain-following equipment. The second was at the invitation of Lieutenant Colonel Freddie Obleser, one of my fellow staff officers at HQ AIRCENT, whom I had met when he was a squadron commander at the German Air Force base at Norvenich which I had visited when I was at CFS in 1963. My friendship with Freddie was to be of great significance many years later when I was the UK Chairman of the Tri-National Tornado Training Committee.

My refresher flying was carried out at RAF Manby in November where I flew thirty-five hours on the Jet Provost Mk 4, in the course of which I renewed my master-green instrument rating. The second was at CFS RAF Little Rissington where I flew twenty-five hours on the Gnat and re-validated my A2 QFI category on that aircraft.

I travelled by train to RAF Valley on 12 January 1970 and was accommodated in the VIP suite of the Officers' Mess whilst taking over from the departing Station Commander, Group Captain Ted Colahan. Ted was a pipe-smoking avuncular man of Irish extraction and a laid-back disposition who was obviously well liked. He gave me a comprehensive tour of the station and of the many varied units based there. The principal unit was No. 4 Flying Training School which had a very interesting history, having been formed in Egypt in 1921. It was now the fast-jet advanced FTS, flying the Hawker Hunter Marks 6 and 7 and the Folland Gnat.

In addition there were two helicopter units, namely C Flight of No. 22 Squadron, the role of which was air-sea rescue, and the detached mountain-flying element of CFS Shawbury. Then there was the Missile Practice Camp, under the operational control of HQ Fighter Command but under Valley for administration and discipline. There were also two non-flying units, the Marine Craft Unit which had two high-speed launches and the primary role of sea rescue, and the RAF Mountain Rescue Team, composed mainly of volunteers, well placed at Valley for rescue missions in Snowdonia.

Finally RAF Valley was a master diversion airfield (MDA), one of about a half-dozen dotted around the UK, which maintained a twenty-four-hour air traffic control and emergency service facility to deal with airborne emergencies every day of the year. I was delighted to learn the extent of my command responsibilities: this was something I could really get my teeth into.

Handover completed, I returned to Little Chalfont to pick up Jane and Karen – and our prize brown Burmese cat, Anyo. The drive to Valley was mostly along the tedious A5 but that through Snowdonia was lovely. We eventually crossed the splendid Menai Bridge onto Anglesey and then started to notice how desolate and derelict everything had become. The villages were drab, grey, mean-looking places, the roads and curb sides were deteriorating and such few trees as there were leaned perilously away from the perpetual strong westerly winds. As we neared Holyhead, things got steadily worse and we wondered what on earth we had let ourselves in for – and for two years.

However, as we finally left the A5 and drove towards Valley things improved and when we entered the camp it was like coming upon an oasis of good order – without the palm trees! We thankfully decanted into the Station Commander's Residence, a modern Type II married quarter of no architectural merit but well placed for the Officers' Mess and with lovely views over a lake at the bottom of our front garden.

I spent the first month in office visiting units and listening to what people had to say, having first interviewed my three wing commanders. The Chief Instructor, Max Bacon, a peacetime Cranwell graduate with a fighter background, struck me as being reasonably able and enthusiastic but ambitious and perhaps a bit over-confident. The OC Admin Wing, Joe Matthews, a navigator, seemed very competent, albeit somewhat authoritarian and fussy, not bad traits for his particular job. The OC Engineering Wing, Fred Wild, a highly qualified electrical engineer, did not impress me, seeming more academic than practical.

It did not take me long to realize that the picture of the station painted by Ted Colahan was not nearly as rosy as he had made out. The major problem was that the FTS had failed to meet the monthly flying task, set by HQ FTC, for months on end. As a consequence, courses were finishing late and a back-log of students waiting to come to Valley was building up to unacceptable proportions. This was due mainly to the poor utilization rate being achieved by the Gnat. In addition, discipline was poor as the station had the highest crime rate in the Command, due mainly to a high incidence of absence without leave. A 'phone call from the Senior Air Staff Officer (SASO) of HQ 23 Group, our immediate masters, had left me in no doubt that I was expected to put things right – or else. Oh dear: had I been presented with a poisoned chalice?

It also became clear that the personnel at Valley either loved or loathed serving there. I had few misgivings about Flying Wing, where I found good morale and strong esprit de corps – and who would not be happy flying two of the most delightful aircraft in the RAF. But I did worry about the ground-crew, who were clearly over-stretched with little reward, and also about the personnel of the detached and lodger units who seemed not to have been properly integrated into the station.

The existing organization of the station had much to commend it in that there was just about every facility anyone could want, perhaps because of the relative isolation of the base and lack of local amenities. There were two excellent messes, a Corporals' Club, and The No. 10 Club for all other ranks, where there were regular dances and concerts. In addition, there was an active wives' club, which ran a thriving thrift shop, as well as clubs for every imaginable activity such as motor/motor-cycle repair, theatre, sub-aqua diving, sailing, boy scouts and girl guides, to name a few. There was also a well-equipped gymnasium, squash and tennis courts, rugby and football pitches, etc., etc.

I was beginning to wonder why morale was so low until I started to talk to NCOs' and airmen's wives, almost all of whom hated being at Valley. The over-riding reason was that there was nowhere to go 'off-camp', and that it was too remote for them to go home at weekends – to see their mums! This complaint was very justifiable; Holyhead, the only large town on the island, was a most unattractive place with few amenities except for a fleapit of a cinema. For reasonable shops and other facilities, one had to go to Llandudno or upmarket to Chester. Despite a reasonable train service between London and Holyhead, almost everywhere else in the country was pretty inaccessible, particularly getting back to camp on Sundays. And, of course, in those days few airmen had cars.

In my second month I started to re-organize the way in which the station was run. Ted Colahan had held a monthly meeting in his office but only with the wing commanders. I moved the venue of that meeting to the Station HQ conference room and invited all squadron commanders, heads of sections, such as the SMO, the CoE Padre, the Education Officer etc., and, most importantly, representatives of the 'lodger' units to attend. This resulted in up to thirty people attending and in giving every unit an opportunity to have a say. I was thus able to get a better grasp of those areas where help was needed. But the main benefit was that it made everyone feel part of the team.

My most urgent task was to find out why aircraft utilization, particularly for the Gnat, was so low. What I found was that, because the Gnat was subject to frequent component failures, the engineers were 'cannibalizing' the Command reserve of those aircraft, which was held at Valley. This was mainly because the number of components held in store was inadequate and the AOG (aircraft on ground) system for getting replacements from the maintenance units was not working properly. The robbing from reserve aircraft was not totally prohibited but, on the scale at Valley, was extremely wasteful of manpower and bad technical practice.

I instructed Fred Wild to stop robbing from the reserve fleet immediately and to restore the aircraft to their proper inhibited state. I undertook to get onto HQ 23 Group to increase our holding of stores and to sort out the AOG system. I also showed Fred how he could better utilize his manpower by liaising with Max

Bacon to evolve a staggered take-off pattern of operations which would eliminate hold-ups whilst awaiting manpower to carry out the refuelling and turn-round procedures.

I next tackled the Chief Instructor and explained to him the advantages of staggered take offs and the need to get together with Fred to work out the details. I also told him that the last scheduled take-off of 1600 hours, laid down by Ted Colahan, was to apply only when the FTS was ahead of its monthly task. After all the airfield was open twenty-four hours a day and, weather permitting, it would be foolish to waste the opportunity to catch up. Finally, I got permission to use the surplus capacity of the Hunter squadron to pick up the smaller AOG spares from the MUS, thus saving days when delivery was by road or rail.

As I expected, Max and Fred were a bit disgruntled with my interference, so it was just as well that, in my third month of command, No. 4 FTS exceeded the Command task for the first time in over a year. I now needed to capitalize on this success, so I drafted a notice for Station Standing Orders congratulating everybody and granting the whole station, except those on duty, a long weekend from after duty on the next Thursday until 1200 hours on the following Monday. I also promised that this concession would be repeated every time we reached the task. In the event we exceeded the task every month for the rest of my tour. The effect on the overall morale of the station was incredible, enthusiasm abounded and absence without leave became a thing of the past. We even managed to take two more students on every course and to seriously reduce the backlog.

* * *

It did not take long for us to appreciate just how important RAF Valley was to the economic and social structure of Anglesey. The RAF community on the base was the third largest in the county, after Holyhead and Llangefni, the county town. We were also one of the largest employers of civilians in an area of high unemployment and, of course, the spending power of RAF personnel and their families contributed much to the local economy.

The station was also a social centre because of its many sporting and entertainment facilities, so sadly lacking elsewhere. Honorary membership of the officers' and sergeants' messes was much prized and those lucky enough to be invited to join could attend dances, games nights and other mess activities. Invitations for non-mess members to attend such functions as the annual Battle of Britain cocktail party were much sought after. This situation tended to subject us to a certain amount of toadying. For example, we had barely moved into the residence before Mrs Mabel Horspool called to welcome us to Valley and to introduce herself as a dear friend of the Colahans. Poor Mabel did not feature on our guest list, not least because we learned she had done the same thing with the last five commanding officers.

Many of the visitors to our house were VIPs of one sort or another. We had one particularly hectic week in May starting on the 16th when the Lord Lieutenant of

Anglesey, Sir Robert Williams Bulkeley, was inspecting our local ATC squadron. As I was invited to the event, he and the CO of the North Wales ATC Wing ended up having tea with us. The very next day the Lord Lieutenant of Merionethshire, John Williams Wynne, who owned vast acres of land and flew his own light aircraft to keep an eye on his thousands of sheep, diverted to Valley when thick fog descended on his airstrip. I met his aircraft, took him home and invited him to share our dinner, which was best end of neck lamb stew, whilst waiting for his chauffeur to collect him. He was very complimentary about Jane's cooking and a few days later sent us a huge, beautiful salmon trout.

A couple of days later some schoolboys climbed up into the superstructure of the Britannia Railway Bridge where pigeons nested. They lit a fire with the intention of smoking out the birds so they could steal their eggs. Unfortunately the fire got out of control and before long the bridge was ablaze, thus severing the most important economic link between Great Britain and Ireland, yet alone Anglesey itself. This catastrophe was extensively covered by the media and was regarded as a national emergency by the Labour Government of the day.

On 24 May a Government delegation flew into Valley from London. It was headed by the Secretary of State for Wales, Mr George Thomas, and the Minister for Agriculture and Fisheries, Mr Cledwyn Hughes, who was also MP for Anglesey. They proceeded to inspect what was left of the bridge before returning to Valley accompanied by some local big-wigs, such as the Chief Constable of Gwynnedd and Alun Williams, Chairman of Anglesey County Council. I was asked if they could gather in a conference room to discuss what action to recommend to the Cabinet. As the conference room was being redecorated, and as there were only eight of them, I invited them to the residence where they could use our dining room.

Deliberations over, we offered them tea and sandwiches which were much appreciated. I also introduced my mother, who happened to be staying with us. George Thomas, that smoothest of politicians, chatted her up and tried his best to persuade her to vote Labour at the next general election – little knowing that her staunch political convictions were far to the right of Genghis Khan and that Winston Churchill was her hero! George Thomas went on to become one of the best ever Speakers of the House of Commons and a Lord to boot.

As a master diversion airfield it was not unusual for Valley to handle civilian aircraft; this had been particularly so during the run up to the Investiture of Prince Charles as the Prince of Wales in Caernavon Castle on 1 July 1969. Ted Colahan and his three wing commanders and their wives were compensated for the upheaval with invitations to attend the ceremony and were allowed to keep the seats provided for the guests which had been especially designed for the occasion. That Royal event was the second time that I had just missed out! However, I did have the pleasure of meeting and greeting Princess Alexandra on her many flying visits to North Wales, usually to stay with her godfather, Sir Michael Duff, the Lord Lieutenant of Caernavon. Jane and I had the pleasure of meeting Sir Michael, who had been a wing commander in the RAF on intelligence duties during the Second World War, when we were the guests of honour at the Welsh premier of the *Battle of Britain* film in Bangor. We became good friends and visited him with the family at Vaynol, his beautiful country seat.

* * *

One of the 'perks' of being the Station Commander was my ability to fly whenever other commitments allowed. I started off by renewing my proficiency to fly the Whirlwind helicopters of the ASR Flight and was then able to fly in and out of the survival camps in the Welsh hills which we ran for every new course. I was usually accompanied by Flight Lieutenant Brian Nice, the flight commander, who had been one of the QFIs at Little Rissington where he was a member of the Red Pelicans, the CFS formation aerobatic team – small world! I flew into every one of the seven camps for the courses which arrived in my time at Valley.

I also renewed my proficiency to fly the Hunter and flew that beautiful aircraft until 4 FTS got well ahead of the tasks, when I started to fly the Gnat. I did not feel guilty about flying mainly for pleasure because I liked to be seen to be doing so and it was the best way to monitor the efficiency of the flying operation, air traffic control, the homing and landing aids, etc. And what a pleasure it was to fly the Gnat which, after the Spitfire and the Hunter, was my next favourite aircraft. It was a very small aircraft about which it was said 'you don't get into it – you put it on'. Its performance was quite exhilarating and its controls were so responsive that it was found necessary to fit rate of roll limiters into the control system lest pilots made themselves dizzy. It was a delight to fly, especially at low level in the North Wales low-flying area which included most of Snowdonia and the village of Port Merion, the mock Italianate creation of the architect Clough Williams Ellis. I also took advantage of the fact that we ran weekend air experience camps for ATC cadets in the summer, flying Chipmunks, my favourite light aircraft on which I had already flown over 900 hours.

As another means of keeping my eye on things, I went out several times on training sessions with our mountain rescue team, learning how to abseil up and down vertical cliff faces. And whenever they wanted a volunteer to act as the casualty that they were to rescue from some perilous situation on the mountain – guess who got the job? Being strapped into a stretcher and lowered 200 feet down a craggy mountain side was not exactly my idea of fun, but it went down well with the team.

I also went out several times in the high-speed launches of the Marine Craft Unit. All our pilots, staff and students, had to practise various emergency procedures on a regular basis, including dinghy drill. I found that these practices were being done rather unrealistically, either in the swimming pool or shallow bays around the perimeter of the airfield. So I initiated a procedure whereby a half-dozen pilots would be taken well out to sea by launch to where it was pretty choppy. They

The Station Commander being rescued by his Mountain Rescue Team.

would then simulate having parachuted into the sea by jumping in from the side of the launch at intervals. Then they would clamber into their dinghies and await their turn to be winched up into a helicopter. I went out with the first such sortie: needless to say I was first into the water and the last to be rescued.

* * *

From a domestic point of view, Jane really came into her own not just as 'the Station Master's wife' but also as President of the very active RAF Valley Wives' Club. She was able to devote time to the numerous activities this involved as Marcus was still at Ratcliffe College and Karen, who had been a day girl at the Arts Education School in Piccadilly, had had to become a boarder at the AET school in Tring because of our posting. Hilary had left Ratcliffe after taking his A-levels but was living with us as he decided to take a year off to retake his Physics exam and improve his grades before going on to train as an Architect. He was tutored by the Station Education Officer, was an enthusiastic member of the sub-aqua club and even got a job at Anglesey Aluminium. Jane liked having him around, as he was more of a help than a hindrance.

Amongst other things Jane presented the prizes at our Sports Days, opened the Coliseum Youth Club and organized a very successful Fashion Show by Browns of Chester in the Officers' Mess which raised £450, split equally between the RAF Benevolent Fund and the Royal National Lifeboat Institution. Many people had doubts about that enterprise but in the event it was a great success, particularly enjoyed by our many lady honorary members. The highlight of the second half, after a break for the wine-and-cheese buffet, was a parade along the catwalk by six of our QFIs in full flying kit with their 'g' suits on the outside. Jane was also involved in organizing a recital of classical piano music by Jane Butler, the sister of our Senior Medical Officer, Ben Butler. This was also a great success, raising money for the Station Charity Fund which was used to support local charities. A typical donation was the Oxy-Tocin infusion machine we bought for St David's Hospital in Bangor. But, of course, Jane's principal activity was being the hostess (and cook) of the many lunch and dinner parties at our house.

As Station Commander, I was entitled to an entertainment allowance which I reckoned amounted, after tax, to rather less than a bottle of gin per week – a meagre fraction of what I actually spent on official entertaining. I was also entitled to the services of a cook from the Officers' Mess but Jane elected to do all our cooking, whether for official or personal entertaining – a personal touch most appreciated by our guests.

I was very lucky in my superiors whilst at Valley. When I took over my immediate 'boss' was AVM Harry Burton, the AOC of No.23 Group based at RAF Ouston. I was not very popular with his staff because what I had achieved in sorting out Valley's problems should have been done by them long before – and I did not hesitate to tell them so. However, in July 1970, my former boss as Commandant of CFS, AVM 'Birdy' Bird Wilson took over as AOC, sorted out his staff and gave me his full support in everything I tried to do.

My ultimate boss was the AOC-in-C of HQ FTC, Air Marshal Sir 'Duke' Mavor. 'The Duke' had attended the Harvard Business School where he had become obsessed by their preaching about the efficiency benefits of a system of management for big business called 'Management by Objectives', or MBO. He was intent on introducing this system into his command and eventually directed that all FTC stations were to adopt this system within six months. This would initially involve all wing and squadron commanders in an incredible amount of work in preparing their 'objectives', which would detract from their getting on with the job in hand. So I applied to HQ FTC to be exempt on the grounds that Valley was already achieving all its objectives, using that ACS system of management – of which the C-in-C had not heard but nevertheless agreed. Many months later, during my farewell interview with him, he asked what ACS stood for; when I replied Applied Common Sense he roared with laughter – I am pleased to say!

The year 1970 turned out to have been a very good one for RAF Valley. Not only did we achieve our flying tasks for nine consecutive months we also did well in a number of other areas. For example we won the MT Efficiency cup, came second in the Fire and Rescue competition and third in the Jolliffe Trophy for airmen's dining halls. In the sporting events, we won the Command cricket and shooting cups and were runners-up in soccer. In the HQ 23 Group championships we won the basketball, cricket, soccer, squash and golf cups and were the badminton runners-up. Finally, our Drama Club came second in the Command Arts and Theatre competition.

These achievements were reflected in the AOC's Inspection report which gave us a glowing report both on and off parade. In fact it would seem that Valley could do no wrong! By the end of the year we were so far ahead of our flying task that I authorized a mass formation of twenty-one Gnats and seven Hunters, to be led by Max Bacon on New Year's Eve to mark his imminent posting. I flew in the lead Hunter with Squadron Leader Ian Porteous, the Hunter CO.

* * *

The euphoria of having completed a successful and incident-free year was shattered in January 1971 when two Red Arrows Gnats were involved in a collision at RAF Kemble in which four pilots were killed. Within a couple of hours of the crash I was appointed President of the Board of Inquiry into the accident with instructions to report to CFS Little Rissington whence HQ FTC had already despatched the terms of reference for the inquiry.

By midday I was driving myself to Little Rissington in my staff car to meet up with the team which consisted of a wing commander QFI pilot and two squadron leaders, one an engineering officer, the other a senior medical officer with aviation medicine expertise. On arrival, I was called into the office of the Commandant, Air Commodore Freddie Hazlewood, who attempted to outline the nature of the findings he expected of the inquiry. That was rather foolish, as my reaction was to think that maybe CFS had something to hide. I had to tell the Commandant that his intervention was out of order and that, amongst other things, the terms of reference charged me to investigate whether there had been any failure of supervision – about which he was clearly worried.

Our next port of call was RAF Kemble and the crash site, which was in the centre of the main runway. The scene was absolutely horrific: from the condition of the aircraft debris it was obvious that the collision had been fully head-on and not a glancing blow. The remains of the aircraft were scattered over a surprisingly small area and had been reduced to small fragments of metal, such was the force of the impact. The biggest identifiable aircraft parts were the four main wheels; everything else had been shattered into smithereens. A team of technicians from Rissington and Kemble were already gathering up the bits which were to be stored in one of the vacant hangars where we would attempt to discover any evidence of possible technical failure. Photographs of the crash site showing distribution of the debris had already been taken.

Also at the crash site was a team of four medical orderlies who were sifting through the debris to collect body parts in plastic bags. They were only youngsters and it was a necessary but appalling job and two of them had been violently sick. The only intact items of the pilots and their clothing were their leather flying boots which had been wrenched off their feet by the incredible force of the deceleration of a head-on collision at a relative speed of about 600 knots. Flesh had been shredded and bones smashed: in fact, the largest intact piece was a lower mandible or jawbone.

As a team the Board was faced with the difficult task of investigating whether there was any evidence to support a finding of pilot error or technical failure and whether there were any other contributory factors. We had also been tasked by HQ FTC to assess the degree of risk involved in all the manoeuvres carried out by the Red Arrows.

Apropos of pilot error we had to consider the experience of the pilots and the nature of that particular flight. The captains of the two aircraft, Flight Lieutenants Euan Perreaux and John Haddock, were both extremely well qualified to carry out the Roulette manoeuvre as they had been the synchro-pair for the past season and had carried out that manoeuvre, in practice and performance, well over a hundred times.

From a spectator point of view, the Roulette is the most exciting and seemingly most dangerous as the aircraft fly towards each other from either end of the runway and just as they appear to be about to collide they both roll 90-degrees to starboard and then rapidly back again, seemingly passing each other with only feet to spare. It is not unusual to hear a great simultaneous gasp from the spectators. In fact, the risk is illusionary as the aircraft nearer the crowd flies at 200 feet down the near side of the runway whilst the other aircraft flies down the far side at 250 feet. To the spectators looking up, they appear to be at the same level whereas in fact there is a runway's width (100 feet) horizontal and a fifty-foot vertical clearance.

The next thing to consider was whether either of the two new pilots could have been flying the aircraft from the rear seat and had made a fatal error of judgement. The main reason for ruling out that possibility was the nature of that particular sortie. For some time the Red Arrows had become concerned about the speed of response and power output at different throttle settings of the Orpheus engines when performing certain manoeuvres. So the team had started flying the various sequences with tradesmen in the rear seats monitoring the settings and responses from the instruments and writing the results on their knee pads.

When it became time to monitor the synchro-pair sequences there were no tradesmen available at Kemble because winter servicing of the majority of the team's aircraft was in full swing at Little Rissington, so the new pilots were used to do the monitoring and writing down the results on their knee-pads. Moreover, not only was this not a training sortie but neither of the new pilots were designated to be in the synchro-pair, so there would have been no point and, anyway, new pilots always fly in the front seats in training sorties because of the restricted view from the rear.

It is all too easy when in doubt, and particularly when a pilot was killed, for Boards of Inquiry to opt for a finding of pilot error, even when there is no evidence whatsoever to support that conclusion. After due consideration of the possibility of physical or psychological problems, and finding no reason to suspect that any of the pilots were unfit to fly because of tiredness, after-effects of alcohol consumption or any form of domestic, financial or other trauma, the Board members were unanimous in ruling out pilot error altogether.

So our next consideration was whether mechanical failure of some sort might have been responsible. In this our investigation was hampered by two things; firstly the total fragmentation of the aircraft and its systems made examination of the wreckage utterly useless. Secondly, and incredibly, there were no witnesses of the crucial micro-seconds immediately before the collision. The ATC officer and his assistant on duty in the tower said that they had both seen the crash but, on interrogation, admitted that they had only witnessed the immediate aftermath, having been alerted by the horrendous noise of the impact, nor was there anyone on the airfield who might have been watching the aircraft. So there was no evidence that either of the aircraft had veered towards the other at the last minute or whether the aircraft were, unaccountably, approaching each other on the same side of the runway.

There were three possible mechanical failures that we considered, namely engine break-up, hydraulic failure and control-column jamming. Only two and a half months previously the leader of the Red Arrows, Squadron Leader Dennis Hazell, was leading a formation of five aircraft coming in to land when his engine suddenly blew up, spewing debris out of the back end. Dennis ejected at low level, sustaining a badly-broken leg. That dramatic engine failure was attributed to salt corrosion of the roots of the compressor blades causing turbine disintegration, a problem only previously encountered at Valley where the airfield is virtually on the sea shore. There the prevention of corrosion was attained by washing the engine with clean water during a ground run followed by a mixture of oil and paraffin every month. It is possible that the Red Arrows had developed this problem as I had permitted them to train at Valley at weekends when Kemble's weather was below limits. The team had followed the Valley prevention method since the accident, so it was unlikely that engine disintegration had been responsible and, anyway, the distribution of debris at Kemble showed no evidence of back-end scatter.

Hydraulic failure without engine failure is always possible and would result in loss of power-assisted control column movement when the stick forces would become heavy and unresponsive but the aircraft would still be flyable. It is also possible that the control column might have become jammed had a screwdriver or spanner been left in the engine compartment during maintenance. However, the Red Arrows had a stringent tool-control system and we checked that their shadow-boards showed that no tools were missing. We also found that the knee-pad pens were tethered and, if dropped, would only dangle rather than drop through into the works. Anyway, as the cockpits were pressurized, there was no access into the engine compartment.

After a hectic week of investigation, the Board was unable to come up with any positive conclusion as to the cause of the accident. This was due to two main factors: firstly, the lack of any eyewitnesses and, secondly, the inability to find any evidence of technical failure due to the total disintegration of both aircraft. Moreover, we found that there were no failures of supervision of either aircrew or technicians. Indeed we found that the Red Arrows had continued to maintain the high standards in their operation first instilled during the leadership of Ray Hanna after the slap-dash approach of Lee Jones.

The final two days at Kemble were spent talking with Flight Lieutenant Bill Loverseed, who had taken over the leadership from Hazell, and his team. We discussed at length the degree of risk involved in every Red Arrow manoeuvre and produced a 'league table'. Naturally, there is an inherent risk in formation aerobatics but this is kept as low as possible by careful selection for the team of only the finest pilots and by a training and practice programme which is second to none. Indeed, we checked the records since 1965 and found that the Red Arrows yearly accident rate was lower than that of all other units flying the Gnat for the complete period. It is interesting to note that we rated the roulette manoeuvre as being one of the least risky. It has been retained in the Synchro-Pair sequence for the last thirty-six years completely without further incident.

We duly completed our report which was endorsed by the AOC-in-C before forwarding it to the Air Force Board. Thankfully, my Board came under no pressure from above to suggest that the most likely cause was pilot error.

* * *

I returned to Valley on 29 January 1971 to find, perhaps a little disappointedly, that the station had continued to run efficiently in my absence. However, such complacency which might have crept in was rudely shattered when we suffered a fatal crash. On 16 May two instructors were carrying out a properly authorized sortie of staff continuation training which included low flying. They were seen to be flying at about 250 feet up one side of a valley in the low-flying area when the aircraft was seen to go into a 180-degree steep turn which was misjudged as they crashed, belly-up, near the top of a ridge called Cwn Penmacho. I flew to the crash site in a helicopter once the rescue team had retrieved the bodies. It became clear what had happened from the marks on the ground and the scattering of the wreckage. This was confirmed by the independent accounts of the two pilots who had been watching the aircraft from above and by eye witnesses on the ground. When in a steep turn neither of the pilots would have been able to see just how close to the high ground they were getting. Another ten feet up and they would have missed the ridge.

A Board of Inquiry was convened and had no hesitation in finding the cause to have been pilot error – with which I could not argue. Fortunately, they found no failure in supervision or any other aspect of our procedures. I addressed all the pilots, staff and students, at the following mornings Met Briefing and told them, amongst many other things, that even the best pilots can make mistakes and that the least we could do was to learn the lesson that we must never allow ourselves to be other than truly professional.

We did our best to honour our two pilots by holding a memorial service in the CoE church on camp conducted by the Padre, Squadron Leader the Reverend

John Jenkyns. It was attended by their wives and their parents and the AOC, AVM 'Birdy' Wilson, flew in for the service. I read one of the lessons and the choir sang beautifully. It was a moving occasion, marred only by the sobbing of one of the wives throughout the service. The other wife shed tears but with great dignity and courage. It was a sad, avoidable waste of two young lives, especially so soon after the Red Arrows' crash in which the two new pilots killed had been ex-Valley QFIs well-known to many of the congregation.

Nor was that the last needless death on the Station during my tour there. Shortly after the crash several airmen had been celebrating one of their birthdays; when the bar closed one of them said that he was going for a walk along the beach to clear his head. Next morning one of the officers out for an early morning jog along the shoreline on the west side of the airfield came across the drowned body of the airman. It appeared that he, slightly worse for wear, had happened upon one of the small boats tethered well above the high-tide line on the grassy bank. He must have untied the boat, pushed it into the water and jumped in. Unbeknown to him the owner had, quite correctly, taken out the drain plug from the bottom of the boat. The outgoing tide took the boat out to sea where it gradually filled up and sank. The dinghy was recovered several days later when it was washed up miles away.

Although I was in my element and enjoyed every minute of being a station commander, these deaths did cast a bit of a shadow. Nor was the Station, successful as it might be, immune from the occasional stupidities that sorely tried my patience. One such concerned the Squadron Leader CO of one of our lodger units, which came under me for discipline, who was having an affair with the wife of one of our administrative officers. They were both members of the Bridge Club and were thus able to tell their respective spouses that they were playing cards when really they were 'playing away'. Nobody was aware of this amour and the RAF does not pontificate on moral issues – unless the behaviour damages the good name of the service.

Eventually the affair ended, much to the dismay of the wife who confided her unhappiness to the wife of the Squadron Leader's deputy who in turn was absolutely furious because she, also a member of the Bridge Club, had been cast off by the same Casanova several months previously. In her fury, the woman scorned confessed her infidelity and the whole story to her husband who in turn reported the matter to the new OC Admin. Wing, John Williams, a stickler for doing things 'by the book' who consulted the *Manual of Air Force Law* which laid down that an officer found to have had a sexual relationship with the wife of a subordinate should be invited to resign or face disciplinary action – which could result in dishonourable discharge.

All this came to a head whilst I was on leave. By the time I returned John had already initiated action by reporting the affair to HQ Fighter Command and it was too late for me to intervene. Had it come to my attention in the first place I would have advocated dealing with the matter quite differently. Clearly, the

Lothario would have to be posted away immediately, preferably to the Outer Hebrides, he should be given a severe reprimand, the affairs would be noted in his service documents and further promotion thereafter would be highly unlikely. In advocating this somewhat softer approach I would be taking two things into account: firstly, the changing mores of society since the *MAFL* was last revised and secondly the future wellbeing of his long suffering wife and family. I need not have worried on that score, as the culprit chose to resign.

I had never forgotten that I had broken a few rules and done one or two silly things in my youth, so perhaps I do lean towards leniency towards all but the most serious misdemeanours. A typical example occurred during a Guest Night in the Officers' Mess, when a graduating course was being dined out. When the dinner and speeches were over, the PMC, Wing Commander Sandy Innes-Smith, left the top table along with myself and our guests, who included a retired general. We went into the bar where normally the rest of the officers would follow. After about fifteen minutes I became aware of the sound of distant music and how few other officers had joined us. Sandy and I went back towards the dining room where, through the glass doors we saw a young girl sashaying along the top table to the strains of David Rose's 'The Stripper'. By this time she was topless and was about to discard her skirt.

Although rather amused, I realized that prompt action was necessary, so I went in unnoticed until I climbed up onto the table whereupon the young lady disappeared as if by magic. The music was still playing, so I sashayed towards the centre removing my bow tie and mess-dress jacket the while. When the music stopped there was a fearful hush so I said 'I don't know why you should have spent good money when you could have made use of local talent', which resulted in some relieved laughter. When they had quietened down, I told them that it was not really a laughing matter because, if the incident became known to the AOC, who was a martinet when it came to social misconduct, an inquiry would be called for and heads might roll, perhaps including my own. So I told them never to mention this incident to anyone, lest the culprits be disciplined. As I got down from the table, I was given a quiet round of applause.

I did not let the matter stop there. I wrote a 'staff in confidence' semi-official letter to every officer on the staff so that everyone should be aware of my views on what I described as a 'disgraceful incident!' I said that, whereas I was prepared to treat it as a youthful prank which misfired, I was more concerned that none of the senior officers present had made any attempt to stop the 'entertainment' or even walk out. Also, that I was not intending to take any action, other than that of which certain individuals were already aware. However, I stressed that if a similar incident was to occur again I would have no hesitation in taking action under Queen's Regulations No.1020.

My own inquiries revealed that the instigator of the incident was the CO of the Squadron of the graduating course. I therefore had him on the mat and read him the riot act, telling him that he was very lucky that I was not taking the matter any

The author hosts a Guest Night to celebrate the Golden Anniversary of No. 4 Flying Training School, the only FTS to have been in continuous operation for 50 years.

further. He seemed suitably contrite and must have learned a lesson because he was twice posted back to Valley in the course of his career, first as Chief Instructor and then as Station Commander. I have often wondered how, in my place, he would have handled a similar incident! He eventually retired as an Air Vice Marshal.

I always enjoyed dining-in and guest nights in the mess, even though I usually had to make a speech. I tried never to tell the same joke twice, unlike my predecessor who, according to Joe Matthews, only knew three jokes and used them over and over again. Perhaps the most important guest night was on 2 April 1971 when we celebrated the fiftieth Anniversary of the formation of No. 4 FTS in Egypt in 1921. Our guests of honour were ACM Sir Walter Dawson and AVM Butler, father of our SMO, Ben, who had both served at No. 4 FTS before the war. Unfortunately the AOC, AVM Birdy Wilson, was unable to attend but I invited the COs of the other four FTSs – if only to gloat that No. 4 was the only one to have had fifty years' continuous service.

My favourite events by far were the ladies' guest nights held twice a year and much enjoyed by our honorary members. In my speeches, before I proposed the toast of 'The Ladies', I always tried to include a short but appropriate odd ode. I must admit that I had no hesitation in plagiarizing and paraphrasing the verses of Ogden Nash and other rhymesters. Perhaps the best received was the following:

> There's a special type of person
> known plurally as 'wives'
> who do their hair in curlers
> and try to run our lives.
> They get up early in the morning
> to cook breakfast for the boys

and keep on having babies
which runs up bills for toys.

There's a special type of person
known singularly as 'wife'.
The Cockneys call her trouble
with lots and lots of strife.
They come in different colours
and are of various shape and size
but underneath the warpaint
there's a blessing in disguise.

There's a special type of person
known officially as 'spouse'
who cooks and scrubs and dusts
and never seems to grouse.
    Though we take them all for granted
they are deserving of our kisses
those special types of person
known affectionately as 'Mrs'.

* * *

As my tour-expiry date of mid-January 1972 approached, time seemed to fly by. In mid-November I was asked by the Editor of *Force Eight*, the station magazine, so called after the Beaufort Scale for 'storm', if I would write another 'Christmas Message' for publication in the December edition. In my draft, I congratulated all personnel on how much had been achieved during the year, especially as we were on course to have attained all our flying targets for a record twelve consecutive months. In addition, our station teams had won just about every sporting competition entered and the Airmen's Dining Hall had come second in the RAF-wide Jolliffe Trophy. The communications centre had won a prestigious Silver Star 'Comstar' award and the MT section had won the coveted MT Efficiency Trophy for the second year running. I also praised the Mountain Rescue Team and C Flight of No. 22 Squadron for having carried out an unprecedented number of meritorious rescues. I attributed these successes to the outstanding spirit and morale of all personnel and to the hard work they had put in.

    No sooner was I putting the finishing touches to my draft than I received a kick in the teeth in the form of a 'phone call from the Air Secretary's Department, telling me that I was posted to the Ministry of Defence with effect from 13 December 1971 to take over as Deputy Director of Air Plans. To rub salt into my aching gums, I was told that my successor would be arriving at Valley in two days for a short hand-over, which was to be effected from 6 December. I got a bit stroppy and said 'I be blowed if I would leave Valley until after Christmas', only to be told that the Assistant Chief of the Air Staff (Policy and Plans) had been approached but had insisted that my arrival could not be delayed.

So bang went all our plans for Christmas and all the festivities planned for our departure, which included a special ladies' guest night in early January so that Jane, who was very popular, could also be dined out in style. I now had to complete the hand-over by 6 December, which left exactly one week in which to arrange somewhere to live and to move in with all our goods and chattels. Luckily the MoD quartering people were able to offer me, as a temporary measure, a vacant MQ at RAF Abingdon.

In the meantime my successor arrived and was staying in the VIP suite of the Officers' Mess. My heart had sunk when I learned who it was to be, as I had known him as the CI of the RAF College at Cranwell when I was at CFS. My impression then was that, whilst he was considered to be academically gifted, he lacked personnel management skills and had the leadership qualities of a wet blanket. Unfortunately so it proved: I learned from friends at Valley that he had lost control and that the station had gone to pot. After about a year he was relieved of his command, having been injured when a light communications aircraft, in which he had been a passenger, crashed on take-off as a result of having been refuelled by Station Flight with AVTUR instead of AVGAS. Luckily his successor was made of sterner stuff and RAF Valley was restored to its proper place in the FTS world – on top!

Luckily, there was a course graduation dining-in night scheduled just before I had to leave. The AOC, who had tried to have my departure delayed, was able to attend and said a few nice things. Before he flew back to his HQ he confided in me that I could expect a little something in the New Year's Honours list. If such a thing was to happen, and I had been disappointed before, it would have been the gilt on the gingerbread of what had been the best two years of my career to date. The job had been challenging, demanding, bloody hard work and occasionally frustrating, but always enjoyable and rewarding.

From a family point of view, our stay at Valley had been much appreciated by Jane who, perhaps for the first time, had been completely comfortable with service life, not least because she liked the responsibilities and privileges of being a Station Commander's wife rather than just a 'camp follower'. Hilary, now at Kingston Polytechnic studying Architecture, having improved his physics grades, had enjoyed his stay with us, having made full use of the facilities available on camp, not least the sub-aqua club. Marcus and Karen had also enjoyed spending their holidays with us. More than anywhere else, we had become fully integrated into the Anglesey civilian community, thanks largely to the many active honorary members of the mess. Our closest friends were Richard and Dilys Cunliffe, who lived nearby in a lovely Georgian manor house with beautiful grounds. Dilys, now long widowed and approaching ninety years old, still comes to stay with us from time to time.

The author commissioned the foremost slate sculptor in Wales to reproduce the RAF Valley crest of a rampant Welsh Dragon as a farewell gift to the Officers' Mess. It was unveiled by Audrey, the wife of the Air Officer Commanding, Air Vice Marshal 'Birdy' Bird-Wilson.

Service life is very transitory and one is soon forgotten when the time comes to move on. But I left my mark at Valley in the shape of a massive five-foot-high slate rendering of the central motif of the station badge which I commissioned from Idris Griffiths, the foremost sculptor in slate who lived in nearly Penrhyndendrath. It depicted a rampant Welsh dragon holding a portcullis. I would have liked a replica of the complete badge which would have included the Latin motto 'In Adversis Perfugium' (a refuge in adversity), which was so appropriate for a master diversion airfield. However, I was persuaded against that by Idris because of the increased cost and weight.

It was truly beautiful and weighed in at 4.5cwt. I invited Audrey Bird Wilson, the AOC's wife, to come to Valley to unveil it and to attend a dinner night in the Mess, which was in fact my last official function. It was just as well that prim and proper Audrey was not around when the 'Works and Bricks' people attempted to manhandle that massive dragon to secure it high up on the Mess wall near the main entrance. The air turned blue but, at least, the oaths were in Welsh!

The handover was completed on time and it was with a heavy heart that I put the finishing touches to my Christmas message which read:

> It is with pride that I hand over to my successor, secure in the knowledge that you will give him the same loyalty and support that I have enjoyed. By the time this magazine is published we will have left Valley. We will leave behind many happy memories and many good friends. When we depart we will drive swiftly less sorrow overtakes us.

Chapter 14

A Short Intermission at the Ministry

When Jane and I arrived at RAF Abingdon we reported to the station HQ to meet the WRAF officer in charge of housing who accompanied us to our new home – a miserable type IV semi-detached married quarter. Having handed over the keys, she left us to unpack and await the barrack warden to carry out the usual inventory check. It really was a dreadful comedown from having been a station commander to being an unwelcome lodger on someone else's patch.

On 13 December 1971 I travelled to the Ministry of Defence (MoD) main building in Whitehall to take over my new job. The journey was not too bad; Didcot to Paddington by British Rail Express 125 which took less than thirty minutes and then by Underground to Westminster, which took a darn sight longer. The biggest snag was that poor Jane had to drive me to the station at some unearthly hour and then await a 'phone call from me telling her which train home I was hoping to catch so that she could meet me at the station, usually at a time when she should have been preparing dinner.

It was quite a daunting task taking over from David Dick because he had graduated from Cambridge with a double first, had come top of his courses at both CFS and the Empire Test Pilots' School and was not only a brilliant pilot but also a bit of a boffin. I had known him for years and knew him as a jolly nice chap – albeit with the air of an absent-minded professor. He had made a name for himself by campaigning for the RAF to become involved in 'Space' when, to most people, space was just pie in the sky.

He could only spare me three days and explained the reason for the unseemly rush. Apparently an Air Commodore in an important Joint Planning Staff appointment had been sacked as being ill-qualified and incompetent. The job was rotational between the Services and the Royal Navy, who were next in line, were pressing to take over, whereas the RAF maintained that they should see out their turn as their original man had only been in post for three months. It was therefore vital that his replacement should not only take over as soon as possible, but should also be of high calibre to restore our good name. David was clearly an excellent choice.

As Deputy Director of Air Plans (DDAP) I had a team of four wing commanders and our principal task was the preparation of staff papers for consideration by the Air Force Board (AFB). The subject matter of these papers could be extremely varied and the need for them could come from the AFB or in response to Parliamentary Questions (PQs). The preparation time for some papers could be quite lengthy, with no particular dead-line or they could be rush jobs, as was usually the case with PQs. I was quite impressed by the calibre of my wing commanders but found that they had been under-used as David who, being a bit of a perfectionist, took too much work on his own shoulders. I was horrified to learn that he was usually at his desk by 8.00am and seldom left the office before 7.00pm. I was determined not to follow that pattern.

It took me two months to clear the plethora of pending files in my security cabinet and to re-organize how my team worked. When the terms of reference for papers arrived David would allot them to individual wing commanders to prepare and produce the paper in draft form. Then, being David, he would rewrite the whole thing himself: no wonder he had to burn the midnight oil! I only allocated the long-term papers to the 'boys', but for the rush jobs I used them as researchers to muster all the relevant facts to support the recommendations and conclusions. Armed with their inputs, I would write the paper myself as I had found, at the JSSC both on the course and later as DS, that I had a knack of writing quickly, concisely and in a logical format. As a result we were able to produce better papers without the previous panic to meet the tighter dead-lines.

* * *

In the meantime I had been worrying the quartering people to find us an appropriate MoD married quarter or hiring within reasonable commuting distance of MoD, where I had my office on the fifth floor with a lovely view of Old Father Thames. They came up trumps, perhaps because I was making a nuisance of myself, with the offer of a house called 'Alfriston' in Fleet in Hampshire which had been the official residence of the Senior Air Staff Officer of HQ FTC when it was located at Shinfield Park. It had been empty for some time since FTC had merged with HQ Technical Training Command at Bampton as HQ Training Command. It was now redundant but was still furnished to two-star standards whilst MoD was deciding what to do with it. I knew the house, because I had been to a couple of drinks parties there when I worked for the SASO in 1965, so I accepted it straight away.

Things were beginning to look up for the Langer family, not least because Hampshire County Council had funded a place for Karen at the prestigious Farnborough Hill Convent. The only niggle was that my name did not feature in the New Year's Honours list and I was a little surprised that an old friend of mine, Group Captain Bob Price, had been appointed CBE. Bob was currently Station Commander of RAF Linton-on-Ouse and CO of No. 1 FTS. During my time at Valley we had met up several times and compared notes and I knew he was doing a good job – so good luck to him.

A couple of days later I was rung by an irate Birdy Wilson who was absolutely furious with the AOC-in-C, ACM Sir 'Duke' Mavor, who had invited the AOCs of Nos. 23 and 25 Groups to submit nominations for awards and Birdy had nominated me for the CBE. As the AOC No. 25 Gp had no nominations, Birdy was told that he could nominate two people for that honour. So he added Bob's name to his recommendation but with the proviso that I was to have priority. He was very apologetic and promised to sort it out.

I had a pretty good idea why the AOC-in-C chose Bob, because they were both bridge-playing fanatics and had teamed up in championship games for several years. I did not tell Birdy this, because I was afraid he might blow his top and do something he might regret later. On the other hand, of course, it could have been 'Duke' getting his own back on me on, having pulled the wool over his eyes when I sought exemption from his 'Management by Objectives' directive.

* * *

I had always dreaded being posted to MoD but after several months in the job I was surprised to find that I actually rather enjoyed it. The commuting from Fleet was pretty painless: 'Alfriston' was less than a mile to the BR station, to which I cycled on 'Mrs Pankhurst', so called because I chained her to the railings. This meant I no longer depended on Jane for delivery and collection. The journey time door-to-door was about an hour, during which time I could rehearse in my mind the framework of the paper I was currently working on. But what I liked most was the nature of the job which was right in the midst of RAF thinking on policy and which gave me an invaluable insight into the workings of Government and how the Air Force Board handled the vagaries of ministerial decisions. Amongst other things, I was also responsible for monitoring the 'long-term costings' which was the projection of the estimate of the amount of the RAF allotment from the annual Defence Budget for the next ten years and the cost of implementing re-equipment with new aircraft and weapons and other plans for the same period. This projection formed the basis of the annual RAF bid for defence money. Needless to say, the estimates were seldom realized, not least because the RN and the Army were always pressing for a bigger slice of the cake. Any discrepancy which could not be matched by savings required adjustment of the long-term costings by deferring the phasing in of the various programmes or by reducing their scale.

After I had been in post for about five months, my Director, Air Commodore Alan Davies CBE, invited me into his office as I was leaving for home. He poured me a glass of his single-malt scotch whisky, which he did not dispense lightly, and said that, whereas he was pleased with my work, the real reason for our chat was to let me know that I had been pre-selected to attend the Imperial Defence College (IDC) course in January 1974. He congratulated me and forecast a bright future ahead. The IDC course was a sure stepping stone to air rank and prestigious appointments, so it seemed that, after my five years in the promotion doldrums, someone up high was working overtime to help me catch up.

* * *

In July 1972 I was rung by AVM Hazelwood, now working for the Air Member for Personnel (AMP), who said in his usual sarcastic manner, 'For some extraordinary reason the Air Force Board have agreed that you should be given the acting rank of Air Commodore if you were to volunteer for loan service in Singapore'. He went on to say that I had the right experience and qualifications for the job. He asked me to give him an answer within the week.

Needless to say, I was very tempted principally, because acceptance meant promotion but also because I had served in Singapore twice before and liked the country very much. Moreover, the job appealed to me because Singapore Air Defence Command was an emergent air force having been formed following Singapore's secession from Malaysia in 1965 after much acrimonious political wrangling. At that time Singapore withdrew all its nationals who were serving in the Malaysian Armed Forces. In 1968 they formed the Singapore Armed Forces, of which SADC was the air force element but, having been left with a motley crew of officers and airmen, they were very reliant on outside help. The main elements were its two fighter squadrons, equipped with Hawker Hunters, and the infrastructure and training organization to support them. Fighters and training – right up my street. And, of course, twenty years previously I had been the training officer of the Singapore Squadron of the Malayan Auxiliary Air Force, one aim of which had been to train a cadre of pilots and technicians for when Singapore decided to form an air force of its own.

However, from my career point of view, it was not so attractive as I would miss out on attending IDC and officers away on loan service tended to be put on the promotion back-burner. Moreover, I was convinced that my present job was giving me a vital insight in how MoD worked which would stand me in good stead if I was to be considered for higher appointments. We were also happily settled in at 'Alfriston', which we liked so much that I had put in a bid to buy the house, as a sitting tenant, should MoD decide to put it on the market. Finally, we would want Karen to continue at the Convent as she was at a critical stage of her education. So, without consulting Jane, I told Freddie of my concerns and that I was not prepared to volunteer.

Two days later I was invited to call on the Air Secretary, Air Chief Marshal Sir John Barraclough KCB CBE DFC AFC, in his office. He welcomed me warmly, offered me coffee and said that he was very disappointed that I had turned down the Singapore job which, in his opinion, was a golden opportunity. He said that AVM Hazlewood had told him of my concerns and he wanted to assure me that, far from hindering my career prospects, the posting would enhance them. He promised that I would be selected for the January 1975 IDC course and that I would almost certainly get a two-star appointment after completion, especially after having been a virtual CAS, albeit of another country's air force. He cited the case of Alisdair Steedman who had been the first CAS of the Royal Malaysian Air Force on loan as an Air Commodore and was now an Air Chief Marshal. He went on to say that I would be given a former RAF residence in Singapore furnished to two-star standards and that there were many other advantages. Finally, he asked me to reconsider and to let him know my decision as soon as possible. What he did not tell me, as I was to find out later, was that two other officers had already been proposed and turned down by Lee Kwan Yew – apparently for the lack of appropriate experience.

Somewhat reassured by the Air Secretary, I discussed the matter with both Jane and Karen, who would have to accompany us and go to the International School. They were both in favour of our going, so I agreed. A signal was sent to the Prime Minister's office in Singapore, via the British High Commission, giving my personal details and a CV. There was a rapid response which read 'If Air Commodore J. F. Langer is the Flight Lieutenant Johnny Langer I knew in the 1950s he has got the job – subject to interview'.

From then on things moved rapidly and on 15 August I flew out to Singapore, courtesy of the weekly RAF VC10 scheduled flight from RAF Brize Norton via RAF Akrotiri (Cyprus) and the staging post of RAF Gan in the Indian Ocean. When we landed at the SADC base that was once RAF Tengah I was met by Group Captain Alan Jenkins, the Air Attaché, and Lieutenant Colonel Peter Stuart, the base commander. Alan looked after me extremely well; not only did I stay with him and his wife in their British High Commission (BHC) MQ but he also took me to see all the right people and places. First on his list was the High Commissioner, Sir Sam Fall KCVO, and his wife, a charming couple with whom we had tea, and then on to see the two Singaporeans who were to interview me. The first of these was Mr Pang Tee Pow, the first Permanent Secretary of the Ministry of Defence (Mindef), and then Dr Goh Keng Swee, the Deputy Prime Minister and Minister for Defence.

Dr Goh was a fascinating character who had graduated with honours from the London School of Economics and had masterminded the economic survival of Singapore after independence, despite its small size (about that of the Isle of Wight) and its total lack of natural resources. Under his guidance, Singapore was fast becoming the powerhouse of the region, based almost entirely on entrepôt trade. Despite his fearsome reputation, about which I had been warned, I found him a shy and rather reticent individual, unlike Mr Pang Tee Pow who, I was to find out, put the fear of God into his subordinates. However, I must have found favour with them both because, even before I left for home, I was told that they looked forward to my return as DAS in January 1973.

My final interview was with Lieutenant Colonel Ee Tean Chye, the nominal head of SADC, who was also base commander of the former RAF Changi. He said that he was looking forward to my arrival as, by his admission, he knew nothing about air force matters as he, along with a number of other ex-Army officers, had been press-ganged into transferring to SADC because of its lack of national senior officers.

The only blot on the horizon was when Alan took me to see the house the Mindef had earmarked for me. It was a dreadful, rundown, old colonial house which was empty and badly in need of total redecoration. For example, the one bathroom had a rusty, old enamelled tin bath which, when the plug was pulled, emptied its water onto the concrete floor and was channelled towards a drainpipe on the outside of the house. So much for the promised ex-RAF residence furnished to two-star standards. Alan was equally appalled and said that he would sort out something more appropriate with the Singapore authorities before I returned.

What I did not know at the time was that the problem was that when the British Forces left Singapore in 1971 the Treasury endeavoured to get Singapore to pay for all the material assets left behind after withdrawal. Singapore argued that they should only pay for those things which they intended to use for their own purposes. These assets included all the residences and married quarters which Singapore did not require for the simple reason that they did not provide married quarters for any of their military personnel. So Singapore refused to pay that element of the settlement and, when the Treasury argued, they invited them to take them away.

Having won the battle, once the British Forces had left, the residences and type I and II MQs were allocated to Ministers and Senior Government officials and the remainder were either sold or rented out to Singaporean civilians or to expatriates working in Singapore.

* * *

I returned to the UK on 19 August, this time courtesy of the BHC who provided me with a Club Class ticket on a BOAC flight so that I would not have to waste time waiting for the return RAF schedule. The aircraft was a VC10 – but what a difference: comfortable, fully-reclining seats, pretty stewardesses, drinks on demand and scrumptious in-flight meals. The route was via Kuala Lumpur, Banderanaike (Columbo), Doha, Cairo and Heathrow. Back at home, I picked up the reins of DD Air Plans, interspersed with briefings from the Far East Department of the Foreign and Commonwealth Office and from the Vice Chief of the Air Staff (VCAS), AM Sir Ruthven Wade, to whom the senior officer of every loan service detachment reported.

In November I was granted the acting rank of Air Commodore so that I could change the rank badges on my uniforms. Towards the end of the month I was 'lunched out' by MoD. I was not sorry to leave, not least because Alan Davies had been deservedly promoted and succeeded by a man whom I had never liked and who went on to become, perhaps, the worst CAS ever.

As SADC had two operational Hunter (Air Defence/Ground-Attack) squadrons I was detached to RAF Manby in December to review my skills at air-to-air gunnery (flag and ciné), air-to-ground gunnery, rocket firing and low-level bombing, none of which I had practised since leaving No. 43 (F) Squadron in 1959.

Refresher flying over, I was given a spot of leave to do the hundred-and-one things necessary when relocating overseas. Luckily my mother would be able to act 'in loco parentis' for Hilary but Karen was to accompany us, despite being at a critical stage of her education. Marcus would also accompany us; he had won the Harvey Fellowship to read Veterinary Medicine at Cambridge University but would not be going up until September 1973. At least we did not worry about what to take with us and what to put into storage as we had been told again that everything would be provided in our new quarter. And then, on New Year's Eve, my name appeared in the Honours List as having been appointed CBE, very welcome, albeit a year late. It took us by surprise and we were not best pleased to have to forego the usual visit to 'Buck House' for the investiture.

One of the reasons why I was pleased to be returning to the Far East was to catch up, in more ways than one, with Sulaiman bin Sujak. The last time we had met was when he had been a Flight Lieutenant BI QFI at Cranwell and came to CFS, Little Rissington to re-categorize in 1963. I was then in my second tour as a Wing Commander. We had kept in touch and, when he was posted to a Canberra squadron in 1964, he asked me to be one of his referees for Personal Vetting, which was necessary as the squadron was on stand-by to relocate to Malaya should the confrontation with Indonesia escalate. Several months earlier the Prime Minister of Malaya, Tengku Abdul Rahman, had attempted to cajole Sulaiman to join their embryo air force but he had preferred a career in the RAF.

For some extraordinary reason, Sulaiman was not given PV clearance on the grounds that, if the worst came to the worst, he would be unwilling to 'wage war' against fellow Muslims. He was then posted from the squadron and given a ground job. Not too surprisingly, he resigned his RAF commission and joined the RMAF wherein his promotion was meteoric. He was now CAS in the rank of Air Commodore and had reached that pinnacle whilst I remained a Wing Commander. Now that I had caught up, I was looking forward to liaising with him, but little did I know that we had passed each other in the air as he winged his way to attend the year-long IDC course in London in the rank of Air Vice Marshal. Foiled again!

Chapter 15

The Far East Again

On 3 January 1973 Jane, Marcus, Karen and I flew out to Singapore, looking forward to the next two years in the sun. We flew by RAF VC10 from Brize Norton with two refuelling stops at Akrotiri, where we were offered drinks in the VIP suite, and Gan, where Jane had been invited to watch the landing from the 'dickey' seat between the two pilots. We were met by the CO of the staging post, Wing Commander Bill Edwards, an old friend, who gave us a tour of his 'Indian Ocean paradise' whilst the aircraft was being turned around. All the RAF personnel at Gan were there for six months' unaccompanied tours so it was, perhaps, only a paradise for those who were single – as indeed Bill was.

The following day we arrived at Tengah where we were met by Lieutenant Colonel Peter Stuart and the new Air Attaché, Group Captain Arthur Peers, who had just taken over from Alan Jenkins. Also there were a number of RAF loan service, expatriate contract and SADC officers, all anxious to take a good look at their new boss. By this time we were pretty whacked, not having slept properly for thirty-six hours, so we were very glad when we were driven to the Hotel Equatorial where we were to stay, all expenses except drinks paid for by Mindef, until our married quarter was ready for us. In the meantime Jane and I were allocated room 504, made famous by the Anne Shelton song, Marcus and Karen being given single rooms nearby.

Two weeks later we were driven to Bradell Hill, a small enclave of houses formerly occupied by British High Commission families, to move into our own 'residence'. As we approached the house it looked very promising, surrounded by attractive trees on high ground at the end of the road. There was a drive-through porch and ample parking, including a badminton court in sufficient grounds to ensure seclusion. It appeared to be an appropriate house for us, which was not too surprising as its last occupant had been the Head of Chancellery, the No. 2 man at the British High Commission. Unfortunately, we were in for a nasty shock!

There was nothing wrong with the house itself, although being of post-war design it lacked the charm of the old colonial-style houses but, at least, it did have some air conditioning upstairs. However, it contained nothing but a mish-mash of the bare essentials of furniture, fittings and equipment. There were beds, a dining table and chairs, a desk in the study, an oven and refrigerator in the kitchen and the most awful three-piece suite in the lounge. There were no carpets or rugs, no pictures, a little disreputable cutlery, no ornaments and only the minimum of kitchen utensils. The downstairs wooden flooring had once been lovely but it was clear that, when the house had been cleared, the BHC furniture had been dragged out, leaving bad scuff marks. It now needed stripping and re-polishing.

We were accompanied by Captain Jimmy Chew, who had been one of my pilots under training in the MAAF nearly twenty years previously. When I complained about the inadequacy of the furnishings, he explained that, because the SADC had no married quarters, everything now in the house had had to be bought from local shops – on a very tight budget. He agreed to do what he could to improve matters but he would need authority from Mr Pang Tee Pow.

During our stay in the Hotel Equatorial, I had been settling into my new job at the Mindef HQ at Tanglin. I had all the appropriate trappings in that I had been allocated a suite of an inner and outer office along with a Chinese secretary named Gwen, who thankfully spoke excellent English, typed quickly and accurately and did shorthand. My pride and joy of a staff car, a Humber Snipe, and my own personal driver, Corporal Zakaria, were available whenever I wanted them: I could even use it for domestic and social purposes, provided I was in the car. I had a mini-flag pole so that I could fly my SADC pennant: all very imposing.

* * *

The first thing I did at Mindef was to call on the First Permanent Secretary, Mr Pang Tee Pow, who was my immediate superior, to inquire whether there were any directives, job specifications or terms of reference to delineate the duties and responsibilities of the Director Air Staff – which was a new appointment. Mr Pang seemed a little surprised that I expected such a thing. He went on to explain that, from the formation of SADC in 1969, he and Minister of Defence, Dr Goh Keng Swee, had been guided by two contract officers who had neither been given, nor had asked for, such information.

The first of these had been Air Marshal Sir Rochford Hughes, an Australian serving in the RAF who had retired from having been the last AOC-in-C of the Far East Air Force (FEAF), which had been disbanded before the final withdrawal of British Forces from Singapore in 1971. His official title, as a civilian, had been Air Advisor to the Singapore Government. The second had been Air Commodore Geoffrey Millington, who had been my Station Commander at RAF Leuchars when I commanded No. 43 (F) Squadron. He had been the best station commander I had ever had and from whom I had learned a lot about man management. He had retired from the RAF and had been the Senior Staff Officer at HQ Mindef in the rank of colonel. Sir Rochford had been responsible for advice on policy and plans whilst Geoffrey had been in charge of air operations and training. Mr Pang went on to say that it had been the Prime Minister's idea that the two posts be combined, and be titled Director Air Staff in the rank of brigadier general, when the contracts of the previous incumbents ended.

As no directives or even guidelines were forthcoming I spent the first two weeks visiting units and meeting people. The biggest SADC air base was Changi which housed the elementary and basic flying training units, the Alouette helicopter squadron, the ATC School and the Technical Training Institute, through which all SADC tradesmen had to pass. The next most important base was Tengah, the home of the two Hunter squadrons and the third was the grass airfield of Sembawang, the home of the University Air Squadron. The former RN and RAF airfield at Seletar was manned by SADC ATC personnel but, at that time, was used principally in connection with the Australia, New Zealand and UK (ANZUK) components of the Integrated Air Defence System (IADS), about which I will write later. In addition, there was the sector operations centre (SOC), the radar station located on Bukit Gombak, the highest point in Singapore, and the mobile Bloodhound surface-to-air missile squadron which had units dotted around the island. The SOC and the Bloodhound II squadrons had previously been RAF units but had been handed over to SADC as operational units in 1971 on withdrawal.

At the beginning of February I was invited to call on the Prime Minister in his office at the *Istana* (Palace). Mr Lee Kuan Yew welcomed me warmly, we talked briefly about old times and then, in complete contrast to Dr Goh and Mr Pang Tee Pow, told me exactly what was expected of me. Incredibly for a politician, he even said that, in 1968, when Singapore ceded from Malaysia, he had made a bad mistake. Faced with the need to form an embryo air force out of the rag-bag of Singaporean personnel of varied rank, trades and all with limited experience, he had approached the RAF to provide loan service personnel for those posts for which there were no qualified Singaporeans. Unfortunately, the UK Treasury's rules laid down that the recipient country should not only pay each individual's wages but also an equal amount for the loss of that person's service to the RAF. When he and Dr Goh, who was then the Minister of Finance, worked out the sums they were amazed by the cost so they decided to advertise in aviation journals worldwide for contract personnel, whom they reckoned would cost less than half of opting for RAF loan service.

The decision to recruit contract personnel turned out to be a recipe for disaster for many reasons. Firstly they were taken on largely on the strength of their CVs and many of them failed to live up to expectations. Secondly, although about half of them were retired RAF officers and SNCOs, the balance was made up with Australians, Indians, South Africans and Israelis and a few others such as former Fleet Air Arm personnel. This polyglot mixture did not add up to a cohesive and efficient work force. Thirdly, as the majority of the contract personnel had had full careers in other services they were fairly old, and in many cases, somewhat out of date. Fourthly, they were more than content to supplement their pensions and were in no hurry to prepare SADC personnel to take over their own cushy jobs.

Mr Lee went on to say that the best of this bad lot were the ex-RAF personnel and that SADC had already started to weed out the weakest of the others and replace them with RAF loan service personnel, who being on two-year tours, had no axes to grind and were more amenable to promoting the advancement of the Singaporeans. He said that my job was to review progress to date and devise ways and means, without prejudicing efficiency and effectiveness, of working towards SADC not having to rely on any outside help – preferably within the next five years. On that happy note he asked me to submit a six-monthly progress report to Dr Goh and wished me the best of luck.

* * *

I gave myself a month or so to continue to learn exactly how SADC worked and where its strengths and weaknesses lay. I hate 'new brooms' who take over and immediately start making fundamental changes without a proper appreciation of the problems faced by their predecessors. In fact I was quite impressed by the progress made by SADC since 1968, but then a lot of the groundwork had been done years before, thanks largely to the help of the British Government and the RAF. Unfortunately, very few of the pilots who had been trained by the Singapore Squadron of MAAF, of which I had been a training officer from 1953 to 1955, had wound up in SADC as most had been snapped up by Singapore International Airlines. However, the air traffic and fighter controllers we had trained now filled the majority of the ATC and FC posts where there was less need for expatriate assistance.

Considerable progress had also been made in the technical trades as most of the recruits had come directly from Singapore University or the Technical Colleges, having graduated with engineering degrees or diplomas. Under the guidance of Group Captain Stanley, an ex-RAF contract officer, these personnel had been welded into an efficient force. Stan had done so well that at the end of his contract he was able to hand over to a Singaporean, Lieutenant Colonel Pat Wong, whom he had groomed to succeed him. The one area where expatriate assistance was required was in the SADC's Technical Institute where the majority of the instructors were ex-RAF SNCOs. The Bloodhound surface-to-air missile squadron was another success in that it was already fully operational, thanks to the RAF Regiment personnel who had stayed behind after withdrawal until the SADC recruits, who had mainly been pressganged from the Army's Territorial Artillery Squadron, were fully up to speed.

The only area where there was still almost total dependence on expatriate assistance was that of flying operations but nevertheless significant progress had already been made. In the initial stages the Singaporean Government had bought a number of Cessna light aircraft which they used for primary flying training, carried out by civilian instructors of the Singapore Flying Club, before sending the successful cadets overseas for basic and advanced flying training. By the time I arrived SADC were already doing their own basic training, albeit with an all expatriate team of loan service and contract instructors. Pilot training is by its nature a very lengthy process; for example, it takes about eighteen months to train an *ab initio* cadet to RAF wings standards and, thereafter, there is still operational conversion training and the very necessary accumulation of experience on squadrons. In my view, progress had been reasonable but, perhaps, could have been quicker.

I was beginning to wonder why, as I had recently found out, the contracts of Sir Rochford Hughes and Geoff Millington had been terminated early when they had obviously done a good job in laying the groundwork for future progress. Group Captain Basil Fox, the ex-RAF contract officer who was Head of the Air Equipment Department, was able to tell me. It appears that Sir Rochford had recommended that the Singaporean Government should purchase a number of Britten-Norman Trislanders, to meet their needs for a search and location and general-purpose light cargo aircraft, from an Australian company who were the Far East agents. The deal was about to be signed when Dr Goh discovered that Sir Rochford had committed the cardinal sin (in Singaporean eyes) of profiting from

The author in the uniform of SADC's No. 6 Tropical Mess Kit.

his position by accepting a directorship of that company. The Ministry promptly cancelled the contract and declared Sir Rochford *persona non grata* whereupon he retired to Australia with his tail between his legs.

Basil also had told me that Geoffrey Millington had been very popular and had been doing a good job but Dr Goh, and others in the Mindef hierarchy, had been shocked by the rather racy behaviour of Geoff's wife, Anne, who had apparently developed a penchant for young officers. They believed that her behaviour was giving SADC a bad name and was not setting the right sort of example. I was not too surprised as, although Anne had been an excellent station commander's wife at Leuchars, she had later become rather flirtatious. The axing of Sir Rochford and Geoffrey Millington was SADC's loss but my gain and it was certainly an object lesson in the rather Victorian mores of the Singaporean Government under the autocratic premiership of Lee Kuan Yew.

When I was ready I called a meeting of all the relevant loan-service personnel who comprised Group Captain Bill Kelly, Head of Air Operations, Wing Commander Jerry Farwell, OC Flying Wing at Tengah, Wing Commander Keith Monson, the Chief Instructor at Changi and all the squadron and flight commanders. I started by congratulating them on having done a good job and on having set high standards. However, the time had now come to begin the most important aspect of loan service, which was to prepare the SADC officers to take over the posts they were currently filling.

As a start I wanted to see the most promising being groomed to take over specific jobs. For example, the two most experienced and suitable candidates should understudy the squadron commanders by being given desks in their offices and being involved in all appropriate decision making. I suggested that the two who best fitted that bill were Captains Mike Teo and Gary Yeo. Everyone seemed somewhat surprised that I was able to nominate them, but then they did not know that Mike and Gary had been amongst the first SADC pilots to undertake advanced training on Hunters at Valley. I had been impressed by them then and had made a point of checking how they had progressed since returning to Singapore. It was agreed that they should be the first COs-in-waiting and that four more should be selected to become flight commanders.

I went on to say that the other SADC officers were to be prepared for qualification as PAIs (Pilot Attack Instructors), IREs (Instrument Rating Examiners) and QWIs (Qualified Weapons Instructors), all of which functions were being carried out currently by loan-service personnel. In addition, all pilots were to be graded in respect of such things as their instrument ratings and, also, according to their experience, competence and ability to authorize, brief and lead formations of up to four aircraft on practice interceptions and/or ground-attack sorties.

I then turned to flying training. I said that it was vital that SADC should start sending suitable pilots to CFS in the UK (or Australia) to become QFIs and I suggested that Captains Tim de Souza and Johnny Norfar should be the first to go, once I had obtained Mindef approval because of the cost implications. I had known both at Valley, where they had struggled to make the grade but were good pilots, although not really cut out to be fighter pilots.

Finally I made them all sit up by telling them that I would seek approval for CFS to be invited to run their rule over all aspects of SADC's flying operations to ensure that the proper standards and practices were being maintained. A general discussion followed, several points were cleared up and they all dispersed with, I believed, a new sense of purpose.

* * *

My first three months in office were marked by two very different but pleasant events. Firstly, in early February, the High Commissioner told me that he was planning to hold an investiture to hand over the awards to the seven British personnel in Singapore whose names had featured in the New Year's Honours list. We fixed a date but a little later he phoned to ask if I would mind if the Investiture was delayed as HRH the Duke of Edinburgh was stopping over in Singapore en route to an official visit to Australia and had confirmed that he would be pleased to do the honours.

Having missed out on another visit to Buckingham Palace, and half-expecting that the insignia of my CBE would arrive by post, this was a very welcome turn of events. The Investiture was held at the British High Commission and was followed by a reception there, both of which were attended not only by Jane but also by Marcus and Karen. But the gilt on the gingerbread was that Jane and I were invited to a dinner that evening at the *Istana*, hosted by Sir Sam and Lady Fall for Prince Philip and his Equerry, Lord Rupert Neville. The only other guest was the Royal New Zealand Navy Vice Admiral who commanded the ANZUK Force; unfortunately his Australian wife was away at the time. It was an excellent, intimate dinner made the more enjoyable by Prince Philip's 'Tales from the Palace', which were hilarious.

The author and his wife who is admiring the insignia of a Commander of the Order of the British Empire (CBE) which had been presented by Prince Philip.

The second event arose because the USS *Enterprise*, the largest aircraft-carrier of the US Seventh Fleet on station in the Western Pacific, was due to pay a courtesy visit to Singapore in early March. Whilst en route the Task Force Commander, Rear Admiral McClendon USN, sent an invitation to Dr Goh Keng Swee to visit the ship. Dr Goh was not too keen, so he talked a reluctant Mr Phua Bah Lee, the Senior Parliament Secretary to the Ministry of Defence, to go in his place. I was invited to accompany him – to my delight! We were duly collected by a Grumman C1A on 2 March and flown to the *Enterprise* in the South China Sea. Unfortunately, Mr Phua was rather apprehensive about the visit, particularly when our pilot carried out the controlled crash, which naval aviators call a landing, on the flight deck. I told him that what he needed was a stiff drink – forgetting that USN ships are 'dry'.

That afternoon the captain laid on a practice emergency scramble and recovery for our benefit, a very impressive performance, especially as there was a heavy swell. Poor Mr Phua never found his sea-legs and felt perpetually queasy. That evening we had a very American but excellent dinner followed by a rather dreary film about Jeremiah Johnson who rose from backwoods obscurity to prominence in US politics. Next morning Mr Phua was not feeling any better, so I arranged for a SADC Alouette helicopter to pick us up rather than staying on board until the ship reached Singapore the following day. I thoroughly enjoyed the brief visit, not least because, being the same rank as the Task Force Commander, I was given VIP treatment.

Another very pleasant event was the visit to Mindef by my old friend Bill Bedford in April. Bill had been the Chief Test Pilot of Hawker-Siddeley Aviation for many years, but was now the Sales Manager for the company, dealing mainly with the Harrier and service support for the Hunter. SADC now had sufficient pilots in the training pipeline to form two additional Hunter squadrons as planned. However, there was a problem in that the Hunter was no longer being manufactured, so Bill had been trying for some time to buy back surplus aircraft from Hunter operators around the world. The purpose of Bill's visit was to confirm, finally, that his efforts had been in vain and therefore Hawkers could not find and refurbish sufficient Hunters to support the formation of two new squadrons. It was coincidental that Bill's son Peter was one of my loan-service QFIs.

Meantime, whilst I was busy enjoying myself, all was not so happy on the domestic front. I had complained to Mr Pang that the furniture and fittings of our new quarter were well below expectations and asked if they could be upgraded. His response was pretty negative and his demeanour was as inscrutable as ever. However, he did arrange to have the exterior walls of the house painted; maybe he had got the wrong end of the stick. I next approached Arthur Peers, the Air Attaché, to see whether the High Commissioner could help out as all their married quarters were beautifully furnished. I knew Arthur of old as he had taken over from me as OC Cadet Wing at Henlow, where he had undone many of the changes I had made. For example, he had stopped the ballroom dancing lessons and had reinstated the archaic rule that the cadets were not to go out in 'civvies' without wearing a hat – both to the dismay of the cadets. I knew Arthur to be a stodgy old fuddy-duddy and expected him to be unhelpful – which he was!

So poor Jane had to contend with a house of which the very spacious open-plan ground floor had meagre, inappropriate furniture with no rugs, carpets, ornaments or lamps of any description – and badly-scuffed wooden flooring. On the advice of the Air Secretary, we had put nearly all of our belongings into store, although luckily we did bring out a canteen of cutlery. It was just as well that Marcus was with us, as he was not going up to Cambridge until September. He was a great help in stripping and polishing the floor and dealing with the electrics when we bought table and bedside lamps.

An early acquisition was our cook-boy and *amah*, Ah Ho and Ah Choy, who looked after the cooking, laundering and housework, leaving Jane free to scour the shops and bazaars for essentials. 'Thieves Market', a downtown flea-market, was a marvellous place to pick up ex-MoD kitchen equipment at very reasonable prices. In the end we spent every spare penny of my pay for the first six months just to put the house into a sufficiently acceptable state for us to even consider entertaining at home. Jane and I decided that we would only buy things that we would want to keep for when we would eventually buy a home of our own, which is why our house resembles the inside of a Chinese emporium.

I was soon to discover that, by accepting loan service, I had been sold a financial pup by the Air Secretary. For example, there were two RAF Group Captains serving in Singapore; the first was Arthur Peers and the second was Tony Carver, who filled a rather cushy ANZUK appointment. Despite their being junior to me their monthly pay was far superior because of their entertainment, servant and other allowances to which I was not entitled. And they had unlimited access to the High Commission's duty-free store. But, at least, I had the best job!

* * *

Shortly before my arrival, Mindef had been tipped off that there were aircraft bargains to be had in the Arizona Desert. After the end of the Korean War the US Department of Defense (USDoD) had stored many surplus USN and USAF aircraft in the desert by cocooning the airframes and inhibiting the engines. The ultra-dry conditions prevented any danger of rust and cocooning prevented wind/sand erosion. Mindful that Hawkers might be unable to find sufficient Hunters to form the two new fighter squadrons, the Embassy staff in Washington had been tasked to investigate and report.

Towards the end of April, Dr Goh told me that the report had arrived and in it were several recommendations which he wanted to discuss. They had identified the Douglas Skyhawk, a USN carrier-borne fighter, as being the most suited to SADC's requirements and which could be purchased at what seemed a very reasonable price. However, there was a sting in the tail in that a condition of the sale would be that an American aviation company would have to be awarded the contract to prepare the aircraft to the buyer's specifications.

Accordingly the Embassy staff had sought tenders for the work from three such companies and two had been submitted, from Douglas, the original manufacturer, and Lockheed, which was the more competitive. Dr Goh asked me to read the report in detail and give him my views. He also asked if I would be prepared to lead a small team to go to the USA should he decide to investigate the possibilities further. I read the report, discussed certain aspects of it with Bill Kelly, Basil Fox and Pat Wong, then told Dr Gok that I had only one reservation in that it was assumed that the preparation, modification and re-equipping of the aircraft would have to be carried out in the USA.

I pointed out the enormous advantages of having the aircraft shipped to Singapore and all the work carried out there. Whether this would be possible would depend upon the American company chosen being prepared to relocate their work-force to Singapore, but the advantages of having SADC's own engineers and technicians observing, participating and finally undertaking the work themselves would be worth any extra cost.

First-class economist that he was, Dr Goh immediately saw the possibility that this proposal could lay the foundations for Singapore becoming a major centre for aircraft maintenance and third-line servicing, not just for Singapore Airlines but for the whole of the Far East. He said that I should leave for the USA as soon as possible and, subject to my agreement that the Skyhawk was the best available aircraft for SADC, my priority was to negotiate the terms for the forty aircraft necessary to support two squadrons of sixteen each and that their preparation should be carried out in Singapore.

Once the decision was taken things moved very rapidly and on 6 May I rendezvoused with my team, which consisted of an engineer, an accountant and a lawyer, at Paya Lebar (Kalang) for the flight to Los Angeles via Hong Kong (courtesy of SIA), Tokyo and Honolulu (courtesy of Japan Airlines). The visit was a resounding success in every respect. I found on arrival that Douglas had pulled out of the project as they were in the throes of a merger with McDonnell Aviation so Lockheed's was the only tender. Their representatives met us at Los Angeles airport and thereafter looked after us wonderfully, booking our accommodation, flying us in company aircraft around the country, arranging meetings and, most importantly, fixing that I could fly a USN Skyhawk.

Our first meeting was with the US DofDef representatives who quoted us a bargain-basement price for the forty aircraft we required and said that they had no objection to the preparation being carried out in Singapore. We accepted their terms, which were well within budget, subject to my decision that the Skyhawk was indeed the right aircraft for SADC.

On the evening of 8 May I was flown to the Naval Air Station at Lemoore in a Cessna 310 flown by 'Spud' Murphy, one of Lockheed's staff pilots. The following day I received a very comprehensive briefing on every aspect of the Skyhawk and its operation from Lieutenant Commander Anderson before my scheduled flight with him the next day in the two-seat training variant of the aircraft.

I am not a test pilot but in the nearly two-hour flight I did my best to put the aircraft through its paces – and was well satisfied. I found it to be more manoeuvrable than the Hunter at low level, responsive on the controls and with sufficient fuel in the internal tanks for flights in excess of two hours, which would be useful when airborne standing patrols were necessary. But it was slower in the climb to 40,000 feet where it lost out in performance terms and it did not have airbrakes, which would give the Hunter an edge when dog-fighting. It had a very robust landing gear, as befits a carrier-borne aircraft, which would be good when teaching inexperienced SADC pilots the rather different landing technique. The only real fault that I found was that it was unpredictable at the point of the stall – especially under high-g loading. Overall, I believed that it would complement the Hunter extremely well, and having two different aircraft types would be a great help when teaching fighter tactics.

I had no hesitation in giving my team the go-ahead to finalize the draft contracts, not least because Lockheed agreed readily that the preparation of the aircraft should be carried out in Singapore, provided that they should carry out a critical path analysis on the first six aircraft in their US plant in order to find the most efficient sequence for the various operations involved in the preparation process. They were even prepared to do so at no extra cost than that in their tender, provided that we gave them a dedicated hangar and all the necessary lifting gear and trestles along with non-technical labour. To their surprise, the Lockheed 'bean counters' worked out that, although their training of the SADC engineers and technicians would extend the time to complete the programme, the overall cost would be less, because a smaller team of highly-paid US personnel could be used.

Having wrapped up everything more quickly than expected, the other three members of the team flew home a day early whereas I stayed on as Lockheed had offered a visit to their 'Skunk Works' in Burbank, California, where they were developing the world's first 'stealth' aircraft. This was an offer I could not refuse. The aircraft, under the presiding genius of Kelly Johnson, was being developed to evade detection by ground or airborne radar by the use of state-of-the-art materials, the razor-edged inclination of the aircraft surfaces to prevent radar reflection and the shielding of the exhausts to prevent infra-red detection. I clambered over the prototype aircraft, which was top-secret and flown only over the desert in an area prohibited to other aircraft: it was a revolutionary design, albeit rather weird-looking, and I was very privileged to have been given a preview.

An added bonus of my trip to the States was that I was able to fly to San Francisco to spend the weekend with my sister Jean and her husband Jack Tate, who lived in Belvedere on a hill overlooking San Francisco Bay with a cabin cruiser moored at the bottom of their precipitous garden. We were joined there by my younger sister Edwina, who lived in nearby Sausalito, and by Carroll Terra, a sister by unofficial adoption, who drove all the way from Davis with her three young children. It was an unexpected and very happy family reunion.

I flew back to Singapore on 15/16 May via Tokyo (courtesy of Pan Am) and Taiwan, Hong Kong and Kuala Lumpur (courtesy of SIA, who kindly upgraded me from business to first-class). When I reported to Mindef I was greeted by a very affable Dr Goh and Mr Pang who obviously were delighted with the outcome of the team visit. From that time on I began to feel that at last I was beginning to have their approval and trust.

The rest of the year flew by and SADC went from strength to strength. The young officers were responding wonderfully to being given responsibilities and vied with each other to be sent on specialist courses overseas. SADC had always played second fiddle to the RMAF but in the IADS exercise held later that year we put up more fighters and achieved higher interception rates than ever before. There was a new sense of purpose helped by the arrival of replacement loan-service officers such as Wing Commander Ray Coleman and Squadron Leaders Sam Toyne and David Wardill who, unlike the 'gung-ho' approach of their predecessors, understood the need to accelerate the experience levels and proficiency of the Singaporeans and had the personalities and attitude to do so.

From a domestic point of view, the Langers were also progressing well. By mid-year, thanks largely to Jane's endeavours and my shrinking bank account, our house was brought up to scratch and we were able to entertain at home. Karen was doing well at the International School and had started ballet lessons again, after having to give up because of the injuries she had sustained in our car accident at Little Rissington. Most importantly, Marcus had a job, albeit as a trainee keeper grade III, at the soon to be opened Singapore Zoo. The director, knowing that Marcus was going up to Cambridge in October to read Veterinary Medicine, used him to look after certain animals, such as Orangutans, and new-born lion cubs in need of special care: so he did not have to spend too much time shovelling up the smelly stuff.

Very sensibly the Prime Minister and Dr Goh appreciated that their embryo armed forces needed a lot of expatriate help but I became increasingly aware of their reluctance to admit it. For example, shortly after my arrival there was to be a 'passing out' parade for a course of pilots who had qualified for their 'wings'. I asked Mr Pang if I could be the reviewing officer, a job which previously had been done only by Ministers or senior officials. He was obviously not keen but said he would ask Dr Goh, who agreed that I should officiate.

The Wings Parade was televised, so after the event Jane and I watched the evening 'news' programme only to find that, whereas I was named in the commentary, all the scenes in which I appeared were either shot from behind me or, when my face was shown, the film had been processed so that I appeared to have a dark countenance, not unlike an Anglo-Indian.

On another occasion, at my instigation, SADC held an Open Day at Changi which featured flying displays by various aircraft, including a flypast by sixteen Strikemaster aircraft. The VIPs and other spectators were to be seated in raised stands on a bank in front of which ran the perimeter track along which the aircraft would taxi to the end of the runway for take-off. Dr Goh accompanied me to the dress rehearsal, which went very well, but he noticed as the Strikemasters taxied past that all the pilots in the cockpit seats nearest to the spectators were expatriate instructors. When he asked why this was I explained that the left-hand seat is where the captain of the aircraft sat and that there were no SADC pilots at Changi competent enough to fly in such a mass formation. He thought for a bit and then asked if the captains could fly from the right-hand seat with the SADC trainee pilot nearest to the crowd. I replied that it was possible as the cadet could operate the undercarriage when necessary. So on the day, on my instructions, the cadet pilots left their oxygen/RT masks dangling so that their black, yellow and coffee coloured faces were clearly visible. It all sounds rather silly but, at least, my agreement earned me a few more 'Brownie' points.

* * *

In late December, my old friend Air Vice Marshal Sulaiman bin Sujak returned to Kuala Lumpur to resume his job as CAS of the RMAF. As he told me later he was horrified at what had happened during his year away at the Royal College of Defence Studies in London. Apparently his deputy, who had stood in for him, was a fervent Islamist and had introduced a new regime in which only Muslims were promoted or appointed to the more senior positions at the expense of the ethnic Chinese and Indians. This had resulted in undermining both efficiency and morale. In addition, to Singapore's dismay, he had revoked our previous permission to operate in southern Malaysian airspace which had severely limited SADC's training programmes. It took him several months to sort things out and to return the RMAF to his secular approach to personnel management and to co-operation with SADC, which was an essential element of the Integrated Air Defence System. When we were finally able to get together, he said that he had great difficulty in not calling me 'Boss' as indeed he had done in Singapore in 1955/56, on 43 Squadron in 1958/59 and at CFS in 1963.

One of the peculiarities of my job was that despite being Commander of SADC I had no direct responsibility for personnel matters, other than those pertaining to RAF loan service. Lieutenant Colonel Ee Tean Chye, the base commander of Changi who was the senior SADC officer, was responsible for the exercise of discipline and the Head of Air Management and Personnel (HAMP), Mr Benny Ortega, a civil servant at HQ Mindef, was responsible for policy and reported, not to me, but directly to Mr Pang. In March, Lieutenant Colonel Ee made an appointment to see me and said that junior SADC officers had genuine grievances about their pay and that, whereas he had approached Ortega on several occasions, he had been unsympathetic and had refused to refer the matter to higher authority. He asked me if I could use my influence and access to Mr Pang to further the pilots' cause.

Ee went on to explain that there were two main grounds of discontent. The first of these was that, as the Singapore armed forces were a unified organization, the basic pay was the same for all officers of the same rank. This created several anomalies; for example, Army officer cadets would be commissioned after only six months' training whilst cadet pilots' flying training to wings and commissioning could take up to two years, losing out on eighteen months' seniority and pay. Moreover, there was no comparison between the level of responsibility of, say, an infantry officer whose weapon was a £100 rifle and a pilot whose weapon was an extremely costly aircraft such as a Hunter.

Another injustice was that all SADC pilot training was to 'fast-jet' standards and that therefore there was a relatively high wastage rate. The best of those who failed to make the grade could be diverted on to helicopters or to the Skyvan squadron but the majority were discharged to civvy street. Thereafter, many of them were recruited by SIA as co-pilots and within a couple of years could be earning twice as much as those who had made the grade.

I sympathized with these legitimate grievances and was rather annoyed that no one had brought them to my notice before. I told Tean Chye that I would do what I could but, frankly, I did not have high hopes as I knew that the Defence Budget was pretty stretched already. So I gave the problem some thought, did some research, consulted with a few people such as Brigadier General Raj, the DGS and nominal head of the SAF, and my old friend AVM Sulaiman, the CAS of the RMAF, who provided me with their pay scales and then I did what I do second best – I wrote a staff paper.

In it I outlined the grievances, and highlighted the long-term problem of recruiting cadet pilots of the right calibre if the disparity with the pay available elsewhere, such as in civil aviation, industry and commerce, was not redressed.

I gave examples and stressed, amongst other things, that RMAF pay scales were nearly double those in SADC. I pointed out that there would be increased liaison with the RMAF in future as the Integrated Air Defence System expanded and that there was a danger that SADC would become regarded as the poor relation.

Finally I proposed a possible solution which would not result in pay increases across the SAF as a whole but would reward endeavour, seniority and qualification. This proposal advocated index-linking basic pay and supplementing it with command, staff and flying pay, plus increments for educational and service achievements such as university degrees, attendance at staff college and passing courses to become qualified flying instructors, etc., etc. When the paper was finalized I gave it to Mr Pang who thanked me and said it would be given due consideration, a polite way of saying that nothing would be done about it. However, I sent a copy to Dr Goh who thought the proposals were excellent and that he would seek extra money for the Defence Budget to enable implementation. And, as with many things in Singapore, once decisions are taken, action follows swiftly and the new pay scales became effective within a couple of months.

In April the first six Skyhawks arrived in crates, having been refurbished and modified in USA to the Singapore specification and with them Lockheed set up their engineering facility in a hangar at Seletar to begin work on the remaining thirty-four which would arrive in batches over the next eighteen months. This was a period of much excitement, a lot of change and a real feeling that SADC was really beginning to become an effective force.

In July it was decided by Dr Goh that SADC should celebrate the fifth anniversary of its formation by holding a Gala Dinner in the grounds of the *Istana* to which the President, Mr Benjamin Sheares, the Prime Minister and other VIPs should be invited. The actual dinner took place on 23 August and was blessed with a beautiful evening. There were about twenty round tables, each set for eight people, positioned around the grounds where the trees were lit with fairy lights. It was a typical Chinese dinner of ten courses, provided by the Majestic Catering Company which looked after most of

The author addresses the guests at a dinner to celebrate the 5th anniversary of Singapore's Air Defence command, of which he was the commander (on loan from the RAF) in the rank of Brigadier.

the Government's diplomatic hospitality. The SAF band played an eclectic selection of music from a sufficient distance to be enjoyable but not to drown conversation.

In the event the President was unable to attend, so the Prime Minister and Mrs Lee were the principal guests at the top table of which Jane and I were the hosts. Dr and Mrs Goh and Brigadier General Winston Choo, who had just taken over as DGS, and his wife were the guests on the next table where Colonel Bill Kelly and his wife were the hosts – and so on down the line. Many of the junior SADC officers were seated at the top tables which really made their day. Jane got on really well with Mr Lee, next to whom she was sitting and I found Mrs Lee, whom I had not met before, a delightful dinner companion. She had met her husband at Cambridge University where they had both read Law and both attained double firsts – obviously a marriage made in Heaven.

At the end of the dinner I made a short speech to welcome the guests to which the Prime Minister responded and proposed a toast to SADC. Afterwards he confided that he was very pleased with the progress SADC had made since my arrival and that he had plans for its further expansion. He said that he believed that a strong Air Force, rather than Army or Navy, was necessary, in the country's geographic, economic and political situation, to ensure that Singapore gained the influence in South East Asia to which he aspired.

By early August I had become a little concerned at not hearing from the Royal College of Defence Studies (RCDS) as they normally contacted those selected for their course six months in advance with a suggested reading list. I therefore sent a signal to MoD, via the BHC, requesting confirmation of my attendance on the January 1975 course. The reply from the Air Secretary was pretty succinct:

> Air Commodore Langer has not been selected for the RCDS but I wish him to report to the MoD as soon as possible to discuss the long-term future of loan service in Singapore and his future career.

So I took a week's leave and flew to London by the RAF VC10 schedule on 29/30 August. I reported to the Air Secretary, now AM Sir Derek Hodgkinson, who asked me why I had expected to be on the course and I told him that his predecessor, ACM Sir John Barraclough, had told me not only that he would reserve a place for me but also that, on completion of the course, I would almost certainly be promoted. Sir Derek seemed rather bemused by what I said and told me that it was longstanding policy that all senior officers returning from loan service and exchange postings would not be promoted until they had been assessed in an RAF appointment because they would have been reported upon by people who had no idea about our standards. He then asked me to report back to him in three days, by which time he would have looked into the background to my complaint.

When I did he told me that I had been misled, not least because my records showed that I had voluntarily forfeited my selection for the RCDS in favour of going to Singapore. However, he assured me that, with my record, further promotion would not be affected by my not having done the course. He then offered me the choice of two prestigious jobs, i.e. Director of Air Plans or Director of Flying Training, which were becoming vacant in May 1975. Needless to say, I chose the latter – which was right up my street. I returned to Singapore somewhat disappointed but with high hopes for the future.

As I approached the last six months of my term I decided to make one last push to speed up the reduction of SADC's reliance on expatriate help. So I drew up a recommended timetable for phasing out the loan service and contract officers currently in place. To cut a long story short, I devised a plan whereby, at the end of five years, all the captain and major posts would be filled with SADC personnel. By then the only loan-service posts would be those of Director Air Staff, Head of Air Operations, OC Flying at Tengah and the Chief Instructor of the Flying Training School, plus a few specialist contract officers, such as Basil Fox who was being retained to look after logistics.

I even recommended that my post of DAS should be downgraded to Colonel and that my successor should be Bill Kelly, currently HAO, who was keen to sign on for an additional six months. This move would not only be good for continuity but also, by downgrading DAS and HAO, would make those posts more accessible to SADC officers in future. I made a few other recommendations, including that the current Hunter squadron commanders should hand over to their SADC deputies immediately and that Captain Stuart White, a contract officer formerly a Fleet Air Arm pilot and QFI, should have his contract extended so he could mastermind the conversions on to the Skyhawk which were about to begin. I also recommended that the two Skyhawk squadrons should be commanded by the best qualified and available SADC pilots.

The only front on which I cautioned less speed was that of flying training. By this time we already had several SADC QFIs and had speeded up the process by sending pilots not only to the RAF CFS but also to that of the RAAF. To date all our QFIs were either category B1 or B2, so I suggested that expatriate help would be needed until at least half of them were categorized A2, an indicator of both above average experience and ability. I had discussed this provisional timetable at MoD with the Air Secretary who had had no reservations.

* * *

For Jane and I, 1973 was a very hectic year and we had neither the time nor the money to go on holiday. However, we did manage to cross the causeway occasionally for weekend over-night stops in the Government rest houses at Malacca, on the west coast with its history, and at Kuantan, on the east coast with its glorious, deserted sandy beaches. But we determined that, in the second half of my tour, we would try to take advantage of where we were, and of my connections, to pay visits to rather more exotic places. Thus in January 1974 we made a flying visit to Hong Kong on a RAF VC10 scheduled return flight which allowed us a two-night stay in the Park Hotel in Kowloon. This gave us just enough time to explore the markets, travel across the New Territories to the Chinese border, and go by Star Ferry to the island where Hong Kong and its harbour nestle at the foot of the mountain, to the summit of which we drove for the marvellous views.

In April we flew to Saigon, this time by RNZAF Bristol Freighter, to stay for two days with old friends, Group Captain Geoff Hermitage, who was Air Attaché there, and his wife Daphne. Geoff was the last RAF air attaché to have an aircraft, in his case a de Havilland Devon, which had its major servicing carried out in Singapore, and in which he was to fly as it was due for an engine change. Our stay with them was actionpacked and included a cocktail party at the Embassy and a flight in the Devon to Na Trang on the east coast which was still functioning as a beach resort. However, the Vietcong were not far away and Geoff had to fly a circuitous route to avoid our being shot at. The highlight of our visit was a boat trip up the Mekong river to see the 'Coconut Monk', a strange Cambodian who had pledged not to cut his hair or his nails until peace returned to the region. In the meantime, he prayed for peace, held audiences and slept at the top of a structure which resembled a space rocket. On the return trip we heard rifle fire from the opposite bank, which caused our two female boatmen to lay prostrate in the boat. All very exciting.

Very exciting, maybe, but my abiding impression of the visit was one of sadness at the dreadful state of Saigon itself. I had passed through four times twenty-five years previously when the country was called French Indo-China. I had found it a beautiful city with wide, tree-lined boulevards, flanked by attractive white villas, along which elegant young ladies would ride their bicycles dressed in the national dress with white straw hats and long white gloves. It was very civilized and very French, with cafés that would not have looked out of place in Montmartre. Now it was a dirty, bedraggled shambles, largely as a result of the American Forces designating it as a rest and recreation centre for their troops, thus spawning the springing up of sleazy bars, cabarets, dance halls and brothels. The Yankee dollar reigned supreme and the local economy had collapsed as had the sewer system. It was with good reason that the river that flowed through the city was called 'cholera creek'. To make matters, worse tens of thousands of refugees fleeing from the Vietcong had flooded in, resulting in the setting up of shanty towns and an explosion of crime because there was no work for them. It was only a matter of months before Saigon fell to the North Vietnamese; I hope that they restored good order as the city was spiralling out of control.

Later in April Jane flew home to check on our mothers, neither of whom was well. She found that my mother had exaggerated as usual and was really just enjoying her ill health; indeed she went on to live to be ninety-three. Unfortunately, Jane's mother had played down her condition for, shortly after Jane's arrival, she had a heart attack and died. This was not only distressing for her but, because she had to wind up her mother's estate, she was not able to return to Singapore for six weeks.

As Christmas neared we found ourselves on our own as Marcus was at Cambridge and Karen had returned to London to study at the Royal Academy of Dancing. In the sweltering humidity that is Singapore, Christmas is a bit phoney, despite the delicious Christmas pudding ice-cream available from Cold Storage and Fitzpatrick's. So we decided to get away from it all by sailing to Brunei on Christmas Eve in the SS *Rajah Brooke*, a venerable cargo vessel with a few passenger cabins which had been plying its trade in the South China Seas for decades. Sailing time was two and a half days each way with two days in port.

As a means of escaping Christmas it was a dismal failure as the other passengers were families with children. The Captain talked me into being Father Christmas so, for the first and last time in my life, I donned the full regalia with the obligatory white beard. With a suitably gruff voice, I quizzed the children on the true meaning of Christmas before rewarding them with presents. However, there were many compensations in that we were treated to the most magnificent sunsets every evening and the boat was often accompanied by dolphins, hammerhead sharks and flying fish. The food was quite good, although on occasions we ate alone at the Captain's table as the flat-bottomed boat rocked and rolled in the heavy swell.

In harbour we continued to live and eat on board but had plenty of time to explore Bandar Seri Begawan, the name of both the port and the capital city. It was a strange mixture of wooden *attap* houses and huts, some on stilts, punctuated by rather grand buildings, paid for by the oil-rich Sultan, such as a superb mosque, schools, hospital and a museum dedicated solely to the life and works of Winston Churchill. We did not meet the Sultan but he flashed past us twice in one of his Lamborghinis. The highlight of our visit was a river trip well into Sarawak to a native longhouse which was fascinating. The highlight for the other passengers and crew was when the *Rajah Brooke* was buzzed by two SADC Hunters. Before sailing, I had left a sealed operations order to be handed to the pilots of the two Hunters equipped with photo-reconnaissance cameras. They were tasked with locating and photographing a cargo vessel which was leaving Brunei on such and such a date and was bound for Singapore with a suspected consignment of drugs on board. The operations order described the vessel but gave no times or route so the pilots would have to carry out a square search. They had no trouble in finding us, much to my relief and the delight of the children on board.

Our final trip was to Bangkok in February 1975: we flew there in an RNZAF Bristol Freighter to stay for three days with Wing Commander Ray Watson, who had been one of my squadron commanders at CFS and was now Air Attaché. Ray and his wife took us to see the Grand Palace, the Temple of the Emerald Buddha and a few of the numerous other '*wats*' dotted around the city. We also took a boat trip to view the floating markets and found out that to travel by river or canal was the only way to avoid the horrendous traffic jams that plague the city. We also dined in a traditional Thai restaurant where the locals sat cross-legged at very low tables. Luckily for our creaking joints they provided tables with pits where Europeans could dangle their legs. After three very interesting days we travelled home by RAAF Hercules to Penang and then by RAAF DC-3 (Dakota) a real relic of a bygone era, having been first brought into service in the 1930s.

Our final few weeks simply whizzed by. I was dined out at Changi where I was presented with a large oil painting by a local artist of a somewhat idealized Bukit Gombak. I was also dined out at Tengah and presented with an inscribed plate of Selangor pewter. Meantime, Jane was very busy supervising the packing of our belongings which ran to fourteen wooden crates for shipment home. This was far in excess of our allowance but the understanding warrant officer in the RAF Movements staff managed to wangle it for us.

At my final interview with Dr Goh he said that the Prime Minister had asked him to tell me how happy he was at the progress that SADC had made recently and was considering eventually making it autonomous with the title of the Republic of Singapore Air Force. Indeed as Jane and I were being seen off for our flight home on

The author, now a Brigadier, meets up with Sqn Ldr Jack Challinor, now Deputy Captain of The Queen's Flight, at Tengah.

1 April 1975, it was announced that the RSAF was to come into being on that very date. It was a proud moment for me, but thereafter everything went pear-shaped when the captain of our VC10 announced that the aircraft was unserviceable with a badly-cracked windscreen and that a replacement would not arrive for at least two days. So we had to return to the Hotel Equatorial for another brief stay with no car and very little local currency. It was a bit of an anti-climax to a tour which had gone from being frustrating at first to ultimately extremely rewarding. I was sorry to leave but pleased to have achieved all I had set out to do. My only regret was that, although I had flown every one of SADC's nine aircraft types, I had been too busy to fly as much as I would have liked. Having eventually arrived at RAF Brize Norton at some ungodly hour four days later, when we looked out next morning from their Gateway Transit Hotel there were two inches of snow on the ground. It was not the warmest of welcomes home after two years spent in the Tropics.

* * *

Postscript

After our return home we kept in touch with several people in Singapore and, after about a year, we learnt the sad news that Group Captain 'Dusty' Rhodes, who had taken over from Bill Kelly as DAS, had been killed in a flying accident, the first major accident since the formation of SADC in 1968. Apparently, he had been carrying out a bombing attack in a Skyhawk on an off-shore target when he pressed home his attack too low and had to pull back sharply to avoid hitting the water. The aircraft went into a high-speed stall, dropped a wing and crashed into the sea. Thus he, a very experienced ground-attack pilot, fell victim to the characteristic of the Skyhawk about which I had warned and incorporated in the pilot's notes.

Shortly after that unfortunate accident, I received a 'phone call from the Singaporean High Commission saying that Mr Pang Tee Pow was in London on SAF business and would like to meet me. We arranged that I would meet him and his team for lunch at their Kensington Hotel during which Tee Pow asked me if I would consider returning to Singapore. I replied that, as much as I would like to do so, I would not be able to until I had retired from the RAF in June 1980. He said that Dr Goh would be disappointed but he made a note about my retirement date.

In October 1979 I had a 'phone call from Mr Tripp who had taken over from Sir Sam Fall as High Commissioner in Singapore but was now back in UK having just retired from the FCO. He said that Lee Kwan Yew had asked him to contact me – so we arranged to have lunch at the RAF Club. He said that the Prime Minister, mindful of the fact that I was soon to retire, had asked him to sound me out about returning to Singapore as Air Advisor. As luck would have it I had just retired, somewhat early, from the RAF in order to take up an offer from a UK Government agency which would enable me to continue working until 1985, at least.

As the years rolled by Singapore became further from our thoughts until, in 1990, Brigadier General Gary Yeo, now Deputy Commander of the RSAF, arrived in London to attend the RCDS course. We got together several times during his stay and the first time Gary and his wife, Ming, came to lunch in our house in Kew he presented me with a book published in 1985 to commemorate the twentieth anniversary of the RSAF from its beginnings as SADC.

Reading the beautifully-illustrated book brought back many happy memories of people, places and events mostly half-forgotten. But the overwhelming emotion was one of total amazement at the incredible progress that had been made since my departure thirteen years previously. For example, they now operated no less than seven fighter squadrons, being one of Hunters, three of Skyhawks, two of F-5E Tigers and one of F-16s – which, incidentally, I had recommended as the eventual replacement for both the Hunters and Skyhawks. The Hunter squadrons had been reduced to one because half the Hunters were now being used in the operational and weapons-training roles. The Skyhawk aircraft had been updated and re-engined with a more powerful one which had improved their performance considerably and, what with the addition of the F-5s and F-16s, the RSAF was now the most potent air force in the SE Asia region.

The Skyvans were still doing valiant service in the search and location role but had been supplemented by a Grumman E2C Hawkeye airborne electronic warfare aircraft. This added a new dimension to the Bloodhound II surface-to-air missiles and the recently-acquired improved Hawk Fire Units, the principal weapons of the Singapore Air Defence Artillery group, operating under the command and control of Air Force Systems Command with its sophisticated radar. In addition, the RSAF now operated Hercules in the strategic and tactical roles and had updated their Alouette helicopter squadron with Bell 212s and Huey UH-IHs. I was most impressed by the political will which had made this rapid expansion possible. This was expressed succinctly by the foreword in the book by the Deputy Prime Minister and Minister for Defence, Mr Goh Chok Tong, who wrote 'Our constraints of men and space are such that the enormity of the defence burden must fall on the Air Force'. What a very wise man! I have yet to find out whether he is a relative of Dr Goh Keng Swee!

The biggest surprise in the book was that the editor and his contributors publicly acknowledged their debt to the people who had helped them to achieve such progress,. Indeed the book was 'Dedicated to those who had influenced and assisted in the development of the Air Force and especially to those airmen and

The author admires a papaya which he planted as a seed when he and his wife moved into their married quarter.

airwomen whose devotion to duty and professionalism have made the RSAF what it is today'. However, having said that, only three loan-service officers were actually named in the text. I quote 'Notable among the Directors Air Staff was Brigadier General J. Langer who was the first DAS and one of the prime movers behind the agreement of the Defence Council to rename the SADC the RSAF'. There was even a photograph of me with Lieutenant Colonel Peter Stuart.

Also written was 'Another whose contribution was substantial was Group Captain M. A. Turnbull who was DAS in the mid-1970s, having been previously the Head of the Air Operations Department'. I had met Turnbull briefly when he first arrived at SADC to take over from Bill Kelly who was in turn taking over from me. Turnbull, an RAAF loan-service Wing Commander acted as DAS when Dusty Rhodes was killed. He must have found favour because Mindef persuaded the RAAF to promote him to Group Captain so he could finish his tour as DAS. The third person mentioned was Squadron Leader Chris Strong, of whom it was written 'he was a personality that all pioneer Hunter pilots will remember. The first CO of No. 140 Squadron, he built up our very first fighter squadron'. I was very disappointed that Group Captain Basil Fox was not mentioned. He had been Head of the Air Equipment Department for many years and who, having handed over that post, continued to serve for about twenty years as Head of Defence Procurement and then as Director of the agency set up by the Singapore Government to handle contracts with civilian aviation companies.

That Singapore was now prepared to acknowledge expatriate help in building up the air force from its inauspicious start in 1968, was a sure sign that the RSAF had the self-sufficiency and confidence to accept their history. It made me proud to have played a small part in their astonishing success.

Chapter 16

The Last Post

I took over as Director of RAF Flying Training (DFT) on 5 May 1975. The Directorate was located in the offices comprising the entire top floor of Lacon House, one of the imposing office blocks lining Theobalds Road in Holborn. My staff was headed by two deputy directors, one looking after elementary, basic and advanced training (DDTF), the other operational training (DDTO). In addition there were five wing commanders and four squadron leaders, all very experienced in their various specializations. There was also a small self-contained unit comprising the editorial and production staff of civil servants, headed by an Aviation Historian, Bruce Robertson, who looked after the compilation of the *Air Clues* magazine and the *Aircraft Recognition Journal*, which were published and circulated RAF-wide under the aegis of DFT.

I had a large office with a lovely old leather-topped desk and a conference table which seated up to twelve people. There was also an outer office for my private secretary, Mrs 'Bobs' Francis, a prim and proper oldish lady who had had to return to secretarial work to make ends meet after her bank manager husband had left her for a younger model after twenty years of marriage. My boss was AVM Eric Cook, the Director General of Training, a nice man with whom I got on very well. He had his office in Ad Astral House, the next office block, along with his two other directors, those of ground and education training. I was delighted with my domain, which I referred to as the 'Penthouse Suite', not least because the offices were set back from the sides of the building thus creating a virtual veranda all around with superb views over central London and particularly of St Paul's.

I soon found out that, in addition to the job specification for DFT, I had two looming extra-curricular tasks. The first was to oversee the introduction into RAF service of the BAe Hawk, the advanced training aircraft which was to replace the Hunter and Gnat in that role. The second longer-term project was the introduction of the Panavia multi-role combat aircraft (MRCA), as yet unnamed, not just into the RAF but also into the German Air Force and Navy and the Italian Air Force on a joint-training basis. Clearly I was going to be a busy boy but, at least, it all sounded quite exciting – little did I realize just how much excitement there would be!

In June I was thrown into the deep-end of the MRCA pool: to explain I must digress. In June 1972 a Tri-national Joint Operational Study Group had been set up to examine the feasibility of carrying out all or some MRCA training on a co-operative basis. The Study Group reported in March 1975, having endorsed the idea of joint training since there were significant standardization and inter-operability advantages as well as financial benefits in the scheme. They proposed

The author chairing a meeting of the Tri-National Tornado Training committee with his German and Italian Co-Chairmen.

that a joint operational conversion unit be set up at RAF Cottesmore and that joint weapons training be carried out at the IAF base at Decimomannu in Sardinia – subject to further investigation of the facilities and potential at that base. They also recommended that the aircraft be named Tornado.

The Study Group report had been circulated to the Chiefs of Air Staff who cleared agreement in principle with their respective Ministries of Defence. Then a high-level meeting was called in June 1975 at the MoD in London to discuss and ratify the proposals. I attended this meeting at which a draft Memorandum of Understanding (MoU) was drawn up. The MoU authorized the setting up of a Tri-National Tornado Training Committee (TTTC) to supervise and co-ordinate all aspects of the development of a joint operational conversion unit at RAF Cottesmore and of a joint weapons training facility at IAF Decimomannu – should that base prove suitable for that purpose.

I was to be chairman of the TTTC with Colonel Karl Heinz Goldberg of the GAF and Sylvio Nardini of the IAF as co-chairmen. There were to be three sub-committees to look after the detailed aspects of operational training, personnel and administration and engineering and supply. There was also to be a Tornado Aircrew Course Design Team, under the chairmanship of one of my DFT officers, Wing Commander Don Oakley, to devise the various ground-school and flying syllabi and advise on training aids. Finally there was to be a Finance Committee which would work in parallel with the TTTC to ensure that we kept within budgetary constraints. The sub-committees and the design team were to report to the TTTC at its meetings, the first of which was to be held in December 1975 in Rome and thereafter quarterly rotating between the three capitals.

* * *

For the first six months in office I had concentrated on settling in as DFT and getting to grips with those tasks not connected with the introduction of the Tornado. On our return from Singapore and after disembarkation leave, we had been allocated a temporary type V MQ at Medmenham, the former 'patch' for the staff of HQ 90 (Signals) Group based in Medmenham Abbey since the Second World War but now relocated elsewhere. Eventually we were offered a type III MQ on the MoD patch at Lees Gardens on the outskirts of Maidenhead. Our fourteen crates had arrived but were being held in storage: now, at last, we were able to take delivery. They filled our garage for weeks whilst we unpacked them and found places for all our Far Eastern treasures.

Although the commuting was a bit of a pain I found that I was enjoying my work as DFT. I think that this was due to the diversity of my responsibilities, the calibre and esprit de corps of my staff and the fact that I was kept extremely busy. However, after a few months, things started to go awry with the arrival of a new DGT, AVM 'Freddie' Sowrey, who was the replacement for Eric Cook who was about to retire. I had met Freddie several times when he was the Wing Commander CO of No. 46 Squadron of Javelin night-fighters and I was the Squadron Leader CO of No. 43 Squadron day-fighters. He was a small man known affectionately as 'Bent Fred' because he suffered from severe cervical spondylosis, resulting in a very hunched posture. Despite this problem he had a reputation as a good pilot and commander. Like many others I admired his indomitable spirit and tenacity.

There is a probably apocryphal story about when he led his squadron into a USAF base in East Anglia on a liaison visit. There was a small party on the tarmac to welcome them fronted by two USAF 'Bird' colonels and the RAF Unit CO. The Americans were somewhat astonished when the strange figure of Fred clambered down from the cockpit and even more so when he turned to assist his navigator, Squadron Leader Bob Olding, to climb down. Bob had some difficulty because he had lost a leg when ejecting from a two-seater Vampire fighter during the Suez campaign. The RAF man overheard one of the American colonels say 'You've got to hand it to these Brits: they don't waste anything'.

We warmly welcomed AVM Sowrey on his arrival but the euphoria turned to dismay when, after a visit to my Directorate in Lacon House, he ruled that we were to move into Ad Astral House where a number of offices had become vacant. This would have made good administrative sense if the space in Ad Astral was adequate and appropriate – which it was not. The offices were spread over two floors and we had to be shoehorned in by much doubling and trebling up. For example, my lovely big office on the sixth floor was replaced by two small offices at the back of the building on the second floor, overlooking a busy side street and the backs of other buildings where the sun rarely shone. It was noisy and smelly from vehicle fumes and waste bins and was too small for other than a small meeting of up to four or five people and my secretary, 'Bobs', was appalled not to be in an outer office, albeit her cupboard of an office was next door. The worst affected were the editorial and publishing staff who had enjoyed a large studio with good light, ideal for their drawing boards and printing presses. They were now crammed into three dingy offices totally unsuitable for purpose.

When I saw what was available for the move I complained bitterly but, alas, to no avail, but with the promise of review if more space became available, which it never did. I had a near riot on my hands by my staff: Jack Holt, the DDTF, who never minced his words, was apoplectic with rage and the previous high morale of my boys sank abysmally, especially as our 'penthouse suite' remained unoccupied. That was bad enough but worse was yet to come!

Somewhat put out by the 'reduced circumstances' of my Directorate following our relocation I determined to spend as much time as possible away from my dreary office. The first opportunity came in December when I travelled to Rome with my Tornado project officer, Wing Commander Mike de Burgh, and another Wing Commander from AMSO's Department who was looking after the 'works and bricks' aspects of preparing RAF Cottesmore for joint operational conversion training. This was the first meeting of the TTTC and, as agreed in June, all the administrative arrangements for the meeting would be undertaken by the host country and that it would be chaired by that country's co-chairman, in this case Colonel Nardini.

The Italians, as a nation, are not renowned for their administrative abilities, at least not since Mussolini made the trains run on time and invented the *autostrada* (motorway) system to open up the country. Just about everything that could go wrong went wrong but, nevertheless, we managed to get through the business in hand by lunchtime on the second day. Whilst our respective project officers were cobbling together the minutes of the meeting, Sylvio took Karl Heinz and me on a lightning tour of some of the city's sights before a quick lunch at a *ristorante* on the outskirts. As we drove back for the 3.00pm meeting to agree the minutes we got stuck in the most appalling traffic jam. We eventually got to the MoD forty minutes late where we learnt that the circus had come to town and that a parade had been authorized through the centre. The lead elephant had taken fright at the cacophony that is endemic to Italian traffic and had run amok, hotly pursued by its *mahout* causing chaos and total gridlock.

* * *

The next away day out of the office came unexpectedly when, in the New Year, the MoD received a request from the British High Commission for the RAF to send a team to review the flying training being carried out by the Nigerian Air Force (NAF). The original request had come from Air Commodore John Yssadoko, who had recently taken over as Chief of the Air Staff and was very dissatisfied at the way in which pilot training was being carried out. The CAS had undergone his training in UK and had attended the RAF Staff College course at Andover; as a result he was very pro-British.

It was decided that I should lead a small team of four consisting of myself, two wing commanders, one a QFI the other an engineer, and Squadron Leader John Winterbourne, a very experienced 'trapper' from CFS. On 9 February we flew out to Lagos from Heathrow in a Nigerian Airlines Boeing 707, which was rather scary until we heard the reassuring Australian voice of the captain. We were met by the Defence Attaché, a British colonel with whom I was to stay whilst the others were to be looked after by British High Commission personnel. The next day we re-assembled and were taken to meet the High Commissioner, Sir Martin le Quesne, who gave us a potted history of Nigeria with particular emphasis on the post-independence political situation. It was a sorry story of corruption and military coups to stop it but which usually resulted in matters getting even worse. I was invited to stay for lunch with Sir Martin and his wife along with Lady Plowden, the educationalist, who was visiting Nigeria on Unicef business, a most interesting occasion.

In the afternoon the team was briefed by the CAS who painted an extraordinary picture of the shambles that was NAF flying training. To summarize, he said that there was no proper aircrew selection procedure or aptitude tests. Most candidates were proposed by politicians, tribal chiefs and other VIPs and the whole system was rife with nepotism and corruption, largely because the military were highly regarded, being second only to politicians in the career 'pecking order'. Elementary flying training was carried out by the British team flying the Bulldog aircraft, basic flying training by Israelis flying an aircraft of which I had never heard and advanced and operational training was carried out by Russians at Kano flying Yaks and MiGs.

I asked how this ridiculous situation had arisen and John explained that Russia and Israel were keen to have a presence in Africa and had offered to supply aircraft free of charge, provided that they ran the training units. The Nigerian politicians concerned, no doubt encouraged by liberal bribes, had accepted these offers without any discussion with the air force. The Israeli training was reasonable but that carried out by the Russians was beset with problems, not least because none spoke English and no Nigerians spoke Russian. In addition, their aircraft servicing was terrible and availability was pathetic. No wonder the top brass in the NAF referred to the Russian unit as 'Fred Karno's air force'! John went on to say that we would be able to visit the Israelis, but that the Russians refused to let us have a look at their set up. What John really wanted from the team was a hard-hitting report highlighting the problems inherent in the present system and recommendations of measures which would improve standards and reduce wastage.

The following day the team was flown to Kaduna in a NAF Fokker F-28 to meet up with the ex-RAF instructors at Camp Bonny, the airfield base of the EFTS. Kaduna is more or less in the middle of Nigeria and was a far cry from the hustle and bustle of Lagos; indeed there seemed to be more camels and mules in the town than motor cars. We were warmly welcomed and given a good briefing on the problems they faced, not least being the poor calibre of the cadet pilots which resulted in a wastage rate of well over 50 per cent. However, we had only been there for a few hours when word came through that there had been yet another military coup and that the capital was in chaos.

A short time later we received a message from the BHC saying that it would be advisable to return and that they had arranged for the NAF to fly us back to Lagos. When we arrived we learnt that the coup had been led by Lieutenant Colonel Dimka, who had the support of a junta of middle-rank army officers, and that their forces had ambushed the staff car of the President, General Mohamed, and had killed him and his bodyguards. They had then taken control of the radio station and the Ministry of Defence as well as certain other buildings such as barracks and key industrial installations. Luckily there were no dissenters in the Air Force, which had taken control of the airport and was thus able to continue to operate. Nevertheless, the country was in turmoil and the senior Government members, mostly the generals who had masterminded that last coup, being fearful for their lives, had dressed in civvies and fled to their tribal or family homes.

Within twenty-four hours Dimka had established sufficient control to broadcast a message to the Nigerian people saying that he now headed a government intent upon eliminating corruption and restoring democracy by holding elections within a year. He said that his forces had 'executed' the former president for having been even more corrupt that the civilian government that his military coup had overthrown.

Whilst this pre-taped message was being broadcast, Dimka turned up at the BHC demanding to see the High Commissioner. Unwisely, Sir Martin agreed to see him. Perhaps he wanted to glean intelligence about the likely success of the coup and its implications. Having heard Dimka's request for political recognition of his junta, Sir Martin, not impressed by his claims, gave him a right wigging about his actions and told him in no uncertain terms to go away and not return until he could substantiate that he had established a 'de facto' government.

The fact that Dimka had visited the BHC so soon after the initiation of the coup became common knowledge, and rumours spread that the UK was behind the coup. This led to the flames of anti-colonial rule being fanned. I happened to be in the BHC on the third day when an unruly mob wielding anti-British placards swarmed around the front of the building and started to throw stones to break windows whilst the Nigerian Police looked on. It started looking nasty whilst I was on the roof with the Defence Attaché who was taking photographs. I saw about a dozen men carrying what looked like a telegraph pole with which they started to pound the entrance door as others started to prepare firebombs which they attempted to throw into the building through the broken windows. Luckily the Nigerians do not play cricket and their bowling was well wide!

By this time the ground floor had been cleared of everybody except a half-dozen Royal Marines who had been issued with ammunition for their fire-arms with strict instructions not to fire unless the rioters broke in and life was in danger. Upstairs, the BHC staff were incinerating documents whilst Sir Martin and others were attempting to contact either the Police HQ or any Nigerian Army HQ which had remained loyal. Eventually, the Chief of Police was located, told of our plight and warned that unless something was done to restore order the situation could become an international incident and he could be in trouble if his force did not react quickly. In no time at all the riot squad arrived and set about the mob with their sticks and batons until it had dispersed.

It was a few more days before the coup was overturned. No thanks to the Top Brass who had fled the capital; the restoration of order was due largely to a few field commanders whose troops had remained loyal and, to a lesser extent, to the police – and to the fact that the coup had been badly planned and executed and was without popular support. A state of martial law was declared and the ports and airports sealed off until the prime movers of the rebellion had been rounded up. Despite this relative order, anti-British feelings persisted and Sir Martin was declared *persona non grata*. So it was decided that my team should return to Kaduna, which had not been affected, until we were able to return to the UK. We were flown up-country on the 15th but it was not until the 22nd when, thanks to the efforts of the CAS, the authorities agreed to release a British Caledonian Boeing 707 freighter to fly us home.

The Nigerian Air Force was largely unaffected by the coup, so we were able, whilst in Lagos, to have many discussions with the air staff and to give CAS our confidential views on how the NAF should proceed in order to rationalize future flying training. I told him that whereas our views were politically sensitive I would submit a formal report in more diplomatic terms which he would be able to show to his political masters to convince them of the need for radical changes. They must have been grateful as, when we were being seen off, we were presented with a host of gifts. As team leader I was given four, comprising a very large wooden carving of a Nigerian warrior holding a spear with an upside-down elephant balanced on his head, a large framed embroidery of Oma's mother (whomsoever she might have been), a necklace of sea-shells denoting that I was now a tribal chief and a beautiful jet black ebonwood carved ceremonial stick. My wing commanders were given three gifts each and Squadron Leader John Winterbourne was lucky enough to get only two. Fortunately, we were waved through customs at Gatwick where we were met by Jane who had been kept fully informed by the FCO whilst I was incommunicado in Nigeria. We subsequently learnt that it was another forty-eight hours before anyone else was allowed to leave Nigeria.

The abiding impression that I took away from Nigeria was one of sadness that, since independence, the country had squandered the legacy of good governance with a succession of inept and corrupt civilian governments, followed by equally ineffective and greedy military regimes. As a country, Nigeria had everything going for it, not least its vast natural resources of oil, timber, minerals and extensive lands given over to cattle-raising and agriculture. And yet, whilst those in power lined their own pockets and lived the life of Riley, the ordinary people had not benefited in terms of healthcare, education or living conditions in general. The picture I remember most clearly was at the weekly farmers' market in Kaduna, to which I was taken by our Nigerian interpreter. The meat stalls were alive with buzzing flies and on each canopy were perched several vultures waiting to swoop down on the offal and other scraps being discarded during butchery.

* * *

I had hoped for some more 'away days' in April as it was Germany's turn to host the TTC but Colonel Goldberg requested to miss his turn for 'political reasons', so it was held in London. It was a good meeting, not least because the sub-committee was beginning to make progress and there were problems to resolve and decisions to be taken. One such decision was that, at the request of Colonel Nardini, the co-chairmen and their project officers should visit Decimomannu to review the extent and cost of the facilities needed for it to be prepared as the joint weapons training unit.

For the UK meeting I managed to get the MoD Hospitality Fund to pick up the tab for a lunch for the delegates. I opted for Simpsons in The Strand as the venue because it was the most quintessentially British restaurant. Simpsons set the standard and thereafter a formal delegates' lunch became accepted with each nation trying to out-do the last one with originality and excellence.

On 23 May Mike de Burgh and I flew out to Rome to link up with our German and Italian counterparts and then on from the IAF base at Ciampino to Decimomannu in Sardinia. It did not take us long to decide that Decimomannu was quite unsuitable as the cost of the works needed to provide adequate accommodation, hangarage, hard-standings and appropriate range facilities would be prohibitive. I found it difficult to understand how the IAF could have thought that the base would be suitable. The answer probably lay in the agreement that the costs of setting up the joint facilities should be borne in proportion to the number of Tornado aircraft purchased. At that time the UK, with 229 ordered, was by far the biggest contributor, Germany paid her fair share whereas, if I remember rightly, Italy would only pay 12 per cent of the costs. So, had we gone ahead, Italy would have inherited a superb base at very little cost to themselves. In the event, at a specially-called meeting in Rome, Italy decided to do their own weapon training and so it was decided later to set up the joint Anglo-German facility at RAF Honington, where the existing facilities were such that the reduced task could be accepted at very little cost.

The last TTTC meeting of the year was held in Bonn in October 1976 and, as expected, was run with the usual Teutonic efficiency with Karl Heinz as chairman. The most excitement during that visit was when he drove Sylvio and I around Nurburgring Grand Prix circuit in his Mercedes at speeds in excess of 100mph. The most unusual event that coincided with the meeting was the kidnapping of a German businessman, Hans Jurgen Schleyer, whom the Red Army Faction held ransom in an attempt to get the government to release some members of their terrorist group from prison. The kidnapping did not affect us but a picture of a blindfold Schleyer with a pistol being held at his head was shown on TV under a banner emblazoned with the initials RAF which, on our return, led to comments such as 'What on earth were you up to in Germany?'

* * *

Whereas 1976 was a busy and rewarding year for me, I regret that it was blighted by an increasingly strained relationship with my immediate boss, AVM Sowrey. It had started with his insistence on my Directorate moving into Ad Astral House with the resulting cramped and inadequate accommodation. Thereafter, there were many silly nuisances which irked us: for example he suddenly realized that the acronym for his appointment, DGT, was the same as that of the Director of Ground Training, So, without consulting us, he had our acronyms changed to DT(F), DT(G) and DT(Ed). The first we learnt of this was when we saw the changes in the MoD telephone directory. Air Commodore Don Calder, who was now DT(G) was furious not least because, had we been consulted, he would have suggested that his title should be changed to Director of Technical Training which would have been more appropriate as the original 'ground' related to when he looked after education as well.

Lack of consultation by a new broom was irksome, as was DGT's seeming lack of interest in what I was doing, even though Tri-national Tornado Training was the most important task being undertaken within his purview. For example, I suggested that he might like to see the minutes of the TTTC meetings but he declined the offer. In many ways I should have been glad but I do not think it was because he had full confidence in my ability to do a good job: it was pure disinterest. In fact the only Directorate in which he showed an interest was that of education, perhaps because as a pseudo-intellectual he felt more at home in that more academic sphere.

It all came to a head over a staff paper prepared for the Air Member for Personnel (AMP), Sir Neil Cameron. Some years previously multi-engined pilot training (MEPT) had been suspended when serious fatigue fractures were found in the Valiant V-bombers as a result of which the fleet was grounded permanently. As there was already a back-log of second-pilots awaiting postings and there were now hordes of Valiant pilots to be absorbed into the remaining V-Force squadrons of Vulcans and Victors, MEPT was put on hold, No. 5 FTS was disbanded and its base, RAF Oakington, put on a care and maintenance status. Unfortunately that decision had coincided with the first scheduled deliveries of the Scottish Aviation Jetstream turbo-prop aircraft which were to replace the aging Varsities: the Jetstreams were therefore put into long-term storage at a maintenance unit.

It was now necessary to consider how, when and where MEPT should be restarted. This was largely an academic exercise. As a start Wing Commander 'Sandy' Innes-Smith, who had been my OC Operations Wing at Valley and was now my statistician, had to calculate the complex problem of how many new second-pilots would be required every year for the next ten years. He had to take into account the projected shape and size of the front-line squadrons over the next decade. The factors to be considered included that Polaris would eventually take over from the V Force as the principal strategic nuclear deterrent and that the V Squadrons would be phased out. They in turn would be replaced by Tornados as the main tactical nuclear deterrent – and, of course, the Tornado does not need second-pilots as the crew consists only of the first pilot and a weapons system operator. Second-pilots would still be needed in the transport and maritime squadrons but the overall numbers would be steadily reducing. I checked Sandy's calculations and that he had used the right parameters and timescales and then handed over the preparation of the draft paper to Jack Holt.

Jack came up with three possible ways of restarting MEPT. They were, firstly, re-activating No. 5 FTS at RAF Oakington, the most expensive option, which could not be recommended in the long term. The second option was to delegate MEPT to either CFS or to the RAF College at Cranwell, of which Cranwell was the preferred solution as they had spare capacity and the choice of so many redundant airfields in Lincolnshire to use as the multi-engine relief landing grounds for the practice of 'circuits and bumps'. The final option was to put MEPT out to civilian flying schools, which was not costed as Jack dismissed it summarily for a number of reasons with which I fully agreed.

As the paper was for AMP to present to the Air Force Board I gave a copy of Jack's draft to DGT in case he wished to comment. A couple of days later AVM Sowrey called me into his office and said that he knew that AMP favoured going out to civilian contract wherever possible as a means of meeting demands for cuts in the Defence Budget from the Treasury. He then told me to rewrite the paper to favour the 'civvy' option. I protested strongly saying 'Surely the whole purpose of writing a staff paper is to muster the facts and discuss the considerations in such a way as to enable superior authority to make informed decisions'. I was merely repeating the mantra that the DS used at JSSC when teaching staff work. DGT retorted angrily that it was not my job to argue with a superior officer's wishes: in other words 'What AMP wants; AMP gets'.

With great reluctance I set about rewriting the whole paper. With the help of Wing Commander 'Chris' Christie we investigated the civvy option in great detail, hoping that we would find compelling reasons to reject it. Chris and I visited the College of Air Training at Hamble, the Oxford Air Training School at Kidlington and the Scottish Training School at Perth. Before our visits I wrote to the three principals, asking them to prepare costings for providing ground-school and flying programmes, the detail of which I attached, for three courses of three-and-a-half months each for fifteen RAF students for three years. In the event the costings turned out to be very similar, no doubt there having been some collusion. However, Hamble had the best weather factor, superior facilities and good accommodation. I regretted this as the principal, an ex-RAF group captain, openly boasted that he was 'a close friend of good old Neil Cameron'. Even more annoying was our discovery that the civvy option using twin piston-engined Cessnas would be marginally cheaper than the cheapest RAF one at Cranwell using the turbo-prop Jetstream.

To cut a long story short I wrote a paper in which I discussed the pros and cons of the options in such a way that it was clear that, whereas the civvy route was cheapest, there were sufficient disadvantages to disregard that option. I deliberately did not make any specific recommendations but made it obvious that I favoured delegation of the task to Cranwell.

When the paper was finalized I handed the top copy to DGT who glanced through it and, to my surprise, actually congratulated me on having done a good job. Several weeks later, following his promotion to Air Chief Marshal (ACM) and prior to taking over as CAS, Sir Neil Cameron handed over the appointment of AMP to AM Sir John Aiken. No sooner had this change occurred than ACM Sir Andrew Humphrey, who was still CAS prior to taking over as Chief of the Defence Staff, summoned DGT and me to attend a meeting of the Air Force Board.

Sir Andrew was absolutely hopping mad and opened the meeting with a tirade about how he had been placed in a most embarrassing situation when the Chief of the Naval Staff (CNS) had put in a bid for the RAF Jetstreams, currently in store, to be transferred to the Royal Navy as replacements for their existing light-communication aircraft, the ageing Percival Prince, known in nautical circles as 'Admirals' Barges'. CNS argued that the RAF had no need for them as they were about to put MEPT out to civil contract. In addition, he stressed that this would save the Defence Budget millions of pounds and that the Treasury strongly supported the idea.

The CNS claim was the first that Sir Andrew had heard about civilianizing MEPT, so he had summoned Sir Neil who told him that no decision had been taken but the DFT had written a paper recommending that course of action. Sir Andrew then addressed the meeting as a whole and said that, whereas there were a few tasks currently undertaken by RAF personnel that could be civilianized, flying training was definitely not one of them. He also added that Sir Neil had promised that no further consideration would be given to such a ridiculous proposal.

He then turned to me saying, 'Langer, you must have been out of your mind to have even thought that such a proposal had any merit at all' and then proceeded to enumerate many of the reasons why it was 'unthinkable', all of which I had included in my paper. Whilst Sir Andrew was ranting I tried desperately to attract DGT's eye but whilst everyone else was looking at me he resolutely refused to do so. I tried to intervene putting my hand up and saying 'But, Sir …' but Sir Andrew said 'No ifs and buts, Langer, and don't try to make excuses. You may leave now as we have other matters to discuss'.

In retrospect I was glad that 'Bent Fred' (who I shall now refer to as BF) did not leave the meeting with me because I was sure that I would have biffed him for not having come to my defence. It would have been very satisfying but would not have done my career much good. Instead I wrote him a demi-official, staff in confidence loose minute, in which I reminded him that it was only at his insistence that I explored the civvy option, which was quite contrary to my own views, and that I had made no recommendations to adopt it in my paper. I requested that he should inform Sir Andrew and Sir John of those facts. The loose minute was a model of restraint but BF did not even have the courtesy to respond to it and when I eventually broached the subject he merely said 'I have taken note of what you wrote' and promptly changed the subject.

I no longer cared what BF thought about me as I had lost all respect for him but I was very concerned that ACM Sir Neil Cameron, for whom I had great admiration, indeed he was one of my few role models, seemed to dislike me intensely. I subsequently found out that somebody had told him that it was I who had tipped off the Royal Navy about the availability of the Jetstreams and had therefore triggered the row between him and Sir Andrew. I never found out who told him that lie – but I had my suspicions!

* * *

A couple of months after the June 1975 meeting, which had authorized planning for Joint Tornado training and had appointed me as Chairman of the co-ordination committee, the then Air Secretary told me that the AFB had suggested to him that I should stay in post as DFT until I retired – as continuity would be vital to the success of the scheme. As I was due to retire in June 1980 on my fifty-fifth birthday that would mean remaining in post for just over five years. I had no objection to this as DFT was, without doubt, the best appointment in MoD for me, given my background and qualifications but I was concerned that it might prejudice my chances of promotion. The Air Secretary re-assured me by saying that there were two exceptions to the plan, firstly should I be promoted and, secondly, if I did not measure up to the job, which left me not knowing whether to be pleased or worried!

I discussed this with Jane and we decided that this would be a good time to get into the housing market before it was too late. So most weekends we would sally forth looking at houses in our preferred areas of the suburbs of SW London or the Home Counties of Surrey, West Sussex and Hampshire. We set ourselves an upper limit of £30K and several pre-requisites; for example, the sitting room had to be big enough to accommodate Jane's boudoir grand piano, it had to be cat friendly for Mao and TD and within easy commuting distance of Central London. We had a pretty good idea of the sort of home we wanted and instructed our estate agents accordingly. Perhaps the primary consideration was that it had to have 'character', which I defined by saying, 'Every time I open the garden gate I want to be able to say how lucky I am to be living here.'

We had several near-misses until we saw an Edwardian semi-detached house in Kew which most nearly met our criteria. The asking price as £28.5K which I negotiated £750 off but we still had to take out a mortgage of £9,000 after we had pooled all our savings. We moved in in November 1976 and almost immediately house prices, which had been static for years, started to soar. We lived at 29 Beechwood Avenue happily for sixteen and a half years when we sold it for £220K.

Towards the end of 1975, when joint Tornado planning was getting pretty hectic, I was handed a very unwelcome extra chore when I was appointed Chairman of the RAF Participation Committee. Although the Air Show season was only from April to September inclusive this was a year-long task because it involved soliciting offers of display resources from not only RAF sources but also from the Royal Navy, Army and aerospace companies for the next season soon after the last one ended. Whilst these were coming in we had to collate bids from the organizers of the four Battle of Britain air shows as well as the bids from Service Units for their open days and from civilian organizations which were putting on commercial displays. Then came the tricky bit of putting together an overall programme of participation for the complete season and inviting comments and suggestions. Finally, after adjustment, there was a meeting of all participants, which I chaired, to confirm or make final alterations.

Ever since the 1950s the Chairman had been the Director of Fighter Operations at MoD; this was because the official RAF formation aerobatic team had always been provided by an RAF fighter station after a competition between the various teams. No. 43(F) Sqn had won the competition several times: indeed the 'Fighting Cocks' team, led by Flight Lieutenant Peter Bairsto, had had that honour when I took over as CO halfway through the 1957 season. The following year saw a change of policy and the first semi-permanent team was the Black Arrows team of Hunter aircraft led by Squadron Leader Roger Topp, CO of No. 111 Squadron. The Black Arrows were authorized to form a team of nine aircraft, which made for a much more impressive display than the previous maximum of five. The Black Arrows were famous for their twenty-two aircraft loop which beat the then record of sixteen by the Pakistan Air Force. However, I must confess that Roger only achieved this record because I lent him two aircraft and pilots to make up his team.

Unfortunately when the Hunters were phased out as front-line aircraft they were replaced by the English Electric Lightning, a superb interceptor fighter with a fantastic rate of climb to the troposphere and beyond. The Flying Tigers of No. 74 (F) Squadron duly took over from the Black Arrows but, alas, the Lightning proved unsuitable as a formation aerobatic aircraft, not least because the high-g manoeuvring was using up their fatigue life at an alarming rate. So the mantle of providing the official team was passed to Flying Training Command and the Jet Provost Red Pelicans took over the role. The team did their best but the limitations of the aircraft made their displays very unimpressive, especially when compared to American, French and Italian teams which still used fighter aircraft. Luckily, the advent of the BAe/Folland Gnat, later replaced by the Hawk, enabled the Red Arrows to take over for the 1965 season and to become regarded justifiably as the world's foremost team.

So there was logic in my taking over the Chairmanship, although the reason given was that the Director of Fighter Operations, Air Commodore 'Micky' Mount, was too busy to cope. In fact, despite my misgivings, I had no such problem as I inherited a young and very capable civil servant who had been secretary to the Committee for the last two seasons and knew the ropes. And, of course, there were many perks, such as the invitations Jane and I received to attend the Battle of Britain and other displays as VIP guests. I was also able to attend the alternating Farnborough and Paris Air Shows, made all the more enjoyable by the invitations to view the displays and have lunch in the BAe chalet courtesy of my old friend Bill Bedford.

* * *

I tried very hard to get on with DGT but I could not forgive the way in which he had dropped me in the mire. Although there was much to admire about him, not least his many outside interests and the way in which he coped with his disability, we were too much like chalk and cheese. I found him somewhat devious, rather indecisive and all too ready to bow to outside pressures for economies and cuts from the Treasury. Unfortunately, the AFB usually passed the burden of cuts onto flying and ground training in order to protect the operational units, an understandable reaction but, in my view, a misguided one which DGT accepted without fighting our corner. I suppose the fundamental difference between us was that he was an academic ditherer whereas I was a hands-on 'doer'.

Petty instances of annoyance continued to irk me; for example, on one occasion he stopped me from attending a vital TTTC meeting in Rome at the last minute for no good reason. A couple of weeks previously we had been notified of a Parliamentary Question (PQ) on a flying training matter for which I had provided the brief for the Minister along with the answers to possible supplementary questions from the floor of the House. The PQ was pretty straightforward but DGT suddenly decided that I should be around to answer any query that might arise should the minister leave reading his brief until the last moment. This was not normal procedure and anyway, as I argued, my deputy Jack Holt could provide any additional information required but BF insisted on my staying. So my other deputy Director, Group Captain 'Des' Richard, who had not been involved in any joint Tornado training planning, had to go to Rome in my place. Needless to say there were no questions!

I was beginning to wonder how much longer our strained relationship could continue when it occurred to me that DGT might be getting on a bit and must soon reach retirement age. So I looked him up in *Who's Who* and saw that, having been born on 14 September 1922, he should be on his way in a couple of months. Indeed a little later it was announced that an old acquaintance of mine, Brian Plenderleith, currently Commandant of the RAF College at Cranwell, would be taking over on 1 September: my cup runneth over for both reasons. The only snag was that, as Senior Director, I would be expected to say a few kind words when we 'lunched' him out in a private room of a nearby pub as arranged for the end of August, a task made the more difficult when it was announced that Bent Fred was to be promoted to Air Marshal (who retire at fifty-eight) and was to be the UK representative of the Permanent Military Committee of the Central European Treaty Organization (CENTO), based in Ankara.

I managed to put together a jokey, light-hearted form of words and ended with the hope that Fred and Mrs Sowrey would find their tour a 'Turkish Delight'. After the lunch BF took me aside and actually apologized for what he called 'the little misunderstanding over MEPT' and then dropped the bombshell that Brian Plenderleith had recently been diagnosed as having a brain tumour which required an urgent operation. In the meantime, I was to act as DGT until Brian had recovered sufficiently to take over. In turn, Jack Holt was to act as DT(F) and Des Richard as Chairman of the TTTC. Luckily we had just held a meeting so there would not be another for four months.

Whilst acting as DGT I came across the file in which my staff paper on MEPT had been placed. I re-read the paper to remind myself exactly what I had written, only to find that it had been altered considerably before being passed on to AMP. BF had completely changed the emphasis of my original, not least by watering down most and deleting others of the disadvantages of going out to civilian contract. He had also added the recommendation that, on balance, the civvy option should be adopted.

I must stress that DGT was quite entitled to make changes, but not before consulting and getting my agreement. Not having done so, and passing it onto AMP under cover of a letter stating that it was DT(F)'s paper, was unpardonable. I was shocked by this discovery but not nearly as incensed as I was when, many many years later, I read the autobiography of Marshal of the RAF Lord Cameron. Unfortunately, Neil Cameron died before he had finished it so it was completed by Air Commodore Henry Probert, who had been DT(Ed) in my time. When Henry was interviewing the now Air Marshal Sir Frederick Sowrey KBE about the time when Sir Neil had been AMP, Fred had the nerve to claim that it was he (and AUS(P)) who had talked AMP out of his plan to put MEPT out to contract. Having thus rewritten that small piece of history, perhaps it was not too surprising that Sir Bent Fred went on, in retirement, to become Chairman and later President of the RAF Historical Society.

To return to 1977, regrettably Brian Penderleith's operation was not successful and he had to retire on health grounds – dying six months later. So after my having been acting DGT for three months it was necessary to regularize the appointment. As I learned later, the Air Secretary had offered the newly-appointed CAS, Air Chief Marshal Sir Michael Beetham, the choice between myself, which he recommended, or Air Commodore Michael Gordon Beavis. Unfortunately for me MGB, as I called him, had served under Sir Michael twice before, in Cyprus and RAF Germany, whereas I was 'John Who?': so he chose the devil he knew.

I duly handed over to MGB, now complete with acting AVM rank, who was somewhat apologetic about his good fortune, saying that I was far better qualified and experienced than he, not least because he had never been in Training Command, was not a QFI and anyway was two years junior to me as an Air Commodore. I had worked with MGB in MoD when I was DD Air Plans and he was an assistant Director of Defence Plans as a wing commander. I liked him then and knew he was a sharp operator, so I was able to assure him that I would be pleased to work for him, not least because I had done my own share of overtaking in the fast lane, albeit I now seemed to be suffering from a loss of power.

* * *

The year 1978 was when everything started to go right and not just because a certain gentleman was now residing in the Middle East. Perhaps the greatest success story was that of the introduction of the Hawk into service. Although I had nominal responsibility the success was due to two main reasons: firstly the excellence of the aircraft itself and secondly to the sterling efforts of BAe/Hawker Siddeley.

The Hawk was the first post-Second World War aircraft to be designed specifically for the advanced training and tactical weapons role. Its predecessors had all been ex-front line fighters, such as the Spitfire, Vampire, Meteor and Hunter: even the Gnat had been designed originally as a single-seat fighter. Most of these aircraft were pretty out of date and did not reflect the requirements of the then current front-line fighters. In practice, the Hawk exceeded all expectations in terms of performance, handling, engineering and ease of maintenance. But perhaps the most astonishing fact for such a high-performance aircraft was that, despite having flown 23,000 hours during my time, there had not been a single accident.

The second reason for success was the work of BAe/Hawker Siddeley who converted a nucleus of QFIs from RAF Valley and the weapons instructors for RAF Brawdy. Wherever the Hawk came into service they provided one of their engineers to assist and advise in the early stages. The total order for the RAF was 175 aircraft but by March 1978 I had taken delivery of the hundredth in a ceremony at Dunsfold Airfield, well ahead of schedule. The higher utilization rates being achieved by the aircraft and the earlier than expected delivery enabled us to accelerate re-equipment plans, to shorten course times and to be able to offer training for overseas customers in support of sales.

By 1978 the Hawk was beginning to attract a lot of attention in aviation journals and interest from potential customers, such as Finland and Indonesia which had already placed orders. The only European competitor to the Hawk was the Franco-German Alpha Jet. The most important interest came from the USA where the US Navy and Marines were looking for what they called the 'VTX advanced trainer replacement'. Hawk and Alpha Jet were both contenders but after initial consideration a short list of four aircraft was released, being Hawk and three US aircraft.

Shortly after this announcement I was contacted by Air Chief Marshal Sir Denis Smallwood, who having retired, had recently taken over as the Military Adviser to

BAe. He told me that the company had been invited to put on a Hawk presentation for the US Department of Defense and US Navy representatives in the British Embassy in Washington and that they would like me to assist by giving a talk on why the RAF had chosen the Hawk and on our experience of operating the aircraft so far. He assured me that BAe would provide airline tickets and accommodation and would pick up the tab for all other expenses.

I felt pretty confident that I could contribute something useful to the BAe sales pitch, not least because I had been involved with the Hawk since its conception as the HS1182AJ project. When I was DD Air Plans in 1972 I had sat in on the specification meetings with the MoD (Air) Operations Requirement Branch and had been invited by ACAS (Pol) to consider and recommend an appropriate name for the aircraft. I had written a tongue-in-cheek loose minute (Appendix A) in which I recommended Hawk as the best option. I had by now converted on to the aircraft and carried out ground-attack sorties, thanks to Mike Beavis, who encouraged me to visit training units and to fly whenever possible. How unlike Bent Fred, who would not permit me to do so, probably because he was jealous of my many visits abroad.

On 7 May I met up with the BAe team which consisted of Colin Chandler (Head of Sales), Bill Bedford (Harrier, Hunter and Hawk sales), John Farley (BAe Chief Test Pilot) and Andy Jones (Hawk Production test pilot). In Washington we were all accommodated in a huge self-catering apartment at No. 1 Washington Square. After a jolly dinner in a nearby restaurant, where we discussed tactics, we returned to the apartment where we had great fun seeing whose paper-dart aircraft could stay airborne longest and travel farthest from our sixth-floor balcony. I won, because I cheated by using paperclips on the nose to increase stability and performance.

The following day we went to the Embassy to look at the arrangements and facilities for the presentation and to have a rehearsal. On the day the proceedings were opened by the British Ambassador (who was the son-in-law of James Callaghan the UK Prime Minister and perhaps the most unpopular man to hold that prestigious diplomatic post). Then Colin Chandler took over to introduce the team and to hand over to me. I spoke for about twenty minutes and answered quite a lot of questions. But undoubtedly the star of the show was Andy Jones who put across his enthusiasm for the Hawk very convincingly. Eventually we all retired to another room for drinks and a sumptuous buffet lunch and had the opportunity for informal talks with the US representatives.

During the drinks 'Splinters' Smallwood, whom I had known since he had been my CO on No. 33(F) Squadron, asked when I was due to retire because, if the Hawk was to win the VTX competition, BAe would like me to consider being their man in Washington. He told me that a decision about the VTX winner should be taken by the end of the year so I promised that I would consider applying for premature voluntary retirement (PVR) should the Hawk win.

* * *

A few weeks after my return from America I had a telephone call from a very worried Colonel Goldberg, saying that the GAF was under pressure from the government to withdraw from the joint Tornado training draft agreement for economic reasons. He said that the deputy commander of the GAF wanted to hold urgent talks with the two of us before opposing that proposal.

On 28 June I flew to Bonn and no sooner had we started talking than in walked the impressive figure of the newly appointed Chief of the Air Staff who was taking over that very week. He took one look at me and said 'Johnny! What on earth are you doing here?' It was none other than General Frederick Obleser with whom I had worked at HQ AFCENT in 1967-69. We had got on very well then, when he was a lieutenant colonel, not least because we were both fighter pilots and I had flown with him in the Lockheed F-104. Freddie invited Karl Heinz and I into his office where we presented the case for remaining joint and then to his residence where, over more than a few bottles of fine Rhine wine and an excellent dinner, we put the world to rights. The following day I flew home and shortly afterwards a very relieved Karl Heinz rang to say that General Obleser had given the politicians a hard time and had convinced them of the real financial advantages and that the proposal had been dropped.

So planning continued and the penultimate meeting of the TTTC was held in Bonn in September 1978. The very last was held in early May 1979 in the Officers' Mess at RAF Cottesmore, which was about to be handed over to the already designated joint permanent staff under the command of Group Captain M. G. Simmons. Our work as a Committee was now complete and we had achieved all of our objectives. It had been far from easy to evolve a plan that satisfied the training needs of the three air forces and some compromises had been inevitable. However, we had surmounted all the many problems in a spirit of goodwill because of our shared conviction that joint training was the most effective way to introduce a major weapons system into the NATO inventory.

Although the Mess was not fully operational we were able to hold our farewell lunch in the dining room as a team of catering staff from HQ Fighter Command had come up to prepare the meal. I had asked the Command Catering Officer if the menu could reflect the 'Best of British'. The team excelled themselves: as we foregathered we were served English sparkling wine from Kent which rivalled all but the most expensive French champagnes. The menu included Scottish smoked salmon, Aberdeen Angus steak, Welsh trifle and Stilton cheese, all accompanied by the freshest of local vegetables and, incredibly, surprisingly excellent red and white wines from English vineyards. Our German and Italian friends could not believe that everything was home-grown, reared, fished or produced! As one delegate said 'When you told us that everything would be typically British we expected fish and chips'.

It was a great shame that the stalwart Karl Heinz was not there as he had retired from the GAF, aged sixty, a few months earlier. His replacement, Colonel Karl Rimmek, read out a message of best wishes from him and then presented me with

The Last Post   249

two books. I was sorry to have to say goodbye to my tri-national team which had done such a good job, having completed our task on time and well within budget. But my final involvement was yet to come when on 8 May there was a ceremony at Cottesmore for the formal signing of the previously draft Memorandum of Understanding, which was attended by the Chiefs of the Air Staffs, Ambassadors, senior government officials and other VIPs. AM Sir Michael Beetham welcomed the guests and then handed over to me to give the keynote address in which I spoke of the background to the joint training concept, the work of the study group and then the problems faced and overcome by the TTTC. Finally, I outlined the timetable for the build-up of the aircraft and aircrew to the steady state in 1980. That was followed by a display of command-less drill by the RAF Regiment team and a flypast by two Tornados from BAe Warton. Suddenly I was the flavour of the month amidst many congratulations and much back-slapping.

* * *

To back track a little: in October 1978 MoD (Air) had received a request from the Bangladeshi Government for someone from the RAF to run the rule over the flying training organization of their air force – and I was given the job. After discussions with the BAF air attaché in London, I boarded a Bangladeshi Biman Boeing 707 at Heathrow on 22 November with some trepidation, not least because when my secretary had made the ticketing arrangements with their Embassy she had told them that I always travelled in business- or club-class. She had been told that, because Bangladesh was an egalitarian republic, their airline had only one class – economy.

When I boarded the aircraft I was very surprised to be shown into a small curtained-off section immediately behind the cockpit with luxurious seats and tables and to be told that the aircraft would be making an unscheduled, non-fuelling stop in Belgrade. When we landed there I was moved back into a reserved seat in the front row of the packed cabin whilst a small party boarded, causing much excitement from those passengers who recognized the figure of their popular President who had been paying an official visit to Yugoslavia. Shortly after take-off, the purser invited me to go forward to meet President Ziaur Rahman, a former general who had led a military coup but had then been elected President in a democratic election in 1977. He was a small, goodlooking and charming man who spoke excellent English. He was very interested in my mission and we got on so well that he invited me to join him in his suite for the remainder of the journey. I was very saddened to read three years later that, after several failed attempts, he had been assassinated in Dhaka in 1981.

When we landed at Dhaka I was met by the First Secretary of the British Embassy who was to look after me for the first night. We drove to his married quarter in a dilapidated old Humber Snipe which was the official car of the Ambassador who was on home leave. When I commented on the state of the vehicle he told me that the FCO had agreed its replacement by a shiny new Daimler ages ago but it was now sitting in its container on the dockside at Dacca in West Africa, to which it had been sent in error.

Over dinner my host and his wife briefed me on the recent history of Bangladesh since its ill-advised creation as East Pakistan when India was granted independence in 1947. He told me of the military coup, led by General Ziaur, which had overthrown the corrupt government and how, since Ziaur had been voted in as President with an overwhelming majority in the elections of 1977, the joint civilian/military government had been steadily introducing secular democracy into the predominantly Muslim nation. Unfortunately, largely as a result of injudicious spending by the original East Pakistan governor, the country was very poor and the threat from Islamic extremists was such that Dhaka had a night-time curfew when only the Army and the Police were allowed on the streets.

The following day I was driven to the military side of the airport, where I noticed a number of MiG 21s scattered about the dispersal in an obvious state of disrepair. I was then flown in a Bell 212 helicopter to the air base at Jessore, the home of the Cadet Training Wing, where I was met by the Officer Commanding, Wing Commander Altaf H. Choudury, who was to look after me for the next few days. He took me on a quick tour of the base which was a model of good order after the ramshackle appearance of the BAF enclave at Dhaka.

Altaf had a visit plan all mapped out which included my being the reviewing officer of a parade of Cadet Wing personnel, briefings on all aspects of the ground and flying training syllabuses, sitting in on ground-school lectures, visiting the cadets' accommodation, eating lunch with the cadets in the Mess and, finally on the last day, addressing all ranks of Cadet Wing on my impressions of its operations.

It did not take me long to realize that my visit was being regarded as an AOC's annual inspection, as in the RAF. Indeed towards the end of my visit Altaf told me that when Bangladesh won its independence most of the Pakistan Air Force personnel based in the East returned to the West, leaving behind relatively few Bangladeshi personnel. The more senior officers were pilots, engineers and administrators but that, as he was the most senior qualified flying instructor, he had been charged with setting up Cadet Wing from scratch. As there was no one in the BAF qualified to supervise flying training, the hierarchy wanted assurance that Altaf was going about things in an efficient and effective manner.

Thankfully I knew that I would be able to write a glowing report because I had been very impressed by everything that I had seen at Jessore. The base itself was extremely well kept, all personnel irrespective of rank and trade were well turned out and an aura of efficiency and keenness permeated every aspect of the operation. On my last day Altaf asked if there was anything else I would like to see or do and I replied that I would like to fly their principal training aircraft which they designated as the PT-6. In fact it was the Chinese-manufactured version of the Russian Yak 18, which was then very popular with aerobatic pilots throughout the world. Altaf agreed readily and we spent a happy half hour showing each other our aerobatic skills.

The following day I bid a fond farewell to Jessore to return to Dhaka, ostensibly to debrief the BAF CAS and to start preparing my report. On the way back by Bell 212 I told the pilot that I had flown many types of helicopter but never the Bell. He asked if I would like to have a go, so on my saying 'Yes, please' he landed in a field, briefed me on the controls and instruments and let me fly it from take-off to landing at Dhaka.

I was in for another surprise next day. During my visit I had told Altaf that when I had been based in India during the war on gliders in the airborne assault role our forward bases from which to mount our operations in Burma had been Chittagong and Cox's Bazar. I had never been to either, which I would have liked to have done, as our two 'ops' had been cancelled. When I was having breakfast in the Mess, Altaf appeared unexpectedly, saying that the CAS had agreed that I should be flown to Chittagong from which I could see one of the most beautiful areas of their country. So Altaf and I were flown to Chittagong in a Fokker F-27 along with my two armed bodyguards who had been assigned to accompany me everywhere during my stay. After a tour of that city, we were flown by helicopter to Kaptai and its National Park which consisted of a maze of inter-connecting lakes nestling amongst hills and valleys which were densely forested. We eventually landed on the helicopter pad of the BAF Rest Centre in the centre of the park. After a leisurely lunch we boarded a steamboat in which we cruised the lakes, admiring the dramatic scenery whilst watching, through binoculars, the wildlife and birds along the water's edge.

After that most enjoyable day out, my remaining time in Dhaka was a bit of an anti-climax: my job was done; all that remained was putting the finishing touches to my draft report. The curfew enabled me to wrap it up as in the evenings I was confined to the Mess. I was glad when I boarded the Bangladesh Biman Boeing 707 night flight to the UK and more so when I found that, although the cabin was all-economy class, two special seats had been reserved at the front for myself and a Junior Minister. Unfortunately, the Minister never stopped talking and I did not manage to get any sleep especially when, approaching London, the aircraft was held in a holding pattern for over twenty minutes. The pilot obviously decided to conserve fuel by flying as slowly as possible and the aircraft was juddering far too close to the stalling speed. By the time we had landed I knew why Pope John Paul II always kissed the tarmac on disembarking – well he did always fly by Alitalia!

When I arrived home I stayed up until it was time to go to bed, by which time I had had no sleep for forty-eight hours and slept like a log, so soundly that, much to Jane's chagrin, I completely missed the ravages of the great storm which blew tiles off the roof and uprooted our white mulberry tree.

* * *

I had had my fifty-third birthday on 24 June 1978 so when I was not promoted in the July list I knew that further advancement was no longer possible as the Treasury rules state that one must have two years left to serve in the new rank.

I was also aware that, because of the three-year wage freeze imposed by the Labour Government, my pension would be very much lower than those who were lucky enough to retire just before the freeze. This was because index-linked pensions were not frozen and therefore were increased annually at a time when inflation was at an all-time high. This was due to the world's economic situation and the Chancellor's incompetence and inability to control it. I had already made enquiries about my pension entitlement and had been advised that it would be around £7,750 per annum, clearly not nearly enough to maintain a reasonable standard of living, so it was imperative that I would have to continue to work after retirement.

Air Chief Marshal Sir Denis Smallwood had been keeping me informed about the progress of the US Navy VTX competition which the Hawk had won easily. However, there was a snag in that Congress had refused to sanction a British aircraft unless BAe linked up with an American aviation company for the conversion of the aircraft to the VTX specification in the USA and for subsequent repair and maintenance. Needless to say, this would require months of negotiation for BAe to find the right partner. Splinters insisted that BAe still wanted me to be 'their man in Washington' but also told me that the post would not be established until negotiations were complete.

I was beginning to get a bit restive as it had been a long time since I had first been offered the Washington job and I was beginning to have doubts about it finally coming to fruition, so I decided to look around to see what else might be on offer in the UK. My first port of call was Group Captain Bert Ambrose whom I had first known at Leuchars. He was now retired but working at MoD (Air) running the P5 section for AMP which helped senior officers find jobs after retirement. He told me that a government intelligence agency, known as Box 500, was looking for a group captain or air commodore to give security advice to those aviation companies which were manufacturing equipment classified as secret or higher. I told him that I knew nothing about intelligence or security, but he persuaded me to go for an interview as it would be good practice should the Washington job fall through.

I duly reported for an interview at a building which I had difficulty in finding as it had no windows at ground level and an anonymous, untitled entrance. Once inside, I was met by the organization's recruiting officer who escorted me to the interview room and introduced me to the five members of the board. One of them opened proceedings by outlining the nature of the job at the end of which I told the board that, now knowing exactly what was involved, I was not interested and that I did not wish to waste their time any further. However, the Chairman persuaded me that the interview should continue – so I agreed. They then proceeded to quiz me about my RAF career, my domestic circumstances, my politics, my hobbies and interests, etc., etc. I am afraid that I treated the interview rather lightly and even managed to provoke the odd smile on their austere faces. When it was over they thanked me for my honesty and my attitude towards their questions.

After that episode I explored various other opportunities, such as fundraising for charities, becoming the bursar of a school or university college; and other equally dull activities, all of which I dismissed with horror at the inevitable tedium. About three months later I was contacted by the Box 500 recruiter who said that I had impressed the board and that there was a post coming up in which they thought I might be interested.

He arranged for me to meet the retiring incumbent, an ex-RAF group captain, who gave me a comprehensive briefing on the job and introduced me to some of the people which whom I would be working. It certainly seemed most interesting, it would be connected with aviation, albeit of the civil kind, and I could do it to the age of sixty and perhaps beyond. The pay as a Grade V Crown Servant would be a fraction of what I would have earned had I gone to Washington, but that would be compensated by my remaining in the UK with easy commuting to central London from Kew. So I decided to accept the job which would start in September 1979, nine months before my retirement date.

After discussions with Jane, who never really fancied living in the USA, and with Mike Beavis, who encouraged me to 'go for it', I put in an application for premature voluntary retirement (PVR). No sooner had I done so than the Air Secretary, ACM Sir John Gingell who later became Black Rod in the Houses of Parliament, called me to his office. He said that he and most members of the Air Force Board felt that I had had a raw deal due to AM Sir Fred Sowrey having 'dammed me with faint praise' in his confidential reports on me and to my having fallen foul of ACM Sir Neil Cameron. He told me that I had already been put forward for two AVM appointments and that, whereas all other members of the AFB had concurred, Sir Neil had vetoed my promotion. He went on to say that now Cameron was no longer CAS, if I was to sign on for eighteen months I would be posted to fill an AVM appointment for the necessary two years.

I told Sir John how pleased I was by his offer but that I would have to give it a lot of thought and would let him know my decision as soon as possible. This really was a dilemma: on the one hand I had set my sights on achieving AVM rank which meant not only more pay and correspondingly a better pension but also the status of that promotion, automatic entry into *Who's Who?*, invitation to CAS's annual briefing of retired Air Officers, etc., etc. On the other hand I now had a job to go to which I could do for more than five years, and possibly longer, which would result in a supplementary pension. Moreover, my new pay scale plus my RAF pension would more or less match the pay of an AVM which I would only be on for two years and I would still need to find work on retirement at the age of fifty-seven.

To help me decide I went to see George Cooper, the senior civil servant who looked after the administration and paperwork for the appointments of AVMs and above. After pressure from me, he reluctantly told me that the job on offer was that of Air Officer Administration (AOA) of HQ Strike Command at RAF High Wycombe. That really was the deciding factor: I had been very fortunate to have had some wonderful jobs, especially the last few, and when I retired I wanted to go out on a high whereas being an AOA would be an extremely disappointing finale. However, I was by now the most senior Air Commodore in the RAF and had been overtaken in the promotion stakes by many who were up to two years junior. For example, Pete Bairsto who had been my A Flight Commander when I was CO of 43 Squadron, was now deputy C-in-C of Strike Command in the rank of Air Marshal and it would be to him that I would report as AOA.

When I told Jane of my dilemma she wisely refused to influence me either way and insisted that it should be my decision alone. My heart wanted the promotion, but my head looked much further ahead than the next two years – and my head won. I would be very sorry to leave the RAF but not sorry to leave my present job which I would have done for four-and-a-half years by mid-September, nearly twice as long as any other. It was a delight to work for Mike Beavis, an excellent boss, but now that the Hawk and Tornado projects were complete there was a feeling of anti-climax. I had more time to visit units and to do a lot more flying, indeed my aircraft tally had risen to fifty-six different types (see Appendix A), but I was ready for a new challenge. So I told Sir John that I could not accept his offer and my application for PVR was approved.

My last day of service in the RAF was to be 28 September 1979 – exactly thirty-seven years from the day I was enlisted. I had thoroughly enjoyed my career, not

The author retired from the RAF in September 1979 after 37 years' service. He was dined out by his directorate in the Officers' Mess at RAF Northolt where he was presented with this large cartoon of him flying a Hawk aircraft with silhouettes of the 56 aircraft types which he had flown during his career in line astern.

least because of the wonderful variety of jobs I had done and the places where I had served. There had been many highs, which had included being a fighter squadron commander, being the Station Commander of the busiest base in the RAF and commanding an air force, albeit not the right one. The lows were few: firstly the failure to carry out operations during the Second World War, despite having volunteered to become a glider pilot; secondly, the loss of my flying category which effectively put back my promotion to Group Captain for five years; finally, having had the misfortune to suffer the deviousness of AM Sir Frederick Sowrey, which caused me to fall at the last fence of the promotion race. On balance, however, the good bits so outnumbered the bad that I would gladly do it all again – for nothing!

I was dined out in style at a Directorate Ladies' Night in the Officers' Mess at RAF West Drayton which both Jane and Karen attended. Dougie Palmer recited an amusing poem about my career which he had concocted and Des Richard made the valedictory speech in his usual dry laconic manner. After that I was presented with a large framed picture of a cartoon drawn by 'Sam', the principal illustrator of the *Air Clues* magazine, showing me flying a Hawk behind which were trailing silhouettes of most of the aircraft I had flown, all cut out from copies of the *Aircraft Recognition Journal*. I could not have asked for a more appropriate and appreciated present which today hangs proudly in my study.

Chapter 17

My Second Career

I reported to Box 500 on 14 September 1979, along with about a dozen other new entrants, to attend the month-long introductory course. Jane was the only member of our family who knew my next occupation; our children did not and had been told the cover story. This led to a slight problem when Marcus and Pat were married. When asked about 'father's occupation' for insertion on their marriage certificate, Marcus should have said 'retired Air Commodore' but professed some uncertainty. Whereupon the registrar asked 'Is he an officer?' to which the answer was 'of course' and then 'Is he an executive?' to which he replied 'I suppose so'. Thus on the marriage certificate I am down as an executive officer, thereby being demoted to the lowest form of animal life in the Civil Service. In fact my new rank was senior specialist officer (Grade V) in the Crown Service.

The introductory course was most interesting and enlightening as it dealt with the activities of the service as a whole and we were addressed by the Directors of every Branch irrespective of in which we would be working. As well as learning all about the service we were also subjected to a number of tests to prove, for example, that we could write decent English in a succinct style. We had to do summaries of long and complicated passages of text and to listen to tapes of conversations and then summarize the important parts without having taken notes. We were all well aware that we were still on probation and would remain so for at least a couple of years.

After the course I was attached to F Branch to work in the sections dealing with communist subversion and Irish Republican extremism. This was to give me first-hand experience of intelligence gathering, recording and use. I was given a desk alongside two relatively new entrants who had been recruited directly from University. They both went on to make a name for themselves for very different reasons. The first was a young lady, the daughter of a former attorney general, who was charming, obviously very intelligent and of a somewhat forthright disposition. Her name was Eliza Manningham-Buller and she went on to become Director General of the Security Service, only the second lady to achieve that distinction. The second was a young man who, despite having been to a grammar school and a good university, seemed to have a large chip on his shoulder. His name was Michael Bethany and he achieved notoriety rather than fame by being caught attempting to peddle his access to intelligence information to the Russian Embassy.

Eventually I reported to C Branch to take over as the *de facto* aviation security adviser to the UK Government, from ex-Group Captain Ken Ritchley who had

The author chatting with Air Marshal Sir Peter Bairsto at a No. 43(F) Squadron reunion dinner. Peter was his A Flight Commander when the author was the Commanding Officer.

done the job for the last seven years. The terms of reference of the post were as follows:

a) The study of unlawful interference with civil aviation in respect of tactics, techniques and weapons;
b) To advise Government Departments and other agencies on aviation security;
c) Liaison with civil aviation authorities and firms on behalf of the Service;
d) To represent the Service on the National Aviation Security Committee;
e) To conduct aviation security training.

Those terms of reference really only covered the basics and I was surprised that there was no detailed job specification. For example, they said nothing about the principal task which was the assessment of the level and nature of the threat and the recommendation of protective security measures commensurate with that threat. Moreover, aviation security training got a mere mention whereas in fact it was going to be my major commitment and the reason why Ken Ritchley had insisted on our having a hand-over period of at least six months. Strictly speaking, the Department of Transport (DoT) should have been running the training programme as they had responsibility for overseeing the implementation and standard of security measures and chaired the National Aviation Security Committee (NASC). They had the executive powers whereas we had no authority and could only advise. They had attempted to set up a training programme but had neither the will nor the expertise and requested that we should take over.

The annual task was to run two two-day courses for UK airport and airline management and senior police; two long courses of nine days for UK security managers and middle-rank police; one ten-day course for security personnel from Commonwealth countries and, finally one four-day course for UK and Commonwealth airlines and for members of the British Airline Pilots' Association (BALPA).

In addition there were about fifteen one-day courses on the recognition of explosive and incendiary devices for airport and airline security staff, the police and personnel from government departments who were required to carry out passenger and baggage searches. These courses were run jointly by myself and Lieutenant Colonel John Coghill, who had made a name for himself in bomb disposal during 'the troubles' in Northern Ireland. The courses were carried out at the Propellant, Explosive and Rocket Motor Establishment (PERME) at Waltham Abbey on the site of an eighteenth-century gunpowder mill from which the highly volatile explosives were shipped by longboats to the Navy at Chatham and the Army at Woolwich. I counted up and found that I would be giving nineteen different lectures in the course of a year – no wonder Ken had insisted on a long handover.

* * *

My branch was the most open of all the branches in the Service as it was the interface with industry and commerce. The main responsibility of the two biggest sections, C2 and C4, related to the giving of personnel and physical protective advice. C2 dealt with those companies undertaking the manufacture of equipments classified secret and above whilst C4 dealt with the larger industries such as railways, the ports, oil and gas and, as in my case, civil aviation.

What I found most agreeable was that most of the C Branch staff were ex-military, many of whom I had known before. For example, the Head of C4 was Colonel David Sutherland MC and Bar who had had a most interesting war, having been a founder member of the Special Boat Service, had worked with the Special Air Service as a member of 8 Commando and had undertaken numerous raids behind enemy lines. His exploits were legendary and one of them, in Rhodes, was later made into a successful film, *They Who Dare*, with Dirk Bogarde playing Sutherland. After the war he assisted the Greek government during the civil war and was awarded the Greek War Cross. He then spent three years instructing at Sandhurst before leaving the Army in 1956 to join the Security Service.

Both C2 and C4 had a majority of ex-service personnel mainly of colonel/group captain rank with a few one-stars and several lower ranks. There were also a few career MI5 officers with specialist qualifications. It was rather like working in a Joint Service appointment in MoD. This feeling was strengthened by the fact that I still caught the same District Line train from Kew along with the same fellow travellers and still changed on to the Piccadilly Line at Hammersmith. The only difference was that I got out at Green Park rather than Holborn: I even got home more or less at the same time.

As when I was DFT, the job entailed quite a lot of travel, especially because the British Airports Authority (BAA) was still nationalized and I had direct responsibility for overseeing the security standards at their seven airports, four of which were in Scotland. The same thing applied to British Airways. And, as I was to find out, I would be attending many overseas aviation security conventions, such as those held by the International Congress of Aeronautical Organizations (ICAO) in Paris and those organized by the Federal Aviation Administration (FAA) in the USA.

Meanwhile, I was struggling to get to grips with the lecture programme. My immediate concern was to take over the two lectures at Waltham Abbey. The programme there consisted of four elements: first I was to talk on the nature of the worldwide threat, giving detailed examples of some of the most spectacular or disastrous attacks against civil aviation, be they hijacking, sabotage or armed assaults. John Coghill would then show samples of the various types of explosives, such as RDX, Semtex and the homemade varieties that can be manufactured from everyday chemicals such as fertilizers and hydrogen peroxide. He would also cover the various types of detonator, detonating cord and a variety of timers such as clocks, watches, altimeters and pressure switches, which could be used to initiate the explosions and how all these components may be put together to form a viable device.

We would then break for lunch in the canteen before going onto the PERME range where John would demonstrate the power of various explosives and how it was possible to cut through a thick steel plate with a shaped charge. He also showed how easy it was to start a blazing inferno with an incendiary device contained in something as small as a cassette tape. Finally, I would finish off by demonstrating the various ways in which people have tried to evade detection when smuggling weapons or devices on board aircraft and the search procedures and techniques necessary to ensure their detection.

On the first Waltham Abbey course I listened to Ken and made notes; on the second I gave the threat lecture with Ken listening and on the third I gave both talks and thereafter Ken left further courses to me. Having crossed that particular hurdle, I thoroughly enjoyed subsequent courses, not least because we were dealing with the most important people in the security chain – those who carried out the vital search tasks. Before long, whenever I visited a UK airport someone would come up and say how much they had enjoyed the course and how useful it had proved.

It took me quite a long time to re-jig all the lectures. Ken had laid firm foundations but his rather dour approach was not my style. I resolved to lighten the approach without undermining the impact. For example, I would start every Waltham Abbey course by saying 'Doubtless you have heard of the "Two Ronnies". Well we are known as the "Two Johnnies" – but our double act is deadly serious. However, we do hope to raise a few laughs along the way'.

I also made my talks more pro-active by involving the audience. For example, instead of just demonstrating the correct passenger search technique, as Ken did, I would invite someone to search me as if I was a passenger at their airport. When he had done so, I would ask if he was satisfied that I was not carrying a weapon or other prohibited item. Having been assured I would take the ballpoint pen from my top pocket, unscrew it and take out a detonator. I would then take off my shoes and take out the insoles which were, in fact, sheet explosive. Finally, I would remove a short length of detonating cord from under my shirt collar. I would then roll up the sheet explosive, secure it with an elastic band, insert the detonator and cord into the centre of the roll and hey presto – you have got a grenade powerful enough to wreck an aircraft cockpit.

* * *

As the aviation security specialist I was required to represent the Service in any national emergency involving aviation in the Cabinet Office Briefing Room A, usually referred to as COBRA. The most important of these was in February 1983 when an Air Tanzania aircraft, en route to Dar-es-Salaam, was hijacked. The hijackers, calling themselves the Tanzanian Democratic Youth Movement, ordered the captain to fly to and refuel at Nairobi, then to Khartoum and Athens where they discovered that the co-pilot was carrying a loaded revolver which they confiscated.

The aircraft left Athens without declaring a destination but was monitored on radar as flying northwards, so in mid-morning COBRA was activated and I was called in on my pager. It was a Saturday and Jane and I were looking at houses in Surrey. We sped home for me to change and have a quick lunch before I drove from Kew to Whitehall in eighteen minutes. The Home Secretary, Mr Willie Whitelaw, had just taken charge but everybody was pretty relaxed as by then their destination had been declared as Paris where we were sure that the French would deal with the incident.

Suddenly everything changed as Paris ATCC reported that the aircraft had over-flown them and was heading our way. I immediately got onto the National Air Traffic Service (NATS) to ensure that they had got the message and to remind them that, if the captain requested landing instructions for Heathrow, the aircraft was to be directed into Stansted, using the call-sign London Airport as in our contingency plans. I also asked them to inform all other major UK airports that a hijacked aircraft was heading our way, destination unknown, so they could brush up on their own reception plans. Later on that evening the Prime Minister, Mrs Thatcher, returned to No. 10 Downing Street and popped into COBRA to see what was going on. She seemed to be relieved to find that Willie Whitelaw, whom she trusted, was in charge but, nevertheless, she made it clear that wherever the aircraft landed in the UK it was not to be allowed to take off again. She was furious that the authorities at Nairobi, Khartoum and Athens had made no attempt to terminate the incident at their airports. She also stated that the aim should be to end the hijack by negotiation and that force should only be used if the hijackers threatened to kill hostages unless their demands, still unknown, were not met, a strategy upon which we had decided long before she had put in an appearance.

Indeed we already had the Metropolitan Police negotiation team and the SAS on stand-by.

Before long the captain requested landing instructions for Heathrow, was diverted to Stansted and landed safely. Everything went according to plan, the aircraft was directed to the designated hard-standing on the far side of the airfield, a land-line was plugged in so that we could talk to the aircrew and negotiations began. These were difficult because the hijackers spoke no language other than their regional dialect and the FCO had difficulty in finding an interpreter. Eventually, it transpired that the main purpose of the hijack was to solicit the help of the UK Government in forcing the resignation of the President of Tanzania, Dr Julius Nyerere, but first they wanted an interview with the former leader of the opposition whom Nyerere had forced into exile and who was now living here, having been granted political asylum. I cannot recall his full name but his Christian name was Jack.

It did not take the police long to find out that Jack was now a mature student at Keele University and that he was not in residence that weekend. It took a little longer to trace him to a clinic which specialized in the detoxification of alcoholics. An official from the Home Office was immediately despatched along with COBRA's directive as to what he could and could not agree at the subsequent meeting with the hijackers. In the meantime he was put on a diet of black coffee.

Having been told that Jack would be produced around noon on the following day, the hijackers relaxed and requested food for themselves and the hostages – and a crate of whisky. The food, and one bottle of whisky, was duly delivered, along with a couple of hidden microphones so that we could eavesdrop on conversations in the cabin. We still did not know exactly how many hijackers there were or how many of them were armed. They had claimed to have pistols and explosives. We also needed to know where the hijackers stationed themselves within the aircraft should an assault become necessary.

Everything was under control until the Chief Constable, Bob Bunyard, informed us that the hijackers had ordered the captain to start up the engines. Mrs Thatcher just happened to be in COBRA at that time and unfortunately she over-reacted, saying that we would become the laughing stock of the world if the aircraft was allowed to take off. She then ordered the Director of the SAS, whose men were in position at the hard-standing, to tell his chaps to shoot out the aircraft's tyres to prevent it taking off. Brigadier Peter de la Billière hurried out to do her bidding.

I was horrified by this order and turned to Director C to explain why, only to be told that one does not argue with the 'Iron Lady'. Nevertheless, I stood up and said, 'Prime Minister, I strongly advise against that course of action', whereupon she glared at me and said 'And who are you and why do you object?' So I told her who and what I was and explained that, as the incident was to be resolved without violence, shooting out the tyres might well provoke it. I told her that aircraft tyres are inflated to 300lb per square inch and if they were shot out whilst taxiing they would virtually explode and the aircraft would rock, giving the impression that an assault was being mounted. The hijackers might then panic and start shooting.

I went on to say that because it was now dark the hijackers had probably realized how vulnerable their position was and wanted to taxi across to the passenger terminal, which was all lit up. Moreover, there was no point in their flying away when they knew that Jack was coming to meet them the next day. I also pointed out that Bunyard, the incident commander, was well aware that the aircraft must not leave and would be blocking the runway and taxi-tracks with petrol tankers and other vehicles – as practised in an exercise in which I had participated only six weeks previously.

Mrs T. pondered a moment then, saying to me 'Be it on your own head', countermanded her order. The aircraft taxied to the terminal, the inner and outer cordons were put in place, communication was re-established and, in a gesture of goodwill, the hijackers released some of the women and children as well as some of the elderly and disabled passengers. By now it was just before midnight and the Prime Minister came in to say goodnight and, amongst other things, thanked me for my advice. She then realized that none of us had had anything to eat since COBRA had been activated and was told that the police canteen, which normally catered for COBRA, shut down at weekends. The only facility was tea and coffee with powdered milk (ugh) and even the biscuit tin had been found to be empty. She disappeared back to No. 10, re-emerging a half-hour later with enough sandwiches for the sixteen of us, which she had made herself, and with a large decorated cake which she had received as a Christmas present.

Sandwiches devoured, Willie Whitelaw decided to stand down COBRA until 9.00 the following morning, having been assured by the Chief Constable that the hijackers and the remaining hostages had bedded down for the night. He kept just three of us on as watch-keepers: a chap from the Home Office, a police superintendent and myself, with strict instructions to let him and our respective bosses know if there were any significant developments.

The following morning Jack, wearing dark glasses and accompanied by his Home Office minder, arrived a little earlier than expected. He boarded the aircraft to talk to the hijackers and gave them certain assurances which we had agreed. Thereupon the hijackers gave themselves up and sought political asylum: the hostages were released none the worse for wear, the incident was considered closed and COBRA stood down. We discovered by questioning the hijackers that there was no such organization as the Democratic Youth Movement; indeed all four hijackers were middle-aged taxi drivers who had dreamt up the name for effect. We also found out that they had had no weapons, their pistols were wooden homemade replicas, until they discovered at Athens that the co-pilot had a loaded revolver which they confiscated, accidentally shooting him in the leg when removing it. A search of the aircraft also revealed that they had had no explosives. Most astonishing of all, the four hijackers had their wives and children on board which we had been unable to discover because Air Tanzania did not keep passenger lists on internal flights.

There were several lessons to be learned from this incident. Although I had decided quite early on that this was a minor politically-motivated incident,

COBRA decided, quite rightly, to treat it as a terrorist act – just in case. Perhaps the most important object lesson was that no weapons should ever be allowed on board, even by officials authorized to carry arms. For example there was a hijack in America many years ago by a single armed passenger. Two other passengers, one an FBI agent, the other a CIA man, both authorized to carry, drew their guns and stood up, whereupon each thought the other was an accomplice and shot at each other. US airlines have long carried armed 'sky marshals': their presence never prevented hijacks but merely increased the chances of violence and the possibility of disastrous cabin decompression. The UK policy has always been to prevent weapons getting on board by effective search techniques and rigorous airside security. Any authorized carriage of weapons and certain other prohibited items must be handed in to the airline by appointment and then stored in the hold in a locked container.

My attendance in COBRA was extremely useful in that I was able to forge a liaison with the SAS and subsequently persuade BA to give their helicopter pilots flight training on the simulators of all their aircraft types. This would enable us to put an SAS man on board a hijacked aircraft as the co-pilot of an exchange crew – should the opportunity arise. BA gave them access to all their aircraft on the ground so they could become familiar with the lay-outs within the aircraft and also how to approach the aircraft without being seen, in case an assault became necessary. Also having been introduced to the Metropolitan Police chief negotiator, Commander David Vanness, I talked him into talking to some of my courses in exchange for my talking to his.

The Air Tanzania hijack was not the first time that I had been called into COBRA, as I had been one of the Service's watch-keepers from the outset of the siege of the Iranian Embassy in 1980. Although there was no direct aviation involvement in that incident, I was useful as, through my contacts at NATS, I was able to arrange that the flight paths of aircraft approaching Heathrow should be routed directly over the Embassy at a lower level than normal so that their noise could mask the sounds of drilling and dismantling of an attic wall from the building next door to enable SAS access. I was also at COBRA following the shooting of WPC Yvonne Fletcher from a window of the Libyan Embassy when she was policing a peaceful demonstration outside the building in April 1984. And I was in COBRA following a bomb explosion at Heathrow, but in that case I was sent to the airport to report back to COBRA which was having difficulty in getting information from the airport police station. In fact the bomb went off in the arrival baggage collection hall of one of the terminals in an item of luggage off a foreign airline. As usual, the police overreacted and wanted to close the whole airport, but I managed to persuade them to close only that terminal until all incoming bags had been screened.

* * *

Going back a bit, during my final interview with the Air Secretary he told me that the RAF was badly underrepresented in the Territorial, Auxiliary and Volunteer Reserve Association (TAVRA) of Greater London. He had been asked to look out for likely candidates who, on retirement, would be working, and preferably living, in or around London. He said that I fitted the bill exactly, particularly because of my joint-service experience, and asked if I would be interested. On learning a little of what would be involved I volunteered, not least because it would enable me to keep in touch with the Armed Forces.

My name was duly put forward and, in no time at all, I was invited to meet the chairman of the London TAVRA, Colonel Alan Niekirk, a former Army officer, now a high-powered solicitor, at the Duke of York's HQ near Sloane Square. Alan gave me a briefing on the role and responsibilities of TAVRAs and then took me to lunch in the Officers' Mess to meet the Vice-Chairman (Army) Lieutenant Colonel Nicholas Eden, son of Sir Anthony, and a few other senior TAVRA members. After lunch Alan said that they would be delighted to welcome me and I duly became a member of the General Purpose and Finance Committee and of three other sub-committees. Within two months I took over as Chairman of the 'Pre-Service' sub-committee, which made sense as it dealt with the Cadet Forces of all three services with units within the bounds of Greater London, of which those of the Air Training Corps outnumbered those of the Sea Cadets and the Army Cadet Force put together. Within six months I was appointed Vice-Chairman (Air) and finally, to my surprise, in January 1983 I was appointed a Deputy Lieutenant of and for Greater London.

The office of Lieutenant goes back many centuries, the first recorded incumbent having been William Latimer who was appointed in 1298 by Edward I to be 'Notre Lieutenant e Soverein Cheveteire' for the northern counties. The first Lord Lieutenant was Lord Russell, who was instructed by the Privy Council in 1594 to put down the West Country revolt against the Prayer Book. Thereafter Lords Lieutenant were appointed on a regional basis whenever trouble threatened. It was, for example, through the Lords Lieutenant that the Home Forces were mustered at Tilbury in 1588 at the behest of Queen Elizabeth I.

The tradition of Lords Lieutenant, and their appointment of Deputies which dates back to 1662, continued without official sanction until 1 April 1974 when under the provisions of the Local Government Act of 1972, it was stated that 'Her Majesty shall appoint a Lord Lieutenant for each county and Greater London'. Today Lords Lieutenant retain their military role through their Presidency of their TAVRAs but the tendency is to involve more civilians as DLs in recognition of their work in local communities and for charities. For example, when I was presented with my scroll of appointment along with five others one of them was David Jacobs who, although a wartime Royal Naval officer, was being honoured for his charitable work.

At that time the Lord Lieutenant was Baroness Nora Phillips who had succeeded MRAF Lord Elworthy. Her appointment, the first ever non-military person, was greeted with great surprise and much indignation by the Colonel Blimps of this world. It was true that her qualifications for the post were pretty meagre. Her main claim to fame was that she was the widow of Morgan Phillips, the Secretary General of the Labour Party, who had died unexpectedly shortly before he was to be created a life peer. The then Prime Minister, Harold Wilson, transferred that honour to his widow, despite the fact that she had only been involved in local politics and as a magistrate. Her subsequent appointment as Lord Lieutenant was considered by many to have been a two-fingered gesture to the 'Establishment', which Harold Wilson loathed. Perhaps Nora's best contribution to politics was that she was the mother of Gwyneth Dunwoody MP, an excellent parliamentarian – albeit of the wrong hue.

For all that, Baroness Phillips played her role unexpectedly well and her diminutive figure, lost in the back seat of her limousine, went scurrying from one engagement to the next, having done her homework and saying all the right things. As she was President of the London TAVRA, I met her frequently and we got on very well together and maybe that was why she invited me to become a DL.

Theoretically the Lord Lieutenant could officially appoint up to 184 DLs because of Greater London's population of about seven million. When I joined their ranks there were about seventy odd, of whom thirty-two were Representative Deputy Lieutenants, one for each of the Boroughs. This was because the Lord Lieutenant and his Vice Lord Lieutenant could not cope with all the many demands made upon them so the Representative DLs would deputize for him at events in their Boroughs. In 1984 I was invited to become Representative DL for Kingston-upon-Thames when Mr Rowan Bentall, life president of the department store group Bentalls of Kingston, was about to reach the retiring age of seventy-five. I met with Rowan who briefed me on what exactly was involved, but I turned down the offer on the grounds that I would be unable to do justice to the job whilst working for the Security Service.

However in March 1987, Field Marshal Lord Bramall, who had taken over from Baroness Phillips, asked me to consider becoming the Representative DL for the Borough of Hillingdon, a post best suited to an ex-RAF officer as there were two RAF stations within the Borough as well as Heathrow Airport, which I knew like the back of my hand.

The author 'seeing' off Diana, Princess of Wales, at RAF Northolt prior to her official visit to Germany.

This time I accepted because I was less than eighteen months away from retirement and, moreover, because of the family connection in that my grandfather J. F. and my father C. E. had both built housing estates in the Borough.

The only snag was that, as a Representative DL, I was expected to wear the Lieutenancy uniform on official occasions. I did a little research and found that the two tailors in the city who made the uniforms charged over £1,000 for the full regalia and that did not include the sword and belt. Although I would have been very proud to wear the uniform, I just could not afford the expense. Luckily those DLs who had served in the Armed Forces in the rank of

The author dressed and 'armed' for meeting and greeting Diana, Princess of Wales, at Heathrow.

full colonel and above could opt to wear their old service uniforms and I found that I could borrow a sword and belt from the Equipment Section of RAF Uxbridge, which looked after the ceremonial requirements of MoD. Problem solved.

* * *

When I joined the Security Service I soon found out, to my delight, that the job would involve a lot of travelling. For the first few years I flew mainly to the UK airports, often by BA's excellent shuttle service. These visits were to get to know the security managers, to be shown their procedural and physical security, to learn of any problems and occasionally to carry out security surveys. Whenever airports were planning to build new terminals or enlarge existing ones the design plans had to be approved by the Department of Transport (DoT) and myself and necessitated many visits during the building phase. I also flew to a number of European airports, particularly Paris (Charles de Gaulle) to attend ICAO and IATA meetings.

My first intercontinental flight was to New York to attend the third International Federal Aviation Administration (FAA) on Aviation Security in May 1983; these were held every two or three years and were attended by representatives from most countries in the Western world. Ken Ritchley, my predecessor, had not attended but Director C was keen for me to go, so I travelled by BA with their Head of Security, Denis Phipps, with the result that we were both upgraded to first class – an unexpected luxury.

The two-day conference was held in the old-fashioned and rather grand Sheraton Hotel, but was otherwise pretty dreadful as the standard of the presentations, with a couple of exceptions, was very poor. Moreover, the conference was an outrageous sales pitch to persuade the delegates to buy American-manufactured metal detectors, x-ray machines, explosive detectors and other security equipment. They also used the conference as a venue for honouring a couple of airline aircrews for their 'outstanding' performance in handling a couple of hijacks by awarding them citations. In fact, all that those aircrews had done was to follow IATA guidelines but I suppose that so many other US aircrews had made such a 'pig's ear' in similar circumstances that when someone got it right the FAA thought it 'outstanding'. I was amazed during the conference at how the Americans had the nerve to portray themselves as being the aviation security experts and that every country should follow their example. In fact, the Americans could only legitimately boast that they were the most experienced in that, since the first hijack of a civil airliner, more than a quarter of all hijacks had originated from US airports as a result of security failures. In the same period there had been only one such hijack from a British Airport.

The two redeeming events during the conferences were firstly, that my younger sister, Liz, flew in from Los Angeles to spend two days with me at the Sheraton and then our old friend Helen O'Connor from Singapore, now widowed and living and working in New York, was able to drive across the city and we had an excellent dinner in a nearby Italian restaurant.

My next big trip was in January 1984 to the Sultanate of Oman at the request of the Foreign and Commonwealth Office (FCO), which was concerned that the Americans were meddling in the economic markets of the Gulf States. One instance was that a US company was bidding for a contract to run aviation security courses for the Royal Omani Police (ROP) which ran airport and airline security. The Americans were by-passing the ROP, which was already negotiating a similar contract with a British company, by going directly to the Minister concerned, no doubt with the promise of a considerable backhander.

On arrival I was met and looked after by Colonel Ray Coombes, a former superintendent of the Cheshire Constabulary, who took me to see all the right people, including Major General Said Rashid al Kalbani, the ROP Inspector General, and his deputy who was responsible for personnel and training. Having managed to get a sneak look at the American proposed training programme, I was able to convince them that, taking into account the fact the Oman had only two airports, the programme was too ambitious, unnecessarily elaborate and far too expensive. Also that British was best, not least because their proposal concentrated on training ROP personnel to carry out the programme themselves and to take over running it – within two or three years. I subsequently learnt that the Americans had been sent packing and that the contract was awarded to a subsidiary of the UK's Control Risks Ltd.

In the course of the visit, at the request to Ray Coombes, I gave two talks on consecutive days on the threat to aviation in the Middle East with a forecast of its likely development and on aviation security in general with particular reference to changing ICAO requirements for international airports. These talks were attended by most of the senior ROP and Customs and Immigration Officials.

The third trip to faraway places was to Philadelphia in April 1985 to attend the fourth FAA Conference. As our eldest son, Hilary, had married and now lived and worked in Philly it would be nice if Jane could accompany me so, when I received my club-class return ticket, I arranged for it to be swapped for two economy-class tickets which cost about the same. It was rather more than fair exchange as we were upgraded to club class both ways anyway.

The conference itself was a great improvement on the last one as the FAA, obviously running out of things to say, had invited speakers from other countries to give some of the presentations. I had been invited to give the UK perspective, so when my time came I gave a two-part talk fully supported by slides. I talked first about the UK perception of the threat to aviation worldwide and how we expected it to develop in the future. I made two forecasts which turned out to have been pretty prescient. The first was that, as airport and airline security measures became more effective, an increasing number of attacks would be mounted from outside the airport perimeter fence. These could be either mortar attacks against airport targets or the use of surface-to-air missile attacks against aircraft. The second was to warn that we should not discount the possibility of suicide bombers, either within terminals or by those travelling knowing that there was a bomb in their hold baggage. If either precedent was set it would require a complete re-appraisal of security measures because, at that time, the Israeli Airline, El Al, was the only airline to screen hold baggage.

In the second half of the presentation I talked about how we went about assessing the threat in the UK and about the importance of the collation of all relevant information about all previous attacks in terms of weapons used, types of explosive, techniques used in attempts to evade detection and the tactics used by hijackers to seize control, to subdue the passengers and to put pressure on the authorities to meet their demands. My audience was astonished when I told them that I had a record of every single hijack, every sabotage attack against aircraft or airports, every assault against passengers, every SAM attack etc., whether successful or thwarted and whether it had been carried out by terrorists, political refugees, criminals or cranks. I explained that only by studying the past could trends be spotted and countermeasures devised to foil them. At the end I was bombarded with questions and had many requests for copies of my script – which I could not meet because I did not have one, merely a framework to act as an aide-memoire: everything else was in my head.

At the end of the conference I found that all the other 'foreign' presenters had been given commemorative brass plaques or citations. As I bade farewell to my opposite number in the FAA, who incidentally had twenty-three assistants whereas I was a one-man band, I asked why I had not been given one. He apologized that I had not been told but that the Chairman of the Conference, Billie H. Vincent the Director of FAA Aviation security, had decided that mine was the best presentation and that it merited a 'Special Citation' as being the 'outstanding' one: and that it could not have been prepared in advance and would be sent to my home address. When it arrived I was so, in American terms, 'honoured and privileged' to receive it that I hung it in the most appropriate place – the downstairs loo!

My final long-range trip was to Tokyo in September 1986 to attend the G7 Economic Summit Meeting, at which the threat of international terrorism was a reserve agenda item for discussion – if time permitted. I was there to brief the UK team, headed by the Chancellor of the Exchequer, as civil aviation had been by far the most frequent target of terrorist attacks for the last thirty-five years. Alas, I was not needed as the meeting did not get around to the subject. However, I enjoyed my first-ever visit to Japan, having been well looked after by a first secretary at the Embassy and his wife who took me to a number of Japanese restaurants to sample the various styles of their cuisine; although I was grateful, I have to admit that I did not particularly like any of it. The other bonus of the trip was that the refuelling stop both ways was at Anchorage. As both stops were in daylight I had an airborne panoramic view of Alaska with its mountains and lakes.

There was one trip which I was very cross to have to miss when the company secretary of British Airways invited Jane and I to be his guests, all expenses paid, on BA's inaugural flight to Buenos Aires. Unfortunately, that flight coincided with one of my Commonwealth courses. Had it been a UK course it could have been postponed but, as the joining instructions for the eighteen students from twelve countries had already been sent out, I had to decline the offer.

* * *

It was incredible how quickly time flew by whilst I was working for the Security Service, perhaps because Jane and I were both so busy. Apart from keeping house and looking after Marcus and Karen when they were at home, Jane also worked as an exam invigilator for the University of London and part-time for an opinion poll and market research company called Telsales.

We also managed to plan to take a few holidays between my courses. Our favourite type of holiday was touring in our own car or flying to some faraway place and hiring. We usually stayed in a different place every night and we certainly covered a lot of ground and visited some remarkable places. We could not understand why anyone would want to spend a week or more in one place, just lazing on the beach by day and doing the clubs in the evening. However, we did take two three-day city breaks, one in Venice in February 1981 and the other in Istanbul in February 1985 which were most enjoyable.

I can remember flights to Hannover in 1985 to explore Saxe Coburg and the Harz Mountains, to Munich in 1986 to re-acquaint ourselves with Oberammergau and Bavaria, including a night stop in Rottenburg, an untouched medieval walled town. We also flew to Malaga to stay with friends who lived near Gibraltar and others who lived near Almeria. But more often we took the car by ferry to Cherbourg to explore north-west France, or to Santander to stay in Portuguese *poussadas* or Spanish *paradores* which, at that time, represented remarkable value for money in some fascinating places.

One of our best holidays was in May 1983 when we flew to New York with Air India to attend Hilary's marriage to Cleirach Partin. After three days in Philadelphia, where we met up with Karen and her then boyfriend Alan in time for the wedding, we hired a car and all four of us set off on an adventure. We first drove through the Amish country of south Pennsylvania before going down the Blue Ridge Mountains, taking in parts of West Virginia and Carolina. Finally we met up with our old friend from Singapore, Helen O'Connor, who now lived in Alexandria, just outside Washington. It was there that we first met the four-star Admiral Wes McDonald, who held the NATO appointment of Supreme Commander Atlantic (SACLANT) – not bad for a USN pilot! He was a widower and, much to our delight, he and Helen married shortly after our visit.

In Karen's back garden prior to going to one of the Royal Garden Parties at Buckingham Palace.

The only black spot on that trip was the flight out with Air India. Originally Jane and I had applied for an indulgence flight on the RAF VC10 scheduled flight to Washington. Having applied much in advance, we had been assured of seats but were thrown off at the last moment to make way for a crowd of Treasury Officials. With forty-eight hours left to go, the only flight I could find which would get us there in time was with Air India. It had originated in Bombay and did not appear to have been cleaned during the turnaround at Heathrow. The toilets were a disaster area with the floors awash with urine as many of the Indian ladies on board were more used to squatting on the floor to perform. However, the curry for lunch was excellent.

What with my extra-curricular duties with TAVRA and as a DL on top of my work for the Service, I was 'on the go' pretty well all the time so it was not too surprising that time flew by and I was in sight of the retiring age of sixty. I was approached by the Personnel Branch who said the Director General and Director C were keen for me to sign on until the age of sixty-five. This was a very tempting offer but, alas, arthritis emanating from my lumbar regions was beginning to worsen and it would be only a matter of time before I would need a hip-joint replacement operation and commuting was beginning to be a bit of a problem. So I compromised and agreed to stay on until September 1987 which would give me eight years' service and a much-needed pension of one-tenth of my final salary to supplement my meagre RAF pension. After retirement, I planned to work as an aviation security consultant which should enable me to wind down gracefully and perhaps move to the country to enjoy our dotage.

Chapter 18

Winding Down

Although my last day of service was not until the 28th I handed over to ex-Group Captain John Woodard, who had been understudying me for six months, on 1 September 1987. I was duly 'lunched out' at The Duke of York's HQ and presented with *The Oxford Illustrated History of Britain* (my choice) and a limited edition (10/25) print of a proof illustration by Peter Scott for his book *The Diary of a Travelling Naturalist* (a lovely surprise).

A couple of months before I was due to retire I had written to a number of organizations and individuals telling them that I planned to set up as an aviation security consultant with effect from 15 September, trading as Langer Associates, and would be available to carry out airport and airline security surveys, aviation security training and associated activities. I included my terms and conditions of employment which I deliberately set low by comparison with possible competitors, mainly because I wanted to get off to a good start. Moreover, unlike most others I was not dependent upon my consultancy earnings. The ploy seemed to work because before long I was turning down jobs which did not interest me.

My very first job was offered to me a month before I left the Service by my old friend, Ken Holmes, who had been the No. 2 aviation security adviser at the DoT. Ken was now the Security Manager (Europe) of KLM and had recently founded the Holmes Aviation Protection Company. He had been approached by Defence Systems Ltd, whose American subsidiary US Defence Systems Inc. had won a competition to carry out an independent evaluation of security at New York's John F. Kennedy International Airport (JFK). He agreed to form a team to commence work on 22 September 1987.

The team consisted of Ken as team leader who was to be responsible for looking at JFK's security organization and management, for liaison with the appropriate US authorities and for co-ordinating the work of the team. I was to scrutinize passenger and baggage procedures, to look at the airport and airlines' aviation security training and to write the report. Pat Carson, the former commander of the Metropolitan Police station at Heathrow, would examine JFK's contingency planning and training and liaise with the NYPD. Finally, Mike Sixsmith, a retired Army major who had joined DSL in 1980, would look at physical security and access control. A formidable team for a formidable task.

Neither Ken nor I had high expectations about the state of security at JFK as we were well aware of the lamentable US aviation security record over the past few decades. But we were still surprised at just how dreadful we found it to be. I won't attempt to even summarize the faults we found but in my first draft report we made exactly one hundred recommendations about things that needed to be done. Of these, seventeen were classed as 'essential' or necessary to meet ICAO guidelines for international airports, sixty-three were classified as 'highly desirable' or needed to achieve good security practice and the rest were just 'desirable'. This classification was to give the US authorities an idea of the priority to give when implementing the recommendations.

Ken handed over a copy of the draft report to the Port Authority of New York and New Jersey, who owned JFK and La Guardia, to study whilst we finished our evaluation and I put the finishing touches to the final report – which was to run to just over eighty closely-typed pages. Three days later Ken and I were summoned to a meeting with the two relevant directors of the Port Authority and the inevitable attorney at law, along with the Airport General Manager. They started by congratulating the team on the comprehensiveness of the report and started trying to wheedle us into toning down the final report – for 'political and financial reasons'! Needless to say, we refused because, as Ken said, what they did with our report was their business but we were not prepared to impugn our integrity by watering down justified criticism. Indeed when we left the meeting I revised the draft to include three more recommendations and a warning of the possible consequences of not heeding our advice.

The Directors had only disagreed with the report on two specific points. Firstly, although they agreed with my overall assessment of the threat to US aviation interests worldwide, they contended that the threat within the USA was very low on the grounds that no terrorist group would be foolish enough to attempt an attack in America when it would be so much easier to do it overseas where security was poor. This has been true up to now, but I had warned them that the main threat now came from Islamic extremist groups and that it was only a matter of time before they would attempt a major attack on US soil, if only for the publicity it would attract.

The Directors' second disagreement was with our recommendation that they should apply the same standards of security on domestic flights as they did on international ones on the grounds that experience has shown that domestic incidents all too often become international events. The team had paid a visit to La Guardia, the New York domestic airport, and found that, in some instances, there was no security at all. This applied mainly to the scheduled shuttle services between the major American cities where passengers were not required to book in or be screened but to simply board the aircraft and pay for their tickets to the cabin staff. In other words they were treating shuttle aircraft like Greyhound buses.

We were so appalled by the standards that we had uncovered that the team debated whether we should send a copy of our report to the FAA – which should have been aware. Unfortunately, when US Defense Systems Inc. had been awarded the contract they had signed a 'confidentiality clause' which legally prevented us doing so. We could but hope that most of our recommendations would be acted upon. Alas, this was not so, even after al Qa'eda had planted two bombs in the basement of the World Trade Center which luckily did little damage and caused only one death and a few minor injuries. The failure of the US aviation authorities to get their act together resulted in the horrific event, now known universally as 9/11, where four domestic flights were hijacked and two of them were flown into the twin towers of the World Trade Center with the loss of around 3,000 lives. The third aircraft hit the Pentagon building while the fourth came down in Pennsylvania when some brave passengers attempted to overcome the hijackers with the result that it crashed short of the target. It was ironic that the HQ of the Port Authority was on the seventy-seventh floor of one of the twin towers. Poetic Justice?

* * *

No sooner had I returned from New York after twenty-six gruelling days than I was offered another job, this time by my old firm, the Security Service. In December 1986 there had been a serious hijack attempt of a Pan Am Boeing 747 at Karachi International Airport (KIA). The 'post mortem' of the event exposed many lapses of security and flawed procedures, including a botched assault by the Pakistan Army that had resulted in the deaths of more hostages than of the Islamic terrorists responsible. A senior Pakistani police officer, who had attended one of my courses in London, suggested to his superiors that John Coghill and I might be invited to hold a four-day course at KIA for the airport security managers and supervisors and for the Airport Security Force, a police outfit, which bore most responsibility for security and reaction. John and I duly flew to Karachi on 20 November 1987 and spent the first day being given a conducted tour of all aspects of their security system. During the course, which was well attended by the right people, I was able to put across those flaws I noted on tour, most of which concerned access control, which was surprising as it was poor access control which had enabled the hijackers to drive through the cargo area to that Pan Am aircraft and hijack it on the ground on the flight line whilst it was loading.

Our visit must have been appreciated as we were invited to return to do the same thing at Islamabad International Airport which served the capital city. John and I did so in November 1988, which was a nostalgic trip for me as the airport had been built on the site of RAF Chaklala, just outside Rawalpindi, my old stamping ground when I was stationed at RAF Fathejang in 1944/45. Moreover, the senior ASF officer actually came from Fathejang, regarded me as a long-lost brother and insisted on taking me to meet his family in the village and to drive me over the now disused airfield. Nostalgia was heightened when, at the weekend, the naval and air attaché at the British High Commission took us to the Rawalpindi Club for lunch and to Sam's Restaurant in Murree, up in the hills, where No. 670 (Glider) Squadron had celebrated VJ Day in August 1945.

Before that second visit to Pakistan I had carried out two overseas airport surveys on my own, which were interesting for different reasons. The first in

February/March 1988 was to Cyprus, at the invitation of Mr Michael Herodotou, the Director of Civil Aviation, to carry out surveys of Larnaca and Paphos airports. When negotiating my terms of contract with the Director, because Jane had never been to Cyprus, I offered to waive my fees if he would pay all the extra expenses if she accompanied me – as my secretary. This related to the airline tickets, the hotel bill and the provision of a hire car. He was only too pleased to agree as he would be getting my services for much less than expected.

Jane accompanied me everywhere, making notes and writing down the names of everyone with whom I had discussions – no easy task with Greek names! It also gave her an insight into my work and particularly of the frustrations of the job which were greater than usual at Larnaca due to the incompetence of the police chief and the fact that all their directives, contingency plans, orders etc., were in Greek – and because Greeks will be Greeks. There were two main exceptions to this: first, Mr Herodotou himself who was very cooperative, charming and hospitable. Secondly, the brightest spark was young Andreas Hadjinicolaou, the training officer of Cyprus Airways who had also attended one of my courses in London. I found no faults whatsoever with their security practices and Andreas was able to tell me of many weaknesses in the airport security which I might not have discovered in the short time available.

I had a final interview with the Director before I left when I gave him a synopsis of my findings. He was not surprised that I had made forty-odd recommendations for improvement and said that he would act on them as soon as he received my final report. Unfortunately, no sooner had I handed over my final report to the FCO for transmission to Cyprus in the diplomatic bag than an aircraft hijacked by Palestinians landed at Larnaca Airport and eventually broke the record by becoming the longest hijack, lasting for ten days of hostage-threatening and negotiation. Everything that could go wrong went wrong in the handling of that hijack in terms of communication, negotiation, media interference, containment, etc., all of which might have been avoided had my recommendations been acted upon – which, of course, the Director had yet to receive. However, well after the event, he wrote me a letter admitting as much and said that the hijack had given impetus to their implementation which was well underway.

The other overseas survey I carried out was in Malta at the behest of the FCO following a request from the Maltese Government. I flew to Luqa International Airport on 16 October and was met by a second secretary from the British High Commission who drove me to my hotel where he briefed me on the political situation in Malta. To over-simplify: there had been a recent general election as a result of which the previous very anti-British prime minister had been voted out. During his premiership, British residents and commercial companies had been harassed and the country had turned to Libya as a supporting ally. Since the election the BHC had made serious attempts to mend fences and had offered trading concessions, financial investment, subsidized training and an independent airport survey at no cost – hence my presence.

He went on to say that Colonel Gaddaffi had been very angry at this turn of events and loss of influence and that lately his agents had carried out a number of attacks in Malta against British interests. He said that it was possible that I could be a target so I should be alert to the threat and to let him know if I noticed anything suspicious.

Undeterred, I proceeded with the survey and was pleased not only with the cooperation I received but also with the existing standards of security. What a difference to the laid-back attitude of the Greek Cypriots; in Malta I found nothing but energy and enthusiasm. There were a few flaws in their system and I did compile forty recommendations – most concerned with the organization, senior management and contingency planning rather than the efficiency of passenger and baggage handling.

I found the Maltese very hospitable and they insisted that I should take time to let them show me some of their national treasures. These included the ancient fortified walled town of Medina, which had remained unchanged since the Middle Ages, and the Basilica with the second largest dome in the world, beaten only by that at St Peter's in the Vatican City. The vast interior was impressive but surprisingly, unadorned other than by a 500lb German bomb which had penetrated the dome, ricocheted around the walls but failed to explode – which, of course, they claimed to have been a miracle.

All these trips were at midday, so I worked from early morning and they went back to work until late so I was left to my own devices at night. This suited me well as I was able to write up my notes from the day's inspections and discussions and to just pop out to the centre of Valletta for dinner. Luckily, after a rather dreary first night's dinner in the hotel, I found an excellent restaurant to which I returned every evening afterwards to sample the country's specialities, such as rabbit pie and superb red snapper fish. Although I did not take the BHC warning about being a target too seriously, I did take certain precautions, learned from Box 500, like checking that I was not being followed, avoiding unlit areas, standing sideways on to the hotel door when inserting the key and then pushing it wide open before entering. Finally, I checked under the bed and mattress for a pressure-activated explosive device. All by the book, all rather James Bond, and rather fun.

During my stay in Malta I had met everyone who mattered from the Deputy Prime Minister, Mr Guido de Marco, the Director of Civil Aviation and the Assistant Commissioner of police downwards. I was only there for six days, so before I left I briefed the Director of Aviation on my overall impressions of security and promised a full report within a couple of weeks. When they received it, via the diplomatic bag, I got a letter from Mr de Marco thanking me and saying that he had not expected such a comprehensive report which he had now read and would recommend that the Airport Security Committee should implement every recommendation.

* * *

Over the past couple of years my creaking right hip had been giving me a lot of pain and, by the end of 1988, I was walking with a pronounced limp. I had been in the hands of the orthopaedic consultant at RAF Hospital Halton for over a year but he had concentrated on trying to sort out my troublesome back before carrying out the now inevitable hip-joint replacement. I had been subjected to epidural injections, x-rays, scans and manipulation, but he had finally come to the conclusion that an operation would be too dangerous as the cause of the problem lay within the spinal cord. The hip-joint replacement operation was carried out successfully in January 1989 and is still going strong.

After the operation I decided to turn down further airport surveys and to concentrate on aviation security training. This is a boring subject, so I will just say that I ran or contributed to courses and seminars for International Military Services Ltd, the Royal College of Military Studies, IATA courses at Bailbrook College, Royal Ordnance, Loughborough University, the FCO and British Airways.

I also ran three courses overseas: the first of these was at Larnaca Airport in Cyprus in March 1992 as a follow up to my survey in 1988. I was invited by the Director of Civil Aviation to run a two-day course for security managers and supervisors and to be shown the changes in their security planning and procedures following the recommendations in my report. The second was in October 1992 in Greece at the behest of the FCO which was concerned at the number of adverse reports from British airlines about the inadequacy of security at Greek airports. With the agreement of Mr G. Tsentos, their Director of the Civil Emergency Planning Division of the Greek CAA, I was to run two one-day courses at the airports of Athens, Heraklion (Crete), Rhodes and Corfu. I would like to think that my visit went well but, in the event, it was rather like 'the curate's egg', being good only in parts. My reception in Athens was lukewarm to say the least. My course was poorly attended, the arrangements for it were pathetic, the audience was unresponsive and cooperation was minimal despite all the airports having been circulated prior to my visit by the Director of Civil Aviation. In contrast, the courses at Heraklion and Rhodes were well-organized and received by an enthusiastic audience in both cases, largely due to the respective heads of security who were pretty keen. The visit to Corfu was a mini-disaster due to the attitude of the airport commander who, before my arrival, had told his staff that the course would be a waste of time. His arrangements were appalling; for example, he told the security personnel that it was up to them if anyone attended. As a result, when I arrived for my first talk there was an audience of seven. I had to get rather cross and threaten to inform the Director of his intransigence before I got a decent venue and audience.

The one saving grace of my Greek adventure was that the CAA had attached one of their administrators to act as my interpreter and to smooth my way through Greek bureaucracy. Thankfully, Stamoulis Petrus spoke excellent English, having spent a couple of years in England studying. He was young and keen and I could not have coped without him. Wherever we went he forewarned the airport of our arrival so we were able to bypass security. When we arrived back in Athens for my flight home on 17 October I bade him a fond farewell before checking into the international terminal where I had to go through the usual security checks. Needless to say they x-rayed and opened my briefcase which contained all my lecture notes, my slides and view-foils and all the exhibits I needed for my lectures. These included, amongst other things, dummy detonators, de-activated explosives and incendiary devices and samples of look-alike types of explosive. Despite my showing them the letters from the British Embassy (in English) and from the Director of the CAA (in Greek), which explained the purpose of my visit, I was marched away to a side room with a police guard whilst they sought authentication from the CAA. As it was a night flight and it was now long after office closing time I did not have high hopes. I was getting pretty frustrated, not least because nobody claimed to speak English when, with no explanation or apology, I was told, in good English, that I could proceed and I just managed to scramble aboard as the doors were closing. I cannot be sure but I believe that my detention was deliberate as Petrus had told Mr Tsentos of my dissatisfaction at my reception and the arrangements for the course and he had probably given the Head of Athens Airport Security a dressing down and my detention was his way of getting his own back.

My very last aviation security training commitment was in January 1994 when Major Peter Timothy of Royal Ordnance/RCMS talked me into accompanying him to Geneva to talk to a group of people from the HQ of the International Red Cross in Geneva. Officially I had retired in June 1993 when we had moved to Filkins, but he asked me as a special favour and I accepted because of the venue. Unfortunately, Timothy had got the Red Cross requirement wrong and what I had prepared was irrelevant. So, having found out what exactly they wanted during our introductory meeting, I had to burn the midnight oil in my hotel bedroom to develop a frame-work for the next morning's talks on how to protect Red Cross vehicles and convoys from attack in battle zones, how to behave if a passenger hijacked an aircraft, how to find which airlines to avoid because of a threat to them or because of their poor security records, and a number of other topics not within my normal remit.

* * *

When not contributing to training courses or seminars or carrying out airport surveys, I developed another string to my bow in that I was invited to write on various aviation security topics for books, conferences, etc. It started before I left the Security Service when I was approached in 1984 by Martin Stanton, who ran the transport security courses at Loughborough University, to comment on the chapter on aviation security for his draft book on airport management. I was not impressed because it was superficial, incorrect in places and omitted many important points – so I completely rewrote the chapter, which was easier than just criticising it. Martin was very pleased, accepted my version without alteration and sent me a cheque for £210 which was completely unexpected.

Three years later I was asked to write a discussion paper for the Home Office on the policing of airports. At first I refused to do so as it was outside my Security Service remit but the Head of the Security Department, Mr Birt, contacted my boss because he said that neither the Home Office nor the Department of Transport had the necessary expertise, especially as the paper was for the Association of Chief Police Officers (ACPO) who had been worrying them for guidance for a long time. Director 'C' agreed that I could do it, but not on behalf of the Service but as a private individual, in my own time, and that I should be paid appropriately. My paper, entitled 'The Categorization of UK Airports', recommended that there should be five categories in descending order of importance as follows:

1. Major international airports which handle airlines under substantial threat worldwide or operate flights on high-risk routes
2. Other international airports
3. Domestic airports which serve international airports or operate flights to and from Northern Ireland
4. Other domestic airports
5. Small community airports and those which operate no scheduled services

The categorization scheme would be linked to the policing requirement, i.e. from basing a police station at the airport with resources for an armed response to no police presence at the airport at all. It would also be linked to the level of security countermeasures to be applied. It was vital that the categorization should be decided by a standing committee with representation from the Home Offices, DoT, ACPO and the Security Service in conjunction with the chief constable of the region in which the airport was located and the appropriate airport director. The categorizations should be kept under review and altered if, for example, there was a change in the threat levels or the nature of the flights. I subsequently learnt that my proposals were accepted by all the authorities concerned.

However my best 'little earner' was the work I did for the various companies for which I ran seminars or contributed to courses. This included course design, the preparation of slides and hand-outs for presentations and lectures, and promotional material for soliciting work from UK airports and airlines and potential overseas customers. This last involved me in a number of presentations to possible overseas clients, one of which stands out. The delegation from Saudi Arabia was very high-powered as it was led by a royal prince and included the odd minister and the inevitable sheikhs. The contract for which Royal Ordnance was tendering, to run aviation courses for the Saudi airlines and airports, would be very financially rewarding, so it was decided to book the newly-opened Queen Elizabeth II Conference Centre in Westminster as the venue. Prior to the presentation, Doug Boucher, RO's administrator, and I went to make the final arrangements at the centre which included the provision of a sumptuous lunch. When discussing the menu with the catering manager I stressed that Saudis are teetotal, so an assortment of non-alcoholic drinks should be available and that under no circumstances should any dish containing pork be served. We agreed that chicken would be the safest bet for the main course.

On the day, after coffee and an introductory welcome and talk by the senior Director of Royal Ordnance, the morning presentation went down very well, the Saudis asked a lot of intelligent questions and seemed impressed with what we were offering. We then all piled into lunch, the tables for which were beautifully set out. After a starter of Scottish smoked salmon, I looked at the menu and my heart sank as the main course was coq au vin. I thought we might get away with it when I saw that the Saudis were tucking in with apparent delight. Then the prince discovered a piece of bacon on his plate, whereupon he turned to the director and asked what was in the recipe, only to be told that coq au vin was a classic French dish where the chicken is cooked in red wine with shallots, carrots and bacon. Wine and bacon! Oh dear! The prince stood up and spoke loudly in Arabic, whereupon all the delegates pushed their plates away as if they had been poisoned. Needless to say Royal Ordnance did not land the contract, all because of the stupidity of the catering manager.

Perhaps my most prestigious writing task was when I was invited by the Singapore Government to prepare two papers for the International Conference on Security in the 1990s, Trends, Concepts and Applications to be held there in May 1991. The topics were 'The threat to Civil Aviation and the Responsibilities of Governments' and 'Civil Aviation Security – the shortcomings', which were right up my street. I not only hoped that my papers would be accepted, which they were, but also that I would be invited to present them, which I was not, as the conference was designed for Near, Middle and Far East delegates only – of which I was unaware. I believe that the papers were used as part of the seminar discussions but there was no reward to me other than, perhaps, publicity.

* * *

Once I had retired from the Security Service my consultancy work allowed me more time to devote to my duties as a Deputy Lieutenant, which had increased significantly since I had been appointed to represent the Lord Lieutenant in the Greater London Borough of Hillingdon. These involved liaising with the three MPs whose constituencies were within the Borough and particularly with the Mayors of Uxbridge, the incumbent of which office changed every year. I also stood in for the Lord Lieutenant when presenting the Queen's Awards to Industry to companies within the Borough.

One very pleasant duty was attendance, with Jane, at the ANZAC Day commemoration service and wreathlaying at St Mary's Parish Church at Harefield, which was held every year on 25 April. Harefield Hospital was where severely injured Australian, New Zealand and Canadian soldiers were treated in the First World War. Many of them died and were buried in the church cemetery in a separate war grave area. After the service the congregation gathered at the War Memorial where I laid the first wreath amongst many others and then the children from the local school placed posies of flowers on every grave. It was always very moving and good to find that the tradition was still being carried on so long after that most terrible of wars. I also used to take the salute at one of the many Remembrance Sunday march pasts within the Borough.

However, most of my duties centred on events with the cadet forces of the three services, including presentation of prizes and certificates, annual inspections, sports days and the like. But there was one job which I considered as the 'perk', which made all my other unpaid, and sometimes rather boring, activities well worthwhile, and that was standing in for the Lord Lieutenant at the departure of members of the Royal Family from Heathrow or RAF Northolt. I was even paid expenses for that most delightful of chores.

I might well have been a little anxious about my first job greeting Royal persons at the airport and then introducing them to the VIPs gathered to say farewell on their departure on an official visit overseas. These VIPs were usually the Ambassador or High Commissioner of the country concerned, and their wives, as well as a representative of the appropriate FCO department and a few other hangers on. I was neither familiar with the protocol nor with the drill of wearing a sword, traditionally with which to defend my charges. I was also a trifle worried that I might forget, or get wrong, the names and ranks of the VIPs when introducing them.

Luckily my very first Royal person, in June 1987, was none other than HM Queen Elizabeth the Queen Mother who was the Commandant in Chief of the Central Flying School. When her limousine arrived at the Royal Suite at Heathrow I saluted and said 'Good morning your Majesty: Air Commodore John Langer standing in for Lord Bramall.' Her first words were 'Don't I know you?' So I reminded here that we had met twice at CFS in the 1960s whereupon she burst out laughing saying 'Ah yes: the saga of the exploding pepper pot!', immediately putting me completely at ease. I then introduced her to the Canadian High Commissioner, and a few others, after which she turned back to me and wanted to know what I was doing now, was I still in the RAF etc., etc., until her aircraft was ready and I escorted her to the steps past the line of reporters and photographers waiting outside. It was a very relaxed and happy occasion.

My next commitment was to look after their Royal Highnesses Prince Charles and Princess Diana at RAF Northolt in November 1987 prior to an official visit to the Federal Republic of Germany. This also was a pretty relaxed occasion as it was a small party with only the Ambassador and Baroness Wechman and the Station Commander in attendance. Charles had been long qualified for his RAF pilot's wings and had recently qualified for a commercial pilot's licence, so he was looking forward to flying the Royal Flight aircraft waiting on the tarmac. This was the first of the eleven occasions over the next five years that I was to look after them either together (six times), or Charles (twice) and Diana (three times) separately, so I got to know them quite well.

In January 1988 I was on duty in the Royal Suite at Heathrow prior to their departure for Australia to help celebrate their bicentennial year and then on to Thailand for the King's sixtieth birthday. There was the usual coterie of VIPs to see them off, headed by the Australian High Commissioner and the Thai Ambassador. Introductions over, Charles was chatting away merrily but Diana took no part and seemed troubled by something: very different to the bright, bubbly young lady I had met for the first time less than three months previously. I asked her if she would like to sit down which she was pleased to do.

Along with many others I had long thought that Charles and Diana had very little in common, not least because of the twelve-year difference in their ages. He was passionate about the environment, conservation, architecture and the usual countryside pursuits, whereas Diana was only interested in music and ballet and, of course, children. However, they had now been married for six years and she had done her Royal duty in producing the eventual 'heir and the spare', so I was rather surprised when she told me that she was dreading the visit to Australia. When I asked why, she replied that Charles was getting increasingly annoyed that wherever they went the media gave her all the publicity, especially in photographic coverage, and that he felt that his contribution to the various events was being sidelined. Indeed, as I escorted him to the aircraft, I was conscious that the newsmen behind the barriers were paying no attention to him but that all eyes and lenses were focused on Diana, who was being escorted by Robin Baxendale, the Head of BAA's Special Services.

From that time onwards, every time we met, I was aware of the tension building up between them. They started to arrive separately, which made meeting and greeting difficult, and then they scarcely acknowledged each other's presence. Diana always made a point of collaring me and talking about her worries. To her credit, not once did she mention the third person in their marriage which she disclosed to the world in that ill-advised interview with Martin Bashir.

As time passed her personality changed from that demure, shy and rather naïve young lady to someone more confident and extrovert. I guessed that their relationship had gone past the point of no return when she started wearing high heels, whereas previously she had worn 'flatties' to minimize the fact that she was so much taller than Charles. Her make-up became more dramatic, her neck-lines became lower and her skirts higher, which was a pity as they revealed that she had knobbly knees.

For all that she remained an attractive and warm person. For example, in May 1992 I was seeing her off on a visit to Egypt at the invitation of Mrs Mubarak. As we awaited her arrival I was chatting to Surgeon Commander Robin Clark, one of the doctors who accompanied their Royal Highnesses on most visits overseas. I asked him if Diana really was as passionate about children as the media coverage of her frequent visits to the Great Ormond Street Hospital and similar events would suggest. He confirmed that indeed she was. In the course of our discussion I happened to mention that Hilary's daughter, Jesse, had been born with almost total kidney dysfunction and about the struggle to keep her alive until she could have a successful transplant, as the previous two attempts had failed. He must have told Diana this because a few weeks later I received a small parcel from her Private Secretary, Patrick Jephson. It contained a framed photograph of the Princess in a ball gown, wearing a diamond tiara inscribed 'to dear Jesse with all my love, Diana'. Even today the very thought of that kindness brings a lump to my throat.

The last time that I saw off both of them was rather embarrassing. It was at Heathrow in November 1992 prior to their visit to South Korea. As was not unusual, Diana arrived late and by the time I had introduced her to the South Korean Chargé d'Affaires the Royal Flight was announced as being ready, whereupon she took my arm and said 'you will escort me to the aircraft, won't you?' and started walking towards the door. I told her that I should be going out with Prince Charles; but she insisted! I looked over towards Charles who, realizing what was going on, nodded assent and invited Lord King, the Chairman of British Airways, to walk out with him. I managed to slow down Diana so that they would arrive at the aircraft first.

In the few minutes that it took she poured out her heart, saying that she and Charles now lived completely separate lives and that she felt an outcast in respect of the Royal Family and that, if it was not for her boys, she would walk out. She then added 'If I did that it would please them as I feel they would be glad to be shot of me'. Although I was surprised that she should have confided in me, I was sympathetic and sensed that she was badly in need of someone to give her a hug. Looking back with the benefit of hindsight, I now realize that I was hearing the first signs of the paranoia that was to plague her last few unhappy, troubled years.

So far I have not written about Prince Charles himself, whom I came to like and respect. I found him charming and easy to get on with, a view not shared by some of his staff. However, I could understand why, after the euphoria of the first few years of his marriage and the birth of their sons, they had grown apart. His character was so different from that of Diana; he was intensely earnest, rather dour and inclined to bore the socks off listeners to his frequent tirades about his pet hates, such as architectural 'carbuncles', or his championing of such causes as the environment and organic farming. He did not have a great sense of humour and was a stickler for protocol. By comparison, Diana was rather lightweight and inclined to frivolity with an irreverent sense of the ridiculous. Now, of course, Prince Charles has mellowed considerably and I believe that, with the help of his new wife, who has weathered her own storms with great dignity, he will make an excellent king.

The very last time I met Diana was in September 1993 at RAF Northolt prior to her visit to Luxembourg. Waiting in the VIP Suite were the Ambassador, Sir

Donald Logan from the FCO and the Station Commander, so we did not have the chance to chat – but as I greeted her on arrival she just whispered 'nothing's changed'. Over the next few years I read with sadness the media revelations, such as the 'Squidgy Tapes', the eventual divorce and finally about the disastrous car crash in Paris. And, as I write this, the Mohamed Fayed-inspired public inquest into her death with his ridiculous and totally unsubstantiated allegations about Royal involvement in her 'murder' is dragging on.

On a happier note, in June 1990 I had stood in for Lord Bramall when HRH Princess Anne visited the London Air Traffic Control Centre at RAF West Drayton to unveil the new Rehost computer. Prior to her arrival, I had had conflicting messages about her journey from Gatcombe. The first said that she would be driving her Bentley, the second said that she would probably hand over to her chauffeur before arrival and would be seated in the nearside back passenger seat. Because of the uncertainty, I had two door-openers, one either side of the parking slot, whilst I stood at the front. Unfortunately, she had been caught up in a traffic jam and, being late, she swept into the station and, rounding the corner at some speed, just managed to stop two inches from my immaculately-pressed trousers – with a wide grin on her face.

I next met the Princess Royal in November 2007 when she was the Guest of Honour at a dinner to celebrate the sixtieth anniversary of the inauguration of the Joint Services Command and Staff College, now located at the Royal Defence Academy at Shrivenham in Wiltshire. Before the dinner she was to unveil a wall plaque to commemorate the event and I was lucky enough, as the most senior 'Cormorant' attending, to be the first person introduced to her after her arrival. I reminded her of the fact that she nearly ran me over seventeen years before at RAF West Drayton. The telling of that tale resulted in much laughter and helped to set the informal tone for the rest of the evening which was a great success.

* * *

I had intended to retire as a consultant after five years on the grounds that I would be getting out of date. However, as I had done a couple of jobs for Box 500 my successor was allowed to keep me up to date with frequent meetings and access to the quarterly reports of aviation security incidents to NASC, which I had originated in the first place. So the eventual decision to retire as a consultant came, in February 1994, after our move to our final roosting nest in Filkins in the beautiful Cotswolds countryside. And it is here that my story must end but, fear not, although I am now well into my eighties, I am still gainfully employed as a tour guide at Kelmscott Manor which, debatably, keeps my brainbox ticking over.

Appendix A

Aircraft Flown

Training Aircraft
de Havilland Tiger Moth
Fairchild Cornell
North American Harvard
de Havilland Chipmunk
Percival Prentice
Hunting/BAC Jet Provost
Hunting Percival Provost
Folland Gnat
SAAB Safir
Victa Winjeel
Siai-Marchetti SF260
Scottish Aviation Jetstream
Victa Air Tourer
Slingsby T61
Hawker Siddeley Hawk
NDN Firecracker

Gliders
General Aircraft Hotspur*
Airspeed Horsa
Waco Hadrian
General Aircraft Hamilcar
Slingsby Sedbergh
Slingsby Cadet

Helicopters
Bristol Sycamore
Westland Whirlwind
Sud Aviation Alouette
Bell 212
Hiller Husky
Aerospatiale Puma

Miscellaneous
Lockheed C-45 Expeditor
Airspeed Oxford
Douglas C-47 Dakota
Taylorcraft Auster AOP9
Avro Anson
Percival Pembroke
Vickers Varsity
English Electric Canberra
Short Sunderland
Beagle Basset
de Havilland Devon
Bristol Freighter
Short Skyvan
Cessna 150, 172, 310
Beagle Bulldog
Beech Baron
Dornier Do28 Skyservant

Fighters
Supermarine Spitfire Mks V, IX, XIV, XVI, 24
Hawker Tempest Mk II
Gloster Meteor F3, F4, T7, T8

---

* Although designed by General Aircraft (GAL), the Hotspur was built by Waring and Gillow, both of whom were furniture manufacturers in peacetime. This followed the GAL factory suffering severre bomb damage in an air raid.

Fighters (*contd*)
de Havilland Vampire F3, FB5, T11
Hawker Hunter F1, F4,F 6, T7
Douglas A4 Skyhawk
English Electric Lightning
Lockheed T-33 Thunderbird
Lockheed F-104 Starfighter
Yak 18/PT6 (Russian/Chinese)
BAC Strikemaster

Naming the HS 1182 AJ

Loose Minute <u>COPY</u>
AF/S2498/1

ACAS (POL)

Copy to: D Air Plans

<u>NAMING THE HS 1182 AJ</u>

1. You asked me to consider suitable names for the HS 1182 AJ and to recommend the most appropriate. As a guideline you indicated that, traditionally, aircraft built specifically for RAF training had been named after seats of learning.
2. A hasty review revealed that few aircraft met that parameter; in fact the Oxford, Harvard, Balliol and Cornell are the only ones that spring to mind. However, there are many that have peripheral academic connotations such as the Tutor, Varsity, Master, Provost, Dominie, Prentice, Proctor and Magister.
3. Even if one disregards the ex-front-line aircraft which became trainers, such as the Hart, Anson, Vampire and Hunter, there still remain many exceptions to that educational theme. Notable examples being the Avro 504K and Tiger Moth, in later years the Chipmunk and Gnat and, in the future, the Jetstream and Bulldog break the tradition.
4. However, in following the learning curve, I first considered universities. The problem here is that of all the University names only Oxford and Cambridge immediately evoke thoughts of the campus. If, for example, one thinks of Durham, the third oldest University, one thinks of the Cathedral. If one thinks of York – the Minster springs to mind; of Edinburgh – the Castle; of Manchester – United or City of football fame; of London – Soho and so on. I even considered Reading because of its academic double meaning and my fancy was taken by Bristol but a 'pair of Bristols' might be open to misinterpretation.
5. The name Kingston had an appeal because it is not only an ancient seat of monastic learning where many Saxon Kings were crowned and buried (the last not necessarily because of the first) but also because Hawker Siddeley make the HS 1182 AJ there. This would retain the academic flavour as there is a Polytechnic there which will soon assume University status and it would also please Hawker Siddeley. However, if we set this precedent then one day we might have to introduce a Warton – which God forbid.

6. Still on the academic theme I considered fringe names such as Monitor, Prefect, Tuck Shop and Fag but rejected them all. I then turned to schools and, in recognition of the introduction of comprehensives, I liked the idea of the Holland Park for a Handley Page aircraft. I then returned to more hallowed grounds and considered that the Harrow might have possibilities. A snag is that a Handley Page Harrow was once in our inventory, but this objection might be outweighed by our being able to call our next formation aerobatic team – the Red Harrows. The verb to harrow also means to harry and to wound which has military relevance.

7. In naming the HS 1182 AJ it is also necessary to take into account its sales potential not only as a trainer but also as a ground attack/counter insurgency aircraft. For this reason the scholastic tag is not entirely appropriate and I have come up with the final thought that the aircraft should be called the Hawk. This name is particularly descriptive of the HS 1182 AJ's air to ground capability, it is alliterative and complementary to Hawker, it evokes thoughts of flight and, although this is debatable, it connects with a seat of learning as a Hawk is the central motif of the crest of the RAF Staff College.

8. To summarize: if one wishes to name the HS 1182 AJ after a University, then Cambridge is the best choice: if a school name is preferred then Harrow is alliterative, descriptive, traditional and acceptable but second hand. But as the sales potential and its roles outside of training must also be considered then perhaps Hawk is the best solution.

(J. F. LANGER)
Gr. Capt. DD Air Plans
Wimbledon College

25 September 1972

Authors note:
This loose minute was a bit 'tongue in cheek' but it was photocopied and circulated widely amidst much mirth – even on the 6th Floor of MoD (Air) when it reached the Air Force Board.

Epilogue

My advice to anyone thinking of writing book-length memoirs is 'don't'. However, if you are mad enough to do so, and you have a story to tell, my further advice is don't leave it until you are an octogenarian because the march of time is inescapable and memory becomes a little fuzzy. It is not necessarily what actually happened all those years ago but more likely 'what the devil was the name of old so and so' or 'was it Da Nang or Na Trang in Vietnam that we visited in when was it'.

In some respects I have had to rely heavily on my four flying log-books which contain a wealth of information which has helped to keep me on the straight and narrow. I also have many books on air force subjects, along with a number of unrestricted documents and letters, and a pile of visit reports, to which I have been able to refer. I also have a wife with a remarkable long-term memory although we often remember events from understandably different points of view.

My final warning is not to underestimate how long the memoirs will take to complete. In my case it has taken the best part of three years but I stress that I have given my writing low priority as I have never allowed it to interfere with normal living: it has been a strictly spare-time task and I don't have much time to spare, even though I seldom read a book or watch TV in the mornings or afternoons. I hope that my writing in dribs and drabs has not resulted in repetition or the tale being disjointed. Perhaps the most important thing to consider before beginning such a task is do you enjoy writing because if you do not it will become a joyless chore. Luckily, apart from the love of flying, I have long got most satisfaction from writing a well-constructed, logically reasoned staff paper, visit report, appreciation or whatever.

I consider myself extremely lucky to have had such a varied, interesting and rewarding career. There were a few lows but they were heavily outnumbered by the highs and, looking back, I have nothing but happy memories. In fact I would be more than happy to do it all over again – provided that I can start at age eighteen and, please God, spare me the arthritis next time round.

GLORIA FINIS